RECONSTRUCTING
THE TALMUD

Joshua Kulp and Jason Rogoff

RECONSTRUCTING THE TALMUD

An Introduction to the Academic Study of Rabbinic Literature

Joshua Kulp and Jason Rogoff

HADAR PRESS

Reconstructing the Talmud: An Introduction to the
Academic Study of Rabbinic Literature, 2nd Edition

Design by Dov Abramson Studio, Jerusalem
2nd Edition Design by David Zvi Kalman

Hadar Press

190 Amsterdam Avenue
New York, NY 10023

www.hadarpress.org

ISBN-10: 1-946611-01-8
ISBN-13: 978-1-946611-01-7

LCCN: 2017930706

Printed in the United States of America

10 9 8 7 6 5 4 3 2 1

TABLE OF CONTENTS

FOREWORD

The study of Talmud was long regarded as an elite pursuit. Consider the following passage from Leviticus Rabbah:

ויקרא רבה פרשה ב	Leviticus Rabbah Chapter 2
...בנוהג שבעולם אלף בני	...It is the way of the world that a thousand people
אדם נכנסין למקרא, יוצאין	enter the study of the Bible, and one hundred of
מהן מאה. מאה למשנה,	them complete it. One hundred enter the study
יוצאין מהן עשרה. עשרה	of Mishnah, and ten of them complete it. Ten
לתלמוד יוצא מהן אחד.	enter the study of talmud and one completes
הה"ד אדם אחד מאלף	it. This is the meaning of the verse: *I have found*
מצאתי...(קהלת ז, כח).	*one out of one thousand...* (Ecclesiastes 7:28)

The picture here is clear: All Jews are expected to have literacy in the Bible, though only a small percentage of them achieve fluency. Of the biblically fluent who begin serious study of the Mishnah, a similarly small percentage attain mastery of the backbone of the Oral Torah. Those masters alone engage with *talmud*, here referring to the process of analytical and analogic reasoning that rests on a foundation of sweeping knowledge of the biblical and rabbinic canon. Similar patterns held for the later understanding of the term talmud—namely, the Babylonian Talmud—which remained the province of a rarified few; historically, only a tiny percentage of all students of Torah have attained mastery of this higher level of learning in any form.

In recent decades all of that has changed. On August 1, 2012, hundreds of thousands of Jews gathered all over the world to celebrate the end of the twelfth cycle of Daf Yomi, the daily schedule of Talmud learning designed to take any person through the entire Babylonian Talmud in seven-and-a-half years. Works by Rabbi Adin Steinsaltz and Artscroll Publications have democratized the Talmud, making its give-and-take accessible to all, including those without fluency in the Hebrew and Aramaic original. What was once a mark of elite achievement has now become, in some circles, a standard of more basic literacy. Various authors and publishers have risen to the challenge by providing tools and support for this growing population to follow the give-and-take of the Babylonian Talmud, to understand its logical structure, and to decode its rich legal and theological lexicon.

This popular embrace of the Babylonian Talmud has also been accompanied by a dramatic rise in the percentage of Jews who have passed through the portals of higher education. In many parts of the English-speaking Jewish world, holding at least one university degree is the norm. As a result, most Jews, especially those with a strong predilection for text learning, have been extensively trained in critical thinking and reading. The university's assumptions regarding historicity, literary criticism, feminism, and anthropology have similarly penetrated the consciousness of most Jews who turn to learn Talmud today. Moreover, for Jews who have learned intensively in a Western mode prior to learning Talmud in depth, the mode of Talmudic discourse can seem foreign and strange, based on assumptions and logical leaps that can seem tendentious and unfounded.

In order to address these issues, other tools are necessary: tools for understanding the culture and practices that gave rise to the words on the printed page; tools for explaining how the Talmud came together as a document, first orally and only later in written form; tools for explaining the literary goals of a Talmudic passage, goals that can sometimes get in the way of—and even trump—its surface-level striving for truth and logical coherence; tools for comparing the different parts of rabbinic literature and for contrasting the major centers of Eretz Yisrael and Babylonia. Only tools such as these can truly quench the thirst of the learner who seeks full understanding of and identification with the Talmudic text as we have it.

Fortunately, these sorts of tools have been around for as long as Talmud has been studied. They have been developed more systematically over the last 150 years in various centers of Jewish learning, both in yeshivot and in universities. Historically-sensitive and academic-Talmudic scholarship began to flourish in Central Europe in the middle of the nineteenth century, spreading to the rest of the Continent and then to other prominent centers in the United States and Israel. Like the study of Talmud itself, this was originally (and has largely remained) an elite enterprise, attractive to a relatively small group of scholars who had mastery of the Talmudic corpus, but who wanted to understand it more fully and to appreciate the brilliance of its creators and redactors.

The time has now come for those tools to be democratized in ways that match the democratization of the body of literature they were designed to study. This volume is a first effort to bring the fruits of critical Talmud scholarship to a broader audience of learners and teachers: those who will not pursue a doctorate in rabbinic literature, but who desire and require guidance to understand what the Talmud is and how it works. The tools of critical Talmud scholarship can make powerful sense of an otherwise perplexing text and give learners a sense of the craft that underlies the Talmud and its creation, above and beyond its basic surface meaning.

For some, this book will function as a textbook and primer in the context of academic learning, making worlds of deeper scholarship accessible through concrete examples. For others, it will serve as a teaching guide, a way of helping students grasp key dynamics in Talmudic passages and rabbinic literature. More broadly, we hope this book will have religious impact, as well; deeper understanding of a text is a necessary prerequisite for identifying with it and allowing oneself to be guided and shaped by its distinctive voice and agenda.

Mechon Hadar is proud to bring this volume to the general public. Our work is committed to erasing the divide between rigorous intellectual inquiry and spiritual seeking. The Talmud sits at the nexus of those two pursuits: it is a foundation stone for all subsequent Jewish religious practice even as it is one of the Jewish people's most impressive intellectual and scholarly achievements. The scholarship modeled in this book is first-rate; we hope and believe it will deepen appreciation and affinity for the Talmud and the brilliant and inventive personalities who created and shaped it.

Rabbi Ethan Tucker
Rosh Yeshiva, Mechon Hadar

INTRODUCTION

Over a thousand years ago, the eleventh century Babylonian rabbi Sherira Gaon eloquently captured in his terse and poetic manner the process by which the Babylonian Talmud was compiled: "Thus generation after generation (*dara batar dara*) the Talmud was gathered together." All classic rabbinic works—the Mishnah, Tosefta, the Midrashim and the two Talmuds—contain the words and voices of multiple generations of sages, but none contain the teachings of as many generations as the Babylonian Talmud, the most majestic and grandiose of all rabbinic compilations. The Bavli, as the Babylonian Talmud is commonly called, is a tapestry of hundreds of voices from diverse places and time periods. It contains legal rulings, biblical interpretations, folklore, and rabbinic legends that developed over the course of many centuries. While each voice was originally issued in a distinct generation, they were "captured" and frozen in time as a single work by editors who lived between the fifth and seventh centuries C.E. The purpose of this book is to guide the modern reader of the Talmud towards a deeper understanding of this extraordinary text by examining its historical development "*dara batar dara*," generation after generation. We sort the historical layers contained in the Bavli, reading each statement closely and understanding it within its particular cultural and historical context. We also compare the Bavli with earlier rabbinic literature, revealing a dynamic world of change, debate, and halakhic diversity far richer and more nuanced than that which is evident when one focuses on the static text found in the printed edition today.

The heart of this book is a critical commentary on nine passages from the Bavli using the techniques developed by critical Talmudic scholars of the last century. This book takes the reader step-by-step through the process necessary to analyze the Bavli's text critically, highlighting the various methodologies and techniques employed by modern academic scholars.

Our commentary aims to bring academic Talmudic scholarship down from the towers (be they of ivory or Jerusalem stone) of academia and make it available to a broader audience. In addition, our goal is to bring this discipline and its findings to an English-speaking audience, one that might not be comfortable reading advanced scholarship in Hebrew. *Reconstructing the Talmud* is an attempt to introduce English readers to the world of Talmudic research and thereby open new avenues of exploring and understanding one of the world's great literary treasures.

The Builder and the Archaeologist: What is Critical Talmudic Commentary?

We will try to illustrate the contrast between traditional Talmudic commentary and modern critical scholarship by analogizing the difference between them to the difference between a builder and an archaeologist. The traditional commentator can be likened to a builder, seeking to make the text most comfortable and convenient to inhabit. In a sense, he[1] is building a house in which he (or another person) might live. A traditional commentator is not especially concerned with determining the relationship between the early stages of the text and the later ones, or even with asking whether such stages exist. Rather, he seeks to understand the logic of each part of the text and how it contributes to the overall structure and flow of the passage. The traditional commentator wishes to harmonize the separate parts of the text, regardless of where these parts are found or where they originated. As a consequence, such a commentator often ends up "reconciling" points within a given sugya that do not easily accord with one another. He ends up harmonizing statements and even entire sugyot that seem to contradict each other. When statements or sugyot are extraordinarily difficult to interpret, the commentator will offer

---

[1] For the sake of convenience and due to the constraints of the English language we have used the pronoun "he" throughout this introduction. Of course traditional Talmudic commentators were all male. This is in no way meant to imply on our part that modern Talmudic study should be the sole province of men.

a strained explanation, one that "makes sense" even if it does not accord particularly well with the source he is interpreting. This harmonization is necessary because the Bavli has served and continues to serve as the foundation for normative halakhic practice. To return to our metaphor, it is less important to the traditional commentator how this house was built in the past; rather he wishes to strengthen the house so that it will continue to stand strong in the future, both for him and for others who wish to dwell within it.

To the academic Talmudic critic who stands "outside" the text, the first goal is to uncover how and when each of the individual components were built and assembled. Like an archaeologist whose interests are not limited to the building or city as it existed in its final form, a Talmudic critic wishes to understand when the cornerstone was laid, how each generation built upon it, and what each layer can reveal to us about the people who gave it shape and dwelled within its walls. The academic Talmudic scholar wishes to reconstruct the form of the text, be it an oral text or written one, as it existed in each and every generation, from its inception to its final concretization. This is not merely an end unto itself, nor is it solely an intellectual exercise. Rather, the Talmudic critic believes that uncovering each historical layer of the text will contribute both to our understanding of that specific layer and to our appreciation of the final edifice. The Talmud contains the voices of many generations of sages and editors, each with its own perspective and assumptions. To the Talmudic critic, understanding the Talmud as a whole depends on differentiating among these layers and appreciating each individually. The critical Talmud scholar recognizes distinct stages of historical development. The Mishnah originally meant one thing, an amora intentionally changed the law that stemmed from the Mishnah, and the Bavli's editors eventually modified the amoraic halakhah/interpretation as well. In contrast, traditional interpreters usually understood the Mishnah solely in accordance with the latest layer of interpretation. When the assumptions and literary sources that were available to any given sage—tanna, amora or anonymous editor—are uncovered, the intentions, values, beliefs and the overall contribution of this sage to the continuously accruing process of the creation of the oral Torah will be better appreciated.

Another hallmark of the Talmudic critic which distinguishes him from the traditional Talmudic commentator is that if at the end of his research the critic fails to understand how a sugya was put together, or what the original, intended meaning of a passage or a portion of a passage was, he should refrain from offering a strained interpretation. A Talmudic critic searches for the original meaning of statements and passages as best as it can be ascertained. When mysteries and puzzles remain, the critic is neither obligated nor expected to offer a strained resolution. The critic does not strive to create harmony in a place where it does not exist. His desire is simply to explain in as objective of a manner as possible the full text and its component parts.

This type of critical research is important for all of rabbinic literature, but it is especially fruitful and effective when the object of inquiry is the Babylonian Talmud. The Bavli is a work that was composed over a period of hundreds of years. Its final editing did not conceal its internal signs of development and the independent sources embedded in it, but it did blur them to a great extent. This requires especially careful and thorough research, but it is research that is possible to undertake. On the one hand, the editors of the Bavli use technical terms to indicate when they are quoting tannaitic and amoraic statements. It seems to have been important to the editors to retain a sense of dialogue and dialectic between earlier and later generations. Indeed, the typical Babylonian sugya progresses chronologically from tannaitic to early amoraic and then to later amoraic sources. Unlike the Mishnah, the Bavli is inherently a stratified text. On the other hand, Babylonian editors did not always quote their sources word for word or preserve them in their original formulation. Rather, they frequently reworded earlier sources, changed their attributions and placed them in new contexts. They also adapted them to their own halakhic and literary needs. In sum, what makes the Bavli so interesting and such a rich source for analysis is its tendency to preserve the boundaries of earlier sources and to blur them at the same time.

Critical Techniques

In this introduction we outline the critical techniques we employ throughout the book, techniques which we believe should be used in any modern critical commentary on the Bavli. Our hope is that this introduction to critical Talmudic commentary and the examples that comprise the chapters of this book will serve as a model for the reader who wishes to apply these techniques to whatever passage he may be learning. This book is not merely a commentary; it is, we hope, an educational paradigm for how to learn the Bavli in a modern and critical manner.

Throughout this introduction we have cited brief examples in which a critical approach can be applied to better understand how a given text developed or what it means. These examples are discussed only briefly and are brought here just to illustrate succinctly the type of analysis in which we are engaging. They are meant more to answer the question of how does a critical Talmudic scholar analyze the Bavli than to provide comprehensive analysis of these passages. For many of these examples, more than one of these techniques must be employed in order to actually understand how the text or its components were conceived and how they developed over time. For simplicity's sake, we have focused on only one technique for each example, though most of these examples have been discussed more fully by other scholars. At the conclusion of each section is a reference to scholarly literature in English devoted to these subjects. These mini-bibliographies are far from comprehensive, but they will provide a starting point for the reader wishing to further his studies.

We begin this introduction by clarifying certain terms used throughout the book. We then offer brief chronological comparisons of distinct compositions: (1) the comparison of the tannaitic compositions, especially the Mishnah and Tosefta; (2) the comparison of the baraitot in the Bavli with their parallels in earlier compositions; (3) the comparison of the Yerushalmi and the Bavli. Next, we discuss the chronology within the Babylonian text itself, explaining the stratification of the Bavli's sugyot and the relationship between sugyot. Lastly, we present some non-comparative critical techniques, namely textual criticism, lexicography, realia, comparisons with non-rabbinic Jewish texts, and literary analysis.

A Clarification of Terms: Stam, Editor, Redactor

In considering the various historical strata of the Bavli, it is helpful to begin by defining a few key terms. First is the "stam," short for the *"stam hatalmud"* or *"stamma degemara,"* a reference to the anonymous voice in the Bavli that frequently creates the discourse between sages, transitions between one source or sugya and another, and interprets the meaning of earlier sources. The term "stam" may be translated as "anonymous," for this voice in the Talmud speaks without revealing its identity. The Bavli may be divided into an "amoraic" layer and a "stammaitic" layer, as we will discuss below.

Next, the term "editor" refers to the Babylonian transmitters who edited the sources they received, be they earlier sources from Babylonia or sources that originated in Eretz Yisrael. We assume that this process of "editing" occurred continuously as rabbinic texts were transmitted, and that each generation of rabbis occasionally passed on their traditions word for word but frequently reworded and revised them.

The term "redactor" refers to those rabbinic sages who were responsible for the organization of the Talmud, deciding which story or statement would be placed into the context of which mishnah. For instance, an earlier sage may have made a statement in one context concerning one topic; a redactor might then transfer the statement to a new context.

These three terms are meant to facilitate the understanding of the various ways in which rabbinic literature developed over the centuries. They do not necessarily refer to activities that occurred in three different time periods or that were performed by three different individuals. Rather, they refer to three different types of literary creativity. The same anonymous sage may take a statement made in one context and move it to another context (as redactor), then modify the words of the statement (as editor) and add some additional words of framework to help it fit its new context (as stam hatalmud). These three processes may occur in different periods, or they may occur simultaneously. What is important to us is that when studying a passage from rabbinic literature, the critical student must always ask whether one of these three processes occurred: Has the statement been edited? Has it been moved from its original context to another? Has discourse been added?

A Word of Caution

We probably should provide a word of caution before presenting the examples found in this introduction. In this type of analysis no single interpretation can be asserted with one hundred percent certainty. We can suggest what statements and concepts originally meant and how sugyot developed over time. But as with material archaeology, textual analysis aims not at certainty but at plausibility. We are reaching nearly two thousand years into the past, trying to reconstruct what the words of the rabbis meant to those who stated them, to those who heard them and to those who edited them. This is an exciting adventure, a chance to recreate the past, to see the Talmudic dialogue as it unfolded in each generation. We hope our suggestions are convincing and that they are historically accurate. But we realize that there will always be room for disagreement and for the existence of other interpretive possibilities. Such has always been the nature of Talmudic commentary, and in this respect critical commentary does not differ from traditional commentary. Nevertheless, the speculative character of this type of inquiry has not prevented us from offering bold suggestions as to the history and the meaning of the material at hand.

Chronological Analysis:
A Comparison of Early and Later Literature

One of the hallmarks of critical Talmudic analysis is the search for chronological development in rabbinic literature, its ideas and its laws. While traditional Talmudic commentators did not deny that halakhah and literature developed over time, they did not consistently search for such development. Traditional commentators regularly imposed ideas created in later stages of rabbinic development upon sages who lived in earlier generations. In contrast, critical analysis stresses that an idea or halakhah should not be assumed to have existed before we can be reasonably sure that it did. Thus, for instance, an idea attributed to a late amora may have been known to a tanna, but we cannot assume that it was.

Of course this raises the question of how to determine chronological layers. This is one of the most complicated questions that critical Talmudic analysis faces. We will outline here a few salient rules of thumb. First of all, as stated, an idea can be presumed to exist only upon its first concrete mention. We should note, however, that occasionally principles or halakhot are named in later generations, but are reflective of the thinking of earlier generations.

Occasionally changes in language assist in dating sources. As we discuss below, this aids especially in separating amoraic statements issued in Hebrew from the stammaitic explanations of those statements which were transmitted in Aramaic. On other occasions we can even trace development within the Hebrew language. However, such occasions are rare.

If the above two criteria were relatively objective, the main techniques for determining chronological development are far more subjective. Legal literature tends to develop in certain ways—from simpler halakhot to more complex ones; from opaque phrases to more explicated ones. Rabbinic literature in particular often seems to have developed from halakhot attached to biblical verses to independent legal formulations. Other techniques for determining chronological development will be explained in the examples that follow.

A. The Relationship between Tannaitic Texts: Mishnah and Tosefta

The tannaim, the sages who lived before the Mishnah was codified around the year 220 C.E., composed two halakhic compositions and a series of halakhic midrashim on four of the five books of the Torah (not on Genesis). We will deal mostly with the two halakhic compositions, the Mishnah and the Tosefta, and the relationship between them.

The Mishnah and the Tosefta are similar to each other in significant ways. They are both organized topically into almost the same tractates.[2] Each tractate is dedicated primarily to a single subject, although digressions are not infrequent. This distinguishes these texts from midrashim, which are organized by the order of biblical verses. Unlike midrashim, the halakhot in the Mishnah and Tosefta usually can be read and understood independently of the biblical verses on which they are based.

For the most part the same sages appear in both compositions such that it is obvious that these two compositions originated among the same rabbinic circles. Furthermore, while we can often speak of a halakhah in one corpus which disagrees with a halakhah in another, the two are fundamentally part of the same halakhic and religious system. Finally, the language of the Mishnah and Tosefta is very similar, and only a trained expert can note salient differences between the two. Thus the similarities between the two far outweigh the differences.

The relationship between these two compositions has been a source of scholarly debate for over a hundred years. Indeed, without much exaggeration, one could say that the question of their relationship is among the most

---

[2] There is no Tosefta for Tractate Avot.

difficult and contentious issues in the academic study of rabbinic texts. The two main positions can be explained as two different ways of understanding the meaning of the word Tosefta.

Tosefta can mean "additional," in which case the Tosefta is a corpus of halakhot which supplements the Mishnah. It forms a sort of early commentary on the Mishnah, and has been even called the first "talmud" on the Mishnah. Those who subscribe to this theory will usually try to understand how the Tosefta comments on, expands upon, disagrees with or simply relates to the Mishnah in general.

The second position understands the word Tosefta as a "gathering" of material, gathered together in order to supplement the material found in the Mishnah. The editor of the Tosefta was familiar with material that was not included in and at times predated the Mishnah. He gathered and organized this material to parallel the Mishnah. Scholars who subscribe to this theory of the Tosefta strive to locate material in the Tosefta that was created earlier than the material in the Mishnah. As evidence, they point to halakhot found in our Mishnah which appear to be edited versions of the earlier material found in the Tosefta. An even more radical assertion of this position is that the Tosefta, *as we know it* (*i.e. as a composed work*), predates the Mishnah.

Our methodology generally follows that of Shamma Friedman, who holds that individual halakhot in the Tosefta are often earlier versions of the parallels in the Mishnah. In addition, Friedman agrees with most scholars who hold that the Tosefta also contains supplements that were added after the composition of the Mishnah. In other words, the Tosefta is a collection of halakhot, some of which were known by the editors of the Mishnah and were redacted into the Mishnah; but the Tosefta as a whole was composed as a supplement to the Mishnah. As such, the Tosefta at times assumes that one knows the material in the Mishnah.

Most importantly, we believe that however one understands the relationship between these two foundational texts, it is incumbent upon one who wishes to learn the development of any given sugya first to study the material as found in the Mishnah and in the Tosefta. Both tannaitic compositions must be studied on their own, without a priori assumptions informed by their interpretation in the Bavli. To put this more simply: when you open a sugya in the Bavli, the first thing you must do is understand the Mishnah on its own, and any relevant material from the Tosefta on its own. Only then is it possible to delineate the various halakhic or other developments that have taken place with regard to the issue at hand.

The tannaim also composed a series of midrashic expositions on Exodus, Leviticus, Numbers and Deuteronomy. There are two midrashic collections on Exodus and Numbers and three on Deuteronomy, a phenomenon which causes us to ask how each midrashic collection is related to one another, as well as their relationship to the Mishnah and Tosefta.[3] We will consider this question when we encounter halakhic midrashim in our commentary on the Bavli. For now we should note that just as understanding a passage in the Bavli requires examination of any parallel material found in the Tosefta and Mishnah, so, too, it requires examination of any parallels in the halakhic midrashim.

Example

משנה פסחים ג:ז	תוספתא פסחים ג:יב
ההולך לשחוט את פסחו ולמול את בנו ולאכול סעודת אירוסין בבית חמיו ונזכר שיש לו חמץ בתוך ביתו אם יכול לחזור ולבער ולחזור למצותו יחזור ויבער ואם לאו מבטלו בלבו.	מיכן אתה אומר ההולך לשחוט את פסחו ולמול את בנו ולוכל סעודת אירוסין בבית חמיו ונזכר שיש לו חמץ בתוך הבית אם יש לו שהות כדי שיחזור חוזר ואם לאו אין חוזר.

Mishnah Pesahim 3:7	**Tosefta Pesahim 3:12**
He who is on his way to slaughter his Pesah sacrifice or to circumcise his son or to dine at a betrothal feast at the house of his father-in-law, and remembers that he has hametz at home: if he is able to go back, remove [it], and [then] return to his religious duty, he must go back and remove [it]. But if not, he annuls it in his heart.	From here you say: He who is on his way to slaughter his Pesah sacrifice or to circumcise his son or to dine at a betrothal feast at the house of his father-in-law, and remembers that he has hametz at home: if he has time to go back, he must go back [and remove it]. But if not, he does not go back.

---

3   For a comprehensive introduction to the tannaitic midrashim see Menahem Kahana, "The Halakhic Midrashim," *The Literature of the Sages: Second Part,* ed. Shmuel Safrai, et al. (Assen: Royal Van Gorcum and Fortress Press, 2006), 3–106.

Both of these halakhot refer to a situation in which a person was on his way to perform a mitzvah right before Pesah and then remembered that he left hametz in his home. Both texts instruct him to return home and destroy the hametz only if he will have enough time to make it back in time to perform his mitzvah. The two passages are nearly identical, but there are two significant differences, both of which demonstrate that this particular passage of the Tosefta predates its mishnaic parallel. First, the Tosefta passage begins abruptly with the technical phrase "from here you say," which is not found elsewhere in the Tosefta.[4] This is a technical term which attaches an apodictic halakhah to a midrash which precedes it. The editor of the Tosefta had before him a source which included the midrash that served as the basis for the teaching (perhaps related to Mekhilta De-Rabbi Shimon b. Yohai 13:7), but he omitted it from the Tosefta and left the independent halakhah concerning hametz. This linguistic difficulty indicates that the version in the Tosefta is earlier because the opposite possibility, that the Tosefta would have added this difficult and abrupt phrase to the Mishnah, is extremely unlikely.

Second, the Tosefta does not mention the concept that one who cannot physically remove or destroy his hametz may "nullify it in his heart." The Tosefta rules that if one does not have enough time to return home, destroy his hametz and still perform the mitzvah he set out to perform (slaughter the Pesah, circumcise his son or participate in a betrothal celebration), he does not return. The Tosefta does not provide a solution to such a problem; the text simply rules that the individual does not return home because the performance of these positive commandments outweigh the obligation to burn the hametz. The author of this mishnah was troubled by the lack of a solution to this problematic situation—either he does not perform the mitzvah he set out to perform and will forever lose the opportunity to perform it, or he leaves hametz in his house on Pesah and thereby transgresses the prohibition that "leaven shall not be found in your house" (Exodus 12:19). To offer some sort of solution the Mishnah "invents" the notion of "nullifying in one's heart." Clearly the authors of the Tosefta were not familiar with this halakhah. Had they known of it, they would not have left the person on his way to perform a mitzvah with hametz still in his possession. The inclusion of this clause in the Mishnah is a sign of halakhic development

---

[4] The scribe of the Erfurt manuscript deletes the phrase because he believes it to be a mistake.

from the earlier toseftan source which does not contain a solution, to the later source in the Mishnah which has one to offer.[5] The Mishnah creatively solves the dilemma of observance of a positive commandment at the cost of transgressing the consequential negative commandment of owning hametz on Pesah. Had the Tosefta disagreed with this solution it would have likely explicitly ruled out the possibility of nullifying hametz in one's heart.

We should conclude this example by noting that this type of development is emblematic of developments from early to later versions of statements and passages. An earlier passage concludes in a somewhat unsatisfactory manner (i.e. he just leaves his hametz there). Later sages/authors offer creative resolutions. By comparing these texts we can uncover the dynamic process through which rabbinic literature and halakhah were created.

Further Reading

Elman, Yaakov. *Authority and Tradition: Toseftan Baraitot in Talmudic Babylonia.* Hoboken: Ktav Publishing, 1994.

Friedman, Shamma. "The Primacy of Mishnah to Tosefta in Synoptic Parallels." In *Introducing Tosefta: Textual, Intratextual, and Intertextual Studies.* Edited by H. Fox et al., Hoboken: Ktav Publishing, pp. 99–121.

Hauptman, Judith. *Rereading the Mishnah: A New Approach to Ancient Jewish Texts.* Tübingen: Mohr Siebeck, 2005.

Walfish, Avraham. "Approaching the Text and Approaching God: The Redaction of Mishnah/Tosefta Berakhot." *Jewish Studies* 43 (2005–2006), 21–79.

B. The Baraitot in the Bavli

The Bavli and Yerushalmi both cite extensively from the Tosefta and the halakhic midrashim. When embedded in one of the two talmuds, these sources are called "baraitot," which is Aramaic for "external"—these are tannaitic sources external to the Mishnah. This term was first used by fourth-generation Babylonian

---

[5] Shamma Friedman, "The Primacy of Mishnah to Tosefta in Synoptic Parallels," *Introducing Tosefta,* ed. Harry Fox et al. (Hoboken: Ktav Publishing, 1999), 113–114.

amoraim and indicates the growing acceptance of the authority of the Mishnah.[6] However, the language and content of these sources as found in the two Talmuds is frequently not identical to that found in the tannaitic corpus itself. That is to say, the Bavli will quote a baraita which clearly is parallel to a halakhah found in the Tosefta, yet the language of the two sources, and sometimes the content of the halakhah, will differ. In such cases, our assumption is that since the Tosefta as a corpus is earlier than the Bavli, so, too, the individual halakhah is found in the Tosefta in an earlier and thus more original form.

This assumption provides a critically valuable technique in analyzing the development of ideas and laws. At times we can see that later editors modify tannaitic sources to match their later assumptions. At other times, they modified these sources in an attempt to harmonize the discrepancies found within tannaitic halakhah.

Some baraitot in the two Talmuds do not have parallels in the tannaitic collections. These baraitot pose a serious problem to the critical commentator, for it is unclear whether they were invented in post-tannaitic times, perhaps even in Babylonia, or whether they are authentic tannaitic teachings external to both the Mishnah and the Tosefta. We believe that the Bavli does contain authentic tannaitic teachings which were not, for whatever reason, included in the tannaitic compositions themselves. However, we also believe that some sources ascribed to tannaim in the Bavli were created in Babylonia after the close of the tannaitic period. Thus a baraita that appears in the Bavli and nowhere else could be an authentic tannaitic creation reflective of second-century Eretz Yisrael, but it could also be a much later amoraic creation that was attributed to tannaim for a variety of reasons. Hence each of these sources must be analyzed carefully for clues regarding its provenance.

Example 1: Change In Language And Content

בבלי פסחים קטז ע"א	תוספתא פסחים י:י
אמר רבי אלעזר ברבי צדוק: כך	מעשה ואמר להם ר' לעזר בר' [צדוק]
היו אומרים תגרי חרך שבירושלים:	לתגרי לוד: בואו וטלו לכם תבלי מצוה.
בואו וטלו לכם תבלין למצוה.	

---

[6] Neil Danzig, "Lehitpathut Hamunah Baraita," *Sinai* 89,5/6 (1981), 240–247.

Bavli Pesahim 116a	Tosefta Pesahim 10:10
R. Elazar b. R. Tzadok said: The spice merchants of Jerusalem would say: Come and take for yourselves the spices for the mitzvah.	It happened that R. Eliezer b. R. Tzadok said to the merchants of Lod: Come and take for yourselves the spices for the mitzvah.

The Tosefta relates a story in which R. Elazar b. R. Zadok went out into the market and encouraged the merchants of Lod to buy the spices necessary for making haroset. This story contains several clues as to the nature of its provenance. First, the fact that this story takes place in Lod and not in Jerusalem indicates that the story occurs after the destruction. Second, haroset was a post-Temple addition to the Pesah meal—the Torah mandates only the Pesah sacrifice, matzah and marror. Third, we know from elsewhere that R. Elazar b. R. Zadok did spend Pesah in Lod at least on one occasion (Tosefta Pesahim 3:11). Thus in the Tosefta R. Eliezer b. R. Zadok is pressing others to adopt what he believes should be used to supplement the foods eaten at the meal.

The Bavli's baraita is clearly parallel to this Toseftan source, but it includes significant changes which furnish the story with a new context. In the Bavli, R. Elazar b. Zadok does not participate in the incident—he relates the story. The incident itself takes place in Jerusalem and instead of the rabbi urging the merchants to buy spices, it is the merchants themselves who call out encouraging their customers to purchase spices for haroset.[7] This deliberate change has two important outcomes. First, the move from Lod to Jerusalem implies that the incident took place when the Temple was still standing, thus intimating that haroset was consumed in the Temple with the Pesah sacrifice. Second, the merchants' call to buy the spices to make haroset would indicate that this was already a widespread and accepted practice. An additional sign that this baraita was reworked in Babylonia and does not appear in its original tannaitic formulation is the addition of the word חרך, spice.[8] This word has its origins in Syriac, a dialect of Aramaic, which was widely spoken in the region beginning only in the fourth century. Due to the relatively late origin

---

[7] The same change is found in Yerushalmi Pesahim 10:3, 37d.
[8] The root ח.ר.ך means charred, referring to the manner in which the spices were prepared. See Michael Sokoloff, *A Dictionary of Jewish Babylonian Aramaic*, (Ramat Gan: Bar Ilan University Press, 2002), 483.

of the word, it would be impossible for the word to have been original to the Tosefta, which was completed by the early third century.[9] Influenced by Babylonian Aramaic, the Bavli added the word into the tannaitic source.[10] Aside from demonstrating how the Bavli reworks an earlier source, this is an important example of how textual studies are an essential component of historical studies and how linguistic studies are an essential component of textual studies. A historian wishing to discover when haroset was added into the Pesah feast should rely on the evidence found in the Tosefta, not in the Bavli.

Example 2: Babylonian Additions To Toseftan Baraitot

Occasionally the Bavli preserves the original baraita from an earlier source but augments it in a way that clearly reflects a Babylonian reality.

An example of this phenomenon appears in the following baraita concerning a man who offers the following stipulation when betrothing a woman:

תוספתא קידושין ג:ט	**Tosefta Kiddushin 3:9**
על מנת שאני תלמיד	On condition that I am a "disciple of the sages"—
חכם אין אומרים לא	we do not say that [he must be] like Shimon ben
כשמעון בן עזיי ולא	Azzai or Shimon ben Zoma. Rather anyone whose
כשמעון בן זומא אלא כל	townspeople treat him [as a disciple of the sages].
שבני עירו נוהגין כן.	

Tosefta interprets "disciple of the sages" to be someone who is regarded as such in his city. Thus the man is betrothed only if he is in fact regarded as a "disciple of the sages" in his city. The Bavli adds on to this baraita:

---

[9] For more on the history and development of Aramaic see Eduard Yecheskel Kutscher, "Aramaic," *Encyclopaedia Judaica*, ed. Michael Berenbaum and Fred Skolnik. 2nd ed. Vol. 2 (Detroit: Macmillan Reference USA, 2007), 342–359.

[10] Shamma Friedman, "Uncovering Literary Dependencies in the Talmudic Corpus," *The Synoptic Problem in Rabbinic Literature*, ed. Shaye Cohen (Providence: Brown University Press, 2000), 41–42.

בבלי קידושין מט ע״ב	**Bavli Kiddushin 49b**

על מנת שאני תלמיד - אין
אומרים כשמעון בן עזאי
וכשמעון בן זומא, אלא כל
ששואלין אותו בכל מקום
דבר אחד בלימודו ואומרו,
ואפילו במסכתא דכלה.

On condition that I am a "disciple of the sages"—we do not say that [he must be] like Shimon ben Azzai or Shimon ben Zoma. Rather anyone whom they ask anywhere concerning one thing from his learning and he can respond, and even from the "tractate of the *kallah*."

Our concern here is not with the emendations to the baraita, such as the change from "anyone whose townspeople treated him [as a disciple of the sages]" to "anyone whom they ask anywhere concerning one thing from his learning and he can respond," but rather with the addition at the end. The "tractate of the *kallah*" was the tractate that was being learned in the Babylonian yeshivot during the month of the "*kallah*"—the biannual gatherings to teach Torah to the masses in Nissan or Elul. The term "*kallah*" seems to denote this biannual gathering. Thus the Bavli adds in that to be a "*talmid*" one need not be able to answer questions from anywhere in the rabbinic tradition, but just from the tractate being learned at that time. The "*kallah*" and the "tractate of the *kallah*" are Babylonian innovations. There is no evidence that this institution existed in Eretz Yisrael and it is never mentioned in Eretz Yisraeli literature.[11]

Example 3: Babylonian Baraitot

Occasionally the Bavli's editors create a baraita, one which does not merely update or modify an original tannaitic teaching, but actually invents one. We term these baraitot "Babylonian baraitot." The following example is from Bavli Sanhedrin 56b. It is found in a sugya concerning which prohibitions must be observed by a "Noahide"—one who is bound by the covenant with Noah, i.e. a non-Jew.

---

[11] See Isaiah Gafni, *Yehudei Bavel Bitekufat Hatalmud* (Jerusalem: Zalman Shazar Center, 1990), 213–225, esp. 216–218.

בעבודה זרה: דברים שבית | With regard to idol worship: Acts for which an
דין של ישראל ממיתין | Israelite court executes, a Noahide is warned (pro-
עליהן - בן נח מוזהר | hibited from doing); [acts for which] an Israelite
עליהן, אין בית דין של | court does not execute, a Noahide is not warned.
ישראל ממיתין עליהן -
אין בן נח מוזהר עליהן.

There is no parallel for this baraita in tannaitic literature. However, the language is paralleled by the language used in Tosefta Avodah Zarah 8:4 to explain the prohibition on fornication:

על גילוי עריות כיצד? | [They are prohibited from] fornication. How
כל ערוה שבית דין | so? Any incestuous relationship that an Israelite
של ישראל ממיתין | court would execute for, a Noahide is warned
עליה בני נח מוזהרין | against—these are the words of R. Meir.
עליה דברי ר' מאיר.

There are two possible ways to explain the existence of the baraita in the Bavli concerning Noahide idol worship. The first, and more likely explanation is that a later editor created this baraita to fill a gap in the Tosefta. He patterned his baraita after the baraita concerning fornication. Since Rava, a fourth-generation amora, comments on this baraita in the Bavli, it must predate him. The less likely possibility is that the Tosefta or some other tannaitic collection originally contained this baraita and it was subsequently lost. The Tosefta as we know it does explain the prohibition on idol worship, but the explanation is completely different from that found in the baraita in the Bavli. The following version is from the Vienna manuscript:

על עבודה זרה ועל ברכת | [A Noahide is liable] for idolatry and for
השם כיצד? גוי שעבד | blaspheming God. How so? A gentile who
עבודה זרה וברך את השם | worshiped idols or cursed God [is to be
לא ניתנה מיתה לבני | put to the sword because] execution was
נח אלא בסייף בלבד. | given to Noahides only by the sword.

The fact that there is a section in the Tosefta that does explain something about the prohibition of idolatry, specifically how a Noahide idolater is to be executed, makes it exceedingly unlikely that the baraita in the Bavli, which concerns itself with the subject of which idolatrous actions committed by a Noahide are pun-ishable, was originally part of the Tosefta and somehow was lost from that text. It is also unlikely that both baraitot were originally part of the Tosefta because the question "how so?" (כיצד) is answered with one halakhah and not two.

Furthermore, we should note a certain difference between the clause con-cerning fornication in Tosefta Avodah Zarah and the clause concerning idol worship in the Bavli. When R. Meir in the Tosefta refers to illicit relations for which Israelites are executed, this is a clear reference to distinctions made in Leviticus 20 between those forms of incest punished by death and those punished by *karet*. The reference point for R. Meir's distinctions is the Torah. In contrast, the list of idolatrous actions punishable by death and those which are merely forbidden appears for the first time in rabbinic literature.[12] That is to say, the reference point for the Babylonian baraita is another rabbinic source. Thus the truly tannaitic text refers to the Torah whereas the later Babylonian text, created to look tannaitic, refers to the Mishnah. This is another sign that the Bavli's baraita is a later development and is not an authentically tannaitic source.

Further Reading

Elman, Yaakov. "Babylonian Baraitot in Tosefta and the 'Dialectology' of Middle Hebrew," *AJS Review* 16:1–2 (1991), 1–29.
Friedman, Shamma. "Uncovering Literary Dependencies in the Talmudic Corpus." In *The Synoptic Problem in Rabbinic Literature*. Edited by S. Cohen. Providence: Brown University Press, pp. 35–60.

C. The Yerushalmi and the Bavli

The two Talmuds—the Yerushalmi and the Bavli—serve as commentaries and expansions of the Mishnah. The former was composed in the Land of Israel, and the latter was composed in Babylonia. The relationship between these two monumental compositions is one of the most fruitful fields of inquiry

---

[12] Mishnah Sanhedrin 7:7; Tosefta Sanhedrin 10:3.

in modern critical Talmudic scholarship, as we demonstrate in nearly every sugya analyzed in this book. However, we first need to clarify our assumptions concerning the relationship between these two texts.

When analyzing any parallel between these two compositions, our a priori assumption is that the literary format of the material in the Yerushalmi predates that of the Bavli. This is true even if the statements are attributed to Babylonian rabbis. Thus, for instance, the words of Rav will be preserved in a more original form in the Yerushalmi, even though Rav is a Babylonian amora. There are two main reasons that this is the case. First, the Yerushalmi was completed and redacted at least several generations before the Bavli. The latest amoraim in the Yerushalmi lived around the end of the fourth century C.E. In contrast, the latest amoraim in the Bavli lived between 100 and 200 years later, and it is likely that the Bavli continued to undergo editing for a long period of time after the death of the last named amoraim. Thus, the Yerushalmi in its totality is an earlier Talmud, one in which we can reasonably expect to find parallel material to exist in a less developed, more original form. Since the Bavli is later than the Yerushalmi, it seems to have been familiar with much of this Eretz Yisraeli material, although not necessarily with the Talmud Yerushalmi itself. The Bavli uses this material for its own halakhic, midrashic and literary purposes.

The second main reason is a corollary to the first—the Bavli underwent an editing process that was far more comprehensive and intensive than did the Yerushalmi. This is evident when we compare the constituent components of sugyot, i.e. baraitot (tannaitic statements) and memrot (amoraic statements) as well as the overall editing of the sugyot themselves. The anonymous voice of the stam is far more present and dominant in the Bavli, shaping the dialectical structure to a significant extent. In contrast, while there is an anonymous voice in the Yerushalmi as well, this voice is less dominant and seems to have intervened less in the structure and wording of the amoraic layer of the Yerushalmi's sugyot. For instance, Yerushalmi sugyot finish without a resolution far more often than do those in the Bavli. They consist primarily of baraitot and memrot, with less discourse about these sources than we find in the sugyot in the Bavli. These are all signs of an earlier Talmud.

For a variety of reasons, the Yerushalmi is often difficult to understand. First, the lack of stammaitic discourse makes the argumentation harder to follow. Second, the text is often corrupt because copyists made numerous errors which went uncorrected. Third, the Yerushalmi was not subjected to the same extensive history of interpretation as the Bavli. By the time commentators began to occupy themselves intensively with the elucidation of the Yerushalmi, the Bavli had been established as the core text in the rabbinic curriculum for centuries. The dominance of the Bavli generally led commentators to explain the Yerushalmi according to words and assumptions found only in the Bavli. Frequently, traditional commentators even emended the Yerushalmi so that its content would correspond to the parallel Bavli sugya. Academic scholars have tried to correct this trend, and in this book we will try to do so as well.

Below are three examples of how comparative studies of the Bavli and Yerushalmi can inform critical analysis.

Example 1: Stam In The Yerushalmi, Amora In The Bavli

Comparative studies of the Bavli and Yerushalmi demonstrate that there are cases in which the Bavli creates a memra—an amoraic statement—from words that exist as anonymous comments on amoraic statements in the Yerushalmi. The following is an example addressed by Shamma Friedman:[13]

בבלי פסחים קיד ע"ב	ירושלמי פסחים י:א (לז, ג)
אמר ריש לקיש: זאת אומרת מצות צריכות כוונה. כיון דלא בעידן חיובא דמרור הוא דאכיל ליה - בבורא פרי האדמה הוא דאכיל ליה, ודילמא לא איכוון למרור - הלכך בעי למהדר לאטבולי לשם מרור. דאי סלקא דעתך מצוה לא בעיא כוונה - למה לך תרי טיבולי? והא טביל ליה חדא זימנא!	חברייא בשם רבי יוחנן צריך לטבל בחזרת שני פעמים. רבי זעורה בשם ר' יוחנן אינו צריך לטבל בחזרת שני פעמים. רבי שמעון בן לקיש אמר אם לא טבל פעם ראשונה צריך לטבל פעם שנייה... מתניתא פליגא על רבי יוחנן: יוצאין במצה בין שכיוון בין שלא כיוון.

---

[13] Shamma Frideman, *Tosefta Atiqta*: *Pesah Rishon* (Ramat Gan: Bar Ilan University Press, 2002), 434–435, n. 52.

Bavli Pesahim 114b

Resh Lakish said: This [the mishnah] proves that commandments require intention, [for] since he does not eat it at the stage when bitter herbs are compulsory, he eats it with [the blessing,] 'Creator of the fruit of the ground,' and perhaps he did not intend [to fulfill the obligation of] bitter herbs; therefore he must dip it again with the express purpose of [eating] bitter herbs. For if you should think [that] commandments do not require intention, why two dippings: surely he has [already] dipped it once?

Yerushalmi Pesahim 10:3 (37c)

Havraya in the name of R. Yohanan say: He must dip lettuce twice. R. Zeora in the name of R. Yohanan says: He need not dip lettuce twice. R. Shimon ben Lakish says: If he did not dip the first time he must dip the second time. A baraita disagrees with R. Yohanan: They fulfill their obligation with matzah whether they had intention or not.

Mishnah Pesahim 10:3 describes eating lettuce twice at the seder. In the tannaitic period, the first dipping was an appetizer course which included lettuce, while the second dipping consisted of lettuce in fulfillment of the commandment to eat bitter herbs (according to Mishnah Pesahim 2:6, lettuce is the preferred form of marror). In the amoraic period, the sages were unaware of certain Greco-Roman eating habits and they began to ask whether it was really necessary to eat lettuce twice. The first opinion, attributed to R. Yohanan in the Yerushalmi, states that one must still dip twice with lettuce. R. Zeora disagrees and says that lettuce need only be dipped once because as soon as it has been consumed one has fulfilled the obligation to eat marror, even if it was in the beginning of the meal. R. Shimon b. Lakish agrees in principle with R. Zeora and explains that dipping is required only later in the meal if it was not done at the earlier stage. The last section of the Yerushalmi quoted here raises a challenge to the first version of R. Yohanan's statement. The reason, according to this explanation of R. Yohanan, to eat lettuce twice is because the first time it is eaten, it is not eaten with the intention of fulfilling a mitzvah. Rather, it is eaten as an appetizer. But there is a baraita that explicitly states, at least with regard to matzah, that one can fulfill one's obligation even without intention. In light of this difficulty, one could conclude that the opinion which requires two dippings of lettuce holds that these mitzvot (matzah and marror) must be fulfilled with the proper intention, whereas the one who holds that the first dipping is sufficient holds that intention is not required.

In the Bavli, the statement from the Yerushalmi that one is or is not required to dip twice has been transformed into a broadly applied abstract concept—"[all] commandments require intention." In addition, the attribution has been switched. In the Yerushalmi, Resh Lakish states that one need not dip twice, whereas in the Bavli he requires two dippings of lettuce. This reversal of attributions between the Bavli and Yerushalmi is a common phenomenon. In any case, these words, "[all] commandments require intention," attributed to the amora Resh Lakish, are actually the words of a Babylonian editor; they are not those of an early Eretz-Yisraeli amora. The abstract concept "commandments require intention" appears four times in the Bavli, each a stammaitic categorization of an earlier amoraic statement. This comparison helps us trace the development of abstract thought in halakhah. Early amoraim issued concrete rulings (one must dip lettuce twice/one need not dip twice) which were extrapolated by later authorities into broadly applying abstract rules (all commandments require intention).

Example 2: Reading The Bavli Into The Yerushalmi

The following passage is an excellent example in which despite nearly identical language, the Yerushalmi and Bavli are in actuality discussing different matters. Mishnah Bava Batra 1:4 states:

כותל חצר שנפל	If the wall in a [jointly-owned] courtyard should
מחייבין אותו לבנותו	fall down, they [the residents] can force the other
עד ארבע אמות.	[resident] to rebuild it up to four cubits high.

This mishnah teaches that residents of a jointly owned courtyard can force the other residents to share in the costs of rebuilding one of the walls of the courtyard that has fallen. Each resident must share in the costs of rebuilding the wall up to a height of four cubits.

Yerushalmi Bava Batra 1:3, 12d, comments on this Mishnah as follows:

כותל חצר שנפל כול':	The wall in a courtyard that fell down:
רב חונה אמר: ובלבד	R. Huna said: As long as it is at the cost
כשעה שבנה עכשיו.	[of material] in which he built it now.
דאין הוה בני דכיפין	[It is clear] that if it was built of
בני לה דכיפין.	stones he rebuilds it from stones.
ברם אין הוה בני דכיפין	But what if it was built of stones and
ובנתיה בליבנין?	now he rebuilds it with bricks?
גבי ליה כיפין וכל	He collects [as if] it were stones and when-
שעה דנפיל בני לה.	ever it should fall, he must rebuild it.

Shlomo Naeh[14] interprets R. Huna as commenting on the mishnah quoted above. The neighbor must repay the one who rebuilt the wall according to the cost of the rebuilt wall, and not according to the value of the wall when it fell down. The continuation of the passage is from the anonymous voice of the Yerushalmi, as can be seen from the switch in language from Hebrew to Aramaic. It is not common for amoraim to use two languages in such circumstances. This is an important criterion (see below) for separating amoraic statements from their later anonymous interpretations. This explanation asserts that if the wall was built of stones and he rebuilds it of the same material, then obviously the other neighbor must repay the value of the stones. But what if it was originally built with stones—the more expensive and stable material—and now he rebuilds it with bricks? The other neighbor should be able to demand that the wall be built with stones, so why should he pay for the bricks at all? After all, he could claim that the inferior material is not to his liking. The Yerushalmi answers that the other neighbor pays as if it had been rebuilt with stones and that the neighbor who rebuilt with bricks must now accept full responsibility to rebuild the wall should it fall again. This is a small modification of R. Huna's rule that he repays according to what was rebuilt.

In contrast to Naeh's explanation, traditional commentators on the Yerushalmi interpreted R. Huna's words as referring to an entirely different mishnah, mishnah three, which reads:

---

[14] Shlomo Naeh, "Behezkat Shelo Natan," *Atarah L'Haim*, ed. Daniel Boyarin, et al. (Jerusalem: Hebrew University Magnes Press, 2000), 151–152.

משנה בבא בתרא א:ג	**Mishnah Bava Batra 1:3**
המקיף את חבירו משלש	One whose [property] surrounds another person's
רוחותיו וגדר את הראשונה	property in three directions, and he builds a fence
ואת השניה ואת השלישית	on one side, and on the second side and on the
אין מחייבין אותו.	third side, he is not obligated to share in the costs.
רבי יוסי אומר: אם	R. Yose says: if he builds a fence on the fourth
עמד וגדר את הרביעית	side, he must share in all of the costs.
מגלגלין עליו את הכל.	

The Ramban, writing in the thirteenth century, was the first to attach R. Huna's statement to this mishnah. To simplify the translation we have used the following transliterations—*nikaf*—the one whose property is surrounded; *makif*—the one whose property surrounds the other person's property.

חידושי הרמב"ן בבא	**Hiddushei HaRamban, Bava Batra 4b**
בתרא ד ע"ב	It seems that this is the meaning [of R. Hu-
נראה שכך פירושו: שאם	na's statement]. That if the nikaf fences the
עמד ניקף וגדר את	fourth side with stones and the makif fences
הרביעית בכיפין והמקיף	three sides with stones, the nikaf has shown
גדר שלש בכיפין גלי ניקף	that he was satisfied with this type of wall.
דעתיה דניחא ליה בבנין	
זה וגבי ליה דכיפין.	
ברם אין הוא הניקף בני	But if the nikaf built with stones and the
דכיפין, והמקיף בנתיה	makif built with bricks which are of less-
דליבנין שהוא בנין פחות,	er quality, the nikaf can say to him: If I pay
יכול ניקף לומר לו אם אני	you for bricks the fence will fall down to-
נותן עכשיו דמי לבנים	morrow and I'll need to build it again.
למחר נופל ואני צריך	
לבנותו פעם אחרת.	

According to the Ramban, the *nikaf* can refuse to pay for the three walls made of bricks because the *makif* used material that is inferior to his fourth wall made of stone. Ramban's interpretation was adopted not only by traditional commentators, but even by Saul Lieberman, in his commentary on the Yerushalmi. However, Shlomo Naeh has shown that this interpretation is very implausible. First, the words in the Yerushalmi, "if it was built," relate to a wall that was already in existence, as in mishnah four, and not to an entirely new wall as in mishnah three. Second, the root בנ״ה, used in the Yerushalmi, is the same root used in mishnah four, whereas mishnah three uses the root גד״ר to describe erecting a fence. Third, the first mishnah of the tractate distinguishes between courtyard walls built of bricks and those built of stones. Clearly, the terms in the Yerushalmi show that R. Huna was referring to mishnah four and not to mishnah three.

Why then did these commentators, including Lieberman, explain the Yerushalmi as referring to mishnah three—building a fence around a property? Lieberman himself reveals the motivation for his own interpretation and that of the Ramban:[15]

> ודברי רב חונא כאן   R. Huna's words here are like his words in
> הם כדבריו בבבלי כאן: the Bavli (Bava Batra 4b): It all goes ac-
> הכל לפי מה שגדר.   cording to how he built the fence.

R. Huna in the Bavli states, "it all goes according to how he built the fence." This statement is clearly referring to mishnah three, the mishnah concerning fences around the field, for the Bavli uses the root גד״ר. But due to the similarity between his statement in the Bavli and his statement in the Yerushalmi, commentators were drawn to interpreting the two statements as referring to the same mishnah. However, such a reading does not make sense based on the Yerushalmi alone.

It is necessary to understand the Yerushalmi in its own context before considering how it relates to the Bavli. R. Huna may have made two different statements with one preserved in each of the Talmuds, or perhaps the Babylonian editors intentionally reworked the original version of R. Huna's statement. In either case, we cannot even begin to compare the two Talmuds critically until we establish the correct interpretation of the Yerushalmi, one free from Babylonian influence. Otherwise, we will fall into the trap of reading the Bavli into the Yerushalmi, rather than reading the Yerushalmi on its own terms.

---

[15] Saul Lieberman, *Yerushalmi Nezikin* (Jerusalem: The Israel Academy of Sciences and Humanities, 1983), 175.

Further Reading

Hayes, Christine. *Between the Babylonian and Palestinian Talmuds*. New York: Oxford University Press, 1997.

Gray, Alyssa. *A Talmud in Exile: The Influence of Yerushalmi Avodah Zarah on the Formation of Bavli Avodah Zarah*. Providence: Brown Judaic Studies, 2005.

Jaffe, Martin. "The Babylonian Appropriation of the Talmud Yerushalmi: Redactional Studies in the Horayot Tractates." In *The Literature of Early Rabbinic Judaism*. Edited by A.J Avery-Peck. Lanham: University Press of America, 1989, pp. 3–27.

Moscovitz, Leib. "The Formation and Character of the Jerusalem Talmud." In *The Cambridge History of Judaism IV: The Late Roman-Rabbinic Period*. Edited by S. Katz. Cambridge: Cambridge University Press, 2006, pp. 663–77.

The Stratification of the Bavli into Historical Layers

When examining the historical development of ideas or halakhot within the Bavli, the first step is to compare the sources in the Bavli with earlier texts. We must ask how the sugya in the Bavli compares with that in the Yerushalmi and how the baraitot in the Bavli compare with those in tannaitic sources. The next step is the separation of the Babylonian sugya into its historical layers: tannaitic, amoraic (and within the amoraic period) and editorial or stammaitic. But there is little value in separating the Bavli into historical levels until the Bavli itself has been compared with Eretz Yisraeli literature.

In this section we will consider how the Babylonian sugya is separated into its component historical layers. This technique has proven especially fruitful in analysis of the Bavli for three reasons. First of all, as stated above, the Bavli is the last of the classical rabbinic creations, and therefore it incorporates sources that were authored at various points throughout the rabbinic period (roughly from the end of the first century C.E. through around 500 C.E.). Second, whereas in Eretz Yisrael the rabbis created multiple compilations and preserved the borders between them (Mishnah, Tosefta, the many halakhic midrashim, Yerushalmi, Genesis Rabbah, Leviticus Rabbah and other aggadic midrashim), in Babylonia all rabbinic statements, passages, and genres were combined into one massive corpus. This resulted in a Talmud that contains many texts that developed over multiple centuries. Finally, the stammaim, the editors and the redactors of the Bavli were both interventionist in their nature and yet at the same time careful to preserve the borders between their words and those of their predecessors. They expanded upon, rewrote, and reorganized some of their sources, and they created new frameworks in which to cast earlier material. But they did not rewrite all of their received material, as did, for instance, Maimonides, who essentially rewrote all of rabbinic halakhah using his own language in the Mishneh Torah. Nearly every page of the Bavli bears clear evidence of multiple historical levels, including passages where amoraim comment on baraitot and where later amoraim comment on the words of early amoraim. Indeed, the Bavli's editors were extraordinarily careful to preserve the chronology of the material they received; rarely does an early amora appear to be commenting on the words of a later amora.

We have divided this section into two parts. In the first we discuss separating the Bavli into two layers, the amoraic and the stammaitic. In the second we discuss the analysis of material that appears in multiple places within the Bavli and how such material may have moved from its original context to secondary and even tertiary contexts.

A. Amoraim and the Stam

For at least a generation, critical Talmud scholars have relied on two fundamental assumptions when analyzing a sugya. The first is that the anonymous voice in the Bavli, the stam, is later than the amoraim. The second is that the stam reinterprets and reorganizes earlier material and even invents statements and then attributes them to earlier rabbis. Critical Talmudic scholars today are trained from the outset to separate a sugya into several layers, the last of which is usually called stammaitic. One of the simplest methods to distinguish these layers from one another is by identifying a change in language.[16]

---

[16] Shamma Friedman compiled a list of fourteen different indicators of stammaitic additions to the text of the Bavli. The list has since been translated from Hebrew into English by Jeffrey Rubenstein. See Rubenstein, "Criteria of Stammaitic Intervention in Aggada," *Creation and Composition*, ed. J. Rubenstein (Tübingen: Mohr Siebeck, 2005), 417–440.

Tannaitic and amoraic statements are almost entirely composed in Hebrew while the stammaitic layer of the text is usually in Aramaic.[17]

The separation of amoraic material and stammaitic material is a particularly fruitful analytic tool, but it is one that must be wielded with caution. The primary complication is that later editors did not merely add their own comments and voices to the sugya. They also reworded the earlier material, such that one must constantly analyze amoraic and even tannaitic material to see if it is authentically early, or if it too has been molded or even invented by the late Babylonian editors. This is accomplished by comparing the Bavli with the Yerushalmi and with other earlier texts, as discussed above, to check for the authenticity and accuracy of the amoraic and tannaitic material in the Bavli. However, many baraitot and memrot are found only in the Bavli and thus cannot be compared with other material. We cannot know for certain whether these sources have been emended or even invented by the stam. Sometimes, but not often, we are aided by lexicographical and linguistic clues. In most cases, we recommend trusting the authenticity of the Bavli's sources, but doing so warily. When we find a statement that is attributed to an amora and found nowhere else in rabbinic literature we assume until proven otherwise that the attribution is accurate—i.e. that the amora actually stated those words or at least gave voice to the idea they express.

Example 1: Contextualization Of Amoraic Statement By The Stam

The following is an example in which the simple meaning of the Mishnah has been reinterpreted by the amoraim and then reinterpreted again by the stam. The example reveals the distinct stages of historical development of a law. As described above, this reading stands in stark contrast to traditional interpreters who understood the Mishnah solely in accordance with the later stammaitic interpretation. Mishnah Ketubot 7:1 states:

---

[17] Hyman Klein was the first to use changes between languages as a basic principle for differentiating between the layers of the text. See Klein, "Gemara and Sebara," *The Jewish Quarterly Review* 38:1 (1947), 67–91, esp. 75–77.

המדיר את אשתו מליהנות	One who vows that his wife may not derive
לו: עד שלשים יום	any benefit from him: For thirty days he pro-
יעמיד פרנס. יתר מכן	vides for her through an agent. More than that,
יוציא ויתן כתובה.	he must divorce her and pay her ketubah.

The mishnah describes a situation in which a man makes a vow, perhaps out of spite or anger, prohibiting his wife from deriving any benefit from his property. A woman subject to such a vow would seemingly not be able to eat any food belonging to her husband or use his money to purchase necessary items such as clothing. Such vows which one person takes to prohibit another from using his property are mentioned throughout the Mishnah and other ancient Jewish literature.[18] In this case, the vow is problematic because a husband has an obligation to provide for his wife (based on Exodus 21:10). How then can a husband take a vow to shirk his own responsibility? This is exactly the question asked by the Bavli (Ketubot 70a): "Since he is obligated to her, how can he prohibit her by vow? Does he have the power to cast off his own obligation?" Nevertheless, despite this difficulty, it is clear that the simple meaning of the mishnah is just that—sometimes vows do have the ability to prevent a person from fulfilling an obligation. Indeed, a distinctly similar law is found in the New Testament (Mark 7:9–13 and Matthew 15:3–6). The following quote is from Mark:

> And he [Jesus] said to them, "You have a fine way of rejecting the commandment of God in order to establish your tradition! For Moses said, 'Honor your father and your mother;' and, 'Whoever reviles father or mother must surely die.' But you say, 'If a man tells his father or his mother, "Whatever you would have gained from me is korban"' (that is, given to God)—then you no longer permit him to do anything for his father or mother, thus making void the word of God by your tradition that you have handed down. And many such things you do."

Jesus rebukes the Pharisees who allow an individual to take a vow that would prohibit his parents from benefitting from him, a direct transgression of the fifth

---

[18] See Moshe Benovitz, *Kol Nidre: Studies in the Development of Rabbinic Votive Institutions* (Atlanta: Scholars Press, 1998), 9–40.

commandment. This is parallel to the Mishnah, in which a husband takes a vow to prevent his wife from deriving benefit from him, despite his obligation to her.

Rav Ashi, a late Babylonian amora, cannot accept that a person could use a vow to shirk his legal responsibility so blatantly. Therefore, he offers a solution that limits the scope of the mishnah:

Bavli Ketubot 70b

בבלי כתובות ע ע״ב
אמר ר' אשי: במספקת
לדברים גדולים, ואינה
מספקת לדברים קטנים.

R. Ashi: [The mishnah] refers to a case where she [earns enough] to provide for her major needs, but she does not provide enough for her minor needs.

According to R. Ashi, the mishnah refers to a case where the wife's handiwork was sufficient to provide her major needs. Thus if a man takes a vow not to provide for his wife and his wife earns enough to basically provide for herself, the vow can stand, at least for thirty days. We can see how R. Ashi radically limits the ability of a husband to take such an oath in the first place. The only case where such an oath would be effective is where his wife did not really rely on her husband for sustenance. If she did depend on him for sustenance, such an oath would have no effect whatsoever.

However, the stam is not satisfied even with this. After all, if she is used to those "little things" and now her husband will not provide them for her, he is still abrogating her rights. In order to resolve this difficulty the stam (whose words are in Aramaic, whereas Rav Ashi's words were in Hebrew) now offers an exceedingly difficult contextualization:

הני דברים קטנים היכי
דמי? אי דרגילה בהו, הא
רגילה בהו! ואי לא רגילה
בהו, פרנס למה לה?
לא צריכא, דרגילה בבית
נשא וקא מגלגלא בהדיה,
דאמרה ליה: עד האידנא
דלא אדרתן גלגילנא
בהדך, השתא דאדרתן לא
מצינא דאיגלגל בהדך.

What is the exact case of these 'minor needs'? If she is used to receiving them, she is used to receiving them. And if she is not used to receiving them, why does an agent provide her with them? This law is necessary for a case where she was used to these things in her father's house and she accepted forfeiting them when moving into her husband's house. [When he takes the vow] she says to him: Up until now when you did not prohibit me by vow, I put up with it. Now that you prohibited me by vow, I cannot accept it any longer.

One can easily see how the broad halakhah in the mishnah—a husband can take such a vow and let it stand for thirty days—has been limited in scope, first by R. Ashi and then by the stam. Bothered by the implications of this vow (just as Jesus was bothered by the implications of the son's vow denying benefit to his parents), R. Ashi and the anonymous editors of the Bavli placed severe limitations on the husband. He can take this vow only if: (1) she earns enough money to provide for all her major needs; (2) she has already forfeited any other luxuries upon moving into his house. Indeed, in such a case, as the stam points out, she will receive more luxuries after the vow (by the provisions of the agent) than she was receiving before her husband took the vow. Most importantly, if the vow in any way impinges on the provisions that she was accustomed to receiving in her husband's home, it is rendered ineffective. This halakhah, far removed from the mishnaic law, is an invention of the stam, influenced by R. Ashi.

Example 2: Aramaic Words Added To Hebrew Statement

Many amoraic statements include words added by the stam. In some cases these words change the meaning of the original statement significantly. The following example discussed by Shamma Friedman demonstrates such a phenomenon.[19]

בבלי בבא מציעא כה ע״ב

מתני׳: מצא אחר הגפה או אחר הגדר גוזלות מקושרים, או בשבילין שבשדות - הרי זה לא יגע בהן.

גמ׳: מאי טעמא? דאמרינן: הני אינש אצנעינהו, ואי שקיל להו - לית להו למרייהו סימנא בגווייהו, הלכך לשבקינהו עד דאתי מרייהו ושקיל להו.

Bavli Bava Metzia 25b

Mishnah: If one found pigeons tied together behind a fence or hedge or on footpaths in the fields, he may not touch them.

Gemara: What is the reasoning? We say, maybe a person put them there and if he takes them, the owners will not have any sign by which to identify them. Therefore, he should leave them there until someone comes and takes them.

---

[19] See Friedman, "Al Derekh Heker Hasugya," *Texts and Studies Vol. I*, ed. H.Z. Dimitrovsky (New York: Jewish Theological Seminary of America, 1977), 302.

ואמאי? ליהוי קשר סימנא!	But why? Let the knot serve as a sign!
אמר רבי אבא בר זבדא אמר	R. Abba bar Zavda said in the name of
רב: במקושרין בכנפיהן, דכולי	Rav: When they are tied by their wings
עלמא הכי מקטרי להו.	[he must leave them there], for that is
	the way that everyone ties them.

According to the mishnah, if one finds pigeons tied up behind a fence or a hedge he should leave them there. When read in the traditional manner, with the stammaitic interpretation including R. Abba bar Zavda's statement, the sugya is interpreted as follows: The assumption is that a person may have left the pigeons there expecting to find them upon his return. The stam then asks why the knot could not serve as an identifying sign should the owner come searching for his birds. That is, the owner could prove that the birds are rightfully his by describing the nature of the knot. Why then should the finder not take them? R. Abba bar Zavda answers that the birds were tied by their wings, which is the way that everyone ties up their pigeons. Such a knot, used so commonly, cannot serve as an identifying sign. The implication is that had the pigeons been tied up in some more unusual way that could serve as a sign, the finder could then take them and attempt to return them to the rightful owner.

However, when we read the sugya critically we can note that R. Abba bar Zavda's statement originally meant something different from the later stammaitic interpretation. To understand the sugya in this way, we need to first separate the Hebrew statement, "when they are tied by their wings" from the Aramaic explanation, "for that is the way that everyone ties them," since these represent two distinct chronological layers. Secondly, we can interpret R. Abba bar Zavda as referring directly to the mishnah and not as responding to the anonymous Aramaic question created by the stam. According to this reading, R. Abba bar Zavda simply explains that if the person found the birds tied up in such a way that it is unlikely that they will move, i.e. tied by their wings, he should not take them—even if they have an identifying mark. In such a case it is preferable to leave the birds where they are so that the owner will be able to find them when he returns. Since they are tied by their wings, there is no chance that they will fly away.

We can prove that the Aramaic words are in fact a later addition to the Hebrew statement because in Yerushalmi Bava Metzia 2:4, 8c, the same Hebrew statement (with a different attribution[20]) appears without the Aramaic addition, suggesting that statement had a prior independent life of its own during the amoraic period, before the stam added its Aramaic explanation.

רב יהודה אמר: ובלבד גוזלות	R. Judah said: As long as they are
מקושרין בכנפיהן.	pigeons tied by their wings.

Thus the amoraim emphasized that the finder should leave the birds there only if they are tied down and will not be able to fly away. Later the stammaim shifted the concern from the potential that the birds might fly away to the lack of an identifying sign. The implication would be that if there is an identifying mark, the finder should take them and then try to return them, even if the birds would not have been able to fly away. To achieve this interpretation, the stam added a framing question before R. Abba bar Zavda's statement as well as an addendum to the statement itself.

Further Reading

Halivni, David Weiss. *Midrash, Mishnah, and Gemara: The Predilection for Justified Law.* Cambridge: Harvard University Press, 1986.

—. *The Formation of the Babylonian Talmud.* Translated, edited and introduced by Jeffrey L. Rubenstein. New York: Oxford University Press, 2013.

Kalmin, Richard. *Sages, Stories, Authors, and Editors in Rabbinic Babylonia.* Atlanta: Scholars Press, 1994.

—. "The Formation and Character of the Babylonian Talmud." In *The Cambridge History of Judaism IV: The Late Roman-Rabbinic Period.* Edited by S. Katz. Cambridge: Cambridge University Press, 2006, pp. 840–876.

---

[20] In the continuation of the Yerushalmi, R. Abba bar Zavda finds a wine jug in a small bag and he takes it. Rav rebukes him for doing so, telling him that he should have left it there so that when the owner returned he would not despair at having lost it. Thus the Bavli took the name of R. Abba bar Zavda from the story and attached it to the amoraic statement itself.

B. Transfer of Material within the Bavli

Often we find that amoraic statements or even entire sugyot appear in multiple contexts within the Bavli, though they differ in language, interpretation, and halakhah. This transfer of material from one context to another is an activity which should be attributed to post-amoraic editors. A critical Talmudic scholar should be wary of the supposition that an amora, for instance, issued the same statement on multiple occasions. While this is of course a possibility, it is equally possible if not more plausible that an editor familiar with an amoraic statement or other such material moved it from its original context and placed it in a new setting.

Example 1: Transfer Of Amoraic Statement

In the following example we will see a statement made by an amora in one context that is moved to a second and then a third context. As we shall see, while it made abundant sense in its original context, it makes little sense in the secondary location and is utterly out of place in the third.

In Bavli Shabbat 22a, we read the following:

בעו מיניה מרבי יהושע	They asked R. Yehoshua ben Levi: Can
בן לוי: מהו להסתפק	one use the decorations of the Sukkah
מנויי סוכה כל שבעה?	during the seven days [of the festival]?

אמר להו: הרי אמרו	He said to them: Behold they said: It is forbidden
אסור להרצות מעות	to count coins by use of the Hannukah lamp.
כנגד נר חנוכה.	

אמר רב יוסף: מריה	R. Yosef said: Master of Abraham! He made
דאברהם! תלי תניא	that which is taught [in a baraita] dependent on
בדלא תניא.	that which has not been taught [in a baraita].

סוכה תניא חנוכה לא	Sukkah has been taught, Hannukah has not
תניא. דתניא סככה	been taught. As it was taught, "If he put up
כהלכתה ועיטרה...אסור	valid *skhakh* and decorated it...he may not
להסתפק מהן עד מוצאי	make use of them [the decorations] until
יום טוב האחרון של חג...	the end of the last day of the festival..."

R. Yosef's complaint in this sugya is easy to understand—R. Yehoshua ben
Levi was asked a question about the sukkah for which there is an explicit
answer in a baraita. Instead of quoting the tannatic source which would have
provided the answer, R. Yehoshua ben Levi answered with an amoraic statement—a source which is not introduced with "*tanya*," a technical term reserved
for tannaitic material. That is, although the answer was taught in a baraita, he
answered based on a source that was not taught in a baraita.

The phrase "Master of Abraham" is an imprecation, presumably invoked
to express R. Yosef's incredulity and outrage. It makes sense in this context,
since the answer indeed appears in a baraita and thus there was no need to
invoke an amoraic source instead. But the full phrase is found in two other
contexts, Ketubot 2a and Bava Batra 134b, where it makes less sense and
cannot be taken literally. In Bava Batra we read:

(1) אמר רב יוסף אמר	(1) R. Yosef said in the name of R. Yehudah in the
רב יהודה אמר שמואל:	name of Shmuel: Why did they say that one who
מפני מה אמרו זה בני	says, "this is my son" is believed? Because a hus-
נאמן? הואיל ובעל שאמר	band who says, "I divorced my wife" is believed.
גרשתי את אשתי נאמן.	
(2) אמר ר' יוסף:	(2) R. Yosef said: Master of Abraham! He made
מריה דאברהם! תלי	that which is taught [in a baraita] dependent on
תניא בדלא תניא!	that which has not been taught [in a baraita].
(3) אלא אי אתמר הכי	(3) Rather, if it was said, this is how it was said:
איתמר אמר ר' יהודה	R. Yehudah said in the name of Shmuel: Why
אמר שמואל: מפני מה	did they say that one who says, "this is my son" is
אמרו זה בני נאמן?	believed? Because he has the ability to divorce her.
הואיל ובידו לגרשה.	

In his opening statement R. Yosef explains in the name of Shmuel that a man who identifies someone as his child is believed. This would exempt his wife—should she ever become widowed—from the need to perform levirate marriage, since only a widow whose husband has left no offspring must marry her husband's brother. According to Shmuel, the reason that the man's statement is accepted is that a husband is believed when he says that he divorced his wife, and divorce would also exempt her from requiring levirate marriage should he die without children. Since he is believed with regard to divorce, he is believed with regard to his child. R. Yosef then raises a difficulty, using the same language he invoked in Shabbat 22a. However, here not only is it strange for an amora to raise a challenge to a statement that he himself transmitted, but the difficulty itself makes no sense. The original statement did not concern a case in which an amora made a halakhah taught in a baraita dependent on one that was not taught in a baraita. Furthermore, R. Yosef does not rectify this problem in section three. This section is no more a baraita than was section one; they are both amoraic statements! It is clear that section two was transferred here from Shabbat 22a in order to serve as a transition from the reasoning in section one to the slightly different reasoning in section three.

The statement was also moved to Ketubot 2a, where its use is even less appropriate:

R. Yosef said in the name of R. Yehudah in the name of Shmuel: Why did they say a virgin is wedded on Wednesday? Because they taught, "if the time [for marriage] has come and they weren't married, she eats his food and she eats terumah." It is possible that if the time had come on Sunday he would [immediately] have to provide her with food. That is why it is taught, 'a virgin is wedded on Wednesday."

אמר רב יוסף אמר רב יהודה אמר שמואל: מפני מה אמרו בתולה נישאת ליום הרביעי? לפי ששנינו הגיע זמן ולא נשאו אוכלות משלו ואוכלות בתרומה, יכול הגיע זמן באחד בשבת יהא מעלה לה מזונות, לכך שנינו בתולה נישאת ליום הרביעי.

R. Yosef said: Master of Abraham! He made that which is taught [in a tannaitic source] dependent on that which has not been taught [in a tannaitic source].

אמר רב יוסף: מריה דאברהם! תלי תניא בדלא תניא.

הי תניא והי לא תניא?	Which was taught [in a tannaitic source]
הא תניא והא תניא.	and which was not taught? They were
	both taught [in a tannaitic source].

אלא תלי תניא דמפרש טעמא	Rather, he made a baraita whose reasoning
בדתניא דלא מפרש טעמא.	had been explained dependent on a baraita
	whose reasoning had not been explained.

In this case, R. Yosef explained the first mishnah in Ketubot (about the day on which a virgin is married) by referencing Mishnah Ketubot 5:3 (about when he must begin to provide food for her and when, if married to a kohen, she begins to eat terumah). `For a reason which we will not get into here, the editors of the Bavli are not satisfied with his statement. In order to raise an objection, they bring the same statement attributed to R. Yosef in two other contexts, "Master of Abraham! He made that which is taught [in a baraita] dependent on that which has not been taught [in a baraita]." However, in Ketubot this statement is utterly out of place, as even the stam notes. Both halves of R. Yosef's statement are taught in tannaitic sources. Clearly R. Yosef did not issue this statement in this context. Rather, the Babylonian redactors imported this statement from another context.

Example 2: Transfer of Stammaitic Discourse

The redactor will at times transfer a selection of stammaitic discourse from one passage in the Talmud to another. He does so in order to supplement a sugya which may be lacking in Talmudic debate. We can at times identify the original location of the discourse because it does not fit perfectly into its new context.

בבלי בבא בתרא צז ע"א	**בבלי חולין פז ע"ב**
א"ר יוחנן משום ר"ש בן יהוצדק:	אמר רב יהודה אמר שמואל:
כדרך שאמרו לענין איסורן,	כל מראה אדמומית - מכפרין,
כך אמרו לענין הכשירן.	ומכשירין, וחייבין בכסוי...
הכשירן דמai?	מכשירין איצטריכא ליה,
	מכשירין נמי,

אי דמיא - אכשורי מכשרי, אי
דחמרא - אכשורי מכשרי!

לא צריכא, שתמדו במי גשמים.

וכיון דקא שקיל ורמי להו
למנא - אחשבינהו!

לא צריכא, שנתמד מאליו.

אי דם - אכשורי מכשר, אי
מיא - אכשורי מכשרי!

לא צריכא, שתמדו במי גשמים;

מי גשמים נמי, כיון דשקיל
ורמי - אחשבינהו!

לא צריכא - שנתמדו מאליהן.

Bavli Bava Batra 97a
R. Yohanan said in the name of
R. Shimon ben Yehozadak: The
same [laws] that have been said [to
apply] with regard to prohibitions
have similarly been said [to apply]
with respect to their rendering objects susceptible to uncleanness.

What [kind] of rendering
susceptible [is meant]?

If it is water, it already renders susceptible; [and] if [it is regarded as]
wine it [already] renders susceptible.

It was only necessary in the case where
it was made into *t'mad* with rain water.
But since he picked up [the rain
water] and poured it into the
vessel [containing the lees], he
[surely] intended them [for use].

Bavli Hullin 87b
Rav Yehudah said in the name of
Shmuel: As long as it is of a reddish color, it makes atonement, it
renders susceptible to uncleanness,
and it must be covered up…

It was only necessary to teach that it
renders susceptible to uncleanness.

But even that statement [is unnec-
essary], for if it is blood it already
renders susceptible to uncleanness,
and if it is water it already renders susceptible to uncleanness!

It was only necessary in the case where
it was made into *t'mad* with rain water.
But even in the case of rain water,
since he picked it up and poured it
into the vessel [containing the lees],
he [surely] intended them [for use].

| It is required [in the case] where the *t'mad* was made without the aid of human effort. | It is required [in the case] where the *t'mad* was made without the aid of human effort. |

In order to understand this sugya, some background is necessary. According to rabbinic law, produce is not susceptible to impurity until it has come into contact with certain liquids, including water and wine. The Bava Batra sugya discusses *t'mad*, a weak wine drink made by passing water through the lees of wine. R. Yohanan says that the first two times that one passes water through the lees, the *t'mad* will cause produce to be susceptible to impurity. The stam questions why this statement is necessary, for both elements of *t'mad*, wine and water, consist of liquids that make produce susceptible to impurity, and therefore it should be obvious that *t'mad* will render produce susceptible as well. The end of the sugya solves this problem by specifying that the *t'mad* was made without any human intervention; rainwater fell directly onto the lees of wine. Rainwater does not cause susceptibility to impurity until it has been moved by human hands. The first two times that this happens to the lees the *t'mad* will have the status of wine and will cause susceptibility. Subsequently, it will become so diluted that it will have the status of uncollected water and will not cause susceptibility. While the resolution of the necessity for R. Yohanan's statement is strained, it nevertheless makes sense.

The sugya in Hullin deals with a mixture of blood and water. Blood is another liquid that renders produce susceptible to impurity. R. Yehudah says that if blood is mixed with water it renders produce susceptible as long as the mixture is reddish in color. The stam asks the same question that appeared in Bava Batra: why is this necessary? After all, both blood and water render produce susceptible. Until this point, the sugya is parallel to Bava Batra but it makes sense in its Hullin context. However, the resolution to this question mentions *t'mad,* the water passed over the lees of the wine, which is irrelevant to this discussion. Clearly, then, the last part of the sugya was transferred directly from the end of the sugya in Bava Batra, where these statements were originally taught. A person reading the sugya in Hullin would be puzzled by the mention of *t'mad.* This can be resolved only by analyzing the sugya in light of Bava Batra. Such a comparative anaylsis reveals that the redactor of this sugya, rather than rewriting his material to fit its new context, simply cut these lines from Bava Batra and pasted them here in Hullin.

In an attempt to make sense of why *t'mad* is mentioned out of context, traditional commentators reinterpret the word *t'mad* as any substance mixed with water. But for critical commentators who compare the source in Hullin with that in Bava Batra, it is obvious that the word "תמדו" or "נתמדו" does not refer to any substance "mixed with water," as the traditional commentators construe them. The word only means "to make *t'mad*," as explained above. But when imported to a new context, a new meaning was forced upon it. [21]

Further Reading

Halivni, David Weiss. *The Formation of the Babylonian Talmud*. Translated, edited and introduced by Jeffrey L. Rubenstein. New York: Oxford University Press, 2013, pp. 168–183.

Critical Techniques

All of the above techniques were comparative in nature. They involved comparing rabbinic statements or passages from one composition with those in another composition, or the separation and subsequent comparison of the various historical layers within the Bavli itself. In employing these techniques, the critical scholar considers how both the style and content of rabbinic literature developed from its origins in the tannaitic period through its final composition in the post-amoraic period. There are additional critical techniques, however, which do not rest on comparative methods. We turn our attention now to the first of these techniques, philology.

I. Philology

Before engaging in what is known as "higher criticism" which analyzes the development of texts and ideas, scholars must first establish the authentic

---

[21] David Halivni, *The Formation of the Babylonian Talmud* (New York: Oxford University Press, 2013), 178.

original form and meaning of a text. This discipline, which has come to be known as philoligy, includes both textual criticism and linguistics. We will give brief examples of both.

A. Textual Criticism

In the Mishnaic and Talmudic periods rabbinic statements and compositions were transmitted and studied orally. For reasons that have been the source of much speculation by contemporary scholars, the rabbis prohibited the writing of oral Torah.[22] However, beginning in the eighth century, the transmission of the Babylonian Talmud shifted to the written page. The move to writing was a slow process which began with the recording of single chapters and tractates; it took centuries for rabbinic literature to be written down in its entirety.

While the writing of rabbinic literature rendered it accessible to a broader audience, one that transcended the walls of the academy, it also made the text more susceptible to errors in transmission. A copyist might erroneously delete words, skip lines or misread a text when copying from one book to another. The most common error of this type is referred to as a homeoteleuton, derived from the Greek word meaning "like ending." In such a case the scribe's eyes skip from one word to the same word on another line, inadvertently omitting the text between the two words. Occasionally the reverse might happen—the scribe's eye skips backwards and he repeats the same line twice. This cannot happen in oral transmission. In addition, scribes may deliberately emend what they deem to be errors in the text, thereby serving as editors as well. Fortunately, there is a wealth of extant ancient manuscripts of rabbinic texts at our disposal, some available in their entirety and some only in fragments. These include European and Yemenite manuscripts and the Cairo Genizah fragments. Additional evidence can be found in quotes by medieval commentators. Collectively, manuscripts and quotes from medieval commentators are referred to as "textual witnesses." Such manuscripts and

---

[22] Shanks Alexander, "The Orality of Rabbinic Writing," *The Cambridge Companion to Talmud and Rabbinic Literature*, ed. Charlotte Fonrobert and Martin Jaffee (New York: Cambridge University Press, 2007), 38–57; Martin Jaffee, *Torah in the Mouth: Writing and Oral Tradition in Palestinian Judaism* (New York: Oxford University Press, 2001).

fragments are useful to critical scholars in recovering the most reliable and error free version of the Bavli (or other text) that is possible. They also aid in distinguishing between differences in texts which are a result of human error and those which are the result of intentional emendation.

In quoting from the Bavli throughout this book, we use the text that appears in the Vilna printed edition. When relevant, we will cite variants found in manuscripts in our commentary.

Example 1: Attribution Of Amoraic Statement

There is an important debate in Pesahim concerning the recitation at the Pesah seder. We learn in Mishnah Pesahim 10:4 that one who recites the Pesah seder "begins with disgrace and ends with praise." All agree that praise refers to the recitation of Hallel at the end of the seder. But what text is recited as words of disgrace? On Bavli Pesahim 116a, two suggestions are offered:

מאי בגנות? רב אמר: מתחלה עובדי עבודת גלולים היו אבותינו. [ושמואל] אמר: עבדים היינו.	What is "disgrace"? Rav says: In the beginning our forefathers were idol worshippers. [And Shmuel] says: "We were slaves."

The printed edition of the Talmud attributes this debate to Rav and Shmuel, two third-century Babylonian amoraim who frequently debate one another throughout the Talmud. However, this attribution appears only very rarely in manuscripts and in the medieval commentators known as the rishonim. The following is a partial chart of the various extant readings:

Manuscript or edition	"Our forefathers were idol worshippers"	"We were slaves"
JTS ENA 1608	Rav	Rabin
JTS EMC 1623	Rav	Rabbah

Vatican 134, Munich 6, Columbia X 893, Ritba, R. Judah b. Yakar, R. Isaiah of Terrani	Rav	Rava
Vatican 109, Rif (printed edition), Ittur, Shibolei Haleket, Rosh, Vilna printed edition	Rav	Shmuel
Rav Netronai Geon, Seder Rav Amram Geon	Rav	?
Oxford 366, Abudarham	Abaye	Rava
Rabbenu Hananel	Rava	Rav Yosef
Munich 95	Anonymous	Rav
Venice printed edition	Anonymous	Rava

Clearly we can see that only one manuscript and a few printed editions of rishonim attribute "we were slaves" to Shmuel, whereas the reading "Rava" (or Rabbah, Rabin, Rav, which are graphically close to Rava) dominates.[23] The attribution to Shmuel was probably an intentional emendation made by copyists due to the prevalence of disputes between Rav and Shmuel and the scarcity of disputes between Rav and Rava. This tendency to change the ascription can also be found in the two textual witnesses that ascribe the dispute to Abaye and Rava, also contemporaries.

Example 2: Error In Printed Edition Of The Yerushalmi

While the use of manuscripts to establish the correct version of texts is important in the Bavli, it is probably even more critical in establishing the correct version of texts that were historically less focused upon such as the Yerushalmi. The version of the Yerushalmi that appears in the printed edition

---

[23] For more on the ramifications of this attribution see Joshua Kulp, "We Were Slaves: Rava's Babylonian Haggadah," *Conservative Judaism* 60, 3 (2008), 59–75.

is riddled with errors. Further complicating the matter is that there are very few textual witnesses to the Yerushalmi: only one full manuscript, some partial manuscripts, Genizah fragments, and some quotes from rishonim. This makes reconstruction of the correct version often difficult if not downright impossible. This is the case, too, for some of the midrashim and the Tosefta, although there are more manuscripts for these works. Finally, since critical understanding of the Bavli is so frequently based on analysis of the texts that preceded it, engaging in textual criticism of the Mishnah, Tosefta, Yerushalmi, and midrashim is of utmost importance even when the ultimate goal is to comment on the Bavli.

Saul Lieberman identified the following example as one of the types of errors found in the printed edition of the Yerushalmi.[24] The first printed edition, Venice 1523, is based almost entirely on the 1334 Leiden manuscript. Before this printing, the manuscript underwent extensive editing by several editors. In this case, the editor did not properly identify a scribal note in the manuscript and removed it from the passage.

ירושלמי פסחים ה:א (לא, ד) – כ"י ליידן רבי יושוע בן לוי אמר תפילות מאבות למדו גרש עד אעפ"כ לא הורידו אותו מגדלותו אלא מינו אותו אב בית דין.	ירושלמי פסחים ה:א - גרסת הדפוס רבי יושוע בן לוי אמר תפילות מאבות למדו אב בית דין.
Yerushalmi Pesahim 5:1 (31d), Leiden Manuscript R. Yehoshua b. Levi said: Tefillot (the Amidah prayers) were learned from the forefathers…*garas*…They did not depose him from his greatness but rather appointed him Av Bet Din.	**Yerushalmi Pesahim 5:1, Printed Edition** R. Yehoshua b. Levi said: Tefillot (the Amidah prayers) were learned from the forefathers, Av Bet Din.

The word "*garas*," (lit. "continuation"), found in the Leiden manuscript of Yerushalmi Pesahim, is a technical term used by scribes to indicate that a portion from another part of the Yerushalmi is meant to be inserted in the sugya. Instead of recopying the entire passage, a scribe begins with the

---

[24] Saul Lieberman, *Al Hayerushalmi* (Jerusalem: Darom, 1929), 22.

first words, writes the word גרש, and then indicates the end of the passage that is to be copied. The term is found not only in the Leiden manuscript of the Yerushalmi, it is also found in Genizah fragments of this text and in other Eretz Yisraeli manuscripts such as the Rome manuscript of Genesis Rabbah. In the case above, the scribe is referring to a passage in Yerushalmi Berakhot 4:1, 7a–c, spanning four columns, which was meant to be inserted at this point in the text. But the later editor who was reviewing the Pesahim passage in the Leiden manuscript erased the scribal note (one can actually see it crossed out in the manuscript). When the printers used this manuscript as the basis for the Vienna printed edition, the result was the nonsensical passage we find in the printed edition of the Yerushalmi, lacking the entire interpolation.[25]

Further Reading

Brody, Robert. "The Talmud in the Geonic Period." In *Printing the Talmud: From Bomberg to Schottenstein*. Edited by S. Mintz and G. Goldstein. New York: Yeshiva University Museum, 2005, pp. 29–35.

Krupp, Michael. "Manuscripts of the Babylonian Talmud." In *The Literature of the Sages Part One*. Edited by Shmuel Safrai. Philadelphia: Fortress Press, 1987, pp. 346–366.

B. Linguistics

There are many examples in the Bavli in which traditional commentators misinterpreted words because they did not have access to the lexicographical and philological techniques that have been developed over the past century. The following are a few examples.

---

[25] The P'nei Moshe, one of the traditional commentators on the Yerushalmi, struggles to decode the passage and comes up with the creative explanation that the words "Av Bet Din" are a convoluted acronym which connects the forefathers to the three prayer services!

Example 1: Unfamiliar Word

Mishnah Sanhedrin 3:3 prohibits various types of gamblers from serving as witnesses; among those mentioned are pigeon trainers. On Sanhedrin 25a the Bavli provides two definitions for the term pigeon trainers in an effort to understand why these individuals are invalid witnesses:

מאי מפריחי יונים?	What are pigeon trainers? Here (in Babylonia)
הכא תרגומה: אי	it has been interpreted, [one who says to anoth-
תקדמיה יונך ליון,	er], "if your pigeon passes mine [you win]."
רבי חמא בר אושעיא	R. Hama b. Oshaya said: It means
אמר: ארא.	[one who employs] *arra*.

The first interpretation describes an individual who races pigeons for prize money. R. Hama b. Oshaya disagrees and suggests that the mishnah refers to *arra*. Traditional commentators were unfamiliar with this foreign word and suggest that *arra* connotes either a pigeon hunter or a snare. Modern scholars have shown that the word actually derives from the Akkadian *arru*, which refers to a decoy-bird used to attract birds away from their dovecote so that they could be captured by the hunter.[26]

We should note here that in the past two decades Talmudic scholarship has been greatly enriched by two Aramaic-English dictionaries by Michael Sokoloff, one of Palestinian Aramaic and the other of Babylonian Aramaic. Scholars in the field are increasingly well-schooled in those languages from which rabbinic literature borrows, including Greek, Latin and Persian. Throughout this book, we rely on this scholarship whenever we encounter such a word or phrase.

Example 2: Dating A Source By Its Language

The critical use of lexicography does not end with deciphering the foreign words in a Hebrew/Aramaic text. At times one can date a text by analyzing

---

[26] David Weisberg, "Late Babylonian Texts and Rabbinic Literature," *HUCA* 39 (1968), 76–77.

its Hebrew vocabulary. Shamma Friedman points this out in his analysis of a well-known source found only in the Bavli (Shabbat 21b) dealing with how many candles a person must light on Hannukah:

תנו רבנן: מצות חנוכה נר איש וביתו.	Our rabbis taught: The mitzvah of Hannukah is one candle for a man and his household.
והמהדרין - נר לכל אחד ואחד. והמהדרין מן המהדרין:	And for the *"mehadrin"*—one can- dle for each and every person. And for the *"mehadrin* of the *mehadrin"*:
בית שמאי אומרים: יום ראשון מדליק שמנה, מכאן ואילך פוחת והולך.	Bet Shammai says: the first day he lights eight and each day he reduces their number.
ובית הלל אומרים: יום ראשון מדליק אחת, מכאן ואילך מוסיף והולך.	And Bet Hillel says: The first day he lights one and each day he increases their number.

Friedman has demonstrated that the original layer of this baraita is the debate between Bet Shammai and Bet Hillel found in the concluding lines. There are many criteria upon which Friedman based this assertion, but among them is his lexigraphical analysis. The word *"mehadrin"* as used in this baraita is a Hebraicized word borrowed from the Aramaic. Traditional commentators understand the word to be related to the Hebrew root הד"ר, meaning beauty, such that this word means "to beautify a mitzvah" as in the phrase *hiddur mitzvah*. There is no corroborating evidence, however, that the tannaim used the word in this manner and the latter phrase, *hiddur mitzvah*, was actually coined by the stam in Bava Kamma 9b.[27] Rather, as Friedman demonstrated, this word in Bavli Shabbat is from the Aramaic root הדר which means to "chase after." The *"mehadrin"* are not those who "adorn" or "beautify" the mitz-vot. They are those who chase after a better way in which to perform them.[28]

---

[27] For an extensive analysis of the root in tannaitic literature see Shamma Friedman, "Mehadrin min haMehadrin," *Leshonenu* 67 (2005): 153–160.

[28] Friedman, "Literary Dependencies," 53–55.

This analysis contributes significantly to our understanding of the development of the laws of Hannukah, for it helps to demonstrate that the opening section of the baraita (from the beginning until the Bet Shammai/Bet Hillel dispute) is a Babylonian addition. The word *"mehadrin"* as it is used in the baraita did not exist in tannaitic Hebrew. The original halakhah/practice was to light eight candles; the houses of Shammai and Hillel argued over how this was done. Generations later, in Babylonia, it seems they decided to reduce the mandated number of Hanukah candles from eight to just one.

Further Reading

Sokoloff, Michael. *A Dictionary of Jewish Palestinian Aramaic of the Byzantine Period.* Ramat Gan: Bar Ilan University Press, 1990.

—. *A Dictionary of Jewish Babylonian Aramaic of the Talmudic and Geonic Periods.* Ramat Gan: Bar Ilan University Press, 2002.

II. Realia

Traditional commentators on rabbinic literature were usually not familiar with the historical, material, cultural and legal contexts of rabbinic literature, referred to collectively by the term realia. The Bavli and every rabbinic composition are, after all, the creations of specific generations of rabbis who lived in a certain geographical place at a certain historical time. For instance, the literature created in the land of Israel (Mishnah, Tosefta, Yerushalmi and midrashim) was under the sphere of influence of the Greco-Roman world, particularly the eastern part of the Roman Empire. The Bavli, on the other hand, was created in Persia, where Sassanian, Iranian and Zoroastrian influence abounded. There is no doubt that they were influenced by their surrounding culture. And so frequently a sugya can be better understood when the external background to certain artifacts and institutions referenced in the sugya have been uncovered.

Example

One of the most fascinating examples of realia enriching the understanding of a Talmudic text is a baraita found in Bavli Berakhot 3a. This baraita teaches that the night is divided into three watches, each of which is accompanied by a sign found in the natural world:

<table>
<tr>
<td dir="rtl">

דתניא: רבי אליעזר אומר:
שלש משמרות הוי הלילה
ועל כל משמר ומשמר יושב
הקדוש ברוך הוא ושואג כארי,
שנאמר ממרום ישאג וממעון
קדשו יתן קולו שאוג ישאג
על נוהו (ירמיהו כה:ל), וסימן
לדבר: משמרה ראשונה - חמור
נוער, שניה - כלבים צועקים,
שלישית - תינוק יונק משדי
אמו ואשה מספרת עם בעלה.

</td>
<td>

It has been taught: R. Eliezer says: The night has three watches, and at each watch the Holy One, blessed be He, sits and roars like a lion. For it is written: *The Lord roars from on high, He makes his voice heard from His holy dwelling; He roars aloud over His [earthly] abode* (Jeremiah 25:30). And the signs are: In the first watch, the donkey brays; in the second, the dogs bark; in the third, the child nurses from the breast of his mother, and the wife talks with her husband.

</td>
</tr>
</table>

According to R. Eliezer's opinion in the first mishnah of Berakhot, one must recite the Shema before the end of the first watch. This baraita creates the impression that a person would have to listen for donkeys braying in order to ascertain when this watch was over. Commentators struggled to understand how this could be possible. In the real world, these sounds would not be heard at the same time every night. How could R. Eliezer possibly have expected anyone to identify the end of the first watch, signifying the last time an individual could recite the Shema, by a sound that could not have appeared with regularity?

Moshe Benovitz has offered a convincing solution to this conundrum by demonstrating that the signs found in the baraita correspond to constellations and not to earthly creatures and sounds. The donkey in the baraita refers to Ursa Major (referred to by the rabbis as *eglah*, "wagon," which is related to the Akkadian *Agalu*, "donkey"), the dogs refer to Hercules (*Kalbu* in Akkadian, cognate to the Hebrew *kelev*), and the woman is a reference to Cassiopeia, who nurses her daughter Andromeda while speaking to her husband Cepheus. The movement of these constellations through the evening sky served as an indication of the passage of time, thereby providing a reliable means of determining the final hour for the evening recitation of Shema.[29]

Further Reading

Elman, Yaakov. "Middle Persian Culture and Babylonian Sages: Accommodation and Resistance in the Shaping of Rabbinic Legal Tradition." In: *The Cambridge Companion to the Talmud and Rabbinic Literature*. Edited by Charlotte Fonrobert and Martin Jaffee. Cambridge: Cambridge University Press, 2007, pp. 165–197.

Kalmin, Richard. *Jewish Babylonia between Persia and Roman Palestine*. New York: Oxford University Press, 2006.

Lieberman, Saul *Greek in Jewish Palestine/Hellenism in Jewish Palestine*. New York: Jewish Theological Seminary, 1994.

Secunda, Shai. *The Iranian Talmud: Reading the Bavli in its Sassanian Context*. Philadelphia: University of Pennsylvania Press, 2014.

Sperber, Daniel. *Greek in Talmudic Palestine*. Ramat Gan: Bar Ilan University Press, 2012.

III. Comparisons with Non-Rabbinic Texts

Traditional Talmudic commentators have tended to interpret rabbinic literature only in light of other rabbinic sources. That is to say, rabbinic interpretations, laws and exegeses existed mostly in a Jewish vacuum. Of course, commentators have always known that the Pharisees competed with the Sadducees during the Second Temple period, for these disputes are mentioned explicitly in classic rabbinic literature. There are also certain heretics, known as *"minim,"* mentioned throughout rabbinic literature and even a hint, here and there, of the competition with Christianity. But for the most part traditional Talmudic commentators read these other cultures exclusively through the lens of those texts that were quoted by the rabbis themselves.

---

[29] Moshe Benovitz, *Talmud Ha-Igud: BT Berakhot Chapter I* (Jerusalem: The Society for the Interpretation of the Talmud, 2006), 65–79.

A critical scholar, in contrast, views rabbinic texts in light of other ancient laws, exegeses and philosophies. The most prominent of these competing systems and the most fruitful for comparison with rabbinic literature are the writings of the sect that lived in Qumran during the Second Temple period—the Dead Sea Scrolls—and the early Christians who became increasingly prominent during the first centuries C.E. It has now become quite commonplace to discuss rabbinic literature, the Dead Sea Scrolls and Christianity in light of one another. Further enriching our knowledge of the period are the extensive writings of Philo, who lived in the early part of the first century in Alexandria and wrote in Greek, and Josephus, who lived during the second half of the first century first in Eretz Yisrael and then in Rome. Our understanding of the exegetical choices made by the rabbis is often illuminated by comparing them with the choices made by other groups. At times, we can sense that the rabbis are polemicizing against other laws, other midrashim and other ways of understanding God, the Bible, and the world. Thus, throughout this book when such an opportunity arises, we shall compare rabbinic interpretation and halakhah with competing views ascribed to other Jews, including the early Christians who themselves arose from a Jewish background. Indeed, early Christians and Jews of the rabbinic period often identified themselves as part of the same religion with competing claims of interpretation of ritual, belief and practice.

Before we cite two examples, we should again note that we must proceed with caution when engaging in such analysis. First of all, these groups were not all contemporaneous. The Dead Sea sect probably ceased to exist before the rabbis began composing the literature that made up the Mishnah. The rabbis never explicitly refer to and were almost certainly not at all familiar with any of the sectarian writings found in Qumran. And while the rabbis clearly knew something about the rise of Christianity, how much they knew, when they knew it and how much competition they felt with early Christians is the subject of fierce scholarly debate. There is a tendency to assume that sects competed with one another simply because they were contemporaneous. But that does not necessarily mean that they knew of each other. Finally, we should avoid the tendency to assume that every rabbinic dicta and story is polemical. Nevertheless, despite these words of caution, comparing rabbinic literature with other religious systems offers, at times, a rich background to our source material.

Example 1: The Dead Sea Sect

In several places in rabbinic literature we find the rabbis urging men to marry their nieces. For instance, Tosefta Kiddushin 1:2 states: "A man should not marry a woman until the daughter of his sister has grown up." Before getting married a man should wait for his niece to reach marriageable age, so that he could possibly marry her. A baraita found in Bavli Yevamot 62b–63a conveys a similar message:

האוהב את שכיניו, והמקרב את קרוביו, והנושא את בת אחותו,והמלוה סלע לעני בשעת דחקו, עליו הכתוב אומר: אז תקרא וה' יענה תשוע ויאמר הנני (ישעיהו נח:ט).	One who loves his neighbors, or draws his relatives near or marries the daughter of his sister or who loans to a poor person at the time of his need, about him the verse says: *Then when you cry the Lord will answer. When you cry, He will say: Here I am* (Isaiah 58:9).

Thus the rabbis seem to be endorsing and even urging men to marry their nieces, and more specifically, their sisters' daughters.

Scholars have long noted that marriage between an uncle and niece was prohibited by the Dead Sea sect. *The Covenant of Damascus,* one of the most famous of the sectarian writings (despite the fact that it was actually found in the Cairo Genizah) reads (column 5:6–11):

וגם מטמאים הם את המקדש אשר אין הם מבדיל כתורה...ולוקחים [ו] איש את בת אחיהם [vacat] את בת אחותו. ומשה אמר אל אחות אמך לא תקרב שאר אמך היא ומשפט העריות לזכרים הוא כתוב וכהם הנשים ואם תגלה בת האח את ערות אחי אביה והיא שאר.	And they also defiled the Temple, for they did not keep apart in accordance with the law... And they marry each one his brother's daughter or sister's daughter. [*Vacat*].[30] But, Moses said: To your mother's sister you may not draw near. For she is your mother's relation.' *Now the precept of incest is written from the point of view of males, but the same (law) applies to women, so if a brother's daughter uncovers the nakedness of a brother of her father, she is (forbidden) a close relationship* (Leviticus 18:13).[31]

In the above passage of this "sectarian" document, the author rails against men who marry their niece. He classifies the practice as a forbidden union which "defiles the Temple" (a reference to the defilement mentioned at the end of Leviticus 18). Clearly, the Dead Sea sect was polemicizing against other Jews who espoused a rabbinic position. This debate is a dispute concerning the proper interpretation of Leviticus 18:13, and may offer window to a larger debate concerning the proper interpretation of Scripture in general.[32] The Torah prohibits a man from marrying his mother's sister, but the text does not explicitly prohibit a woman (the niece) from marrying her uncle. The author of the scroll explains that although the Torah is addressed to the male (the nephew), the prohibition against a man marrying his mother's sister implies the prohibition for a woman to marry her parent's brother (the uncle). In contrast, the rabbinic reading limits the prohibition to that mentioned explicitly in the Torah (nephew/aunt) and therefore permits uncle/niece marriage.[33] This issue was fiercely debated by ancient Jews, certainly by those who composed the Dead Sea Sect. With this background in mind, we might possibly understand at least one of the reasons that the rabbis emphasized the value of marrying one's niece—it was a polemic against the practices or more precisely the prohibitions of other Jews with whom they vehemently disagreed.

Example 2: Rabbinic Literature And The New Testament

There are numerous examples of how passages in the New Testament and passages in rabbinic literature can illuminate one another. This is true, too, of other early Christian texts from the first through fourth and even fifth and sixth centuries. Much scholarly literature has been devoted to such issues,

---

[30] This notation refers to an empty space left by the scribe to indicate a division in the text.

[31] Translation from Aharon Shemesh, *Halakhah in the Making* (Berkeley: University of California Press, 2009), 80-81.

[32] See Daniel Schwartz, "Law and Truth: On Qumran-Sadducean and Rabbinic Views of Law," *The Dead Sea Scrolls: Forty Years of Research*, ed. Devorah Dimant and Uriel Rappaport (Leiden: E.J. Brill, 1992), 229–240.

[33] For more see Aharon Shemesh, *Halakhah in the Making*, 80–95.

including the Jewish background of Christianity, the Christian influence on Judaism, and the rabbinic response to Christianity.

It is important to note that in reading rabbinic texts in light of early Christian sources, we are not positing a direct response from one group to the other. Proving that rabbis argued against the followers of Jesus or that Christians were familiar with the rabbis of the Mishnaic and Talmudic period is notoriously difficult (although at times possible). Our point is far more limited but allows for a broader scope of comparison. A student of rabbinic literature can deepen his understanding of a particular issue by examining the New Testament and other Christian literature which engage with the same questions.

The issue we will explore here is the washing of hands before eating ritually pure food. According to rabbinic law, a person must wash his hands before eating, even if the body has already been purified. Unwashed hands defile food, causing them to have second-degree impurity. This would impact only food that has special status, i.e. *terumah* or sanctified produce, but would have no effect on ordinary produce (*hullin*).

In Mishnah Eduyot 5:6, we learn that there was (at least) one rabbi who did not agree that hands could be purified as if they were separate from the body (text based on Kaufman manuscript):

ואת מי נדו? אליעזר בן	And who did they excommunicate? Eliezer ben
הנד שפקפק בטהרת ידים.	Hanad[34] who doubted the purification of hands.

This Mishnah suggests that the requirement to wash one's hands before eating was a charged issue. Rarely do we hear of someone being excommunicated for disagreeing with the majority opinion. But doubting the efficacy or necessity of washing hands was an offense worthy of excommunication.

A passage in the New Testament demonstrates that this issue was already contentious in an earlier period. The following passage is from Mark 7 (there is a parallel in Matthew 15:1–20):

> Now when the Pharisees gathered to him, with some of the scribes
> who had come from Jerusalem, they saw that some of his disciples ate

---

[34] The printed edition mistakenly reads the name as the more common Hanokh, which is graphically similar to Hanad.

with hands that were defiled, that is, unwashed. For the Pharisees and all the Jews do not eat unless they wash their hands properly, holding to the tradition of the elders, and when they come from the market-place, they do not eat unless they wash... And the Pharisees and the scribes asked him, "Why do your disciples not walk according to the tradition of the elders, but eat with defiled hands?"...

And he called the people to him again and said to them, "Hear me, all of you, and understand: There is nothing outside a person that by going into him can defile him, but the things that come out of a person are what defile him."

Since the inception of Christianity, there have been disputes concerning the meaning of Jesus's statement, "There is nothing outside a person that by going into him can defile him." Indeed of all of Jesus's "halakhic" statements this has probably been the most contentious and potentially significant. Was Jesus denying all of the Jewish dietary laws, including the distinction between animals that may be eaten and those that may not? Was he denying the purity laws? What exactly was his argument with the Pharisees?

Recently, Yair Furstenberg wrote an insightful article arguing that the meaning of the first half of Jesus's statement should be understood in light of a rabbinic innovation that the body could be defiled by eating impure food.[35] This notion is not found anywhere in the Bible, and Jesus was certainly correct when he stated that, at least in the Bible, "There is nothing outside a person that by going into him can defile him." This was a rabbinic innovation, one which is debated in Mishnah Tahorot 2:2:

רבי אליעזר אומר: האוכל אוכל ראשון ראשון אוכל שני שני אוכל שלישי שלישי.	R. Eliezer says: He who eats food with first-degree uncleanness contracts first decree uncleanness. [He who eats food with] second-[degree uncleanness contracts] second-[degree uncleanness. With third-[degree uncleanness contracts] third-[degree uncleanness.

---

[35] Yair Furstenburg, "Defilement Penetrating the Body: A New Understanding of Contamination in Mark 7:15," *New Testament Studies*, 54 (2008), 176–200.

רבי יהושע אומר: האוכל	R. Yehoshua says: He who eats food with
אוכל ראשון ואוכל שני	first-[degree] or with second-[degree unclean-
שני. שלישי, שני לקדש	ness contracts] second-[degree uncleanness].
ולא שני לתרומה.	With third-[degree uncleanness, he contracts]
	second-[degree uncleanness] in regard to
	holy things but not in regard to terumah.

The particulars of this mishnah do not really concern us here. What is significant is that both rabbis agree that a person who eats impure food will be defiled. This is exactly the viewpoint against which Jesus argued, and it aids in understanding why the argument is connected in the Gospels to hand-washing. According to the rabbis, by not washing one's hands, one will defile any food touched. Such food will enter and defile the body. Jesus, on the other hand, argued that hand-washing was unnecessary because impure food cannot defile the body.

These three texts all help us understand one other. The text from Mishnah Eduyot about excommunication should be viewed in light of the argument against handwashing from the Gospels which itself is only comprehensible in light of the debate in Mishnah Tahorot (and other texts which show that the body can be defiled by eating impure food, such as Mishnah Zavim 5:9). Taken together these texts reflect a fundamental dispute concerning the purity laws—is the body defiled by the consumption of impure foods? Does one need to wash one's hands before eating in order to prevent the defilement of the body? Jesus's statement in the Gospels of Mark and Matthew teaches us that Eliezer ben Hanad was denying a major principle in the rabbinic purity laws, one which defined the Pharisaic custom already in the first century. It is not surprising that denial of such a central tenet would have made this rabbi worthy of excommunication. And Rabbi Eliezer and Rabbi Yehoshua's argument in Mishnah Tahorot solve the riddle of just what Jesus was arguing against when he claimed that the body cannot be defiled by what the mouth consumes.

Further Reading

Bar-Asher Siegal, Michal. *Early Christian Monastic Literature and the Babylonian Talmud*. New York: Cambridge University Press, 2013.
Hirshman, Marc. *A Rivalry of Genius: Jewish and Christian Biblical*

Interpretation in Late Antiquity. Albany: S.U.N.Y. Press, 1996.

Schremer, Adiel. *Brothers Estranged: Heresy, Christianity and Jewish Identity in Late Antiquity.* New York: Oxford University Press, 2010.

Shemesh, Aharon. *Halakhah in the Making: The Development of Jewish Law from Qumran to the Rabbis.* Berkeley: University of California Press, 2009.

Sussman, Yaakov. "The History of Halakhah and the Dead Sea Scrolls," *Discoveries in the Judean Desert* 10 (1994) 179–200.

IV. Literary Reading of Aggadot

The final critical technique we shall consider is the literary reading of rabbinic aggadot, stories by and about the rabbis.[36] Traditional commentators generally believed that these stories were reliable descriptions of the rabbis' lives. Indeed, this at least partially explains why rishonim very rarely comment on aggadot. They assumed that these were historical accounts to which they had little to add, beyond clarifying terms or details.

The earliest critical scholars rightfully rejected this point of view, but clung to the possibility that there was nonetheless a "historical kernel" to the text. While these earlier scholars were aware that aggadot tended to develop over time as subsequent generations embellished and exaggerated them, they believed that at the heart of the stories there usually, if not always, lay a historical core. They maintained that the task of the academic scholar was to strip away the layers of embellishment and thereby reveal what actually happened. They understood that these stories did not occur as we encounter them. For instance, R. Yehudah Hanasi did not actually engage in the conversations with the Roman emperor that the aggadah recounts (Avodah Zara 10b). But they assumed that R. Yehudah Hanasi must have had dealings with the Roman government. Similarly, they understood that R. Akiva probably did not have such a vast number of students who died from the plague (Yevamot 62b), but he must have had at least some students who were among the death toll.

---

[36] We do not address here the literary reading of biblical/midrashic aggadot that reconstruct and augment the stories of the Tanakh.

A rejection of this "historical" approach was spearheaded a generation ago by Yonah Fraenkel. Fraenkel demanded that these stories be analyzed not for their political or historical context, but for their literary craftsmanship. Frankel asked the types of question that scholars of literature were accustomed to ask of the stories which they analyzed. How does the storyteller shape his story? How do the characters develop from the beginning to the end of the story? What is the author's point of view? How are literary devices, such as repetition, foreshadowing, and wordplay employed? Are there allusions to other stories? What is the overall theme of the story? There are many such questions one can ask, and to some extent this type of analysis is more subjective than some of the more "technical" critical techniques listed above. Nevertheless, we believe that this type of analysis can enhance our understanding of rabbinic aggadot.

We should also note that such analysis can and should be combined with source analysis. Shamma Friedman, who has analyzed a number of Babylonian aggadot, summarized this approach by stating that instead of searching for the historical kernel, one should search for the literary kernel.[37] That is to say, the first thing to do when analyzing a Babylonian aggada is to check whether the Babylonian editors have used themes found in Eretz Yisraeli literature or even in other earlier texts embedded elsewhere in the Bavli. Jeffrey Rubenstein has been especially prolific and insightful in his literary and source-critical analysis of Babylonian aggadot. Especially noteworthy is his theory that the rabbinic activity in these aggadot, many of which describe tannaim, is actually reflective of the rabbinic academy as it existed in the time of the aggadah's composers. While a scholar may not be able to use these late aggadot to draw conclusions about the lives of the tannaim being portrayed, scholars might, in the end, be able to use them to uncover the concerns and anxieties of the anonymous sages living at the end of the amoraic period, i.e. the men who composed these stories. In other words, these stories reveal more about their authors than about the figures they purport to depict.

Finally, such analysis also entails comparisons with literary and thematic techniques found in other cultures, especially those contemporary with the rabbis. The type of literature composed by the rabbis was not created in a

---

[37] Shamma Friedman, "Literary Development and Historicity in the Aggadic Narrative of the Babylonian Talmud: A Study based upon B.M. 83b–86a," *Community and Culture*, ed. Nahum Waldman (Philadelphia: Gratz College, 1987), 67–80.

vacuum. It can be assumed that the methods of storytelling used by rabbis were to a certain extent common to their culture. Cross-cultural analysis, when possible, enriches our understanding of rabbinic literature, for notions concerning various themes such as magic, suffering, birth, death, luck, etc. were at times shared by the rabbis with their neighbors and at other times debated.

Example

The following brief aggadah is from Bavli Kiddushin 29b. We have included the baraita that precedes it so that we can analyze the aggadah in context.

תנו רבנן: הוא ללמוד ובנו ללמוד - הוא קודם לבנו; ר' יהודה אומר: אם בנו זריז וממולח ותלמודו מתקיים בידו - בנו קודמו.

Our rabbis taught: He [the father] needs to learn [Torah] and the son needs to learn—he takes precedence over his son. R. Yehudah says: if his son is quick to learn and sharp and he can remember his studies, his son takes precedence.

כי הא דרב יעקב בריה דרב אחא בר יעקב שדריה אבוה לקמיה דאביי, כי אתא חזייה דלא הוה מיחדדין שמעתיה, אמר ליה: אנא עדיפא מינך, תוב את דאיזיל אנא. שמע אביי דקא הוה אתי.

Like R. Yaakov son of R. Aha bar Yaakov, whose father sent him to learn with Abaye. When he [R. Yaakov] came back [his father] saw that his traditions were not so well honed. He said to him: I'm better than you; you stay here for I am going to learn. Abaye heard that he [R. Aha bar Yaakov] was coming.

הוה ההוא מזיק בי רבנן דאביי, דכי הוו עיילי בתרין אפילו ביממא הוו מיתזקי, אמר להו: לא ליתיב ליה איניש אושפיזא, אפשר דמתרחיש ניסא. על, בת בההוא בי רבנן, אידמי ליה כתנינא דשבעה רישוותיה, כל כריעה דכרע נתר חד רישיה.

There was a demon in Abaye's academy, that would cause harm even when two people would come in during the day. He [Abaye] said to the members of the study house: No one should let him be a guest in their house, for maybe a miracle will occur. He [R. Aha bar Yaakov] entered and slept in that study house. The demon appeared to him as a seven-headed monster. Each time R. Aha would bend his knees [in supplication] one of the monster's heads would fall off.

אמר להו למחר: אי לא   He [R. Aha] said to them: If a miracle had not
איתרחיש ניסא, סכינתין.   occurred, you would have put me in danger.

Rather than offering a lengthy analysis of this rich and suggestive aggadah, we wish to point out some of the issues and themes that lend themselves to literary analysis. The main character in this story is clearly R. Aha bar Yaakov. The central irony seems to be that this extremely learned rabbi has a son whose "traditions are not well honed." This is the same tension addressed by the opening baraita, about whether a father or son takes precedence when it comes to learning Torah. The story problematizes the situation by showing just how dangerous and fraught such a situation would be.

A literary analysis of the story would address such questions as: How does the storyteller portray R. Aha bar Yaakov as dealing with this problem? Is his decision meant to elicit the reader's outrage or sympathy? How does our perspective shift during the story? We might separate the story into scenes to see how the characters relationship to one another changes from scene to scene. What is the meaning of the presence of a demon in the academy? Is the academy a dangerous place? Why is Abaye presented as using R. Aha to deal with this dangerous situation? Is Abaye's action a response to R. Aha's telling his son to stay home while he goes out to learn? How does the Talmudic context of the story influence its meaning? One can sense that the answers to these questions will be relatively subjective. But this should not deter the critical reader from asking and attempting to answer them.

Source analysis might involve investigating whether the seven-headed monster is found elsewhere in the Bavli. We might expand this search to see how demons are portrayed in the Bavli. If there are any parallels to the story (there are none that we know of), we would consider how the context of the Bavli may have influenced the events of the story itself.

Finally, cross-cultural analysis might examine contemporary tales to see if non-Jewish contemporaries of the rabbis used the image of this particular demon in their legends. What beliefs were current in the milieu in which the rabbis crafted their tales?

Further Reading

Friedman, Shamma. "A Good Story Deserves Retelling," *JSIJ* 3 (2004), 55–93.

Richard Kalmin. "The Modern Study of Ancient Rabbinic Literature: Yonah Fraenkel's Darkhei Ha'aggadah Vehamidrash," *Prooftexts,* 14,2 (1994), 189–204.

Rubenstein, Jeffrey. *Stories of the Babylonian Talmud.* Baltimore: Johns Hopkins University Press, 2010.

—. *The Culture of the Babylonian Talmud.* Baltimore: Johns Hopkins University Press, 2003.

—. *Talmudic Stories: Narrative Art, Composition and Culture.* Baltimore: Johns Hopkins University Press, 1999.

—. (edited) *Creation and Composition: The Contribution of the Bavli Redactors (Stammaim) to the Aggada.* Tübingen: Mohr-Siebeck, 2005.

The Organization of this Book

Each chapter of this book is dedicated to a single Talmudic sugya, which is studied by employing the critical methodologies discussed in this introduction. Every chapter stands on its own and can be read and studied independent of the others. Furthermore, the chapters can generally be read in any order, although there are occasional cross-references.

Chapter One, focusing on the opening sugya in Tractate Sukkah, is the most programmatic chapter in the book, in the sense that it is the clearest example of how a modern talmudic scholar can apply academic analysis to a sugya in the Bavli. The specific topic addressed in this sugya (Sukkah 2a–3a) is the maximum height of a sukkah, and the interplay between the justification for a height limit and the conditions under which the limit may be waived.

The Chapters Two and Three are both examples of how Greco-Roman laws and customs were reinterpreted and sometimes misinterpreted in later stages of rabbinic literature. Chapter Two deals with how the tannaitic prohibition of having an afikoman at the conclusion of the Pesah seder was eventually transformed into the custom of eating a piece of matzah at the end of the meal (Pesahim 119b–120a). Chapter Three focuses on how the rabbis adapted the Greek legal document known as a prosbul into Jewish law and then transformed it into a way to avoid the consequences of loan remission in the sabbatical year. The chapter also explores the fascinating Talmudic discussion (Gittin 36a–36b) concerning the authority of rabbis to legislate laws that seem to contradict those in the Torah.

Chapter Four, authored by Ethan Tucker, highlights how the stammaitic editors adapted sources from early generations and used them to fashion literarily cohesive passages, discourse in which the argument flows from one section to the next. Most importantly, while the fashioning of these passages was primarily undertaken with a literary or aesthetic goal in mind, the end result had a deep impact on halakhic development. The specific case analyzed here is taken from Pesahim 102a–103a and is concerned with the question of whether two different rituals (such as birkat hamazon and kiddush) can be recited over a single cup of wine.

In Chapter Five we turn our attention to a more social/historical issue, the role of women in rabbinic thought and halakhah. Specifically we focus on women's participation in formal meals and their obligation to recite birkat hamazon (Berakhot 20b). At the end of this chapter there is an appendix authored by Alieza Salzberg, in which she broadens the lens to a general discussion of how modern scholars analyze issues of gender in rabbinic literature.

Chapter Six focuses on the comparison of Eretz Yisraeli literature with Babylonian literature, specifically with regard to the topic of interrupting mourning customs for a festival (Moed Katan 20a). The first half of the chapter is textually oriented, demonstrating that the earlier halakhah found in the Mishnah, Tosefta and Yerushalmi was indeed transformed in the Bavli. The second half of the chapter is written by Shai Secunda, who discusses the possibility that this specific halakhah was changed in Babylonia due to Zoroastrian influence.

Whereas most of the previous chapters focused on either a specific halakhah or talmudic passage, chapter seven concentrates on a principle, namely that a mitzvah cannot be performed through a transgression. In Tractate Sukkah 29b–30a this principle is applied to the case of a stolen lulav but it has broader implications as well. In this chapter we not only trace how the literature expressing this principle was created and developed, but how its creation and expansion influenced late and post-Talmudic rabbinic ideas.

Academic study of rabbinic texts is usually strongly associated with the use of manuscripts to determine, as best as possible, the most authentic version of any given text. In chapter eight we deal with a passage from Bavli Berakhot 11b that simply cannot be understood without resort to manuscripts. This passage deals with the blessings recited over the study of Torah: The first half contains an amoraic debate over which texts must be preceded by a blessing, and the second half presents several suggested versions of these blessings.

Finally, we conclude the book by analyzing an extended aggadic passage, the story of R. Pinchas b. Yair and his famous donkey (Bavli Hullin 7a–b). In contrast to traditional commentators who tended to ignore the non-halakhic sections of the Talmud, modern commentators have greatly enriched our appreciation for these stories as literary/cultural creations, reflective of rabbinic concerns. We show how the Babylonian storytellers modified their sources to create a richer, more focused tale, and how in this case they used the tale to explore the place of magicians and miracle workers in a monotheistic world. In an appendix to the chapter, Avigail Manekin-Bamberger discusses some of the ways modern scholars have created a revolution in our understanding of the role that magic played in the Jewish and more specifically rabbinic world.

CHAPTER ONE

THE LITERARY DEVELOPMENT OF A SUGYA: THE TWENTY CUBIT HIGH SUKKAH

SUKKAH 2A–3A

Analyzing a Talmudic Sugya

This chapter stands out in the book because there is no particular "issue," halakhah, or even methodology that we seek to demonstrate. Rather, we seek to answer the question that lies at the heart of why we wrote this book—how does a modern talmudic researcher critically analyze whatever sugya he/she may be studying? In our study of this sugya we try to show step by step how such analysis is done, analyzing the source material that comprises the sugya in chronological order. Since the sugya begins with a mishnah, we analyze the mishnah on its own terms and then in light of the parallel in the Tosefta. Next we move on to the Yerushalmi, a chronologically earlier source than the Bavli. We then proceed to discuss the Bavli, consistently separating the strata that comprise it, all the while comparing the Bavli with the Yerushalmi. With this two-pronged approach (separation of amoraic and stammaitic levels and comparison with Yerushalmi) we can gain a sense of how the understanding of the mishnah, halakhot, and related literature developed throughout the Talmudic period. Of course other methodologies and approaches are used throughout the chapter, and it is impossible to truly atomize one step from any other. Nevertheless, the chapter follows a fairly straightforward progression through the chronological development of Talmudic literature.

This is, in a nutshell, a program for how to interpret the Talmud critically. While we may not arrive at earth-shattering conclusions, we do hope that the type of analysis we engage in here can be replicated by the reader in the study of other sugyot.

The Mishnah and Its Original Meaning

The sugya we will deal with in this chapter is based on the first line of the first mishnah in Sukkah, which stipulates the maximum height of a kosher sukkah: "A sukkah which is taller than twenty cubits high is invalid. And Rabbi Yehudah validates [it]." The Bavli offers several explanations as to why the sages disqualify a sukkah whose *skhakh*[1] is more than twenty cubits high. These explanations are particular to the nature and purpose of a sukkah: They suggest that if the sukkah is higher than twenty cubits, some essential element of the sukkah or the experience of dwelling in it will be lacking.

However, the earliest and probably original interpretation of this debate is likely that which is found in the opening sugya of Yerushalmi Sukkah (1:1, 51a) and Yerushalmi Eruvin (1:1, 18b) which draw an analogy between the Sukkah and the Temple:[2]

> R. Aha in the name of Rav: the rabbis derive [the limit of the height of the sukkah] from the opening of the Sanctuary (היכל) and Rabbi Yehudah derives it from the opening of the Hall (אולם).

According to the Yerushalmi, a sukkah cannot be higher than the height of a specific Temple structure. This idea appears nowhere in Mishnah Sukkah or the Bavli, but it is not without precedent. Mishnah Middot 4:1 states that the opening of the Sanctuary, the inner building in the Temple structure, was twenty cubits high. This same measure is mentioned in the opening halakhah of Tosefta Eruvin which states: "a *mavoi*[3] that is more than twenty cubits high, more than the height of the opening of the Sanctuary, must be reduced." Thus

---

[1] Often the word "sukkah" in the mishnah and other rabbinic sources is synonymous with "*skhakh*," the sukkah covering made of vegetation that has been detached from the ground.

[2] See also Bavli Eruvin 2a–b.

[3] A *mavoi* is an alleyway that empties out into the public domain. Courtyards open into the alleyway. The sages prohibited carrying from the courtyard into the alleyway unless an eruv (a shared meal) was set up in one of the courtyards. In addition, they required the placement of some recognizable sign (a beam or post) at the exit from the alley to the public domain so that people would not carry into the public domain, which was prohibited.

there is evidence that the tannaim derived halakhot concerning the maximum height of certain structures from the height of the Sanctuary. R. Aha, the amora, goes one step further than the Tosefta and posits that just as the maximum height of the *mavoi* was derived from the opening of the Sanctuary, so, too, was the maximum height of the sukkah.[4] The Yerushalmi subsequently raises an objection to this analogy, which may explain why it does not appear in the Bavli. Nevertheless, it seems likely that the size of the entrance of the Sanctuary was indeed the original source of the twenty cubit prohibition.[5]

There is an important implication to this assertion. The amoraim in both Talmuds qualify the sages' prohibition of a sukkah whose height is greater than twenty cubits. As we shall see in depth below, several amoraim posit that under certain circumstances, even the sages of the Mishnah would validate a twenty cubit high sukkah. These qualifications would not seem possible if the source for the twenty cubit rule were the size of the entrance to the Sanctuary. Just as the entrance to the Sanctuary was not and could not be higher than twenty cubits, so, too, the sukkah could not be higher than twenty cubits. In contrast, if the reason for the twenty cubit limit is that an overly high sukkah somehow detracts from the sukkah experience, then there may be conditions under which a sukkah higher than twenty cubits would be valid. Thus the absence of the Sanctuary explanation for the mishnah in the Bavli, and its rejection in the Yerushalmi, paved the way for other amoraim to narrow the applicability of the Mishnah's law.

The Yerushalmi

The structure and many of the elements of the Bavli's sugya are already present in the Yerushalmi (Sukkah 1:1, 51d). Hence, an examination of the Yerushalmi will shed light on the Bavli and will especially serve to highlight how the stam edited its sources to shape the Babylonian sugya.

---

[4] Similarly, the Bavli derives the minimum height of a sukkah from the height of the ark and its covering. See Sukkah 4b–5a.

[5] See Jeffrey Rubenstein, "The Sukkah as Temporary or Permanent Dwelling: A Study in the Development of Talmudic Thought," *Hebrew Union College Annual* 64 (1993), 149, n. 33; Shmuel Safrai, *Mishnat Eretz Yisrael: Masekhet Sukkah* (Jerusalem: Mikhlelet Lifshitz, 2010), 32.

The first Yerushalmi sugya on the mishnah attempts to derive the twenty cubit limit from the *mavoi* and the entrance to the Sanctuary, as we saw above. After an extended discussion, the following passage begins:

AMORAIC STATEMENT EXPLAINING SOURCE OF MISHNAH

(1) רבי אבהו בשם רבי יוחנן: התורה אמרה: בסוכות תשבו (ויקרא כג:מב) עד עשרים אמה את יושב בצילה של סוכה מעשרים אמה ולמעלן את יושב בצילן של דפנות.

(1) R. Abbahu [said] in the name of R. Yohanan: The Torah says: *In Sukkot you shall dwell* (Leviticus 23:42): Up until [a height of] twenty cubits you sit in the shade of a sukkah. From twenty cubits and above you sit in the shade of the walls.

FIRST AMORAIC LIMITATION OF DISPUTE IN MISHNNAH

(2a) אמר רבי יונה: הדא דאת אמר בנתונה למעלה מעשרים אמה לדפנות, אבל אם היתה נתונה למטה מעשרים אמה לדפנות כשירה.

(2a) R. Yonah said: That which you say [that a sukkah higher than twenty cubits is invalid] is only when it [the *skhakh*] is twenty cubits higher than the walls, but if it was placed lower than twenty cubits from the walls, it is valid.

DIFFICULTY ON SECTION 2A

(2b) אמר ליה רבי יוסה: על דעתך דאת אמר בדפנות הדבר תלוי, ניתני סוכה שהיא נתונה למעלה מעשרים אמה לדפנות פסולה.

(2b) R. Yose said to him: According to your opinion, that the validity depends on the walls, it should teach, "a sukkah that is placed more than twenty cubits above the walls is invalid."

SECOND AMORAIC LIMITATION OF MISHNAIC DISPUTE

(3) רבי בא בשם רב: בשאינה מחזקת אלא כדי ראשו ורובו ושולחנו, אבל אם היתה מחזקת יותר כשירה.

(3) R. Ba in the name of Rav: [The debate] is when it [the sukkah] can contain his head, most of his body, and his table. But if it can hold more, it is valid [even if it is above twenty cubits].

THIRD AMORAIC LIMITATION OF MISHNAIC DISPUTE

(4) רבי יעקב בר אחא בשם רבי יאשיה: בשאין דפנותיה עולות עמה, אבל אם היו דפנותיה עולות עמה כשירה.

(4) R. Yaakov bar Aha in the name of R. Yosha-ya: [The debate] is when its walls do not go up with it [to the top] but if its walls go up with it, it is valid [even if it is above twenty cubits].

DIFFICULTY FROM BARAITA

(5) והא מתניתא פליגא: אמר רבי יהודה מעשה בסוכתה של הילני המלכה בלוד שהיתה גבוהה יותר מעשרים אמה והיו חכמים נכנסין ויוצאין בה ולא אמר אדם דבר. אמרו לו: מפני שהיא אשה ואין אשה מצוה על המצות. אמר להן: אם משם ראייה והלא שבעה בנים תלמידי חכמים היו לה.

(5) But does not a baraita disagree: R. Yehu-dah said: It happened with Queen Helena's sukkah in Lod that was higher than twenty cubits and the sages went in and out of it and no one said anything. They said to him: That is because she is a woman and a wom-an is not obligated in the commandments. He said to them: If that is proof, then did she not have seven sons who were sages?!

EXPLICATION OF DIFFICULTY

(6a) אית לך מימר בסוכתה של הילני בשאינה מחזקת אלא ראשו ורובו ושולחנו?
(6b) אלא בשאין דפנותיה עולות עמה.
(6c) מסתברא מה דאמר רבי יאשיה לית היא פליגא, דכן ארחיהון דעתירייא מיעבד דפנתא קלילין די ייא קרורה עליל.

(6a) Can you say that Queen Helena's sukkah was only big enough to fit one's head, most of one's body and one's table?
(6b) Rather, [the debate] is when the walls do not go up with it.
(6c) It therefore seems that the baraita does not disagree with what R. Yoshaya said, for it is typical for rich people to make the walls light so that cool [air] may come in.

The Yerushalmi begins with an amoraic statement offering biblical proof for the notion that a sukkah over twenty cubits high is invalid. The Torah commands Jews to dwell in sukkot. The rabbis understand "sukkot" to be synonymous with the *skhakh*. Sitting under *skhakh* means that the *skhakh* must provide the shade. Above twenty cubits the shade will be provided by the walls and not by the *skhakh*.

We should note that this is not necessarily empirically true (see Tosafot 2b s.v. יש בה יותר), nor does R. Abahu's statement seem to be based on empirical evidence. If the sukkah is wide enough, it is certainly possible for the shade to come from the *skhakh* even if it is over twenty cubits high. And if the sukkah is extremely narrow, even if the *skhakh* is under twenty cubits high, the walls will provide the shade. We can assume that R. Abahu was aware of these empirical realities. His preference for using this verse as a midrash to explain the mishnah is that it is topical to Sukkot and it expresses one of the main values underlying the rabbinic understanding of the sukkah—the *skhakh* must provide shade.

R. Yonah (2a) is the first to limit the debate in the mishnah. He seems to interpret "higher than twenty cubits" in the mishnah to mean "higher than [the walls by] twenty cubits." The sages disallow a sukkah whose *skhakh* is more than twenty cubits above the walls. But if the *skhakh* is less than twenty cubits above the walls, the sages would agree with R. Yehudah that it is valid, even if the *skhakh* is more than twenty cubits above the ground. Were we to look for a realistic setting in which such a sukkah might be built, we might consider a case where *skhakh* was rolled out of a high window from an upper floor of a building.[6] While the side of the building could be considered one of the walls of the sukkah, the other walls would have to be built, and it might be difficult for them to be within twenty cubits of the *skhakh* above. R. Yonah says that in such a case the sages do not consider this "floating" *skhakh,* more than twenty cubits removed from most of the walls, to be part of the sukkah. But if the walls are less than twenty cubits from the *skhakh,* then the sukkah can be considered one integral whole, *skhakh* and walls together. R. Yonah is concerned, or at least interprets the sages in the mishnah as being concerned, lest the *skhakh* not be considered part of the sukkah. As we shall see below, this is similar to R. Yaakov bar Aha's statement (4).

R. Yose (2b) rejects R. Yonah's limitation due to its incompatibility with the language of the mishnah, which makes no mention of walls. It is possible that this rejection is at least part of the reason that R. Yonah's statement did not make its way into the Bavli.

---

[6] A similar case is found in Tosefta Sukkah 2:3.

> ⚫ **Queen Helena** ruled the Assyrian kingdom of Adiabene (located in modern day Iraq) in the first century CE. According to Josephus, she was married to her brother Monabazus I. Josephus describes the conversion of the Royal house to Judaism as the result of the influence of a Jewish merchant. After her conversion, Helena moved to Jerusalem where she remained until the end of her life. Some archeologists claim that her palace and remains were uncovered in excavations in the City of David. In any case, it is highly unlikely that there was any historical interaction between the sages and the royal family. For more on the story of the Adiabene family in the book of Josephus see, Lawrence Schiffman, "The Conversion of the Royal House of Adiabene in Josephus and Rabbinic Sources," *Josephus, Judaism and Christianity,* ed. Louis H. Feldman, et al. (Detroit: Wayne State University Press, 1987), 293-312.

R. Ba in the name of Rav (3) provides the second limitation to the mishnaic dispute. This limitation essentially legislates the mishnaic halakhah out of existence. The sages disqualify a twenty cubit sukkah only if its breadth and width are at the absolute minimum (or close thereto; see Mishnah Sukkah 2:7). The sukkah is just large enough to contain one's head, most of one's body and one's table.[7] Such a sukkah, extraordinarily high and at the same time of bare minimum width, would certainly be nearly impossible to build. But if the sukkah is any wider than this minimum, there is no height limit.

R. Yaakov bar Aha in the name of R. Yoshaya (4) provides yet another limitation to the mishnaic debate. His limitation seems to be a more stringent variation of R. Yonah's limitation offered above (2a). If the walls reach the *skhakh,* then all the sages agree that the *skhakh* can be above twenty cubits. The sages invalidate the sukkah only if the walls do not reach the *skhakh* and the *skhakh* is above twenty cubits. In contrast, R. Yonah was far more lenient and allowed the *skhakh* to be twenty cubits above the walls.

The Yerushalmi objects (5), citing a baraita from the Tosefta concerning Queen Helena's sukkah. We will deal with the baraita itself and its various versions below in our discussion of the Bavli, where it also appears. In this baraita R. Yehudah and the sages argue over whether Queen Helena's sukkah

---

[7] Tables in mishnaic times would have been far smaller than our tables and are comparable to what we could call a tray. See the illustrations found in Dennis Smith, *From Symposium to Eucharist* (Minneapolis: Fortress Press, 2003), 15–17.

serves as a proper precedent for a valid sukkah. They all agree that Helena's sukkah was over twenty cubits high. To R. Yehudah, the fact that the sages did not say anything to her is evidence that a twenty cubit sukkah is always valid. The sages, on the other hand, discount this sukkah as having value as a halakhic precedent because women are exempt from the mitzvah of dwelling in the sukkah. In the context of our sugya, clearly the queen's sukkah was much wider than the minimum width (head, most of body and table). Hence we see that despite the fact that the sukkah was not of minimum width, R. Yehudah and the sages continued to dispute. Thus this baraita rejects Rav's opinion from section three.

The sugya concludes (6) by fleshing out the difficulty brought from the baraita (5). Unlike the parallel found in the Bavli, in the Yerushalmi there is no resolution offered. Rav's position is rejected and R. Yoshaya's is accepted, for the Yerushalmi acknowledges that it is normal for a queen to dwell in a sukkah whose walls do not come up to its roof.[8]

There are several aspects of the Yerushalmi that will distinguish this sugya from the Bavli parallel discussed below. First and foremost, the Yerushalmi does not correlate between the amora who offers scriptural basis for the mishnah (1) and the amoraim who offer limitations of the mishnah (sections two, three and four). Second, there is only one limitation which uses breadth and width to limit the mishnaic dispute (section three). Finally, the Queen Helena baraita is clearly brought as a challenge to one amoraic opinion, and that opinion is eventually rejected. With these points in mind, we now turn our attention to the Bavli sugya.

The Bavli

The Bavli's sugya begins with the attempt to find scriptural basis for the prohibition of a twenty cubit sukkah. We will first cite the sugya in its entirety and then offer an explanation of it and its construction.

---

[8] We should note that ending a sugya with amoraic opinions rejected is more common in the Yerushalmi than the Bavli.

SECTION 1, PART 1

OPENING QUESTION

מנא הני מילי?

From where do we know this?

AMORAIC STATEMENT 1

(1) אמר רבה: דאמר קרא:
למען ידעו דרתיכם כי בסכות
הושבתי את בני ישראל
(ויקרא כב: מג), עד עשרים
אמה - אדם יודע שהוא דר
בסוכה, למעלה מעשרים אמה
- אין אדם יודע שדר בסוכה,
משום דלא שלטא בה עינא.

(1) Rabbah said: Scripture says: *That your generations may know that I caused the children of Israel to dwell in sukkot* (Leviticus 23:43). [In a sukkah] up to twenty cubits [high] one knows that he is dwelling in a sukkah, but above twenty cubits one does not know that he is dwelling in a sukkah, since his eye does not perceive it.

AMORAIC STATEMENT 2

(2a) רבי זירא אמר: מהכא,
וסכה תהיה לצל יומם מחרב
(ישעיהו ד:ו), עד עשרים אמה
- אדם יושב בצל סוכה, למעלה
מעשרים אמה - אין אדם יושב
בצל סוכה, אלא בצל דפנות.

(2a) Rabbi Zera says: From here: *And there shall be a sukkah for shade during the daytime from the heat* (Isaiah 4:6). [In a sukkah] up to twenty cubits [high] one sits in the shade of the sukkah, but in one higher than twenty cubits he sits not in the shade of the sukkah but in the shade of its walls.

AMORAIC CHALLENGE TO STATEMENT 2 AND RESOLUTION

(2b) אמר ליה אביי: אלא
מעתה, העושה סוכתו בעשתרות
קרנים, הכי נמי דלא הוי סוכה?

(2b) Abaye said to him: But if so, one who made his sukkah in *Ashteroth Karnayim*—it would also not be a [valid] sukkah?

(2c) אמר ליה: התם, דל
עשתרות קרנים - איכא
צל סוכה, הכא דל דפנות
- ליכא צל סוכה.

(2c) He answered him: In that case, remove the *Ashteroth Karnayim* and there will be the shade of the sukkah, but here, remove the walls, and there will be no shade of a sukkah.

Tannaitic Source   Amoraic Source   Stammaitic Source

AMORAIC STATEMENT 3

(3a) ורבא אמר: מהכא בסכת
תשבו שבעת ימים (ויקרא
כג:מב). אמרה תורה: כל
שבעת הימים צא מדירת קבע
ושב בדירת עראי. עד עשרים
אמה - אדם עושה דירתו
דירת עראי, למעלה מעשרים
אמה - אין אדם עושה דירתו
דירת עראי, אלא דירת קבע.

(3a) Rava said: From here: *In sukkot you shall dwell for seven days* (Leviticus 23:42). The Torah states: All seven days leave your permanent abode and dwell in a temporary abode. [With a booth] up to twenty cubits [high] one makes his abode a temporary one; [in one] higher than twenty cubits, one does not make his abode temporary, but permanent.

AMORAIC CHALLENGE TO MEMRA 2 AND RESOLUTION

(3b) אמר ליה אביי: אלא
מעתה, עשה מחיצות של
ברזל וסיכך על גבן - הכי
נמי דלא הוי סוכה?

(3b) Abaye said to him: But if so, if he made walls of iron and covered them with *skhakh*, it would also not be a valid sukkah.

(3c) אמר ליה, הכי קאמינא לך:
עד עשרים אמה, דאדם עושה
דירתו דירת עראי, כי עביד ליה
דירת קבע - נמי נפיק. למעלה
מעשרים אמה, דאדם עושה
דירתו דירת קבע, כי עביד ליה
דירת עראי - נמי לא נפיק.

(3c) He answered him: This is what I am saying to you: [In a sukkah] up to twenty cubits, which is the way in which one makes a temporary abode, even if he makes it permanent, he has fulfilled his obligation; [but in one] higher than twenty cubits, which is the way in which one makes a permanent abode, even if he makes it temporary, he has not fulfilled his obligation.

SECTION ONE, PART TWO

STAMMAITIC EXPLANATION OF RELATIONSHIP
BETWEEN THREE AMORAIC STATEMENTS

(4a) כולהו כרבה לא אמרי
- ההוא ידיעה לדורות היא.

(4a) All do not agree with Rabbah, for that [verse] refers to the knowledge of [future] generations.

Tannaitic Source   Amoraic Source   Stammaitic Source

(4b) כרבי זירא נמי לא
אמרי - ההוא לימות המשיח
הוא דכתיב. ורבי זירא: אם כן
לימא קרא וחפה תהיה לצל
יומם, ומאי וסכה תהיה לצל
יומם - שמעת מינה תרתי.

(4b) Nor do they agree with R. Zera, for that verse refers to the Messianic age. And as for R. Zera? [He could answer]: If so, let verse say "And there shall be a covering (חופה) for shade during the day." Why then does it say, *And there shall be a sukkah for shade during the day?* Learn from there two points.

(4c) כרבא נמי לא אמרי
- משום קושיא דאביי.

(4c) They also do not agree with Rava because of the difficulty raised by Abaye.

SECTION TWO, PART ONE

AMORAIC STATEMENT 1 LIMITING DISPUTE IN MISHNAH

(5a) כמאן אזלא הא דאמר רבי
יאשיה אמר רב: מחלוקת בשאין
דפנות מגיעות לסכך, אבל
דפנות מגיעות לסכך - אפילו
למעלה מעשרים אמה כשרה.

(5a) With whom does the statement made by R. Yoshaya in the name of Rav agree: the dispute [concerning the height of a sukkah] is when the walls do not reach the *skhakh*, but when the walls do reach the *skhakh* [both agree] that even if it is higher than twenty cubits, it is valid?

(5b) כמאן? כרבה, דאמר:
משום דלא שלטא בה עינא,
וכיון דדפנות מגיעות לסכך
- משלט שלטא בה עינא.

(5b) With whom? It is in accordance with Rabbah whose reason is that the eye does not perceive it, and since the walls reach the *skhakh*, the eye does perceive it.

AMORAIC STATEMENT 2 LIMITING DISPUTE IN MISHNAH

(6a) כמאן אזלא הא דאמר רב
הונא אמר רב: מחלוקת בשאין
בה אלא ארבע אמות על ארבע
אמות, אבל יש בה יותר מארבע
אמות על ארבע אמות - אפילו
למעלה מעשרים אמה כשרה.

(6a) With whom does the statement made by R. Huna in the name of Rav agree: The dispute is when [the sukkah] is only four cubits by four cubits, but where it was more than four cubits by four cubits [both agree] that even if it is higher than twenty cubits it is valid?

| Tannaitic Source | Amoraic Source | Stammaitic Source |

(6b) כמאן? כרבי זירא,
דאמר: משום צל הוא, וכיון
דרויחא - איכא צל סוכה.

(6b) With whom? It is in accordance with R. Zera whose reason is of shade; since it is broad, there is shade from the sukkah (*skhakh*).

AMORAIC STATEMENT 3 LIMITING DISPUTE IN MISHNAH

(7a) כמאן אזלא הא דאמר
רב חנן בר רבה אמר רב:
מחלוקת בשאינה מחזקת אלא
כדי ראשו ורובו ושולחנו,
אבל מחזקת יותר מכדי ראשו
ורובו ושולחנו - אפילו למעלה
מעשרים אמה כשרה.

(7a) With whom does the statement made by R. Hanan bar Rabbah in the name of Rav agree: The dispute is when [the sukkah] only fits his head, most of his body and his table but when it fits more than his head and body and table [both agree] that even if it is higher than twenty cubits it is valid?

TANNAITIC SOURCE BROUGHT AS CHALLENGE TO AMORAIC STATEMENT 3 (AND PERHAPS AMORAIC STATEMENT 2)

(7b) כמאן? דלא כחד.

(7b) With whom? It is in accordance with no one.[9]

(8a) מיתיבי: סוכה שהיא
גבוהה למעלה מעשרים אמה -
פסולה, ורבי יהודה מכשיר עד
ארבעים וחמשים אמה. אמר רבי
יהודה: מעשה בהילני המלכה
בלוד, שהיתה סוכתה גבוהה
מעשרים אמה, והיו זקנים נכנסין
ויוצאין לשם, ולא אמרו לה
דבר. אמרו לו: משם ראייה?
אשה היתה ופטורה מן הסוכה.
אמר להן: והלא שבעה בנים
הוו לה. ועוד: כל מעשיה לא
עשתה אלא על פי חכמים.

(8a) They objected: A sukkah which is higher than twenty cubits is not valid, but R. Yehudah validates it up to a height of forty or fifty cubits. R. Yehudah stated: It happened with Queen Helena in Lod that her sukkah was higher than twenty cubits, and the elders were going in and out of it and they did not say a word to her. They said to him: Is this a proof? She was a woman and not obligated in the [commandment of] the sukkah. He answered them: Did she not have seven sons? And furthermore, she acted only in accordance with sages.

Tannaitic Source	Amoraic Source	Stammaitic Source

9 We have skipped an anonymous section which analyzes why each of these three amoraim (R. Yoshaya, R. Huna and R. Hanan bar Rabbah) disagree with each other. This section is not relevant to our discussion. We should note that it is not clear whether R. Yoshaya disagrees with R. Huna or R. Hanan bar Rabbah. See Tosafot 2b s.v. בשלמא.

STAMMAITIC EXPLANATION OF BARAITA

(8b) למה לי למיתני ועוד כל מעשיה לא עשתה אלא על פי חכמים?

(8b) Why does it have to teach, "And furthermore, she acted only in accordance with sages?"

(8c) הכי קאמר להו: כי תאמרו בנים קטנים היו, וקטנים פטורין מן הסוכה, כיון דשבעה הוו - אי אפשר דלא הוי בהו חד שאינו צריך לאמו. וכי תימרו: קטן שאינו צריך לאמו - מדרבנן הוא דמיחייב, ואיהי בדרבנן לא משגחה - תא שמע: ועוד כל מעשיה לא עשתה אלא על פי חכמים.

(8c) Thus he said to them: If you will say [with regard to her seven sons] that her sons were minors and minors are exempted from [the obligation of] the sukkah, since she had seven, there must have been at least one who was [old enough] not to be dependent on his mother; and if you will object that a child who is not dependent on his mother is only obligated by rabbinic law, and she did not observe rabbinic law, come and learn, "And furthermore, she only acted in accordance with sages."

STAMMAITIC EXPLANATION OF DIFFICULTY

(9a) בשלמא למאן דאמר בשאין דפנות מגיעות לסכך מחלוקת - דרכה של מלכה לישב בסוכה שאין דפנות מגיעות לסכך משום אוירא. אלא למאן דאמר בסוכה קטנה מחלוקת, וכי דרכה של מלכה לישב בסוכה קטנה?

(9a) It goes well according to the one who says that the dispute was in the case where the walls did not reach the *skhakh,* since it is the custom of a queen to sit in a sukkah whose walls do not reach the *skhakh* because of [the circulation] of air; but according to the one who says that the dispute was only in the case of a small sukkah, is it then customary for a queen to sit in a small sukkah?

FIRST AMORAIC RESOLUTION OF DIFFICULTY

(9b) אמר רבה בר רב אדא: לא נצרכה אלא לסוכה העשויה קיטוניות קיטוניות.

(9b) Rabbah b. Ada said: It was necessary only in the case of a sukkah constructed with many small compartments.

| Tannaitic Source | Amoraic Source | Stammaitic Source |

DIFFICULTY RAISED AGAINST RESOLUTION

(9c) וכי דרכה של מלכה
לישב בסוכה העשויה
קיטוניות קיטוניות?

(9c) But is it customary for a queen to sit in a sukkah with many small compartments?

SECOND AMORAIC RESOLUTION OF DIFFICULTY

(9d) אמר רב אשי: לא נצרכה
אלא לקיטוניות שבה.

(9d) R. Ashi said: It was necessary only in the case of the small compartments in it.

STAMMAITIC INTERPRETATION OF BARAITA IN LIGHT OF R. ASHI'S COMMENT

(9e) רבנן סברי: בניה בסוכה
מעליא הוו יתבי, ואיהי יתבה
בקיטוניות משום צניעותא, ומשום
הכי לא אמרי לה דבר. ורבי
יהודה סבר: בניה גבה הוו יתבי,
ואפילו הכי לא אמרי לה דבר.

(9e) The sages hold that her sons sat in a proper sukkah, while she sat in one of the compartments due to modesty, and hence they said nothing; while R. Yehudah holds that her sons sat with her, and still they said nothing.

| Tannaitic Source | Amoraic Source | Stammaitic Source |

Providing Midrashic Support

This sugya may be divided into four sections. The first section, which extends until the end of 4c, consists of two historic layers. The earliest layer is comprised of the attempts of three amoraim of the third and fourth generations to provide scriptural basis for the sages' prohibition of building a sukkah with *skhakh* more than twenty cubits above the ground. Rabbah (section 1), a prominent third-generation Babylonian amora, finds scriptural support in Leviticus 23:43, specifically in the Bible's word for "shall know." Those dwelling in a sukkah must know that they are in a sukkah. Sukkot are recognizable by their *skhakh*, and therefore the *skhakh* must not be so high that it is difficult for the eye to make out.

R. Zera (2a), another third-generation amora, finds scriptural support in Isaiah 4:6, specifically in the word "shade." The *skhakh,* not the walls, must provide the shade. If the *skhakh* is more than twenty cubits high, it is unlikely that the *skhakh* itself will ever be the source of shade.

Finally, Rava (3a), a fourth-generation sage, finds support in Leviticus 23:42, and in the words "seven days." The Torah implies that one should build a sukkah that can stand for seven days, not one that is a permanent structure. A sukkah that is higher than twenty cubits will usually require a permanent base to support it, and therefore it is invalid.

These three amoraim do not seem to disagree with each other in any substantive way. And indeed there are many passages in the Talmud in which multiple amoraim provide scriptural support for a tannaitic law without disagreeing with each other halakhically. At most we could state that the different amoraim emphasize different aspects of the mitzvah to dwell in the sukkah. Rabbah emphasizes the general awareness that one must have that he is dwelling in a sukkah. R. Zera emphasizes that the *skhakh* must provide shade. And Rava emphasizes that a sukkah should have an impermanent quality to it. But none of the amoraim would question that a sukkah whose *skhakh* is higher than twenty cubits is invalid.

The second historical layer of this passage consists of difficulties that Abaye, a fourth-generation Babylonian amora, raised on R. Zera and Rava (2b, 3b). Whereas R. Zera's comment was midrashic in nature, Abaye's challenge adds a normative/halakhic tone to the sugya. R. Zera's derashah could lead to a halakhic problem—if one builds a sukkah in between two large hills such as those of *"Ashterot Karnayim"* (a reference to Genesis 14:5), then it follows that since the *skhakh* is not providing the shade, the sukkah should be invalid. As Abaye notes, R. Zera's derashah implies that the *skhakh*, not the walls, must provide shade, but there are no tannaitic sources that present such a demand. The tannaim only demand that the *skhakh* not allow in more sun than shade.[10] Against Rava, Abaye raises the difficulty that Rava's derashah implies that the sukkah must be impermanent. As we shall see, there are no tannaitic halakhot that make such a claim. In both cases, R. Zera and Rava (or the editors on their behalf) offer resolutions to Abaye's difficulties (2c, 3c). Indeed, it does not seem that Abaye actually intended to reject R. Zera and Rava. Clearly Abaye did not really believe that R. Zera would invalidate a sukkah whose access to sun is blocked by the hills; nor did he really believe that Rava would invalidate

---

[10] Mishnah Sukkah 1:1; 2:2.

a sukkah whose walls are made of metal. Rather, his role was more of that of devil's advocate,[11] pointing out some logical flaws in their argumentation.

The analysis of the amoraic statements concludes with stammaitic discourse (section four). Underlying the section is the typical stammaitic assumption that when amoraim offer different midrashic justifications for a given halakhah each amora actually disagrees with the other. As we have seen, there is no real reason to assume that Rabbah, R. Zera or Rava actually disagreed with each other with regard to any halakhic matter. However, part of the stammaitic interpretation of virtually all sources includes dealing with the broad problem of superfluity. In this case: If the first amora (Rabbah) satisfactorily provided a midrashic basis to the mishnah's halakhah, why would another amora offer another verse? Based on this question, the stam posits that each of these amoraim disagree with each other. As we shall see in our analysis below, this assumption impacts their interpretation of the next set of amoraic statements as well.

Limiting the Dispute in the Mishnah

The next section, 5a–7b, is comprised of two historical layers. The first is an amoraic layer consisting of three memrot (amoraic statements), and the second is the brief but critically important stammaitic envelope that surrounds each memra. The amoraim themselves limit the scope of the debate in the mishnah. The stam takes each memra and attempts to pair it with one of the memrot that explained the mishnah in section one. One can easily see here the distinction between the amoraic layer, which is entirely in Hebrew and always attributed to an amora, and the stammaitic editorial remarks which are mostly in Aramaic (כמאן אזלא ה) and are anonymous.

We will begin by analyzing the three memrot themselves, separate from their stammaitic envelope. The first memra, attributed in the Bavli to R. Yoshaya (5a), is also found in the Yerushalmi, where it is also attributed to R. Yoshaya. However, in the Bavli it is transmitted by R. Yoshaya in the name of Rav, whereas in the Yerushalmi it is transmitted in the name of R. Yaakov bar Aha in the name of R. Yoshaya. It is likely that the Yerushalmi's ascription

---

[11] This is a role which Abaye frequently plays. A simple search on the Bar-Ilan Responsa project reveals that Abaye says "אלא מעתה" 37 times.

is more original. This statement probably did not originate with Rav, as did the other two memrot in the Bavli. Rather, somehow the transmitters of the Bavli (be it in oral or written form) were influenced by the other statements in the Bavli and ascribed this statement to Rav as well.

The second (6a) and third (7a) statements seem to be two different versions of Rav's statement from the Yerushalmi. R. Hanan bar Rabbah's version (7a), that the debate deals with the case when the sukkah can only contain his head, most of his body and his table, is found nearly word for word in the Yerushalmi, where it is attributed to R. Ba in the name of Rav. The Yerushalmi concludes that R. Ba's statement is implausible, due to the tradition in the Tosefta concerning Queen Helena's sukkah. It seems likely, therefore, that the Bavli developed an alternative, slightly more plausible version of Rav's statement, which was transmitted in the name of R. Huna. According to this version Rav limited the debate to a sukkah that is four cubits by four cubits. These dimensions are obviously taken from Tosefta Sukkah 2:2: "Rabbi [Yehudah Hanasi] says: any sukkah that does not have four cubits by four cubits is invalid."

The later historical layer in this section is the stam's attempt to correlate each memra with one of the memrot from the previous section. The reasoning found in this section is pure stammaitic invention and does not appear anywhere in the Yerushalmi. And as is typical in such cases, the stam's reasoning is often forced and causes Rashi some difficulty. For instance, according to the stam, R. Yoshaya's statement (5b), if the walls reach the *skhakh* then one will notice the *skhakh* more easily, matches Rabbah's interpretation in section one, that one must notice the *skhakh*. It is hard to see how this is empirically true—will one really notice the *skhakh* simply because the walls go so high as well? Rashi (s.v. משום דלא שלטא ביה עינא) seems to address this problem by positing that the matching of R. Yoshaya with Rabbah is based more on the process of elimination than on any substantive connection between the two. For according to R. Zera's interpretation of the mishnah (shade must come from *skhakh* not walls), higher walls would lessen the likelihood that the sukkah would get its shade from the *skhakh*. Similarly, according to Rava's interpretation of the mishnah (the sukkah needs to be temporary), higher walls would make the sukkah more, not less, permanent. Rashi (s.v. משום צל) employs similar thinking in his interpretation of the pairing of R. Zera (shade must come from *skhakh*) with R. Huna (the debate is only when the sukkah is four cubits by four cubits).

The editorial procedure of the stam in this sugya is typical of the editing of the Bavli in many places. One of the goals of the stam seems to have been to take individual amoraic statements and link them together to form discourse, in other words, to form a sugya. Another stammaitic goal seems to have been to reveal the underlying reasons of amoraic statements and thereby allow the pairing of statements that originally were not linked. While there are times that the stam seems to have a strong halakhic agenda, i.e. he favors one amoraic or tannaitic opinion over another, this does not seem to be the case here. Rather, the stam's comments have more of a literary and analytic function. However, as we shall see below, the stam's remarks had (as they often do) deep impact upon the post-Talmudic halakhic tradition.

Queen Helena's Sukkah

The sugya continues (section eight) with the baraita from the Tosefta concerning Queen Helena's sukkah, which is brought as a difficulty against the amora who limited the debate to a small sukkah (R. Hanan b. Rabbah, 7a).[12] After some stammaitic analysis, there are two amoraic traditions that attempt to resolve the baraita. Our analysis will focus first on the baraita itself, which appears in three different versions throughout rabbinic literature:

Variant traditions of the Baraita

תוספתא סוכה פ"א ה"א	ירושלמי סוכה פ"א ה"א	בבלי סוכה ב ע"א
אמר ר' יהודה מעשה	אמר רבי יהודה מעשה	אמר רבי יהודה: מעשה
בסוכת הילני שהיתה גבוהה	בסוכתה של הילני המלכה	בהילני המלכה בלוד,
מעשרים אמה, והיו זקנים	בלוד שהיתה גבוהה	שהיתה סוכתה גבוהה
נכנסין ויוצאין אצלה, ולא	יותר מעשרים אמה, והיו	מעשרים אמה, והיו זקנים
אמר אחד מהן דבר.	חכמים נכנסין ויוצאין בה,	נכנסין ויוצאין לשם,
	ולא אמר אדם דבר.	ולא אמרו לה דבר.
אמרו לו: מפני שהיא אשה	אמרו לו: מפני שהיא אשה	אמרו לו: משם ראייה? אשה
ואשה אין חייבת בסוכה.	ואין אשה מצווה על המצוות.	היתה ופטורה מן הסוכה.

אמר להן: והלא שבעה בנים הוו לה. ועוד: כל מעשיה לא עשתה אלא על פי חכמים.	אמר להן: אם משם ראייה והלא שבעה בנים תלמידי חכמים היו לה.	אמר להם: והלא שבעה בנים תלמידי חכמים היו לה וכולן שרויין בתוכה.
R. Yehudah said: It happened with Queen Helena in Lod that her sukkah was higher than twenty cubits, and the elders were going in and out of it and they did not say a word to her.	R. Yehudah said: It happened with Queen Helena's sukkah in Lod that was higher than twenty cubits and the sages when in and out and they did not say anything to her.	R. Yehudah said: It happened with Helena's sukkah that was more than twenty cubits high and the sages went in and out and did not say anything to her.
They said to him: Is this a proof? She was a woman and not obligated in the [commandment of the] sukkah.	They said to him: That is because she is a woman and a woman is not obligated in the commandments.	They said to him: That is because she is a woman and a woman is not obligated in the [commandment of the] sukkah.
He said to them: Didn't she have seven sons? Furthermore, she acted only in accordance with sages.	He said to them: If from there, then there is proof, for were not her seven sons sages.	He said to them: Were not her seven sons disciples of the sages, and they were all dwelling in it.

Shamma Friedman points out that in the Tosefta and in the Yerushalmi Queen Helena has seven sons who are "disciples of the sages (תלמידי חכמים)."[13] In contrast, in the Bavli she has seven sons but they are no longer disciples of the sages. He explains that the difference is the result of intentional emendation of the baraita by the Babylonian editor, who was uncomfortable with the notion that Queen Helena, reputedly a convert from Adiabene, would have seven sons all of whom were rabbinic sages! Instead, Helena herself is said to have performed,

---

[13] Shamma Friedman, "Habaraitot Shebetalmud Habavli Veyahsan Letosefta," *Atarah L'Haim*, ed. Daniel Boyarin, et al. (Jerusalem: Hebrew University Magnes Press, 2000), 173–174.

"all of her actions according to the sages." According to Friedman, the editors took the notion that Helena listened to the sages from Mishnah Nazir 3:6:

> It happened that Queen Helena, when her son went to war, said: "If my son returns in peace from the war, I shall be a nazirite for seven years." Her son returned from the war, and she was a nazirite for seven years. At the end of the seven years, she went up to the land [of Israel] *and Beit Hillel instructed her to be a nazirite for a further seven years.* Towards the end of this seven years, she contracted ritual defilement, and so altogether she was a nazirite for twenty-one years.

While Friedman highlights exactly what changes the Babylonian editors made to the toseftan tradition, Richard Kalmin offers a broad explanation as to why they would have emended this source.[14] Kalmin reads the Bavli's editorial work in light of the differing attitudes between Babylonian and Eretz Yisraeli sources regarding converts in particular and in light of their differing attitudes towards rabbinic interaction with non-rabbis in general. The Eretz Yisraeli source has little problem depicting the descendants of converts as sages. This is due to the general willingness of Eretz Yisraeli rabbis to "admit non-Rabbis into their midst." The Bavli omits this depiction, in line with its general "portrayal ...of a rabbinic movement that was closed to non-Rabbis... [In] the Bavli's version there is no mention of converts who have become Rabbis." Thus in general the Babylonian emendations to this particular story are part of a broader phenomenon reflected in the Bavli's tendency to edit out stories of interaction between rabbis and non-rabbis.

The Amoraic Resolution to the Difficulty

We now turn our attention to section nine, in which the amoraim discuss the baraita about Helena. First, we note that in the Yerushalmi this baraita is brought as a challenge to Rav, who limits the debate in the mishnah to an

---

[14] See Kalmin, "The Adiabenian Royal Family in Rabbinic Literature of Late Antiquity," *Tiferet LeYisrael*, ed. Joel Roth, et al. (New York: Jewish Theological Seminary, 2010), 61–77.

extremely small sukkah. Obviously, a queen would not dwell in such a small sukkah, and therefore his limitation is rejected. While both Talmuds contain sugyot that occasionally end with the rejection of an amoraic interpretation, this is more typical in the Yerushalmi. And indeed, in the Bavli two Babylonian amoraim attempt to solve this difficulty.

Rabbi Abin bar Rav Ada[15] (9b) resolves the challenge posed by the baraita to R. Hanan bar Rabbah by suggesting that the sukkah in which Queen Helena sat was made of small compartments.[16] Supposedly, Helena would have been sitting in one small compartment, and it was this type of sukkah over which R. Yehudah and the sages disputed. The stam then raises another difficulty: does a queen sit in a sukkah made of small compartments? R. Ashi (9d) resolves the difficulty by saying: "It was only necessary [in reference] to the small compartment in it." In other words, the sukkah was large and was not entirely made of small compartments, but Queen Helena sat in one of the smaller compartments. The stam concludes (9e) by explaining R. Ashi's statement—the elders did not object to Helena because she was sitting in one of the compartments. Her children sat in the larger section of the sukkah, which may be more than twenty cubits high, according to R. Hanan bar Rabbah. R. Yehudah insists that at least one of her sons was with her in the small compartment. Therefore, the silence of the elders proves that they validated a high sukkah, even if it was narrow.

We note that while the Yerushalmi simply accepted that the baraita rejects the amoraic limitation on the mishnaic dispute, later Babylonian amoraim employ forced reasoning to defend an amoraic opinion, even at the cost of a simple reading of the baraita. This is again typical of late Babylonian amoraim, who commonly offer tendentious interpretations of tannaitic material.

The Impact of the Stam on Post-Talmudic Halakhah

In both Talmuds the amoraim limit the scope of the debate between the sages and R. Yehudah in the Mishnah. It seems that for some reason the amoraim

---

[15] This is the reading found in most manuscripts. The printed edition reads "Rabbah bar Rav Ada."

[16] A קיטון is a small room. See for instance Mishnah Middot 1:6; Yerushalmi Ketubbot 4:7, 28d; Bavli Menahot 33b

felt strongly that a twenty cubit sukkah should be valid, but were hesitant to rule like R. Yehudah, because his was a minority opinion opposed by the sages. By severely limiting the scope of the debate, they were able to validate a twenty cubit sukkah and still maintain that the halakhah was according to the majority opinion, that of the sages. In the Bavli none of these amoraic opinions is rejected. In fact, as we have seen, later Babylonian amoraim, R. Avin b. Rav Ada (9b) and Rav Ashi (9d), offer forced interpretations of a baraita in order to justify even the opinion that limits the debate in the mishnah to an extremely small sukkah. The stam, too, does nothing to intimate that any of these opinions limiting the mishnah's invalidation of a twenty cubit sukkah is not to be accepted as halakhically valid. Indeed, one can safely conclude that the Bavli validates a twenty cubit sukkah, as long as its length and width are not at an absolute minimum.

Nevertheless, in contrast to the amoraim, many post-Talmudic authorities[17] rule that a twenty cubit sukkah is never valid. This halakhic development may be traced to the stam's failure to match any of the limitations of the debate with Rava's opinion that a sukkah must be a temporary dwelling place (3a). The immediate intent of the stam was probably to note that none of the amoraim in the second part of the sugya (sections 5–7) agree with Rava's reasoning from the first part of the sugya (sections 1–3). However, post-Talmudic authorities also argued the converse—Rava does not agree with any of the limitations on the debate offered by the amoraim later in the sugya. And for two main reasons many rishonim felt that the halakhah should be in accordance with Rava. First, Rava is the latest amora in this section, and therefore the rule "the halakhah is accordance with the latest opinion" applies.[18] Second, it is Rava who holds that the sukkah must be a temporary structure, which is the majority opinion elsewhere in the Talmud.[19] The Talmud seems to accept the interpretation that the sages and R. Yehudah argue over whether the sukkah must be an imperma-nent or permanent dwelling place, the sages holding the former position and

---

[17] See R. Yitzchak Alfasi and the comments of Rabbenu Nissim.

[18] The principle of adjudication, הלכתא כבתראי—the law follows the later opinion, is first found in the writings of the geonim. The rationale behind the concept lies in the fact that the later opinion must have been aware of the position of the earlier authority and still maintained his ruling. For more see Israel Moses Ta-Shma, *Creativity and Tradition* (Cambridge: Harvard University Press, 2006), 142–165.

[19] Yoma 10b; Sukkah 21b.

R. Yehudah the latter. If the halakhah accords with the majority opinion, we can conclude that a sukkah must be an impermanent dwelling place.[20] Hence, if one accepts that the halakhah is in accordance with Rava, and one takes into account that according to the stam Rava would not accept any limitation on the mishnah, it follows that Rava holds that the sages always disqualify a twenty cubit sukkah. As Maimonides writes (Laws of Sukkah and Lulav 4:1): "The measure of the height of a sukkah is not less than seven handbreadths and not more than twenty cubits." There are no exceptions.

The Sukkah as an Impermanent Dwelling Place: Rava's Legacy

Jeffrey Rubenstein has traced the development of the notion that the sukkah is an impermanent dwelling place, as claimed by Rava in our sugya. In Mishnah Maasrot 3:7 and Tosefta Eruvin 5:5, R. Yehudah considers the sukkah a permanent structure. Therefore, a sukkah requires a mezuzah. If one brings one's produce into a sukkah on Sukkot he must tithe before eating, as if he had brought it into a house which makes produce liable for tithes. Finally, R. Yehudah obligates those dwelling in the sukkah to participate in an eruv (the communal meal that allows one to carry into a courtyard on Shabbat). Rava, according to Rubenstein, picks up on R. Yehudah's consistent conception of the sukkah as a permanent structure, and develops it one critical step further. Whereas R. Yehudah himself focused on the *function* of the sukkah—during the festival the sukkah *functions* as a permanent dwelling place—Rava focuses on the dimensions of the sukkah. Rava explains that the sages, who consistently disagree with R. Yehudah and conceive of the sukkah as an impermanent dwelling place, also demand that the *dimensions* of the sukkah have an impermanent quality. This is the first time in rabbinic literature, according to Rubenstein, in which we learn that the structure of the sukkah must be impermanent. Rubenstein writes, "Here Rava invents the concept of a sukkah as a permanent dwelling as it came to be known in Jewish tradition. Prior to Rava, no such tradition

---

[20] See for instance Sukkah 7b where Abaye ascribes the position that the sukkah must be a permanent dwelling place to a list of specific tannaim. The implication is that the normative majority position is that the sukkah must be an impermanent dwelling place. See the Ran's commentary on the Rif, 1b, s.v. ‏קבע בעינן‎.

existed."[21] Rava understands that R. Yehudah requires a permanent structure and in so doing, he defines the sages' opposition as being a result of their belief that the sukkah must be an impermanent structure.

The one wrinkle with Rubenstein's explanation of Rava is that it is possible to see at least some of the roots of Rava's thinking in R. Yehudah's rulings in Mishnah Sukkah itself. For instance in Sukkah 1:6 we read: "One may make *skhakh* out of wooden planks, the words of R. Yehudah. And R. Meir prohibits." In the mishnah which follows, R. Yehudah offers an interpretation of Bet Shammai and Bet Hillel that could lead to a more permanent sukkah structure than does R. Meir's understanding of the earlier debate. In 2:2, R. Yehudah says that if one leans his sukkah on the legs of a bed, the sukkah must be able to stand on its own to be valid. While any of these mishnayot could be interpreted in other ways, it is possible that R. Yehudah's opinion that a sukkah should be *conceived* of as a permanent dwelling place informed his rulings that a sukkah could (and maybe even should) be built with more permanent structural features than the other sages permit. In other words, what Rubenstein sees as a complete invention of Rava, a fourth-generation amora, could have roots in Mishnah Sukkah itself.

All the same, Rubenstein is certainly correct that Rava's statement is innovative. Nowhere in earlier literature do we hear of any *demand* that the sukkah be an impermanent dwelling place. Abaye's challenge to Rava is justified—if the sukkah must be a temporary dwelling place, why are all sorts of permanent structures, such as iron walls, allowed? Further evidence that Rava's words are an innovation is found in our sugya itself. All of the amoraim who limit the scope of the debate in the mishnah would be more likely to allow permanent sukkot (larger ones, or a sukkah where the walls reach the *skhakh*) than impermanent ones. Thus even if R. Yehudah himself allowed more permanent structures, the other sages certainly did not demand impermanent structures. The twenty cubit limit was clearly not originally meant to prevent the sukkah from becoming a permanent structure. Nevertheless, the stammaitic impact on the understanding of this mishnah was determinative. Just as the halakhah was set according to Rava, so, too, was the popular interpretation of this mishnah—a twenty cubit sukkah is invalid because a sukkah *must* be a temporary dwelling place.[22]

---

[21] Jeffrey Rubenstein, "The 'Sukkah' as Temporary or Permanent Dwelling," 149.
[22] See for example Maimonides' and Bartenura's commentary on the Mishnah.

Chapter Two

From Symposium to Seder: The Afikoman

Pesahim 119b–120a

Introduction

Today people commonly refer to the matzah eaten at the end of the Pesah seder as the afikoman. As we explore the original meaning of the word afikoman and its subsequent development, we shall see that this is a misnomer. The Mishnah and Tosefta, which contain the earliest mention of the term, prohibit concluding the seder meal with an "afikoman." In both of these texts "afikoman" is a loan word from Greek which means drunken revelry. And so the tannaim were not mandating that the meal be completed with a piece of matzah. Rather, they were prohibiting anyone from concluding the meal with drunken revelry, the typical conclusion to a Greco-Roman banquet, which served in many ways as the paradigm for the rabbinic seder.

The amoraim in both Talmuds go on to list particular activities which are part of the afikoman/drunkenness prohibition, including playing musical instruments, traipsing from house to house, and eating the salty foods that traditionally accompanied the drinking of wine. In the later stages of the development of the Babylonian sugya which deals with the meaning and prohibition of the afikoman, we will encounter a halakhah which uses the term afikoman to prohibit eating *any food* after concluding the meal with matzah. While tannaitic and most amoraic sources *prohibit* the revelry they call afikoman, in the medieval period the word afikoman came to refer to the piece of matzah that was mandatorily eaten at the end of the meal. Thus what was originally a prohibition came to be a mitzvah! The origins of this strange halakhah will be the focus of this chapter.

There are numerous methodological and literary considerations that are relevant to understanding the development of the laws of the afikoman and the Babylonian sugya that deals with the issue. First, the word "afikoman" comes from Greek and therefore must be understood in light of our knowledge of the Greek language and of Greco-Roman eating customs. Second, this sugya is an excellent example of the chronological development of the meaning of a word from tannaitic and early amoraic literature through late Babylonian literature. Third, the Babylonian sugya provides an example of how later amoraim modified early amoraic statements to match their understanding of tannaitic literature as well as normative practice. Finally, this is perhaps the best illustration we provide in this book of the halakhic impact of the stam on subsequent religious practice.

Prohibition of Afikoman

The earliest form of the seder is described in the tenth chapter of Mishnah Pesahim.[1] Mishnah 10:8, the last mishnah that describes the seder ritual, reads:

ואין מפטירין אחר הפסח	And they may not conclude with
אפיקומן.	an afikoman after the Pesah.

A more expanded version of this halakhah is found in Tosefta Pesahim 10:11:

אין מפטירין אחר הפסח	And they may not conclude with an afikoman
אפיקומן כגון אגוזין תמרים	after the Pesah, like nuts and dates and
וקליות. חייב אדם לעסוק בה־	parched grain. A person must study the laws
לכות הפסח כל הלילה אפלו	of Pesah all night, even if it is just him and his
בינו לבין בנו אפלו בינו לבין	son, or him by himself, or him and his student.
עצמו אפלו בינו לבין תלמידו.	

In his commentary on Yerushalmi Pesahim quoted below, Saul Lieberman explains the word "afikoman" as a Greek loan-word referring to the

---

[1] See Joshua Kulp, "The Origins of the Seder and Haggadah," *Currents in Biblical Research* 4, 1 (2005), 109–134.

drunken revelry which would typically occur at the end of a Greco-Roman style banquet. According to Lieberman, this is how Jews during the tannaitic period would have used and understood the term. The Tosefta associates the afikoman with nuts, dates and parched grain because they were the typical foods eaten to increase the appetite for drinking which would lead to the revelry of the afikoman. We should emphasize that the Tosefta does not define the afikoman as these specific foods; rather it provides examples of aspects of the afikoman in which it is forbidden to engage after the Pesah meal. Essentially the Tosefta is asserting that it is forbidden to conclude the banquet with even these "harmless" elements of the afikoman, for the eating of these foods is intended to lead to the more harmful aspects of the afikoman, the drunkenness and debauchery associated with the end of the banquet.

After noting that eating foods that are part of the afikoman is also prohibited, Tosefta Pesahim goes on to offer an alternative to engaging in an afikoman—a Jew should spend the rest of the night of Pesah learning Torah in fulfillment of the commandment to "study the laws of Pesah." The second half of the Tosefta is thus not simply an additional legal statement mandating the study of Torah on the first night of Pesah. Rather, it is a guide to replacing the Greco-Roman custom of afikoman with the Jewish custom of studying Torah.

The notion that the study of Torah should be substituted for Greco-Roman post-banquet customs is illustrated by the following quote from Yerushalmi Hagigah 2:1, 77b. The story takes place after a circumcision.

מן דאכלון ושתון שרון	When they had finished eating and drink-
מטפחין ומרקדקין.	ing, they began to clap and dance.
אמר ר' ליעזר לר' יהושע	R. Eliezer said to R. Joshua: Instead of occu-
עד דאינון עסיקין בדידון	pying ourselves with their [customs], let us sit
נעסוק אנן בדידן.	and occupy ourselves with our own [customs].
וישבו ונתעסקו בדברי	And they sat and occupied them-
תורה.	selves with words of Torah.

While this source does not use the term, this seems to be an apt description of what Mishnah and Tosefta Pesahim term the "afikoman." Such revelry would have included "eating, drinking, clapping and dancing."

The two Talmuds also allude to some of these practices in their definition of afikoman:

ירושלמי פסחים י:ו, לז ע"ד	Yerushalmi Pesahim 10:6, 37d
רבי סימון בשם רבי איניני	R. Simon in the name of R. Inini
בר רבי סיסיי: מיני זמר.	b. R. Sisi: types of music.
רבי יוחנן אמר: מיני מתיקה.	R. Yohanan said: various sweets.
שמואל אמר: כגון ערדילי	Shmuel said: like mushrooms and
וגוזליא דחנניא בר שילת.	pigeons for Hanania b. Shilat.

בבלי פסחים קיט ע"ב	Bavli Pesahim 119b
מאי אפיקומן?	What is afikoman?
אמר רב: שלא יעקרו מחבו־	Rav said: That they must not get up and
רה לחבורה.	move from one group to another.
ושמואל אמר: כגון אורדילאי	Shmuel said: like mushrooms for
לי וגוזלייא לאבא.	myself and pigeons for Abba.
ורב חנינא בר שילא ורבי	R. Hanina b. Shila and R. Yohanan
יוחנן אמרו: כגון תמרים	said: dates, parched grains, and nuts.
קליות ואגוזים.	

Although only the Bavli sugya specifically asks the question "What is an afikoman?" it is clear that both sugyot are addressing the same matter. R. Simon's explanation in the Yerushalmi, "types of music," is an obvious reference to the post-banquet singing and dancing alluded to above. Rav's explanation in the Bavli, referring to the prohibition on travelling from one eating party to another, is also found in Yerushalmi Pesahim 10:4, 37d as part of the answer to the "stupid" son's question.[2] The stupid son asks "what is this" (Exodus 13:14), a question referring to Pesah, and the Yerushalmi instructs the father, "teach him the laws of Pesah, that one does not conclude the Pesah meal with an afikoman—that he should not get up from this eating party and join another

---

[2] See Joshua Kulp, *The Schechter Haggadah* (Jerusalem: The Schechter Institute of Jewish Studies, 2009), 210.

eating party." Both versions of this statement define "afikoman" as the typical carousing which might occur at the conclusion of a Greco-Roman banquet.

Explaining the tannaitic and amoraic sources that mention the "afikoman," Saul Lieberman offered the following interpretation alluded to above, which was subsequently accepted by all critical scholars:

> [The rabbis] were familiar with Greek customs and their banquet manners, that when the festivities would reach their peak, they would burst into others' homes to force them to join in the continuing party, and they called this *epikomazein*. The Mishnah warns that one does not conclude the Passover meal with an *afikoman-epikomazein*, and this is the interpretation of the Babylonian and Eretz Yisraeli Talmud.[3]

Building upon Lieberman's interpretation, subsequent scholars[4] have explained that the other interpretation found in the Tosefta and in the two Talmuds—that *afikoman* refers to various types of desserts—are consistent with Lieberman's explanation, for these were "types of delicacies served after a meal, especially to whet one's thirst." In other words, the afikoman is the general term referring to the practice of drunken revelry, and the Tosefta and amoraim identify specific foods or practices that were associated with it. Even sweet foods (R. Yohanan in the Yerushalmi) were heavily salted to encourage drinking. The mushrooms and fowl mentioned by Shmuel in both Talmuds are both foods known for absorbing salt without being particularly filling, similar to fried mushrooms and barbecued chicken wings served at bars today. Indeed, in Greco-Roman meals the foods served after the meal and intoxicating drink went hand in hand. The prohibition of an afikoman thus encompasses all of the elements associated with a party—food, drink, music, and entertainment.

We should emphasize that the sages prohibit eating *specific* foods at the end of the meal because *these* foods encourage drinking. The prohibition is not against eating any food whatsoever after the Pesah sacrifice. We should

---

[3] Saul Lieberman, *HaYerushalmi Kifshuto* (Jerusalem: Darom, 1934), 521.

[4] Baruch Bokser, *The Origins of the Pesach Seder* (Berkley: University of California Press, 1984), 132 n. 62; Joseph Tabory, *Pesah Dorot* (Tel Aviv: Hakibbutz Hameuhad, 1996), 65–66.

emphasize, too, that the word "afikoman" does not mean "dessert"—rather, it refers to the specific practice of drunken revelry, an interpretation found in both Talmuds. Furthermore, these prohibitions relate to the post-Temple period when Jews (at least most of them) were no longer eating a Pesah sacrifice.[5] Thus the prohibition of the afikoman, drunken revelry, has nothing to do with the laws of the Pesah sacrifice; it is connected to the particular social setting of the post-Temple seder, usually patterned after but in this case differentiated from the Greco-Roman banquet.

Eating the Pesah Sacrifice at the End of the Meal

There is a second issue which was not originally connected to the prohibition of engaging in an "afikoman," but which became interrelated in the Bavli (and subsequently in common understanding) because it too concerns the conclusion of the Pesah meal. According to the rabbis all sacrifices, including the Pesah sacrifice, should be eaten either על השבע "when already satiated" or לשבע, "to satisfaction." This issue arises at several points in tannaitic literature, including Tosefta Pesahim 5:3, in connection with the *hagigah* (festival) sacrifice, which according to rabbinic interpretation was supposed to accompany the Pesah sacrifice:

חגיגה הבאה עמו היא	The hagigah which accompanies it is
נאכלת תחלה כדי שיהא	eaten first so that the Pesah can be
פסח נאכל על השובע.	eaten when already satiated.

Since all sacrifices must be eaten "when already satiated," there is a problem on Pesah—which of the two sacrifices should be eaten first, the *hagigah* or the Pesah? The Tosefta answers that the Pesah sacrifice is eaten second so that by the time one eats it, one is already partially satiated by having eaten the *hagigah* sacrifice. The amoraim (Yerushalmi 6:5, 33c) push this a bit further, asking why choose to eat the Pesah second and not the *hagigah*:

---

[5] See Mishnah Pesahim 10:5; Tosefta Yom Tov 2:15; Mishnah Betzah 2:7; Mishnah Pesahim 7:2 and the discussion in Kulp, *The Schechter Haggadah*, 238–240.

ולא יאכל הפסח לשבע?	And let the Pesah not be eaten to satisfaction?
ר' יוסי בי ר' בון בשם	R. Yose b. Rabbi Bun, R. Yaakov bar Dosai [said]:
ר' יעקב בר דסיי: שלא	So that he should not come to break a bone.
יבא לידי שבירת עצם.	

The answer is that if one is ravenously hungry when eating the Pesah, one might break a bone, which is explicitly prohibited (Exodus 12:46). Since there is no prohibition on breaking the bone of a *hagigah* sacrifice, it is better to eat that sacrifice first, not "while already satiated." It seems that were it not for that special halakhah, there would be no mandate to eat the Pesah last.

The Mekhilta de-Rabbi Ishmael (a tannaitic midrash on Exodus) also deals with concept of eating until satiated.

מכילתא דרבי ישמעאל	**Mekhilta de-Rabbi Ismael**
דפסחא פרשה ו	**Pisha Chapter 6**
"על מצות ומרורים	*On matzah and bitter herbs you shall eat it*
יאכלוהו" (במדבר ט:יא):	(Numbers 9:11): From here they said the
מכאן אמרו הפסח נאכל	Pesah is eaten until satiated but matzah and
אכילת שבע ואין מצה	bitter herbs are not eaten until satiation.
ומרור נאכלים אכילת שבע.	

We should note that the term here is "אכילת שבע" and not "על השבע", the term found in the Tosefta. While determining the precise meaning of this halakhah is difficult, it seems likely to mean that one should eat enough Pesah sacrifice to be satiated. It seems that this halakhah is not concerned with when during the meal the Pesah sacrifice is eaten, but rather with the quantity of Pesah sacrifice that must be eaten. When eating a meal based on the Pesah sacrifice, there is a mitzvah that one should make sure to eat a sufficient quantity such that one is satiated. In the post-temple period when the meal is based on matzah and bitter herbs and the Pesah is absent, this mitzvah is no longer relevant.

The demand that sacrifices be eaten while already satiated is found without a particular connection to the Pesah sacrifice in Sifra Tzav 2 (a tannaitic midrash on Leviticus) and in a close parallel in the Bavli. The version found in the Bavli explicitly uses the term "על השבע", "when already satiated." While the midrash is found on a verse that discusses the minhah (grain) sacrifice, it is likely that the intention is that the same rule should be applied to all sacrifices.[6]

בבלי תמורה כג ע"א	Bavli Temurah 23a
מה יאכלו (ויקרא ו:ט) מה תלמוד לומר? מלמד שאם היתה אכילה מועטת אוכלין עמה חולין ותרומה, כדי שתהא נאכלת על השבע.	*They shall eat* (Leviticus 6:9): What does Scripture say? This teaches that if there is only a small amount of food, they should eat with it non-sacred food and terumah, so that it can be eaten when already satiated.
יאכלוה (שם) מה תלמוד לומר? שאם היתה אכילה מרובה, אין אוכלין עמה חולין ותרומה כדי שלא תהא נאכלת על הגסה.	*They shall eat of it* (ibid): What does Scripture say? That if there was a lot of food, they do not eat with it non-sacred food and terumah, so that it should not be eaten when [one's stomach is] already full.

This baraita demands that sacrifices be eaten when already satiated (על השבע) but not when one is already so full that eating more has become undesirable (על הגסה). We cite this source because its ideas concerning when to eat the Pesah sacrifice and how it should be eaten will be referenced in the Bavli's interpretation of the afikoman, which we deal with below.

In conclusion, there are two similar laws in tannaitic literature concerning the proper manner of eating all sacrifices. First, a person should eat them to satisfaction (לשבע). If there is not enough sacrificial meat to fill one's stomach, then one should consume other foods as well. Second, sacrifices should be eaten while already satiated (על השבע). These two halakhot can be interpreted in a complementary fashion. If there are multiple foods at a sacrificial meal, an appetizer should be eaten first, so that the sacrifice is eaten when satiated and also so that it is eaten to satisfaction. But one should always be cautious not to eat the sacrifice at a point in which it would be considered eating when already completely full (על הגסה).

Most importantly, we should emphasize what is not found in tannaitic literature, but will be found in the Bavli—the notion that the Pesah sacrifice (or

---

[6] Saul Lieberman, *Tosefta Kifshuta: Moed* (New York: Jewish Theological Seminary, 1962), 571–572.

any other sacrifice) must be the last food eaten at the meal. Tannaitic sources do say that the Pesah should not be the first thing eaten in the meal, unless it is the only food. But there is no insistence in tannatic literature that it should be the last food eaten. There is no specific prohibition on dessert (unless it is the type of dessert meant to encourage drunken revelry) or on eating any other food after the Pesah has already been eaten. Likewise, there is no insistence that the taste of the Pesah be left in one's mouth (a notion found in the Bavli). Rather we have two simple halakhot mandating that the sacrifice be treated like a proper main course. That is, it should be preceded by an appetizer, and as a main course, the sacrificial meat should be the food which induces satiation. Like any proper main course, it may certainly be followed by dessert. Even Tosefta Pesahim, which prohibited an afikoman, did not prohibit eating all foods after the Pesah. It prohibited only the eating of foods specifically associated with drunken revelry. There is no tannaitic prohibition of eating other types of foods.

"As Long as He Eats an Olive's Worth of Matzah at the End"

A halakhah found in Tosefta 2:20 has been understood by traditional commentators as alluding to the notion that a certain food must be eaten at the end of the meal. But this time instead of the Pesah, it is the matzah.

אין יוצאין בחליט ולא	They do not fulfill their obligation [to eat
בחמעיסה ולא בספגנין	matzah] with a dumpling or with sour
ולא בדבשנין ולא	dough or with sponge cakes or with hon-
באסקריטין אבל ממלא	ey cakes or with dough-paste, but he may
כריסו מהן ובלבד שיאכל	fill his belly with them as long as he eats
כזית מצה באחרונה.	an olive's worth of matzah at the end.

The Tosefta lists various bread-like items with which one cannot fulfill the obligation to eat matzah on Pesah.[7] They are not hametz, so they may be eaten on Pesah. But since they are either boiled or contain ingredients besides

---

[7] In Mekhilta De-Rabbi Ishmael Pisha 10 p. 35, these pastries are excluded because they are not לחם עני "bread of affliction." See also Mishnah Hallah 1:6. See the discussion in Lieberman, *Tosefta Kifshutah Moed*, 503.

flour and water, they are not simple baked loaves of matzah and cannot count towards fulfilling the mitzvah of matzah.

This passage concludes with the injunction to eat an olive's worth of matzah "at the end." But at the end of what? Based on the Babylonian passage we shall examine below, this phrase is understood by traditional commentators to mean "at the end of the meal." According to the Bavli, the Pesah sacrifice was eaten at the end of the meal, and therefore matzah, too, should be eaten at the end of the meal. In other words, matzah is eaten at the end of the meal in memory of the Pesah which, according to the Bavli, was also eaten at the end of the meal.

There are several significant problems with this interpretation. First of all, in the context of the Tosefta itself, this interpretation is not at all clear. The section of Tosefta Pesahim in which this halakhah is found (2:17–21) is not talking about what must be eaten at the end of the meal or about the order (*seder*) of the meal, but rather about which various forms of bread-like foods can count as matzah and which cannot. It would seem strange that such an essential halakhah—that matzah must be the last thing eaten at the end of the meal—would be buried among a long list of what counts as matzah.

Second, the transfer of laws connecting the Pesah to the matzah is attested in the later strata of rabbinic literature, from the fourth generation of amoraim, but it would be surprising to find it in a text as early as the Tosefta. An example of such transference can be found in Bavli Pesahim 120a: "Rava said: One who ate matzah after midnight in this day [after the destruction of the Temple] according to R. Elazar ben Azaryah, he has not fulfilled his obligation." Rava's halakhah relates to Mishnah Pesahim 10:9 according to which one should not eat the Pesah sacrifice after midnight, since from this time on it is considered to be a "remnant" (see Exodus 12:10) and therefore cannot be used to fulfill one's obligation. Rava transfers this halakhah concerning the Pesah to the matzah—one should not eat matzah after this hour, even though it is not a sacrifice and the laws of remnant do not apply. Rava, a fourth century Babylonian amora, has indeed transferred the laws of the Pesah to matzah. But, as stated above, this phenomenon is not found at all in tannaitic literature.

Third, as we saw above, the tannaim did not actually mandate that the Pesah be eaten at the end of the meal, or that it be eaten last. They simply taught that it may not be eaten on an empty stomach and that it must be eaten until satiation. Furthermore, in the other descriptions of the seder, such as those found in the tenth chapter of Mishnah and Tosefta Pesahim, the matzah is brought in the beginning of the meal, along with the other mandatory foods (bitter herbs and haroset). Were there a halakhah that mandated eating the matzah at the end of the meal, it should have been mentioned elsewhere. This is all the more true because eating matzah at the end of the meal would be a strange practice in the cultural context of tannaitic literature—in all of the descriptions in Greco-Roman literature of food served after the main course, there is no mention of plain bread.[8] It also creates numerous halakhic problems, many of which were dealt with extensively by post-talmudic commentators: If the mandatory matzah is eaten at the end of the meal, why do we say the blessing over the matzah in the beginning of the meal?[9] Must one also eat the marror and the "Hillel sandwich" at the end of the meal?[10]

It seems highly unlikely, then, that "at the end" refers to the end of the meal. Instead, we posit that the Tosefta is referring to the end of *the appetizer* course. In tannaitic texts the meal began with a series of appetizers, ending with an appetizer that precedes the bread.[11] Mishnah Pesahim 10:3 states, "They bring in front of him, he dips with lettuce until he gets to the appetizer that precedes the bread (*parperet hapat*)." Tosefta Pesahim 10:5 and 9 clearly state that an appetizer course, including meat and lettuce, were eaten before the meal. This course may also include dumplings and various types of cakes, but as our Tosefta source states explicitly, such doughy foods do not count as matzah. At the end of this course one must eat an olive's amount of the "mandated" matzah, the matzah with which one fulfills his obligation. According to this explanation, the Tosefta source does not transfer laws of the Pesah to laws of the matzah. It merely states that appetizers made from dough do not count in the performance of the mitzvah of eating matzah.

---

[8] Interestingly, in the description of the last supper Jesus gives his disciples first the bread and then the wine. See for instance I Corinthians 11:23–25; Mark 14:22–23; Matthew 26:26–27. Of course, this is not to say that the last supper was a seder, but just that normative practice dictated that a meal began with bread.

[9] See Rashbam Pesahim 119b, s.v. אין מפטירין.

[10] See for instance the Tur Orah Hayyim 477.

[11] According to Tosefta Berakhot 4:8, three seems to have been a standard number of appetizers before a formal meal. For a discussion of the appetizer course see Kulp, *The Schechter Haggadah*, 183–188.

Bavli Pesahim 119b–120a

We should begin by summarizing the halakhot we have seen until this point. At the tannaitic level there exist two distinct ideas: (1) a prohibition against concluding the seder banquet with an "afikoman," a practice which may have included bursting into other people's homes to augment the celebration and may have involved eating specific foods in order to whet one's thirst for wine at the end of the meal; (2) the Pesah should not be eaten on an empty stomach and should be eaten to satisfaction. These two halakhot are not in any way connected.

Bavli Pesahim 119b–120a transforms and reinterprets the texts that transmitted these two ideas. First, the Bavli understands that the Pesah must be the *last food* eaten at the meal. The reason given is that the taste of the Pesah should remain in one's mouth after the meal. Second, the afikoman prohibition is re-interpreted as a prohibition against eating *any food* after the Pesah, and in the post-destruction period, after matzah. The two originally distinct ideas (eating Pesah when already satiated and the prohibition on afikoman) become conflated in the Bavli—the Pesah or matzah must be the last food eaten in the meal because it is prohibited to have an afikoman, which is interpreted as food, after the Pesah or matzah have been eaten. Let us now examine this complicated sugya in its entirety:

AMORAIC STATEMENT

(1a) אמר רב יהודה אמר
שמואל: אין מפטירין
אחר מצה אפיקומן.

(1a) R. Judah said in the name of Shmuel: One may not conclude with an afikoman after the matzah.

STAMMAITIC DIFFICULTY

(1b) תנן: אין מפטירין
אחר הפסח אפיקומן. אחר
הפסח - הוא דלא, אבל
לאחר מצה - מפטירין.

(1b) We learned [in a mishnah]: one may not conclude with an afikoman after the Pesah. After the Pesah is when this is prohibited, but after the matzah one may have an afikoman.

| Tannaitic Source | Amoraic Source | Stammaitic Source |

110

RESOLUTION

(1c) לא מיבעיא קאמר:
לא מיבעיא אחר מצה -
דלא נפיש טעמייהו, אבל
לאחר הפסח דנפיש טעמיה,
ולא מצי עבוריה - לית
לן בה, קמשמע לן.

(1c) It was not even necessary to state: It was not even necessary to state that after the matzah [there is no afikoman], since its taste is not substantial; after the Pesah, whose taste is substantial and cannot [easily] be wiped out [I might have thought] that it would not be prohibited [to have an afikoman], hence [the mishnah] teaches us [that it is prohibited].

PROPOSED TANNAITIC SUPPORT FOR AMORAIC STATEMENT

(1d) נימא מסייע ליה:
הסופגנין והדובשנין
והאיסקריטין - אדם ממלא
כריסו מהן, ובלבד שיאכל
כזית מצה באחרונה. באחרונה
- אין, בראשונה - לא!

(1d) Shall we say that the following supports him: [As for] sponge cakes, honey-cakes and, dough cakes one may fill his stomach with them, providing that he eat an olive's worth of matzah at the end. [This implies], only at the end, but not at the beginning!

REJECTION OF SUPPORT

(1e) לא מיבעיא קאמר:
לא מיבעיא בראשונה -
דקאכיל לתיאבון אבל
באחרונה דילמא אתי
למיכל אכילה גסה - אימא
לא, קא משמע לן.

(1e) It was not even necessary to state: It was not even necessary to state that [if he eats it] at the beginning [that he has fulfilled his obligation], since he eats it with an appetite; but at the end, lest he may come to eat it as mere gorging, I might say [that he does not thereby fulfill his obligation] hence it teaches us [that he does].

ALTERNATIVE VERSION OF OPENING AMORAIC STATEMENT

(2a) מר זוטרא מתני הכי:
אמר רב יוסף אמר רב יהודה
אמר שמואל: מפטירין
אחר המצה אפיקומן.

(2a) Mar Zutra transmits it in this manner: R. Yosef said in R. Yehudah's name in Shmuel's name: One may conclude with an afikoman after the matzah.

Tannaitic Source   Amoraic Source   Stammaitic Source

SUGGESTED SUPPORT

נימא מסייע ליה: (2b)

אין מפטירין אחר הפסח
אפיקומן, אחר הפסח - דלא,
אבל אחר מצה - מפטירין.

(2b) Shall we say that the following supports him: one may not conclude with an afikoman after the Pesah. After the Pesah is when this is prohibited but after the matzah you may have an afikoman.

REJECTION OF SUPPORT

לא מיבעיא קאמר: (2c)
לא מיבעיא אחר מצה
- דלא נפיש טעמיה,
אבל לאחר פסח אימא
לא - קא משמע לן.

(2c) It was not even necessary to state: It was not even necessary to state that after the matzah [there is no afikoman], since its taste is not substantial; after the Pesah, [I might have thought] that it would not be prohibited [to have an afikoman], hence [the mishnah] teaches us [that it is prohibited].

DIFFICULTY

מיתיבי: הסופגנין (2d)
והדובשנין והאיסקריטין
אדם ממלא כריסו מהן,
ובלבד שיאכל כזית מצה
באחרונה. באחרונה -
אין, בראשונה - לא!

(2d) They raised an objection: [As for] sponge cakes, honey-cakes and dough cakes, one may fill his stomach with them, providing that he eat an olive's worth of matzah at the end. [This implies], only at the end, but not at the beginning!

RESOLUTION

לא (2e) לא מיבעיא קאמר: לא
מיבעיא בראשונה - דקאכיל
לתיאבון, אבל באחרונה
דאתי למיכלה אכילה גסה
- אימא לא, קא משמע לן.

(2e) It was not even necessary to state: It was not even necessary to state that [if he eats it] at the beginning [that he has fulfilled his obligation], since he eats it with an appetite; but at the end, lest he may come to eat it as mere gorging, I might say [that he does not thereby fulfill his obligation] hence it teaches us [that he does].

| Tannaitic Source | Amoraic Source | Stammaitic Source |

Before we critically analyze this sugya and its various levels, we will offer a traditional explanation. The sugya opens with Shmuel's statement that it is forbidden to have an afikoman after the matzah. The stam objects to his statement with the citation from the mishnah (1b) which explicitly prohibits afikoman only following the Pesah sacrifice, but does not necessarily prohibit an afikoman after matzah. Shmuel (or the stam) resolves this question (1c) by commenting that one can logically derive that it is prohibited to have an afikoman after matzah because eating an afikoman will cause the taste of the matzah to dissipate. But the mishnah had to explicitly teach the prohibition of an afikoman after Pesah because its taste would remain in one's mouth even after eating other foods. The stam provides proof for Shmuel (1d) from Tosefta Pesahim 2:20 which the stam interprets to mean that ritually acceptable matzah must be eaten at the end of *the meal*. The requirement to eat matzah at the end of the meal indicates that eating any food after the matzah is prohibited. The stam rejects the support from the baraita (1e) by explaining that the Tosefta teaches a different halakhah altogether. Without this baraita one might have thought that one could eat matzah only at the beginning of the meal, when one has a strong appetite. The baraita teaches that one can fulfill the mitzvah of eating matzah even at the end of the meal—this is not prohibited for fear that he would eat the matzah when already full. Thus matzah is linked with sacrifices which, as we saw in the quote from Bavli Temurah above, should not be eaten when one's stomach is already full. The second part of the sugya (2a–2e) mirrors the first but uses Mar Zutra's teaching that one *may* have an afikoman after the matzah as its starting point. All of the assumptions from the first version of the sugya are reversed.

The editors of this sugya interpret the mishnah (and other tannaitic sources) to mean that it is forbidden to eat any food after the Pesah. In their eyes, Shmuel adds that it is similarly forbidden to eat *any* food after matzah. The reason for this prohibition is that the taste of the ritually important food (Pesah or matzah) should remain in one's mouth after the meal has been concluded. Mar Zutra, who teaches that one can have an afikoman after matzah, holds that while there is a requirement that the taste of the Pesah sacrifice remain in one's mouth, there is no such requirement for matzah. The traditional understanding of Shmuel's statement clearly emerges from the stam's interpretation in the sugya. According to this understanding, were one to follow Shmuel's halakhah which prohibits afikoman after matzah (1a), matzah would have to be eaten at the end of the meal, as is the traditional practice today.

However, there is another way to understand Shmuel's statement, one that accords with the tannaitic halakhah and the amoraic opinions found in the Yerushalmi and in the previous section of the Bavli. Mishnah Pesahim 10:8, "And they may not conclude with an afikoman after the Pesah," prohibited concluding a meal centered around the Pesah sacrifice with an afikoman. Shmuel simply clarifies that this prohibition remains in effect even after the meal is no longer centered around the Pesah—just as it is forbidden to have an afikoman, meaning to eat salty food which is intended to lead to drinking and revelry, after a meal that centered around the Pesah, so, too, is an afikoman forbidden in a meal centered around matzah. In other words, Shmuel does not mandate or even imply that matzah must be eaten at the end of the meal, a halakhah that is strange in light of the fact that bread/matzah is always eaten at the beginning of a meal. He simply states that the afikoman prohibition is still in force even when the central food has shifted from Pesah sacrifice to matzah.

The later (mis)interpretation of afikoman, that the prohibition is against eating *any food* after the Pesah or matzah, seems to originate with Mar Zutra, a fifth century Babylonian amora. In section 1b Mar Zutra reverses Shmuel's statement and says *"we may conclude* with an afikoman after the matzah." Mar Zutra obviously would not have allowed drunken revelry, the original meaning of "afikoman," after the seder. Rather, he interprets afikoman as referring to any food. With this understanding in mind, Shmuel's original statement, "they may not conclude with an afikoman after the matzah," would imply, to Mar Zutra, that after eating matzah no food of any sort may be eaten. Whereas earlier amoraim who associated afikoman with various types of food (nuts, date, parched grain, mushrooms and pigeons) understood that only the types of food that are meant to encourage drinking and are typically part of the post-banquet revelry are prohibited, Mar Zutra interprets afikoman as *any type of food*. The word has lost its Greco-Roman context and Shmuel's statement is now read as forbidding *any eating* after matzah. Since this is a strange notion—we always begin a meal with bread and then eat other foods, including the main course—Mar Zutra was forced to reverse Shmuel's statement and *allow* an afikoman after matzah. This reversal in and of itself would not have carried with it any significant change in actual practice—people would eat their obligatory matzah at the beginning of the meal and conclude their meal with whatever foods they saw fit. However, as we shall see soon, Mar Zutra's reversal carries with it deep implications with regard to how the first version of Shmuel's statement is understood.

As to why Mar Zutra did not understand the original meaning of Shmuel's statement, there are two possible main reasons. First of all, as a late Babylonian amora, there is little reason to expect that Mar Zutra would be familiar with a Greek word like afikoman.[12] Second, Shmuel himself associated afikoman with mushrooms or pigeons. While we may understand that Shmuel meant that one should not eat *these specific foods* at the end of the seder meal because they encourage drunkenness and revelry, it is certainly possible that Mar Zutra understood this statement more broadly—one should not have *any food* at the end of the seder meal.

According to this new interpretation of afikoman, the original version of Shmuel's statement implies that it is forbidden to eat *anything* after eating matzah. This may be accomplished only be eating matzah at the end of the meal, a halakhah which, as stated above, seems strange in light of both contemporaneous and contemporary eating practices. Who eats matzah for dessert? Nevertheless, influenced by Mar Zutra's interpretation of afikoman, the editors of the passage reinterpret tannaitic halakhah in order to understand why matzah must be eaten at the end of the meal. Sections 1b–1e and 2b–2e are all stammaitic reinterpretations of the two main tannaitic sources we explained above, Mishnah Pesahim 10:8 and Tosefta Pesahim 2:20. Section 1b deduces from the mishnah that an afikoman is prohibited only after eating the Pesah sacrifice. But after eating matzah, the stam infers, an afikoman would be permitted. Thus the mishnah has been reinterpreted in light of Mar Zutra's understanding of afikoman as any food eaten at the end

---

[12] A similar phenomenon occurs in the late Babylonian explanation of the word כבנומרון/ כבני מרון found in Mishnah Rosh Hashanah 1:2. Lieberman, *Tosefta Kifshutah Moed*, 1022–1023, derives the word from Greek and interprets it to refer to a band of soldiers, "numeron." This matches Shmuel's explanation in the Bavli, "like the soldiers of the House of David." However, Bavli Rosh Hashanah 18a reads: "This is how they interpreted it—like the offspring of sheep (כבני אימרנא)." Rashi interprets this to mean that on Rosh Hashanah the children of Israel are counted like sheep being tithed. This also caused the reading to shift from כבנומרון, an obvious Greek word, to כבני מרון, which is Hebrew. Thus we have another example in which Shmuel understands the original explanation, whether through his knowledge of Greek or through an interpretive tradition, but the stam does not.

of the meal. Section 1c rejects the leniency in regards to the matzah and even provides a reason for the prohibition—the Pesah and matzah both must be eaten specifically at the end of the meal so that their taste may be left in one's mouth. The sugya continues in sections 1d and 2d with a reinterpretation of the Tosefta. Instead of "the end" referring to the conclusion of the appetizer courses, the baraita is understood to mandate eating matzah at the end of the meal. While it does not state so explicitly, commentators interpret the requirement to conclude with matzah to be an echo of the laws of נאכלת על השובע, "eaten when already satisfied," found in tannaitic sources. The Bavli understands this rule as implying that ritually significant foods should be eaten in this manner so that their taste remains in one's mouth once the meal is concluded.[13]

In this sugya, afikoman has been reinterpreted, Shmuel's statement has been reversed and a new halakhah is born—matzah must be the last thing eaten at the seder meal. We should note that there was no amora who legislated that matzah be eaten at the end of the meal; rather the halakhah was born out of stammaitic interpretation of amoraic and tannaitic statements. As such, it is impossible to know whether the stam actually intended for matzah to be eaten at the end of the meal, as became the post-talmudic practice.

In summary, we should emphasize here the two crucial changes in interpretation and halakhah that we have seen in this sugya, and the order in which they occurred. The first is the late amoraic misinterpretation of Shmuel's statement and subsequent reworking of the statement by Mar Zutra. This is an example of how late amoraim allowed themselves to literally rewrite earlier amoraic statements so that they would accord with their own understanding of the issue. The second major shift is the stammaitic reinterpretation of tannaitic halakhah to accord with Mar Zutra's understanding of the afikoman. Here we have an example of how early tannaitic halakhah is (mis)interpreted by later editors. Only by separating the historical layers of the literature can we gain an appreciation of the original meaning of these sources and their development over time.

---

[13] We should note that this is not necessarily an accurate interpretation of this concept. There may be a demand to eat ritual foods "when already satiated" in order to concretize the ritual significance of the food. The food is being eaten not because it is necessary as food, but because it is of ritual significance.

Stammaitic Interpretation and Historical Study

Because the history of the Pesah seder is of interest to such a broad array of scholars, including those occupied with the early history of Christianity and its relationship with Judaism, the proper understanding of the halakhah of the afikoman is of special importance. As we saw above, Saul Lieberman was the first modern scholar to interpret the afikoman prohibition in light of its Greco-Roman context. Here we see how a knowledge of Greek and of Greco-Roman literature can aid in the interpretation of literature composed in the then-Hellenistic land of Israel. We have also seen that the notion that one eats matzah at the end of the meal is a late stammaitic innovation. The tannaitic, or amoraic seder for that matter, did not conclude with the eating of a piece of matzah to symbolize the Pesah sacrifice.

Some modern scholars have projected this late practice onto early tannaim. For instance, Lawrence Hoffman writes regarding the tannaitic period, "the laws regulating the eating of the Pesah were accordingly applied to the consuming of matsah, and, since one such law was that a piece of the Pesah be eaten last, it was decided that a piece of matsah, k'zayit in bulk, be consumed at the end of the meal. This now became known as the afikoman."[14] Hoffman interprets the tannaitic afikoman in a manner found only in the Bavli.

An even more dramatic (and mistaken) example can be found in Israel Yuval's recent study of the origins of Christianity and rabbinic Judaism.[15] At first, Yuval (240 n. 102) compares the afikoman to the Christian "missa," a ceremony that marked the end of the prayer service in the first centuries C.E. in which, "The bishop blessed the worshipers, and they kissed his hand" (ibid). Somehow, Yuval believes that the Mishnah's injunction that, "one does not conclude the Pesah with an afikoman" is directed against this practice, as if it means, "one does not conduct a ceremony of 'sending away' to conclude the sacrificial meal by eating the matzah of the afikoman" (ibid). Here Yuval interprets the afikoman as matzah, an interpretation not found until the Middle Ages. Later in this same chapter Yuval claims that the word

---

[14] Lawrence Hoffman, "A Symbol in the Seder," *Passover and Easter: Origin and History to Modern Times*, ed. Paul Bradshaw and Lawrence Hoffman (Notre Dame: University of Notre Dame Press, 1999), 112.

[15] Israel Yuval, *Two Nations in Your Womb* (Berkeley: University of California Press, 2008).

"afikoman" should be derived from the Greek "*aphikomenos*" which means "the One who Comes." "The eating of the afikoman thus signifies the anticipation of coming of the Messiah (246)." In other words, the afikoman is a Jewish Eucharist. Finally, he suggests that when the Mishnah states that one does not conclude the Pesah with an afikoman, the meaning is that the afikoman matzah should be eaten with the Pesah sacrifice rather than after it, the first symbolizing the future redemption ("the One who comes") and the latter the historical redemption (the Exodus). He concludes, "this rule may relate to the anti-Christian polemic of the second century C.E. (ibid)." Of course, this interpretation is rooted in a misidentification of the afikoman. Only in the post-talmudic period do we hear of anyone referring to the matzah eaten at the end of the meal as the afikoman, whereas Yuval moves this appellation up not only the rabbinic period, but to the Temple period itself, when the Pesah sacrifice was consumed. While medieval Jews may have understood this matzah as having messianic symbolism (indeed everything at the Pesah seder can be understood as having messianic symbolism!), the proper cultural context of the original afikoman is an opposition to Greco-Roman banquet customs and not to Christianity's messianic belief in Jesus.

The Impact of the Stam on Post-Talmudic Halakhah

In the case of the afikoman, the stammaitic influence on post-talmudic halakhah was completely determinative. That is to say, all post-talmudic authorities understand the afikoman to be *any food* whatsoever and not just the specific foods listed by the amoraim as being part of the afikoman pro-hibition. All post-talmudic authorities posit that the Pesah sacrifice was the last food eaten at the sacrificial meal in order that its taste should remain in one's mouth. And finally, all post-talmudic authorities interpret the first ver-sion of Shmuel's statement to mean that Shmuel prohibited eating anything at all after the mandated matzah: Just as the Pesah was eaten last so that its taste would remain in one's mouth, so, too, the matzah must be the last food eaten at the seder meal.

The only real debate in the post-talmudic period is one of halakhah and not interpretation. At the conclusion of the sugya, the reader is left with two versions of Shmuel's statement, the first one prohibiting eating anything after the mandatory matzah, and Mar Zutra's revision which permits it. Phrased differently, the sugya does not rule whether the mandatory matzah is eaten at the end of the meal and after this matzah all food is prohibited (as per Shmuel's original formulation) or whether the matzah eaten at the beginning of the meal is the mandatory matzah with which one fulfills one's obligation and therefore one may eat after this matzah (as per Mar Zutra's revision).

This issue was debated by the geonim and the rishonim.[16] According to the Rambam, *Laws of Hametz and Matzah* 5:13, the obligatory matzah is that which is eaten at the end of the meal, in accordance with the first version of Shmuel. Hence, if one did not eat matzah at this point, one has not fulfilled one's obligation and must go back, wash hands, say hamotzi, and again eat matzah. In contrast, the students of Rashi relate an interesting incident in which Rashi forgot (!) to eat the matzah at the end of the meal and only remembered after having recited birkat hamazon. Rather than wash his hands, bless over the matzah, eat, and then again recite birkat hamazon (which would have forced him to drink another cup of wine) Rashi did nothing, relying on the fact that the obligatory matzah was that in the beginning of the meal (Mahzor Vitry Pesah 74). According to Rashi, eating matzah at the end of the meal is an obligatory custom, but if one does not do so, one has still fulfilled the biblical obligation to eat matzah with the matzah at the beginning of the meal. Rashi held, then, that the halakhah accords with Mar Zutra's version of Shmuel's statement.

Early rishonim tended to refer to the matzah eaten at the end of the seder as "the matzah of the afikoman." They did not call this matzah "afikoman" for all rabbinic sources explicitly forbid the consumption of an "afikoman." But already the Tosafists begin to drop the words "the matzah of the" and to just call the matzah eaten at the end of the meal "afikoman."[17] This meaning of the word "afikoman" was subsequently ensconced in rabbinic and popular parlance (see for instance the Shulkhan Arukh, Orah Hayyim 563 and 567). Thus, when one hears at the end of the meal, "time for the afikoman," it is clearly time for a last piece of matzah, not time to engage in drunken revelry!

---

[16] See Tabory, *Pesah Dorot*, 128–129.
[17] See Kulp, *The Schechter Haggadah*, 266.

Chapter Three

Greek Texts, Rabbinic Contexts: The Prosbul

Gittin 36a–36b

Introduction

Contemporary scholars and rabbis often cite the enactment of the "prosbul" as the paradigmatic example of rabbinic abrogation of Torah law.[1] The typical and traditional understanding of the history of the prosbul outlines its halakhic development from the Bible to the Mishnah. Deuteronomy 15:1–3 mandates the remission of loans every seven years at the sabbatical (*shemittah*) year in an effort to provide relief for the poor. The Torah itself, aware that a lender would hesitate to loan money given that his loan will be remitted in the sabbatical year, warns against refraining from offering loans as the *shemittah* approaches. Mishnah Sheviit 10:3 explains that when Hillel (beginning of the first century, C.E.) saw that despite the Torah's warnings people were refraining from lending and thereby transgressing the Torah's laws, he instituted something known as a prosbul to rectify the problem.

In this chapter, we will present David Bigman's reassessment of the connection between Hillel's enactment (*takkanah*) of the prosbul and the shemittah year.[2] Basing himself both on a parallel Greek institution and a close reading of tannaitic texts concerning the prosbul, Bigman argues that Hillel had no intention to use the prosbul to circumvent the remission of loans in the seventh year as is mandated by the Torah. Rather, Hillel was

---

[1] See for instance, Eliezer Berkovits, *Not in Heaven: The Nature and Function of Halakha* (New York: Ktav Publishing House, 1983), 75.

[2] David Bigman, "Ba'ayah Hilkhatit o Tikkun Hevrati? Al Mashmaut HaProsbul," *Akdamut* 20 (2008), 155–166.

simply attempting to correct a general problem of lenders refraining from offering loans because of difficulty in collection. The original prosbul was a mechanism to ease collection of debt should the borrower default. It was only later in the tannaitic period, long after the original enactment of the prosbul, that it became linked to loan remission in the sabbatical year.

The second half of the chapter will focus on the post-Hillel understanding of the prosbul. Already towards the end of the tannaitic period we find sources which assume that the *original intent* of Hillel's *takkanah* was indeed to resolve the problem of loan remission on the sabbatical year. This understanding was adopted by all subsequent rabbinic sources. Once the prosbul was understood as a means to avoid the consequences of the sabbatical year, subsequent sages were faced with the complex dilemma of justifying such a radical *takkanah,* one which seems to abrogate explicit Torah law. At the core of this discussion rest two different approaches to innovations in halakhah, as we will explore below.

Mishnah Sheviit Chapter Ten

Mishnah Sheviit chapter 10 is the primary tannaitic text dealing with the prosbul. The chapter in its entirety discusses various agreements and debts which are not subject to the Torah's laws of loan remission. Included in this list is the prosbul:

משנה ב
...המלוה על המשכון
והמוסר שטרותיו לבית
דין אינן משמטין.

Mishnah Two
...One who loans and takes a pledge, and one who hands over his debt documents to a court, [these debts] are not remitted.

משנה ג
פרוזבול אינו משמט. זה
אחד מן הדברים שהתקין
הלל הזקן כשראה שנמנעו
העם מלהלוות זה את זה
ועוברין על מה שכתוב
בתורה: השמר לך פן יהיה
דבר עם לבבך בליעל
וגו' (דברים טו:ט).

Mishnah Three
[A loan secured by] a prosbul is not remitted. This was one of the things enacted by Hillel the elder when he observed that people were refraining from lending to one another, and thus transgressing what is written in the Torah: *Beware, lest you harbor the base thought, [The seventh year, the year of remission, is approaching, so that you are mean to your needy kinsman and give him nothing]* (Deuteronomy 15:9).

התקין הלל לפרוזבול.

Hillel enacted the prosbul.

משנה ד

Mishnah Four

זהו גופו של פרוזבול: מוסר
אני לכם איש פלוני ופלוני
הדיינים שבמקום פלוני
שכל חוב שיש לי שאגבנו
כל זמן שארצה. והדיינים
חותמין למטה או העדים.

This is the formula of the prosbul: "I turn over
to you, so-and-so, judges of such and such a
place, that any debt that I may have outstanding, I shall collect it whenever I desire." And
the judges sign below, or the witnesses.

Mishnah two provides two examples of types of loans which are not remitted
in the sabbatical year. The second is a case in which the lender has transferred his loan documentation over to the court. Mishnah three opens with
a statement, similar in wording to the previous mishnah, which declares that
a loan secured by a prosbul is not subject to remission. The mishnah then
explains that Hillel saw that lenders were refraining from offering loans and
as a result he instituted the prosbul. As a prooftext it cites Deuteronomy 15:9,
which describes the reluctance of lenders to lend money lest their loan be
remitted. Mishnah four provides the text of the prosbul, a single document
in which the lender transfers all of his outstanding loans to the court, thereby
allowing him to collect whenever he so desires. Traditional commentators
debate the relationship between the act of transferring loan documentation
found in mishnah two and the prosbul described in mishnayot three and
four. Rashi (Bavli Makkot 3b) explains that the transferring of documentation is the essence of the prosbul. Thus mishnah three describes the origins
of the transaction mentioned in mishnah two. The Tosafot (ibid) disagree
and argue that the prosbul functions in a similar manner to the mechanism
of transferring loan documentation but it is an independent institution.[3]
Irrespective of their interpretation of the relationship between the mishnayot,
all traditional commentators agree that the impetus behind the institution
of the prosbul was to circumvent loan remission in the sabbatical year. This
assumption will be called into question in detail below.

---

[3] See Ritva Makkot ad. loc. The textual variants in the wording of the prosbul
declaration in the Mishnah play an important role in the debate. For more see David
Henshke, "Keitzad Mo'il haProsbul?" *Shenaton HaMishpat HaIvri* 22 (2004), 71–106.

The Greek Roots of the Prosbul

The word prosbul is from the Greek *prosbole*, a combination of two words: (1) before (*pros*); (2) the assembly of counselors (*bole*).[4] Nearly a century ago, Ludwig Blau was the first to note that in Greek papyri found in Egypt the term prosbul refers to the transfer of debt obligation by court order.[5] According to its usage in these documents, if a borrower defaults on a loan when a prosbul is in place, the court has the right to publicly auction off his assets and then use the profit to pay back the creditor. Most subsequent scholars have accepted Blau's identification of the rabbinic prosbul with the Greek prosbul.

However, even if scholars have successfully recovered the Greek origins of the word prosbul, there remains a significant problem—the Greek prosbul seems to work differently from the prosbul enacted by Hillel. According to the Mishnah, the lender transfers *all* outstanding loans to the court, thereby allowing the lender himself to collect at any time. In the Greek version, should a single borrower default on a loan, the *court* sells off the borrower's assets in order to pay back the lender. The difference between the two mechanisms led scholars to provide various suggestions as to how Hillel modified the Greek prosbul in order to respond to the problem of sabbatical loan remission. The general consensus was that Hillel relied on the Greek precedent. But unlike the Greek prosbul in which the court takes an active role in the collection by actually selling off the debtor's assets, the rabbinic mechanism is merely a legal fiction specifically enacted in order to avoid the consequences of the sabbatical year. The lender *symbolically* transfers his outstanding loans to the jurisdiction of the court. This transforms the collection of the loan into an act of the court, like a fine, which is not subject to the laws of sabbatical year

---

[4] See Daniel Sperber, *A Dictionary of Greek and Latin Legal Terms* (Ramat Gan: Bar Ilan University Press, 1984), 155. For rabbinic folk etymologies of the word see the comments of R. Hisda and Rava on Bavli Gittin 36b.

[5] Ludwig Blau, "Prosbol im Lichte der Griechischen Papyri und der Rechtsgeschichte," *Festschrift zum 50 Jahrigen Bestehen der Franz-Josef-Landesrabbiner-Schule in Budapest,* (Budapest, 1927), 96–151. More recently see S.R. Llewelyn, *New Documents Illustrating Early Christianity: A Review of the Greek Inscriptions and Papyri Published in 1982–83* (Macquarie University, N.S.W: Ancient History Documentary Research Centre, Macquarie University, 1994), 225–232.

remission. But in reality the lender would collect the loan himself without the involvement of the court.[6]

Hillel's Prosbul

Recently, David Bigman argued that Hillel's original *takkanah* was *identical to the Greek prosbul.* Lenders were refraining from lending because borrowers were simply defaulting. This social problem was unrelated to the sabbatical year. In response to the problem of loan default, Hillel instituted the Greek prosbul, which allowed the courts to auction off the borrower's property in order to repay the loan. This *takkanah* encouraged lenders to lend to the poor by offering them a guarantee that they would be able to recover their money. This is a revolutionary understanding of Hillel's *takkanah*. According to Bigman, Hillel's prosbul was not a legal fiction; it was a real legal institution, patterned *directly* after its Greek parallel. That is, rather than a fictitious means by which to circumvent the Torah's laws, it was an extra-biblical legal way of allowing for more effective loan collection, thereby encouraging lending. Furthermore, the prosbul would only be necessary in certain circumstances— when the borrower defaulted on his loan. There was no need for a prosbul to accompany every loan document. As we shall see below, it was only later tannaim who proposed that the prosbul could be instituted more generally as a means to avoid remission in the sabbatical year.

Bigman provides three types of evidence from various tannaitic sources to support his theory. First, chapter ten of Mishnah Sheviit describes the effect (or lack thereof) of the sabbatical year on certain monetary arrangements and debts. These include a debt to a store owner or a debt of wages (mishnah one), an arrangement for the division of slaughtered meat (mishnah two), and legal fines (mishnah two). These arrangements and debts are normal occurrences that did not arise specifically in connection with the sabbatical year. Since the mishnah lists the prosbul as another example of a type of debt which is not remitted by the sabbatical year, it too should be understood as an institution that exists independently of the sabbatical year. Furthermore, the language used by the Mishnah, "a prosbul is not cancelled," mirrors the

---

[6] Henshke, 92–98.

language used to describe other cases in the chapter, all types of arrangements which were not created in response to the sabbatical year.

Second, some tannaitic sources describe the prosbul as an agreement between a specific borrower and lender, thereby limiting its scope. Unlike Mishnah Sheviit, which portrays the prosbul as a mechanism which lumps together all of the lender's outstanding loans, Tosefta Sheviit 8:9 describes the prosbul as applicable to a single loan:

(1) ללוה קרקע ולמלוה אין קרקע כותבין עליו פרוזבול.	(1) If the borrower owns land and the lender does not own land, a prosbul may be written.
(2) למלוה קרקע וללוה אין קרקע אין כותבין עליו פרוזבול.	(2) If the lender owns land and the borrower does not own land, a prosbul may not be written.
(3) לו אין קרקע ולערבין לו קרקע ולחייבין לו קרקע כותבין עליו פרוזבול.	(3) If he [the borrower] does not own land but his guarantors or debtors own land, a prosbul may be written.

The Tosefta (and Mishnah Sheviit 10:6)[7] requires the borrower (or his guarantors/debtors) to own land in order for a prosbul to be written. Traditional commentators explain that land is necessary because the lien placed on the borrower's land by the debt makes it as if the debt has theoretically already been paid back at the time of the loan. Possession of land demonstrates that the borrower has the means to repay the loan, such that even if he has not yet done so, it may be considered paid off. This traditional explanation further supports the notion of the prosbul as legal fiction: When the lender goes to collect the loan on behalf of the court after the sabbatical year, it is as if he is collecting a loan that was already collected before the sabbatical year. But this explanation is difficult because it adds an additional legal fiction to the

---

[7] The parallel source in the Mishnah, however, allows the lender to symbolically transfer a piece of his land to the borrower in order to execute the loan with a prosbul. This transforms the necessity for the borrower to own land into a sort of legal fiction, which accords with the later tannaitic attitude towards the prosbul as we shall explain below.

process. Furthermore, it is not clear why a prosbul would be necessary if a loan using land as security is considered as already having been repaid.[8]

According to Bigman's understanding that the prosbul was a general means through which the lender could collect his debt, the Tosefta's halakhah makes considerably more sense. The Tosefta requires the borrower to own land so that the court will have property to auction off in the event he defaults on his loan. Additionally, the Tosefta passage describes the prosbul as a document written for a single lender and a single borrower. The prosbul is written for each individual loan; the lender does not group all of his outstanding loans under one prosbul, as the Mishnah describes.[9] Thus, according to Bigman's reconstruction, Hillel's original takkanah was simply an adoption of the Greek prosbul into rabbinic halakhah. It allowed the lender to collect his debts more effectively, and it had nothing to do with the sabbatical year's remission of loans.

Third, mishnah five in the same chapter of Sheviit indicates that the prosbul exists independently of the sabbatical year:

פרוזבול המוקדם כשר   A pre-dated prosbul is valid, but a
והמאוחר פסול...   post-dated one is invalid…

A prosbul must be dated in order to determine precisely which debts are included in the transfer to the court. Bigman's interpretation of the prosbul fits the halakhah in this mishnah precisely. As explained above, the mishnah understands the prosbul to be an agreement between a single borrower and single lender. The mishnah permits a prosbul which pre-dates the final loan among a group of loans, all to the same borrower. Such a pre-dated prosbul is valid because the pre-dating is solely to the detriment of the lender, who will be able to use the court to collect only for those loans that were given before the document was written. If a loan was given after the date on the document, it will not be subject to the prosbul and the lender would not be able to use the leverage of the court to collect that particular outstanding loan. However, a post-dated prosbul is invalid because the post-dating would

---

[8] Rashi Bavli Gittin 37a s.v. אלא על הקרקע explains that lenders generally refrain from loaning to borrowers without land, and Hillel would not have applied the prosbul to such rare cases.

[9] Cf. Mishnah Ketubot 9:9, which seems to describe a situation involving a prosbul between a single lender and a single borrower.

be to the benefit of the lender and to the detriment of the borrower, since it would enable the lender to use the court to collect even those debts which came into effect after the signing of the prosbul.

In contrast to this reasonable explanation, traditional commentators were forced to explain this mishnah in light of their understanding of the prosbul as an enactment intended to circumvent the sabbatical remission of loans. Thus they explained that a post-dated prosbul is one that was actually written months before the sabbatical year (for example in Adar) but was post-dated to the end of the year (Elul) to include all subsequent loans. The difficulty with this interpretation is that it is hard to imagine why anyone would write such a prosbul. If the sole intention of the prosbul was to protect loans from remission, it would only make sense to write such a document immediately before the sabbatical year in order for the lender to include all of his outstanding loans. In other words, whereas Bigman is able to explain why one would write and post-date a prosbul, the traditional explanation is forced to explain, rather improbably, that "post-dating" refers to a prosbul written at a time in which there would be no benefit to the lender to write such a document.

From Ease of Loan Collection to Avoidance of Loan Remission

The shift from the original meaning of the prosbul as a way to ensure the collection of debt to its use as a mechanism to circumvent the sabbatical year seems to have begun already in the tannaitic period. The clearest evidence for a connection between the prosbul and the *shemittah* year is found in Tosefta Sheviit 8:10:

אימתי כותבין פרוזבול? ערב ראש השנה של שביעית.	When does one write a prosbul? On the eve of Rosh Hashanah which precedes the sabbatical year
כתבו ערב ראש השנה של מוצאי שביעית אף על פי שחוזר וקרעו לאחר מכן גובה עליו והולך אפילו לזמן מרובה.	If one wrote it on the eve of Rosh Hashanah following the sabbatical year, even though he will subsequently tear it up, he may collect on account of it for a long time.

These halakhot unequivocally link the writing of the prosbul to *shemittah*. The Tosefta mandates that the prosbul be written as close as possible to the sabbatical year in order to ensure that all outstanding loans will be included under the prosbul. Presumably this understanding of prosbul refers to a document that groups together all of one's loans and turns them over to the court on the eve of the sabbatical year.

The presentation of the prosbul as a grouping together of all of one's loans is explicit in Mishnah Sheviit 10:4: "This is the formula of the prosbul: 'I turn over to you, so-and-so, judges of such and such a place, that any debt that I may have outstanding, I shall collect it whenever I desire.'" This particular mishnah presents the prosbul as more of a legal fiction than a realistic arrangement between one borrower and one lender. However, while this mishnah lends itself to the interpretation that the lender transfers his loans to the court as a means to circumvent sabbatical remission, such an explanation is not mandatory. Mishnah four may simply represent an intermediate stage in the development of the Jewish form of the Greek prosbul. While Hillel's original prosbul was an agreement between one lender and one borrower, the process may have later been simplified such that the lender could make such an arrangement for all of his debts simultaneously in one document.

In light of Bigman's understanding, we can now summarize the tannaitic prosbul from its inception through its subsequent development. Hillel first instituted the prosbul to function in the same manner as the parallel Greek legal mechanism. It provided lenders with a guarantee that if a borrower defaulted on a specific loan, the court would step in and auction off his property in order to repay the debt. Hillel's prosbul encouraged lenders to loan money by guaranteeing their ability to recover in case of default. Another incentive for lenders was that the prosbul was not subject to sabbatical loan remission, because such a loan was considered to be under the court's jurisdiction.[10] Later, but still in the tannaitic period, Hillel's prosbul developed from an "insurance policy" for individual loans between one lender and one borrower, to a grouping together of *all* of a lender's outstanding loans to various borrowers and their

---

[10] Bigman explains that the only difference between the transfer of documentation to the court and the prosbul is that in the case of transfer the court collects the debt, and with a prosbul the lender acts in place of the court and collects the debt himself. See Bigman, 6 n. 11.

simultaneous transfer to the court. Thus, with one prosbul, a lender would be ensured of his ability to collect on all of his outstanding loans. Subsequently, or perhaps even simultaneously, the prosbul developed into a specific means to circumvent the sabbatical year. Instead of being a document meant to ensure debt collection in case of default, the prosbul became a means by which a lender could prevent remission in the sabbatical year. Thus the prosbul was transformed from a document that happened not to remit in the sabbatical year, to a document that was specifically written to avoid sabbatical year remission.

The editing of the Mishnah blurred the lines between the different stages of development of the prosbul. The inclusion of the prosbul in a chapter concerning sabbatical year loan remission and the prooftext from the relevant passage in Deuteronomy creates the impression that Hillel's enactment was originally created in order to resolve the problem of lenders refraining from offering loans prior to the sabbatical year. However, as we have seen, there are other extant tannaitic sources that present the prosbul in its original, Greek light. We shall now turn our attention to the midrashic collections which portray the prosbul as a document explicitly created to prevent loan remission.

"So Expounded Hillel"

Sifre Deuteronomy (piska 113), a tannaitic midrashic collection composed in the Land of Israel, contains a midrash which exempts from remission any loan in which the lender transferred the documentation to a court:

את אחיך תשמט ידך	*Your hand must remit what is due you*
(דברים טו:ג), ולא	*from your kinsman* (Deuteronomy
המוסר שטרותיו לבית	15:3)—and not one who transfers his
דין. מיכן אמרו: התקין	documents to the court. From here they
הלל פרוסבול.	said Hillel instituted the prosbul.

According to the midrash, the Torah's use of the phrase "*your* hand (ידך)" teaches that loan remission applies only when the money is owed to the lender himself. If the lender transfers the loan documentation to a court, it is no longer in his "hand," and therefore the loan need not be remitted. The editors of the Sifre seem to have understood the prosbul as a mechanism created explicitly for the

> ⊛ **Mekhilta** Deuteronomy is a tannaitic midrash on Deuteronomy that did not survive in its entirety. It was first reconstructed by R. David Tzvi Hoffman in Germany and published under the title Midrash Tannaim in 1908. He based his edition on quotes found in the Midrash Hagadol, a medieval collection of midrashim, as well as on fragments found in the Cairo Genizah which had been published by Solomon Schechter. Since Hoffman's publication new fragments of the midrash have been discovered and published.

purpose of circumventing sabbatical remission. To demonstrate this point they use the technical term מיכן אמרו ("from there they said") to awkwardly connect the relevant clause from mishnah Sheviit 10:3 to its scriptural source as expounded in the midrash.[11] The midrashic editor implies that Hillel enacted the prosbul based on the preceding midrash, according to which one who transfers his loan documents to the court does not have his loan remitted. Thus Hillel enacted the prosbul in order to standardize the transfer of debt documents to the court so that sabbatical year remission would be avoided.

The midrash on the same verse in Mekhilta Deuteronomy makes the connection between the prosbul and the exegesis on Deuteronomy even more explicit.[12] Unlike the Sifre, which only connected Hillel's enactment with the exegesis, this version of the midrash attributes this exegesis to Hillel himself:

ואשר יהיה לך את אחיך	*Whatever is due from your kinsmen* (Deuteron-
(דברים טו:ג), לא המוסר	omy 15:3)—[but] not one who transfers his
שטרותיו לבית דין. מיכן	documents to the court. From here Hillel insti-
התקין הלל פרוזבול. וכך דרש	tuted the prosbul. And thus expounded Hillel:
הלל: ואשר יהיה לך את אחיך	whatever is due from your kinsmen—[but] not
לא המוסר שטרותיו לבית דין.	one who transfers his documents to the court.

Taken in its entirety, this midrash states that Hillel enacted the prosbul based on his own exegesis of the Torah—"thus expounded Hillel." According to this source, there were two steps in the creation of the prosbul. First, Hillel expounded the verse which teaches that the Torah itself exempts from remission

---

[11] See David Weiss Halivni, *Midrash, Mishnah, and Gemara* (Cambridge: Harvard University Press, 1986), 135 n. 48.

[12] On the use of this midrash as an authentic tannaitic teaching see Henshke, 80 n. 36.

deeds which have been transferred to the court. Then, based on the Torah's exemption, he instituted the prosbul. The forced connection between the mishnah and the midrash creates the awkward description of the prosbul as both a *takkanah*, which in most cases represents an independent enactment of the sages, and a midrash, with its origins in Scripture.[13] The amoraic literature discussed in the next section is primarily preoccupied with categorizing the prosbul as one of the two.

Integrating Innovation

By the amoraic period the prosbul was universally understood as having been created specifically to avoid remission in the sabbatical year and thereby avoid the consequences of *shemittah*. Once this understanding took root, the sages were faced with the challenge of explaining the boldness of this innovation. How could Hillel create a mechanism that abrogates Torah law?

Some amoraim adopted the interpretation that Hillel enacted the prosbul on exegetical grounds. According to this interpretation, the prosbul fulfilled the intent of the Torah; it did not abrogate it. Others disagreed, arguing that the prosbul is indeed an abrogation of the law, just not of Torah law. They claimed that Hillel had the legal authority to enact the prosbul for by his time the status of the sabbatical year had been demoted to that of rabbinic law. It was no longer Torah law. Thus, Hillel's *rabbinic* enactment could justifiably override the *rabbinically* ordained remission of loans. The analysis below highlights these conflicting approaches as they appear in both Talmuds.

Yerushalmi Sheviit 10:2, 39c

Yerushalmi Sheviit combines two distinct sugyot with conflicting approaches to the prosbul:

---

[13] Menahem Kahana suggests that there are a limited number of cases in rabbinic literature which indeed use the term "התקינו" to refer to an enactment with its origins in Scripture. See Kahana, *Sifre Zuta Deuteronomy* (Jerusalem: Hebrew University Magnes Press, 2002), 188.

(1a) ואשר יהיה לך את אחיך תשמט ידיך (דברים טו:ג)—ולא המוסר שטרותיו לבית דין. מיכן סמכו לפרוזבול שהוא מן התורה.

(1a) *But you must remit whatever is due you from your kinsmen* (Deuteronomy 15:3)— not one who transfers his debt documents to the court. From here they supported the prosbul that it is from the Torah.

(1b) ופרוזבול דבר תורה?

(1b) And is the prosbul really from the Torah?

(1c) כשהתקין הלל סמכוהו לדבר תורה.

(1c) When it was instituted by Hillel they supported it from the Torah.

(2a) אמר ר' חונה: קשייתה קומי רבי יעקב בר אחא: כמאן דאמ' מעשרות מדבריהם, ברם כאמן דאמר מעשרות מדבר תורה והלל מתקין על דבר תורה?

(2a) R. Huna said: I asked before R. Yaakov b. Aha: [This is fine] according to the one who says that tithes [in our day] are mandated by rabbinic law. However, according to the one who says tithes are [still] a Torah obligation—did Hillel make an enactment against Torah law?

(2b) אמר רבי יוסי: וכי משעה שגלו ישראל לבבל לא נפטרו מן המצוות התלויות בארץ והשמט כספים נוהג בין בארץ בין בחוצה לארץ דבר תורה?

(2b) R. Yose said: And from the time Israel was exiled to Babylonian were they not exempted from commandments that are dependent upon the land of Israel; and yet the remission of loans is in effect both inside and outside of the land?

(2c) חזר רבי יוסי ואמר: וזה דבר השמיטה שמוט—בשעה שהשמיטה נוהגת דבר תורה השמט כספים נוהג בין בארץ בין בחוצה לארץ דבר תורה, ובשעה שהשמיטה נוהגת מדבריהן השמט כספים נוהג בין בארץ בין בחוצה לארץ מדבריהם.

(2c) R. Yose returned and said: This is the nature of the remission: remit—when the sabbatical year is a Torah prohibition, the remission of loans is in effect inside and outside of the land by Torah law; when the sabbatical year is a rabbinic prohibition, the remission of loans is in effect inside and outside of the land by the words of the rabbis.

(2d) דתני: וזה דבר השמיטה שמוט.

(2d) As it was taught: This is the nature of the remission: remit.

רבי אומר: שני שמיטין
הללו—שמיטה ויובל—בשעה
שהיובל נוהג שמיטה נוהגת
דבר תורה. פסקו היובילות,
שמיטה נוהגת מדבריהן.
אימתי פסקו היובילות?
יושביה (ויקרא כה:ו), בזמן
שיושביה עליה לא בזמן
שגלו מתוכה. היו עליה אבל
היו מעורבבין שבט יהודה
בבנימן ושבט בנימן ביהודה,
יכול יהו היובילות נוהגין,
תלמוד לומר: יושביה, לכל
יושביה, נמצאת אומר כיון
שגלו שבט ראובן וגד וחצי
שבט המנשה בטלו היובילות.

Rebbi says these two sabbaticals—*shemittah* and the jubilee—when the jubilee is in effect, *shemittah* is in effect according to Torah law. Once the jubilee has ceased [to be observed], *shemittah* is in effect by the words of the rabbis. When did the jubilees cease [to be observed]? [As it says:] *its inhabitants* (Leviticus 25:6), when its inhabitants are on it [the land] and not when they have been exiled from it. If they were on it, but the tribe of Judah was mixed with the tribe of Benjamin and the tribe of Benjamin with the tribe of Judah, perhaps the jubilee would still be in effect? Scripture teaches: its inhabitants, for all its inhabitants. You now [must] say that once the tribes of Reuben, Gad, and half of Manasseh were exiled, the jubilee was canceled.

The Yerushalmi begins with an exegesis of the verse similar to that found in the tannaitic midrashim, but with two differences.

Sifre Deuteronomy	**Yerushalmi**
את אחיך תשמט ידך, ולא המוסר שטרותיו לבית דין מיכן אמרו התקין הלל פרוסבול.	ואשר יהיה לך את אחיך תשמט ידיך ולא המוסר שטרותיו לבית דין מיכן סמכו לפרוזבול שהוא מן התורה.
Your hands must remit what is due you from your kinsman—and not one who transfers his documents to the court. From here they said Hillel instituted the prosbul.	But you must remit whatever is due you from your kinsmen—not one who transfers his debt documents to the court. From here they supported the prosbul that it is from the Torah.

The first difference is that the Sifre uses the phrase, "From here they said," whereas the Yerushalmi uses the phrase, "from here they supported." The second is that the Yerushalmi explicitly says that the prosbul is "from the Torah." The first difference is probably attributable to the second difference.

The Yerushalmi serves to tighten the connection between the enactment of the prosbul and the exegesis from Deuteronomy. The two are not only connected, as is the case in the Sifre; in the Yerushalmi the prosbul is explicitly derived from the Torah.

The anonymous voice of the Yerushalmi (1b), aware that the language of the Mishnah seems to indicate that the prosbul is an enactment of Hillel, challenges the assertion that the prosbul is considered to be from the Torah. He responds to his own question (1c) stating that the institution of the prosbul is indeed a rabbinic enactment, but that after it was enacted the rabbis also bolstered its status with a midrash from the Torah. Thus while its origins may lie in rabbinic legislation, it derives its efficacy from the exegesis of a biblical verse.

R. Huna opens the second half of the sugya (2a) by noting that the understanding in section one is acceptable only if the tithes "in this day" (to be explained below) are only of rabbinic status. But if we hold that the commandment of separating tithes is from the Torah, then we would have to question how Hillel would have the authority to override Torah law. R. Huna's question requires some explanation. He is referring to a dispute among the sages concerning tithes and other commandments which are performed only in the Land of Israel. What is the status of such commandments following the destruction of the First Temple? Some sages maintain that the returning exiles voluntarily accepted upon themselves the requirement to tithe, but that following the destruction of the First Temple, the Torah no longer mandated tithing. The same status is then applied to other commandments which are performed only in the Land of Israel, i.e. *shemittah*. Therefore, if tithes are no longer mandated by the Torah, then the remission of loans, a subset of the general shemittah laws, is also longer mandated by the Torah (see Yerushalmi Sheviit 6:1, 36c). If such is the case, then we can accept Hillel's authority to make such an enactment. But if tithes and the various laws concerning the sabbatical year maintain their status as Torah law, then how could Hillel issue an enactment that contravenes Torah law?

R. Yose's initial assumption (2b) further sharpens R. Huna's question by arguing that loan remission is a commandment that is independent of the settlement of the Land of Israel. The Israelites maintained their observance of loan remission even when they were in exile in Babylonia, despite the fact that they could not observe the other commandments that require one to be in the Land of Israel. Thus loan remission maintains its biblical status even if tithes are no longer mandated by the Torah.

R. Yose recants (2c) from his earlier insistence that loan remission continues to be of biblical status by equating the status of the other sabbatical year laws with loan remission. Since the other sabbatical year laws (such as the prohibition against working the land) are currently of rabbinic status, the sabbatical remission of loans is also of rabbinic status. The sugya continues with a citation of the midrash (2d) upon which R. Yose's statement's was based. Rebbi [Yehudah Hanasi] explains that the status of the sabbatical laws is dependent upon the jubilee laws. The jubilee is mandated by the Torah only when the land is settled by all its inhabitants (see Leviticus 25:6), i.e. all of the tribes of Israel. Even if there is a return to the land, the tribes must remain distinct and within their original borders (including those tribes whose inheritance was on the Eastern bank of the Jordan) in order for the jubilee to be in effect. Since this was not the case following the exile of the ten tribes during the first Temple period, subsequent to that period both the jubilee and the sabbatical year have only rabbinic status. In conclusion, the Yerushalmi resolves that Hillel's enactment did not actually override a biblical commandment, but only a rabbinically ordained one.

Sections one and two of the sugya in the Yerushalmi represent two distinct and utterly independent justifications for how Hillel could issue an enactment that seems to circumvent Torah law. Section one, like the tannaitic midrashim, argues that prosbul is itself Torah law and that Hillel's innovation is based in exegesis. In section two, R. Yose argues that Hillel's authority to enact the prosbul is valid only when the sabbatical year is rabbinically ordained, as was the case in Hillel's time. Thus Hillel did not circumvent Torah law; he merely circumvented rabbinic law. The fact that only the second section of the sugya appears in the parallel in Yerushalmi Gittin (4:3, 43c) corroborates the two sections' independence from one another.

Mishnah Gittin 4:3: *Tikkun Olam*

Since there is no Bavli tractate for Sheviit, the Bavli's discussion of the prosbul is found elsewhere in the Talmud. Mishnah Gittin, chapter four, lists the prosbul among the rabbinic decrees which remedy problematic economic and social situations, מפני תיקון עולם, which may be translated as, "in order to properly order the world."[14] Mishnah 4:3 reads:

הלל התקין פרוזבול	Hillel instituted the prosbul be-
מפני תיקון העולם:	cause of *tikkun olam.*

There is nothing in this mishnah that connects the institution of the prosbul with the sabbatical year. Rather, the mishnah accords with Bigman's interpretation of the origins of Hillel's *takkanah*. Hillel instituted the Greek prosbul into rabbinic law, which allowed for the courts to auction the borrower's property to repay a defaulted loan. This encouraged lenders to loan money, which ultimately served the needs of the entire society.

Bavli Gittin 36a

The Bavli, like the Yerushalmi, already understands the prosbul as an enactment specifically intended to circumvent the sabbatical year. With this understanding in mind, the Bavli asks two questions. The first question, similar to that found in the Yerushalmi, is how Hillel had the authority to abrogate Torah law by instituting the prosbul. The second question is found only in the Bavli and is a follow-up to the first. The Bavli questions the authority of the post-Temple sages to reinstitute the laws of loan remission, when these laws were already suspended.

CITATION OF RELEVANT MISHNAH

(1) תנן התם: **פרוסבול**	(1) We have learned elsewhere: [A loan
אינו משמט.	secured by] a prosbul is not remitted.

Tannaitic Source	Amoraic Source	Stammaitic Source

---

[14] Today this concept has come to mean good deeds such as charity done in order to "repair the world." In the Mishnah, its meaning was more specific and it usually refers to rectifying problems created because of marital laws or economic injustices.

זה אחד מן הדברים שהתקין | This was one of the things enacted by
הלל הזקן שראה את העם | Hillel the elder when he observed that
שנמנעו מלהלוות זה את זה | people were refraining from lending to one
ועברו על מה שכתוב בתורה: | another, and thus transgressing what is
השמר לך פן יהיה דבר עם | written in the Torah, *Beware, lest you harbor*
לבבך בליעל וגו' (דברים טו:ט). | *the base thought, etc* (Deuteronomy 15:9)

עמד והתקין פרוסבול. | Hillel enacted the prosbul. And this is the
וזה הוא גופו של פרוסבול: | formula of the prosbul: "I turn over to you,
"מוסרני לכם פלוני דיינין | so-and-so, judges of such and such a place,
שבמקום פלוני, שכל חוב | that any debt that I may have outstanding,
שיש לי אצל פלוני שאגבנו | I shall collect it whenever I desire." And
כל זמן שארצה." והדיינים | the judges sign below, or the witnesses.
חותמים למטה או העדים.

QUESTION

(2a) ומי איכא מידי | (2a) Is there anything that according to
דמדאורייתא משמטא שביעית | the Torah the seventh year remits and yet
והתקין הלל דלא משמטא? | Hillel instituted that it is not remitted?

AMORAIC RESPONSE

(2b) אמר אביי: בשביעית | (2b) Abaye said: During the sabbatical
בזמן הזה ורבי היא דתניא: | year in our time, and it is according
| to Rebbi, as it has been taught:

SUPPORT FROM BARAITA

(2c) רבי אומר: וזה דבר | (2c) Rebbi says: *This shall be the nature of*
השמיטה שמוט (דברים ט, ב). | *the remission; [every creditor] shall remit.*
בשתי שמיטות הכתוב מדבר, | The verse speaks of two kinds of remission,
אחת שמיטת קרקע ואחת | one the remission of land and the other
שמיטת כספים. בזמן שאתה | the remission of money. When you remit
משמט קרקע אתה משמט | land you remit money; when you do not
כספים, בזמן שאי אתה משמט | remit land you do not remit money.
קרקע אי אתה משמט כספים.

| Tannaitic Source | Amoraic Source | Stammaitic Source |

STAMMAITIC ADDITION

(2d) ותקינו רבנן דתשמט | (2d) And the rabbis instituted that it shall be
זכר לשביעית. ראה הלל | remitted in order to keep alive the memory
שנמנעו העם מלהלוות זה את | of the Sabbatical year. When Hillel observed
זה עמד והתקין פרוסבול. | that the people were refraining from loaning
| one another he instituted the prosbul.

QUESTION

(3a) ומי איכא מידי | (3a) But is it possible that according to the
דמדאורייתא לא משמטא | Torah the seventh year does not remit and
שביעית ותקינו רבנן דתשמט? | the rabbis instituted that it does remit?

AMORAIC RESPONSES

(3b) אמר אביי: שב | (3b) Abaye said: It is [a case
ואל תעשה הוא. | of] "sit still and do nothing."

(3c) רבא אמר: הפקר | (3c) Rava said: Whatever is declared
בית דין היה הפקר. | ownerless by the court is ownerless.

| Tannaitic Source | Amoraic Source | Stammaitic Source |

Before we offer a source-critical interpretation of this sugya, we will explain it according to Rashi and other traditional commentators. After referencing Mishnah Sheviit 10:3–4, the stam questions (2a) Hillel's authority to enact the prosbul because it seems to be an abrogation of Torah law. Abaye responds (2b) by explaining that Hillel's *takkanah* follows the opinion of Rabbi Yehudah Hanasi (2c) who rules that the sabbatical year laws do not apply after the destruction of the Temple. However, this would seem to render the prosbul superfluous; if the laws of *shemittah* are no longer applicable, loans would not be cancelled in the first place. So why would a prosbul be necessary? This is resolved (2d) by the claim that the rabbis restored the commandment to a rabbinic level lest the laws of the sabbatical year be forgotten. This explanation raises a different question (3a): what gives the rabbis the right to reinstitute a Torah commandment when doing so might deprive the lenders of their money? Abaye again responds (3b), explaining that it is not an actual revival of the Torah commandment; rather, the rabbis encourage debtors to refrain from repaying their loans. No one is actually "doing" anything. They are just "sitting still" and not performing the act of repaying their loan. Rava disagrees (3c), explaining that reinstituting the remission of loans is within rabbinic jurisdiction, as rabbis have the power to declare all property ownerless and transfer it to any party they choose. In the case of loans, the rabbis would have the power to consider the money as if it had been simply transferred to the borrower—his debt would be released. Rashi notes that Rava's statement also answers the first question in the sugya (2a). Rava argues against Abaye (2b), positing that the prosbul is effective even according to those sages who disagree with Rebbi and consider loan remission a Torah commandment after the destruction of the Temple. The rabbis' authority to declare all property ownerless is itself biblically ordained.[15] Therefore, they could use the prosbul to force the borrower to return the money to the lender even after the loan has been remitted. The act would simply be considered a transfer of property, which is within their jurisdiction.[16]

"The Sabbatical Year in Our Time"

As is often the case, Rashi's explanation smoothes over the major difficulties present in the sugya. First, Abaye's response to the question, "in the Sabbatical year during our time" (2b) presents chronological difficulties. The phrase "in our time" most commonly refers to the period following the destruction of the Temple. This is a typical rabbinic way of dividing historical periods, and Abaye would have considered himself as living in the post-Temple period. But Hillel died in the first decade of the Common Era, around sixty years before the destruction. How could Abaye apply "in our time" to an enactment that was made by Hillel when the Temple was still standing?[17] A second chronological difficulty is that Abaye explains that Hillel follows the opinion of Rebbi despite the fact that Rebbi lived two hundred years after Hillel.

---

[15] The prooftexts are brought in an amoraic dispute immediately following Rava's statement.

[16] See also the Tosafot 36a s.v. מי איכא.

[17] See Meiri Magen Avot no. 15 who tries to argue that the phrase בזמן הזה is not meant to be taken literally and in fact refers to the Second Temple period.

The terminology used also presents a difficulty. The sugya opens by questioning Hillel's authority to create the institution of prosbul. The formulation "it is according to Rebbi" implies that Hillel relies on Rebbi's midrash—when *shemittah* is inoperative, loan remission is also inoperative. However, usually when the Bavli attributes a position to a single authority, it implies that there are those who disagree with that position. In this case we would expect the Bavli to be implying that if a sage did not accept Rebbi's connection between *shemittah* laws and loan remission, he must also reject the institution of the prosbul.[18] After all, without Rebbi's midrash, the prosbul could not, according to the typical use of this term, be effective. But we have no indication that any sage ever rejected the efficacy of the prosbul. There is disagreement in both Talmuds about the nature and scope of the *takkanah*,[19] but there is no disagreement as to its efficacy.

Another substantial difficulty is the line of reasoning found in the second half of the sugya. The stam argues that the rabbis reinstituted loan remission even though Torah law no longer mandated it. The prosbul, however, renders the entire reinstitution irrelevant. The stam paints an outlandish picture of rabbinic enactments: the rabbis restore the institution of loan remission only to circumvent it with the prosbul. The justification of this strange progression—that it is necessary in order to prevent the laws of the sabbatical year from being forgotten—does not seem strong enough to explain such tortuous turns in the law.

Reconstructing the Bavli

The difficulties detailed above are likely a result of the fact that the entire sugya is a construction of the anonymous Babylonian editors, the stam. The stam transferred section two of the sugya from its original context elsewhere in the Bavli and appended to it the invented amoraic debate that is section three. Suggesting that statements ascribed to amoraim are actually stammaitc, i.e. post-amoraic inventions, is a radical suggestion, but it is not without precedent. Shamma Friedman devotes an entire article to stammaitic creations

---

[18] Henshke 73. MS Aras 889 sensitive to this problem deletes the word ורבי.
[19] See Yerushalmi Sheviit 10:6–7, 39d and Bavli Gittin 37a.

attributed to amoraim, in which he argues that the statements of amoraim should be analyzed with the same scrutiny as tannaitic material that appears in the Bavli. [20] Just as the late editors of the Bavli will occasionally "invent" a baraita, so, too, will they occasionally invent an amoraic statement.[21] If a statement attributed to an amora expresses ideas that are more characteristic of the abstract reasoning so typically found in stammaitic thinking, there is a strong possibility that it might be a stammaitic creation.

The creators of this sugya in Gittin were bothered by the same problem addressed in the earlier sources—what gave Hillel the right to abrogate Torah law? However, they were either not familiar with the halakhic midrashim which describe the prosbul as being based on midrash, or they rejected them. And while the stam was familiar with a baraita attributed to Rebbi, it is not the same baraita that appears in Yerushalmi Sheviit, nor is it a reworked version of it. Thus there is no evidence that the Bavli was aware of the Yerushalmi's sugya either.

David Henshke, in his article on the development of the prosbul, has already noted that the first part of the sugya was transferred by the redactor to Gittin from Moed Katan 2b.[22] The redactor used this preexisting sugya in order to explain that the prosbul is effective because loan remission is of rabbinic origin following the destruction of the Temple. Noting that the sugya's original context was Moed Katan resolves the chronological and terminological difficulties we had above with Abaye's statement (2b). Here is the sugya as it appears in Moed Katan:

(1) תנן: מַשְׁקִין בֵּית הַשְׁלָחִין בְּמוֹעֵד וּבַשְּׁבִיעִית.

(1) It was taught in the Mishnah: An irrigated field may be watered during hol hamoed or the sabbatical year.

| Tannaitic Source | Amoraic Source | Stammaitic Source |

[20] Shamma Friedman, "Al Titma al Hosafah Shenizkar Bah Shem Amora," *Talmudic Studies: Investigating the Sugya, Variant Readings and Aggada* (New York and Jerusalem: Jewish Theological Seminary, 2010), 57–135.

[21] For examples see the introduction to this book, pp. 29, 32.

[22] Henshke, 72–76.

QUESTION

זריעה וחרישה (2a)...

בשביעית מי שרי?

(2a) ...Who permits sowing or plowing in the sabbatical year?

AMORAIC RESPONSE

אמר אביי: בשביעית (2b)

בזמן הזה, ורבי היא. דתניא:

(2b) Abaye said: During the sabbatical year in our time, and it is according to Rebbi, as it has been taught:

SUPPORT FROM A BARAITA

רבי אומר: וזה דבר השמטה (2c)

שמוט - בשתי שמיטות הכתוב

מדבר, אחת שמיטת קרקע ואחת

שמיטת כספים. בזמן שאתה

משמט קרקע - אתה משמט

כספים, ובזמן שאי אתה משמט

קרקע - אי אתה משמט כספים.

(2c) Rebbi says: This shall be the nature of the remission; [every creditor] shall remit. The verse speaks of two kinds of remission, one the remission of land and the other the remission of money. When you remit land you remit money; when you do not remit land you do not remit money.

ALTERNATE AMORAIC RESPONSE

רבא אמר: אפילו תימא (2d)

רבנן, אבות אסר רחמנא,

תולדות לא אסר רחמנא...

(2d) Rava said: You may even say [it follows the view of] the rabbis and that the Merciful One forbids principal [types of work], the Merciful One does not forbid derivative [types of work]...

Tannaitic Source   Amoraic Source   Stammaitic Source

The sugya in Moed Katan has no connection whatsoever to Hillel or the prosbul. Rather, it is concerned with the prohibition of working the land during the sabbatical year. The amoraim were troubled by the leniency in the mishnah which allows for watering an irrigated field during the sabbatical year, when land improvement is forbidden by Torah law. Two amoraim, Abaye and Rava, each offer a way of resolving this difficulty. Abaye (2b) explains that the mishnah follows Rebbi (2c), who accords rabbinic status to the sabbatical year following the destruction of the Temple. Rava disagrees and explains that the mishnah may even follow the opinion of the rabbis who maintain the biblical status of the sabbatical year after the destruction but allow for the performance of land improvement not explicitly forbidden by the Torah. The textual difficulties found in Gittin are absent in the sugya in Moed Katan. The phrase "in our time" refers to the period after the destruction of the Temple when the leniency of the mishnah came into practice, and not to the period of Hillel, when the Temple still stood. Additionally, the phrase "it is Rebbi" is appropriate because Abaye rejects Rava's attribution of the mishnah to the rabbis. Abaye must explicitly state that in his opinion, the mishnah is only according to Rebbi's lone view. The textual problems arise in Gittin because the editor moved the sugya from its original location to a new context where it does not make sense.

Returning to Gittin, the stam appended an explanation to the baraita (2d) in order to explicitly connect the passage to the prosbul. The addition clarifies that while according to the Torah the laws of loan remission are no longer in effect, the sages reinstituted them so that they would not be forgotten.[23] It was only after the rabbinic reinstitution of those laws that Hillel enacted the prosbul to circumvent loan remission. The stam creatively uses a preexisting source to explain that the sabbatical laws are only of rabbinic status. However, in doing so, he creates the jarring anachronism which suggests that Hillel follows Rebbi and the circular logic whereby one enactment (Hillel's *takkanah*) serves as an antidote for another enactment (the rabbinic reinstatement of the sabbatical laws in a time when the Torah no longer mandates them).

Thus Abaye's explanation of the mishnah in Moed Katan becomes an answer in the Gittin sugya for how Hillel had the authority to enact the prosbul. Similar to the sugya in the Yerushalmi, Rebbi's midrash serves to relegate *shemittah* laws to rabbinic status, which then allows Hillel to issue a *takkanah* to override rabbinic law. The stam, however, goes one step further in his questioning of this process. Once he explores the subject of rabbinic legislation circumventing Torah law, he asks a new question: what gave the rabbis the authority to reinstitute loan remission when according to the Torah, as expounded in Rebbi's midrash, it is no longer operative (section 3a)?

---

[23] Note the change to Aramaic which indicates that the explanation is not part of the baraita.

Here it is important to note that this question is radically different from the original question concerning the legitimacy of Hillel's abrogation. The first question in the sugya (which is paralleled in the Yerushalmi) is interested in what gave Hillel the right to create a prosbul. The answers justify a practical *takkanah* which reflects what seems to have actually been a historical stage in rabbinic legislation (even if this was not Hillel's original intent). In contrast, the second question is interested in what gave the rabbis the right to reinstitute sabbatical loan remission such that Hillel's prosbul was even necessary. The stam's question aims to explain a *fictional* development in halakhah that never had any practical ramifications. The stammaitic discourse in section 2d creates the impression that there was a moment in history when the sages decided to theoretically reinstitute loan remission in order to prevent *shemittah* from being forgotten. But obviously there never was such a historical moment. The question of what gave the rabbis the right to do so (3a), a question unique to the stam, could not possibly have been addressed by the amoraim Abaye and Rava at the end of the sugya, as they appear to do in the current formulation of the sugya.[24]

Further evidence that despite the appearance of named amoraim, section three is entirely of stammaitic provenance may be found in the nature of the responses attributed to these amoraim. Abaye and Rava's answers employ broad legal principles which are characteristic of stammaitic thinking.[25] The principle that it is preferable to transgress by omission rather than commission (3b) can be applied to a variety of very different situations. In this case it explains that the transgression of not paying back the loan is justified since it is only a case of omission. Likewise, according extensive power of appropriation to the court, Rava's answer to the question (3d) gives broad license to the judicial system that could be used to explain virtually any power that the court takes upon itself. In this case, it explains how the rabbis could allow the borrower to not pay back his loan when loan remission is no longer mandated. The stam ascribes the first of these answers to Abaye and the second to Rava.

---

[24] Generally the amoraim do not respond to questions of the stam, though there are certain exceptions. However, in this case it is clear that the amoraim would not be concerned with the line of questioning that they seem to address.

[25] The principle of "sit and do nothing" is attributed to one side of an amoraic dispute in Yevamot 90a but it does not appear to be amoraic. The analysis of that sugya is beyond the scope of this chapter.

> ⊗ **A loan document** found in the Judean Desert which has been dated to 54/55 CE contains an attempt to avoid the consequences of Sabbatical year loan remission, but is certainly not a "prosbul." In this loan the borrower states, "I will repay it on or within…though this is a year of release." For a description of this document see J.T. Milik, *Discoveries in the Judean Desert* vol. 2 (Oxford: Clarendon Press, 1961), 100–104. For a discussion of this document in the context of the history of the prosbul see S.R. Llewelyn, above n. 5.

Assumedly the stam chose Abaye because he was already mentioned above. And since Rava is Abaye's most frequent disputant, as seen in the transferred sugya from Moed Katan, the second opinion was ascribed to him.[26]

Conclusion

From the late tannaitic period, the discussion of Hillel's prosbul was dominated by the theoretical-legal question of what gave Hillel the authority to issue a *takkanah* which abrogates Torah law.[27] The practical issue of how to encourage wealthy members of society to loan to the poor, clearly the impetus behind the original *takkanah,* faded into the background as the rabbis used the prosbul as a chance to reflect on their own authority in the face of Torah laws. In fact, based on the evidence that we find in the Talmud, the actual use of the prosbul seems to have been limited in scope and of little interest to the amoraim. Shmuel (36b) attempts to limit the locations where a prosbul may be written and declares his desire to abolish it. R. Hiyya b. Abba and the students of R. Ashi (37a) ignored the prosbul entirely and simply relied upon an oral agreement. Indeed, we have found only two cases where it is directly related that a sage actually used a prosbul.[28]

---

[26] Abaye and Rava also debate loan remission in the sugya on 37a mentioned above.

[27] For more on this subject see Christine Hayes, "The Abrogation of Torah Law: Rabbinic *Taqqanah* and Praetorian Edict," *The Talmud Yerushalmi and Graeco-Roman Culture,* ed. Peter Schafer (Tubingen: Mohr Siebeck, 1998), 643–674.

[28] In Yerushalmi Ketubot 9:9, 33c, R. Hiyya bar Abba finds a prosbul belonging to R. Yonatan. He chases after him to return it, to which R. Yonatan responds that the prosbul was not even necessary to collect on his debt. On Bavli Gittin 37a R. Ashi is described as writing a prosbul.

With a great degree of caution and caveats about how general conclusions should not be drawn from singular examples, we would like to suggest that this shift in discourse is emblematic of a shift in actual rabbinic power. Little is known about the historical Hillel, but he clearly lived in a time where Jewish autonomy and legal authority was greater than it was during the later part of the tannaitic period, after the failure of both the Great Revolt in 70 C.E. and the Bar Kochva revolt in 135 C.E. Hillel's prosbul was not an attempt to demonstrate his own authority vis a vis the Torah's laws; it was an attempt to improve the economy of an actual society.

In the later portions of the Talmudic period, in both the Yerushalmi and to a greater degree in the Bavli, rabbis became especially obsessed with their own *theoretical* authority. Later rabbis become more self-reflective upon their own texts and practices, and due to their lack of external political power they perhaps became to a certain degree less responsive to actual historical situations. Briefly put—earlier rabbis enacted and shaped the prosbul, and later rabbis reflected on their right to do so. This is a general trend worth examining in other passages in rabbinic literature. Is there a shift from an emphasis upon the practical to a reflection on the theoretical? The answer to such a broad question cannot be resolved through one example, but it certainly bears investigation.

Chapter Four

The Stammaitic Impact on Halakhah: Two Sanctifications, Two Cups of wine

Pesahim 102a–102b

By Ethan Tucker

This chapter focuses on a passage from Bavli Pesahim in order to gain insight into a somewhat puzzling aspect of contemporary Jewish wedding celebrations. Bavli Ketubot 7b–8a records a series of six blessings, referred to as "the grooms' blessing," which are recited during the week-long celebration following a wedding. These six nuptial blessings are appended to the end of birkat hamazon and recited over a cup of wine, which itself requires a blessing, bringing the total number of berakhot to seven—*sheva berakhot*. The Shulkhan Arukh (Even HaEzer 62:9) records conflicting opinions as to the number of cups of wine required to perform the ritual: There are those who require two *separate* cups of wine—one for the six grooms' blessings and one for birkat hamazon—while others allow for all seven blessings to be recited over a single cup. The same debate over the number of cups of wine exists regarding the wedding ceremony itself. Jewish weddings include two main ritual segments: *erusin*—the blessings that precede the formal act of betrothal; and *nisuin*—the seven blessings that mark the beginning of the marriage. While originally these two segments did not occur simultaneously (like the modern practice of engagement and marriage), contemporary Jewish weddings join the two together with only a brief break in the middle. And yet most halakhic authorities rule that each of these set of blessings is recited over a *separate* cup of wine.

Using two cups of wine in such close proximity is odd and problematic for two main reasons. First, there might be a concern of a ברכה לבטלה or a ברכה שאינה צריכה—blessings said in vain or blessings that are not necessary. The general principle is that a person does not make a blessing twice over the same food or drink unless there has been a significant break between the two periods of eating or drinking. If the blessing over wine, בורא פרי הגפן, is recited over each cup—as is the case with the wedding blessings under the wedding canopy—this concern comes into play. Second, there would seem to be aesthetic reasons to combine two adjacent rituals over a single cup of wine, enabling the full liturgical set to flow together without awkward breaks between the various components.

Our analysis of the sugya in Pesahim will help clarify the origins of the practice of using two separate cups of wine for these rituals. We begin by analyzing the sugya and its development and then We evaluate the ramifications of this analysis on later halakhic practice. As this chapter will demonstrate, reconstructing the creation of Talmudic passages can be enormously fruitful for understanding later developments in halakhah. This is true for understanding the development of halakhah in the Talmudic period itself and it is equally significant for understanding post-Talmudic disputes, which are often grounded in conflicting readings of sugyot comprised of various historical strata.

One Cup, Two Rituals

At the root of the halakhic debate concerning the number of cups necessary for the *sheva berakhot* is the issue of using a single cup of wine to perform two distinct rituals. Mishnah Berakhot 8:5 records an early tannaitic dispute regarding the order of blessings at the conclusion of Shabbat:

בית שמאי אומרין, נר ומזון ובשמים והבדלה; ובית הלל אומרין, נר ובשמים ומזון והבדלה.	Beit Shammai say: [The order of blessings is:] lamp, food, spices and havdalah; Beit Hillel say: lamp, spices, food and havdalah.

The mishnah refers to a havdalah ritual similar to the one still used today, involving wine, fire, spices and a liturgical pronouncement marking the end of Shabbat. The specific situation under discussion is a case where people were eating a meal on Saturday night at nightfall and they wanted to combine birkat hamazon and havdalah and say them both over the same cup of wine. Beit Hillel and Beit Shammai disagree about the order of the procedure but both clearly allow the recitation of all of the blessings over a single cup of wine. Tosefta Berakhot 5:30 records a different version of the dispute and then continues with a description of a related case:

הנכנס לתוך ביתו במוצאי שבת מברך על היין ועל המאור ועל הבשמים ואומר הבדלה.	When one enters his home on Saturday night, he blesses on the wine and on the fire and on the spices and says havdalah.
ואם אין לו אלא כוס אחד מניחו לאחר המזון ומשלשלן כולן אחריו.	And if he has only one cup [of wine], he puts it aside until after the meal and attaches all of [the havdalah blessings] to the end [of birkat hamazon and says all the components over that single cup of wine].

The baraita deals with someone coming home upon or after the end of Shabbat. The normal way to do things would be to make havdalah on wine before sitting down for a meal. However, if he has only one cup of wine, he would thereby lose the opportunity to say birkat hamazon over a cup of wine, which the baraita assumes is desirable, if not obligatory.[1] Therefore, the baraita suggests a different procedure for one who has only one cup of wine: He delays making havdalah until after he eats his meal and then combines havdalah together with birkat hamazon so that both rituals are performed over a single cup of wine. Again, the tannaitic source seems to have no problem combining distinct rituals such that they are recited over a single cup of wine.

One Does Not Say Two Sanctifications Over A Single Cup

The source from which the medieval halakhic authorities derive their concern over using a single cup of wine to perform two distinct rituals is found on Bavli Pesahim 102a–b. The sugya appears in the context of discussions of

---

[1] Reciting birkat hamazon over a cup of wine is common and expected in many rabbinic sources. See Mishnah Berakhot 6:5–6; 8:5,8; Tosefta Berakhot 5:30; Mishnah Pesahim 10:7; Rava and R. Hanan's discussion on Bavli Pesahim 117b; Bavli Berakhot 52a; Bavli Pesahim 105b.

kiddush, havdalah and other rituals and actions that surround the beginning and end of sacred days.[2]

OPENING BARAITA

(1) תנו רבנן: בני חבורה שהיו מסובין וקדש עליהן היום, מביאין לו כוס של יין ואומר עליו קדושת היום ושני אומר עליו ברכת המזון[3], דברי רבי יהודה.

(1) Our Sages taught: When a group was reclining [i.e. eating a formal meal] and the holiness of the [Shabbat] day came upon them, a cup of wine is brought and kiddush is said over it. Birkat hamazon is said over a second [cup of wine].[3] This is the view of R. Yehudah.

ר' יוסי אומר: אוכל והולך עד שתחשך. גמרו: כוס ראשון מברך עליו ברכת המזון והשני אומר עליו קדושת היום.

R. Yose says: They may continue to eat until it grows dark. When they finish, he says birkat hamazon over a first cup [of wine] and over the second cup he says kiddush.

QUESTION

(2) אמאי? ונימרינהו לתרוייהו אחדא כסא!

(2) Why? They should say both [kiddush and birkat hamazon] over a single cup!

| Tannaitic Source | Amoraic Source | Stammaitic Source |

---

[2] The text here follows the standard printed Vilna edition. Relevant variants from the textual tradition will be noted.

[3] Ms. Oxford reads instead: כוס של יין ראשו' אומ' עליו ברכת מזון והשני אומ' עליו קידוש היום. For a discussion of this variant, see Rashi Pesahim 102a s.v. ושני and Tosafot Pesahim 102b s.v והכי גרסינן.

[4] This attribution, as is, is a historical impossibility, as R. Huna is R. Sheshet's senior and, according to BT Ketubot 69a, was the latter's teacher. This fact was already noted by R. Yaakov Emden in his gloss on this passage. R. Shmuel Strashun points out that the Rif and the Rosh report this tradition in the name of R. Huna b. R. Yehudah. I will simply refer to this position as that of R. Sheshet throughout.

EXPLANATION

(3) אמר רב הונא[4] אמר
רב ששת: אין אומרים שתי
קדושות על כוס אחד.

(3) R. Huna[4] said in the name of R. Sheshet: One does not say two sanctifications (*shtei kedushot*) over a single cup.

(4) מאי טעמא?

(4) What is the reason for this?

CLARIFICATION

(5) אמר רב נחמן בר
יצחק: לפי שאין עושין
מצות חבילות חבילות.

(5) R. Nahman b. Yitzhak said: because we do not bundle up mitzvot.

OBJECTION FROM A BARAITA

(6) ולא? והא תניא:
הנכנס לביתו במוצאי שבת
מברך על היין ועל המאור
ועל הבשמים ואחר כך
אומר הבדלה על הכוס
ואם אין לו אלא כוס
אחד מניחו לאחר המזון
ומשלשלן כולן לאחריו.

(6) We do not? Is it not taught: When one enters his home on Saturday night, he blesses on the wine and on the fire and on the spices and then says havdalah over a cup [of wine]. And if he only has one cup [of wine], he puts it aside until after the meal and attaches all of [the havdalah blessings] to the end [of birkat hamazon and says all the components over that single cup of wine].

RESOLUTION

(7) אין לו שאני.

(7) [The case of] not having [more than one cup of wine] is different.

FIRST OBJECTION TO RESOLUTION

(8) והא יום טוב שחל
להיות אחר השבת, דאית
ליה, ואמר רב: יקנ"ה!

(8) But when Yom Tov begins on Saturday night, when one does have enough wine and yet Rav said: [One says] YKNH (Yayin—Wine; Kiddush; Ner—Candle; Havdalah) [combining Kiddush and havdalah over a single cup of wine]!

| Tannaitic Source | Amoraic Source | Stammaitic Source |

RESOLUTION

(9) אמרי: מדלא אמר זמן
מכלל דבשביעי של פסח
עסקינן, דכל מאי דהוה
ליה אכיל ליה, ולית ליה.

(9) They said: Since [Rav] did not mention the blessing over time (Z=Zman=sheheheyanu), we must be dealing with the seventh day of Pesah. [By that point,] he has consumed everything he has and he does not have [more than one cup of wine].

SECOND OBJECTION TO RESOLUTION

(10) והא יום טוב ראשון
דאית ליה ואמר אביי:
יקזנ"ה, ורבא אמר יקנה"ז!

(10) But on the first day of Yom Tov, one does have [more than one cup of wine] and [with respect to the blessings said when the first day of Yom Tov begins on Saturday night] Abaye said [one says] YKZNH and Rava said [one says] YKNHZ!

RESOLUTION

(11) אלא הבדלה וקידוש
חדא מילתא היא ברכת המזון
וקידוש תרי מילי נינהו.

(11) Rather, [it must be that] havdalah and kiddush are one thing, whereas birkat hamazon and kiddush are two things.

NEW STARTING POINT

(12) גופא: יום טוב שחל
להיות אחר השבת: רב אמר
יקנ"ה, ושמואל אמר ינה"ק...

(12) Returning to the previous subject: When Yom Tov begins on Saturday night [what is the order of blessings?] Rav says: YKNH [Yayin=wine; Kiddush; Ner=Lamp; Havdalah], Shmuel says: YNHK...

| Tannaitic Source | Amoraic Source | Stammaitic Source |

The sugya begins by describing a group of people eating together on Friday afternoon close to the beginning of Shabbat. R. Yehudah rules that a cup of wine must be brought so that kiddush can be recited as soon as Shabbat begins. A second cup will be used for birkat hamazon (though it is unclear if this happens immediately or after another round of eating). R. Yose allows the group to continue eating without making kiddush. Only when they finish do they bring out two cups of wine, the first to be used for birkat hamazon and the second for kiddush.

The stam then asks (section two) why one needs *two cups* of wine, given that birkat hamazon and kiddush are being recited consecutively and could both be said over a single cup of wine. R. Sheshet (section three) explains the requirement of two cups: "One does not say two sanctifications (*shtei kedushot*) over a single cup." The exact parameters of this phrase are not clear, but it seems that each of these rituals counts as a sanctification and therefore demands and is entitled to its own cup of wine.

R. Nahman b. Yitzhak (section five) explains the religious world view that lies behind this prohibition: there is something inappropriate about bundling two mitzvot together. Granting birkat hamazon and kiddush each their own cup of wine, R. Nahman seems to be saying, treats each with greater respect and endows each with its own integrity.

The stam then objects (section six): Is it really true that we do not combine two sanctifications over one cup? In fact, the baraita cited here seems to prescribe just that: It requires (or at least sanctions) combining havdalah and birkat hamazon over a single cup of wine. But this seems to violate the rule just laid out—these are two distinct rituals that should each have their own cup. The stam offers the obvious resolution that a case where only one cup of wine is available is an exception (section seven). While the bundling of rituals is normally not allowed, here there is no choice.

The stam refutes this resolution by referring to a ruling of Rav (section eight) concerning the proper order of blessings when a person needs to do kiddush and havdalah on the same evening, as in the case of Yom Tov that begins on Saturday night. Rav rules that one begins with the blessing over the wine, proceeds with kiddush and then, before drinking, continues with the blessing over fire and the havdalah passage.[5] Rav rules that one may combine havdalah and kiddush over a single cup of wine, a seeming violation of the principle of not saying two sanctifications over a single cup. The stam responds (section nine) by positing that the absence of the *shehehiyanu* indicates that Rav refers to the last Yom Tov of Pesah. By the last day of the holiday, one's resources—including one's stores of wine—are likely depleted from a full week

---

[5] The absence of spices is debated by later commentators, but this is not significant for the current discussion.

of celebration. Therefore, Rav's halakhah again refers to the exceptional case of having only one cup of wine which the Talmud has already acknowledged differs from the normal situation.

The Talmud continues by again attempting to refute the resolution found in section seven, now citing Abaye and Rava's prescriptions for how to structure a back-to-back kiddush and havdalah scenario, with lineups of blessings that *do* include the blessing *shehehiyanu* (section ten). The presence of *shehehiyanu* proves that these amoraim refer to the first day of the festival when wine is still in abundance. Nonetheless, all of the blessings are recited over a single cup of wine, proving that two rituals can *always* be combined over one cup.

The sugya concludes by resorting to a different resolution (section eleven): Kiddush and havdalah are "one thing" and can thus be recited over one cup of wine, as we see in the teachings of Rav, Abaye and Rava. By contrast, birkat hamazon and kiddush are "two things" and cannot be combined and recited over one cup, which accounts for the protocol of two cups in the opening baraita concerning people eating Friday afternoon leading into Shabbat.

Difficulties

Despite the logical flow of the above presentation and explanation of the sugya, a close look reveals a number of difficulties in its assumptions and conclusions. The first issue concerns Rav Sheshet's statement in section three. R. Sheshet explains that the opening baraita's insistence on two cups is grounded in the principle that one may not recite two sanctifications over one cup. He implies that kiddush and birkat hamazon are each considered a sanctification. R. Nahman supports this by explaining (section five) that the problem lies in making miztvot into "bundles," presumably because each mitzvah should have its own integrity. But in the Mishnah, Tosefta and sugya which follows the quote above (and begins in section twelve) generation after generation of sages assume that kiddush and havdalah can be and often are recited over a single cup of wine. How could R. Nahman and R. Sheshet be completely unaware of these tannaitic and amoraic disputes when they formulated their broad principles about not combining two distinct rituals over one cup?

The second issue revolves around the sugya's interpretation of the second baraita (section six), which is cited because it concludes with a ruling that allows for two different rituals to be said over a single cup of wine. The resolution of limiting this to the case of a person who has only one cup of wine (section seven) is so obvious it is hard to understand why the Talmud would bring a challenge from this text in the first place.[6] Furthermore, a far better challenge could have been brought from Mishnah Berakhot 8:5 (cited above). Both Beit Shammai and Beit Hillel agree that havdalah and birkat hamazon can be said over one cup of wine, a halakhah not limited to a case where only one cup is available.[7] It is puzzling why, then, the Talmud would cite a weaker, easily refuted source, when a stronger one was so obviously available.

Finally, the seemingly neat resolution (section eleven) with which the sugya concludes leaves significant questions unanswered. According to this resolution two rituals can be combined over one cup of wine if they are essentially "one thing," as in the case of kiddush and havdalah. But if they are "two things," like kiddush and birkat hamazon, they cannot be combined. This resolution leaves two related questions unanswered, one theoretical and one practical. First: what makes two rituals, in this case kiddush and havdalah, essentially one thing?[8] Second, the practical question that follows from the above: Can havdalah and birkat hamazon be recited over one cup even when such a combination is not necessary due to lack of wine? This question is related to the status of the resolution which follows the baraita (section seven). At the conclusion of the sugya there are two possibilities for the status of this resolution: (1) The resolution in section eleven replaces the earlier resolution such that we now interpret the baraita as always allowing birkat hamazon and havdalah to be recited over one cup of wine. (2) The exception of of section seven remains, in which case birkat hamazon and havdalah can be combined only when two cups are unavailable.

---

[6] The rishonim also object to the assumption in section nine that the last day of Pesah similarly falls into the category of having only one cup of wine. See Rashbam and Tosafot Pesahim 102b s.v. דאית ליה.

[7] See Tosafot Pesahim 102b s.v. מיתיבי.

[8] For a variety of answers to this question, see: Rashi Pesahim 102b s.v. קידוש; Rambam, Laws of Shabbat 29:13; Sefer Hamikhtam Pesahim 102b s.v. גמרו; Maharam Halavah Pesahim 102b s.v. דהא.

Mentioning Shabbat in Birkat Hamazon

In order to account for these difficulties we need to look at parallel sources, beginning with two parallels to the opening baraita:

תוספתא ברכות ה:ג-ד
אורחין שהיו מסובין
אצל בעל הבית וקדש
עליהן היום ועקרו עם
חשיכה לבית המדרש
חזרו ומזגו להם את הכוס
אומרין עליו קדושת
היום דברי ר׳ יהודה.

Tosefta Berakhot 5:3–4
Guests who were reclining [at a formal meal] with their host and Shabbat began. If they leave as it is getting dark to go to the Beit Midrash, when they return, a cup of wine is poured and they say sanctification of the day (kiddush), according to R. Yehudah.

ר׳ יוסה אומר: אוכל
והולך עד שעה שתחשך.
מזגו לו כוס ראשון מברך
עליו ברכת המזון.

R. Yose says: They continue to eat into darkness. [Later,] a first cup of wine is poured and he blesses birkat hamazon over it.

מזכיר של שבת בברכת
המזון. והשני אומר
עליו קדושת היום.

One mentions Shabbat in birkat hamazon. Over the second cup, he says sanctification of the day (kiddush).

תוספתא ברכות ג:ח
לילי שבתות ולילי ימים
טובים יש בהן קדושת
היום על הכוס ויש בהן
קדושת היום בברכת המזון.

Tosefta Berakhot 3:8
On the nights of Shabbat and Yom Tov, there is a sanctification of the day (kiddush) over the cup [of wine] and there is a sanctification of the day in birkat hamazon.

שבת ויום טוב ראש
חודש וחולו של מועד
יש בהן קדושת היום
בברכת המזון ואין בהן
קדושת היום על הכוס.

[On the days of] Shabbat and Yom Tov, Rosh Hodesh and Hol Hamoed, there is sanctification of the day (kiddush) in birkat hamazon but there is no sanctification of the day over a cup [of wine].

The first text here is another version of the opening baraita of the sugya, with one very important addition: The final line emphasizes that the birkat hamazon said after this meal that began before Shabbat started must include a mention of Shabbat, since the meal is ending on Shabbat. In other words, Shabbat is sanctified in two ways once the meal is ended. First, by mentioning it in birkat hamazon and second, by saying kiddush. The second Tosefta passage is the source for the requirement to include *kedushat ha-yom*—sanctification of the day—in birkat hamazon on Shabbat. It refers to the special passage mentioning Shabbat that is added to birkat hamazon, known today as *retze.*[9]

These texts provide a background for R. Sheshet's statement (section three). R. Sheshet was not claiming that birkat hamazon in general is a kind of sanctification; rather, birkat hamazon when said *on Shabbat* contains a sanctification of the day (*retze*). It is thus the two sanctifications *of Shabbat* represented by the addition to birkat hamazon and kiddush that cannot be combined over a single cup.

R. Nahman's explanation (section five) is also brought into sharper perspective by these two toseftan passages, and in light of the following parallel as well:

בבלי סוטה ח ע״א	Bavli Sotah 8a
אין משקין שתי סוטות כאחת	We do not administer the potion to two sus-
ואין מטהרין שני מצורעין	pected adulteresses at once, nor do we purify
כאחת ואין רוצעין שני	two people with scale disease at once, nor
עבדים כאחת ואין עורפין	do we pierce the ears of two slaves at once,
שתי עגלות כאחת לפי שאין	nor do we break the necks of two calves at
עושין מצות חבילות חבילות.	once, because we do not bundle up mitzvot.

---

[9] See also Talmud Bavli Berakhot 48b, where the insertion for Shabbat into birkat hamazon is also described as קדושת היום—a sanctification of the day. Berakhot 49a rules that one who forgets to mention Shabbat in birkat hamazon but remembers before proceeding with the final blessing of הטוב והמטיב says the following: ברוך שנתן שבתות למנוחה לעמו ישראל באהבה לאות ולברית. ברוך מקדש השבת. The closing of this blessing uses the verb קדש and is identical with the close of the kiddush, showing that the addition of Shabbat into birkat hamazon and kiddush are truly just two facets of the same ritual.

This baraita,[10] quoted by the Talmud, clarifies that the concern of "bundling mitzvot" has to do with trying to save time or resources by performing two *identical* acts simultaneously. It is specifically the *similarity*, or more to the point, the *identity* of the two actions that makes it problematic to combine them. This then maps perfectly onto our now deeper understanding of R. Sheshet: The scenario in the opening baraita of our sugya is one in which two sanctifications of Shabbat are required. Each act of sanctification must be performed properly, with its own cup of wine, since Shabbat is to be sanctified separately in the context of kiddush and in the context of birkat hamazon, with all the trappings of a full cup of wine for each.

Note that neither R. Sheshet nor R. Nahman was expressing any general concern about combining two rituals over a single cup of wine. Theirs is a specific ruling regarding the necessity of maintaining the distinction between two different forms for sanctifying Shabbat, just as there was a concern for the double performance of identical mitzvot in the Sotah text.

In fact, once the sources are read in this way, it is possible to see that the baraita allowing one to combine havdalah and birkat hamazon on Saturday night (section six) and Rav's statement allowing one to combine havdalah and kiddush (section eight) were almost certainly known by the amoraim R. Sheshet and R. Nahman b. Yitzhak. Indeed, these later amoraim may well have been explaining the need for two cups in the opening baraita specifically in light of the fact that the second baraita has no problem combining havdalah and birkat hamazon and Rav has no problem combining havdalah and kiddush—if these rituals can be combined, why cannot kiddush and birkat hamazon work the same way? R. Sheshet and R. Nahman provide a theory for why the case in the first baraita is different: it deals with *shtei kedushot*—two sanctifications of Shabbat—and is thus different from the other case which combined two distinct rituals over a single cup of wine. R. Sheshet and R. Nahman were well aware of the tannaitic and early amoraic traditions that allow for various combinations of rituals over a single cup of wine. Those cases involve two rituals for two different things and would have been irrelevant to their concern about two rituals which accomplish the same thing.

---

[10] The parallel in Sifre Zuta Naso p. 19 attests to the tannaitic authenticity of the baraita.

Historical Reconstruction

We would like to suggest that this sugya's building blocks were originally two independent sugyot with a tannaitic base and amoraic glosses. The first sugya would have consisted of the following:

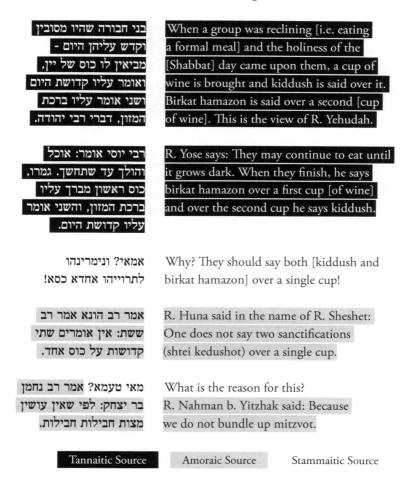

בני חבורה שהיו מסובין וקדש עליהן היום - מביאין לו כוס של יין, ואומר עליו קדושת היום ושני אומר עליו ברכת המזון, דברי רבי יהודה.	When a group was reclining [i.e. eating a formal meal] and the holiness of the [Shabbat] day came upon them, a cup of wine is brought and kiddush is said over it. Birkat hamazon is said over a second [cup of wine]. This is the view of R. Yehudah.
רבי יוסי אומר: אוכל והולך עד שתחשך. גמרו, כוס ראשון מברך עליו ברכת המזון, והשני אומר עליו קדושת היום.	R. Yose says: They may continue to eat until it grows dark. When they finish, he says birkat hamazon over a first cup [of wine] and over the second cup he says kiddush.
אמאי? ונימרינהו לתרווייהו אחדא כסא!	Why? They should say both [kiddush and birkat hamazon] over a single cup!
אמר רב הונא אמר רב ששת: אין אומרים שתי קדושות על כוס אחד.	R. Huna said in the name of R. Sheshet: One does not say two sanctifications (shtei kedushot) over a single cup.
מאי טעמא? אמר רב נחמן בר יצחק: לפי שאין עושין מצות חבילות חבילות.	What is the reason for this? R. Nahman b. Yitzhak said: Because we do not bundle up mitzvot.

Tannaitic Source	Amoraic Source	Stammaitic Source

In this reconstructed sugya the baraita describing the use of two cups of wine when a meal enters into Shabbat is the foundation for some amoraic reflection on the conceptual basis for this practice.[11] As stated above, the amoraim specifically address the question of why the two rituals cannot be recited over one cup.

The second originally independent sugya would have consisted of the following sections:

הנכנס לביתו במוצאי שבת מברך על היין, ועל המאור, ועל הבשמים, ואחר כך אומר הבדלה על הכוס. ואם אין לו אלא כוס אחד - מניחו לאחר המזון ומשלשלן כולן לאחריו.	When one comes home on Saturday night, he blesses on the wine and on the fire and on the spices and then says havdalah over a cup [of wine]. And if he has only one cup [of wine], he reserves it until after the meal and attaches all of [the havdalah blessings] to the end [of birkat hamazon and says all the components over that single cup of wine].
יום טוב שחל להיות אחר השבת. אמר רב: יקנ"ה... אמר אביי: יקזנ"ה, ורבא אמר יקנה"ז...	And when Yom Tov begins on Saturday night [what is the order of blessings?] Rav says: YKNH...Abaye says: YKZNH, Rava says: YKNHZ...

| Tannaitic Source | Amoraic Source | Stammaitic Source |

The baraita about the order of the blessings of havdalah and reciting it and birkat hamazon over one cup of wine serves as the jumping off point for an amoraic debate as to what the order would be if Saturday night was also the start of Yom Tov. Since this baraita is the *only* tannaitic text to discuss the order of the blessings of havdalah without any reference to food (Mishnah Berakhot 8:5 mentions food), it is the logical context in which to discuss how to merge kiddush with havdalah at the beginning of a meal, when birkat hamazon would obviously not be recited.

Rather than leave these two baraitot, both found in Tosefta Berakhot chapter five, with their amoraic commentary as is, the redactor chose to integrate them into a larger structure. Many of the passages in chapter five of the Tosefta are cited in series in the first section of the tenth chapter of Bavli

---

[11] The stammaitic questions were added to the sugya in order to clarify the impetus for the amoraic statements made directly on the baraita.

Pesahim. Those passages form a kind of skeleton of pre-existing material about kiddush, havdalah and eating across Shabbat time boundaries, on which the Talmud's redactors build and expand. The fact that these two sugyot share a topic—balancing eating and sanctification rituals when crossing ritual time boundaries—led the redactor to weave the two together.

Below we reconstruct the sugya noting the historical order in which the separate elements would have been redacted into the sugya:

תנו רבנן: {1a} בני חבורה שהיו מסובין וקדש עליהן היום - מביאין לו כוס של יין, ואומר עליו קדושת היום ושני אומר עליו ברכת המזון, דברי רבי יהודה.

Our Sages taught: {1a} When a group was reclining [i.e. eating a formal meal] and the holiness of [the Shabbat day] came upon them, a cup of wine is brought and kiddush is said over it. Birkat Hamazon is said over a second [cup of wine]. This is the view of R. Yehudah.

רבי יוסי אומר: אוכל והולך עד שתחשך. גמרו, כוס ראשון מברך עליו ברכת המזון, והשני אומר עליו קדושת היום.

R. Yose says: They may continue to eat until it grows dark. When they finish, he says birkat hamazon over a first cup [of wine] and over the second cup he says kiddush.

{3} אמאי? ונימרינהו לתרוייהו אחדא כסא!

{3} Why? They should say both [kiddush and birkat hamazon] over a single cup!

אמר רב הונא אמר רב ששת: אין אומרים שתי קדושות על כוס אחד.

R. Huna said to R. Sheshet: One does not say two sanctifications (shtei kedushot) over a single cup.

מאי טעמא?

What is the reason for this?

אמר רב נחמן בר יצחק: לפי שאין עושין מצות חבילות חבילות.

R. Nahman b. Yitzhak said: Because we do not bundle up mitzvot (*havilot havilot*).

Tannaitic Source	Amoraic Source	Stammaitic Source

{4a} We do not? {1b} Is it not taught: When one enters his home on Saturday night, he blesses on the wine and on the fire and on the spices and then says havdalah over a cup [of wine]. And if he only has one cup [of wine], he puts it aside until after the meal and attaches all of [the havdalah blessings] to the end [of birkat hamazon and says all the components over that single cup of wine].

ולא? והא תניא: {4a}
הנכנס לביתו במוצאי {1b}
שבת מברך על היין, ועל
המאור, ועל הבשמים,
ואחר כך אומר הבדלה על
הכוס. ואם אין לו אלא כוס
אחד - מניחו לאחר המזון
ומשלשלן כולן לאחריו.

{4a} [The case of] not having [more than one cup of wine] is different.

אין לו שאני. {4a}

{4b} But when Yom Tov begins on Saturday night, when one does have enough wine and yet Rav said: [One says] YKNH (Yayin—Wine; Kiddush; Ner—Candle; Havdalah) [combining Kiddush and havdalah over a single cup of wine]!

והא יום טוב שחל {4b}
להיות אחר השבת, דאית
ליה, ואמר רב: יקנ"ה!

They said: Since [Rav] did not mention the blessing over time (Z=Zman=sheheheyanu), we must be dealing with the seventh day of Pesah. [By that point,] he has consumed everything he has and he does not have [more than one cup of wine].

אמרי: מדלא אמר זמן -
מכלל דבשביעי של פסח
עסקינן, דכל מאי דהוה
ליה אכיל ליה, ולית ליה.

{4c} But on the first day of Yom Tov, one does have [more than one cup of wine] and [with respect to the blessings said when the first day of Yom Tov begins on Saturday night] Abaye said [one says] YKZNH and Rava said [one says] YKNHZ!

והא יום טוב ראשון, {4c}
דאית ליה, ואמר אביי:
יקזנ"ה, ורבא אמר יקנה"ז!

Rather, [it must be] that havdalah and kiddush are one thing, whereas birkat hamazon and kiddush are two things.

אלא: הבדלה וקידוש
- חדא מילתא היא,
ברכת המזון וקידוש
- תרי מילי נינהו.

| Tannaitic Source | Amoraic Source | Stammaitic Source |

גופא, {2} יום טוב שחל	Returning to the previous subject: {2} When Yom
להיות אחר השבת. רב	Tov begins on Saturday night [what is the order of
אמר: יקנ"ה, ושמואל	blessings?] Rav says: YKNH [Yayin=wine; Kiddush;
אמר: ינה"ק...אביי אמר:	Ner=Lamp; Havdalah], Shmuel says: YNHK...
יקזנ"ה, ורבא אמר: יקנה"ז.	

Tannaitic Source	Amoraic Source	Stammaitic Source

In this sugya, the redactor has beautifully woven together the two earlier sugyot by making two major moves: (1) He used the second baraita (section 1b) as a challenge to the amoraic glosses in the first part (section three), exploiting the fact that the second baraita also deals with grouping two rituals around one cup, even though this seems to force a reinterpretation of the phrase *shtei kedushot* and a broadening of the sense of *havilot havilot* from its parallel usage in Sotah. (2) He created a literarily and mnemonically appealing three-part challenge/resolution structure that incorporates the next three major pieces of material (section 4a-4c): the baraita, Rav's statement and Abaye and Rava's statements.

The amoraic material in this sugya about how to structure kiddush and havdalah appears in the subsequent sugya in the Bavli (beginning in section two above) and was thus originally independent of this sugya's use of parts of it (sections 4b and 4c) as challenges against the baraita.[12] These opinions were not cited because they serve as the *best* prooftexts for the argument constructed by the Talmud, nor because they actually refer only to the last day of Pesah. Rather, their teachings were core materials located in close proximity prior to this sugya taking final form. In cases such as this, the material's later insertion into another literary unit leads to challenges and resolutions that are somewhat forced and artificial. For example, the third answer (4c) essentially eliminates the need for the first answer (4a). In any event, their inclusion accomplishes the literary goal of linking these units together in a larger structure, even if it leaves somewhat vague definitions of "one thing" (חדא מילתא) and "two things" (תרי מילי).

---

[12] This conforms to the pattern noticed by Talmud scholar Avraham Weiss, *Lekorot Hithavut Habavli: Gufa Veamar Mar* (Jerusalem: Makor, 1969). The term גופא, while presenting itself as returning the reader for a second look at material that was introduced for another purpose, in fact usually highlights material that was historically present at an earlier stage of development.

A few important interpretational shifts happen as a result of the two sugyot being redacted into one. First of all, when the baraita from the second sugya concerning havdalah and birkat hamazon (1b) was used as a challenge to R. Nahman's explanation—"Because we do not bundle up mitzvot"—the concept was expanded to apply to any case that involves combining two rituals over one cup. It was no longer limited to a concern of doing the *same* ritual (i.e. *kedushat hayom*) over a single cup as was the case in the original baraita (Friday night kiddush and *retze* in birkat hamazon). The only halakhic dispensation for using a single cup for any two rituals would be the situation described in the baraita, when he does not have two cups of wine.

The biggest upheaval that occurred as a result of the combination of the sugyot is the complete reversal of when mitzvot should not be bundled. As a result of the "one thing" resolution (4c), the sugya ends up concluding that there is a bigger problem in combining things that are different (birkat hamazon and kiddush) than things that are similar (havdalah and kiddush). This stands in complete opposition to the original concern of "We do not bundle up mitzvot" as it is understood in the baraita in Sotah and in R. Nahman's words. The baraita prohibited the simultaneous performance of two *identical* rituals, and R. Nahman used the concept to explain why birkat hamazon and Kiddush on Friday night cannot be recited over a single cup of wine—they are both *kedushot*, two versions of the same thing. Paradoxically, by the time the Bavli's sugya has been completed, birkat hamazon and kiddush cannot be combined because they are different and not because they are the same!

The Impact of Redaction on Halakhah

The redaction that this sugya underwent had a deep impact on practical halakhah, specifically on the case of Jewish wedding rituals. Below we will show how divergent reading strategies that stem from different approaches to the impact of the editing of the sugya produced different halakhic results.

The simplest path through the linear logic of the redacted sugya leads to the following conclusion: One may not combine two rituals over one cup of wine *unless* (a) one only has one cup of wine *or* (b) the two rituals are considered "one thing." More specifically, birkat hamazon and kiddush, which the sugya explicitly labels as "two things," must be said over two cups of wine. Birkat hamazon and havdalah would also have to be said over two cups of wine unless (a) one considers them to be "one thing" or (b) one has access to only one cup of wine. Indeed, many medieval authorities rule just this way.[13]

But, as we saw in our reconstruction of the sugya, there are deep roots to the tradition of saying birkat hamazon and havdalah over a single cup (Mishnah Berakhot 8:5). Even according to the sugya's final redaction, this ruling would be preserved by stipulating that birkat hamazon and havdalah are "one thing" and that this replaces the resolution of a case in which only one cup is available (section seven), which would have limited the permission to combine them to a case where he had only one cup. This interpretive debate is precisely what drives a practical dispute between Rambam and Ra'avad. Rambam codifies the Talmudic material we have seen as follows:

רמב"ם הלכות שבת כט:יב-יג	**Rambam Laws of Shabbat 29:12–13**
היה אוכל בשבת, ויצא השבת והוא בתוך סעודתו—גומר סעודתו, ונוטל ידיו, ומברך ברכת המזון על הכוס, ואחר כך מבדיל עליו...	If someone was eating on Shabbat [afternoon], and Shabbat concluded as he was in the middle of his meal, he finishes his meal, washes his hands and recites birkat hamazon over a cup [of wine] and then recites havdalah over it...
היה אוכל וגמר אכילתו עם הכנסת שבת, מברך ברכת המזון תחילה; ואחר כך מקדש על כוס שני. ולא יברך ויקדש על כוס אחד—שאין עושין שתי מצוות בכוס אחד, שמצות קידוש היום ומצות ברכת המזון, שתי מצוות של תורה הן.	If he was eating and completed his meal just as Shabbat was about to begin, he first recites birkat hamazon [over a cup of wine] and then recites kiddush over a second cup. He should not recite birkat hamazon and kiddush over a single cup because we do not perform two mitzvot over a single cup, for the mitzvah of kiddush and the mitzvah of birkat hamazon are two [separate] biblical mitzvot.

Ra'avad comments upon the bolded phrase above: "בשאין לו אלא אותו כוס—This applies when he only has that single cup of wine." Ra'avad is bothered by Rambam's blanket authorization to recite birkat hamazon and havdalah over a single cup of wine, for the sugya specifically asserts that this violates the

---

[13] See Rashbam Pesahim 106a s.v. ושמע מינה.

principle of performing two rituals over a single cup. The baraita's authorization to combine the two was limited—as its own language indicated—to a case where only one cup of wine was available (section seven). Ra'avad's legal conclusion here closely hews to the linear flow of the sugya.

But Rambam consciously omitted the condition of having a single cup of wine, likely sensing the broader authorization for combining rituals over a single cup in the tannaitic sources and in the amoraic material about combining kiddush and havdalah. Instead, he used the sugya's conclusion to arrive at a creative reading of "one thing" as referring to a set of two rituals only one of which has biblical status (in this case, birkat hamazon, havdalah being of rabbinic status). While this is almost certainly not the plain and original sense of "one thing," Rambam's interpretation returns to a certain extent to the earlier strata of the sugya, where combining rituals over a single cup is in fact rarely problematic, especially in the case of birkat hamazon and havdalah. Rambam thus returns to the plain sense of the baraita (section six) and jettisons the requirement to have only one cup of wine left in order to combine these rituals. This debate is thus a result of how these halakhic authorities choose to read the sugya. Furthermore, the halakhic choices of these rishonim align with their biases as to whether to prefer the underlying sources of the sugya (Rambam) or to allow the sugya's literary frame to redefine the terms of those sources (Ra'avad).[14]

The halakhic impact wrought by the editors becomes even more striking in the context of Jewish wedding rituals. Originally, the legal procedures of *erusin* (betrothal) and *nisuin* (marriage) were separated by as much as a year. *Erusin* marked the bride's status as bound to the groom, such that a divorce would be necessary to dissolve the union, but co-habitation and other elements of marriage became permissible and took effect only after the *nisuin*. Each of these rituals involves blessings and a cup of wine. In the middle ages, the two ceremonies were compressed into one, as they remain in common practice to this today. Once they were combined, it is clear that many communities simply recited both the *erusin* and *nisuin* blessings over a single cup of wine.

---

[14] See M.S. Feldblum, "The Impact of the 'Anonymous Sugyah' on Halakic Concepts", *PAAJR* 37 (1969), 20–21; idem. "Pesakav Shel HaRambam Le'or Gishato Lehomer Hastami Shebabavli," *PAAJR* 46–47 (1980), 111–120; Yaakov Levinger, *Darkhey Hamahshavah Hahilkhatit Shel HaRambam* (Jerusalem: Herbew University Magnes Press, 1965), 155–181; David Sykes, "Stiyotav Shel HaRambam Memekorotav Bahalakhah," *Diney Yisrael* 13–14 (1986–1987), 113–151.

We have reports to this effect from R. Meshullam b. Natan[15] and R. Menahem Hameiri of Provence.[16] This tradition, despite being an innovation in light of the joining of *erusin* and *nisuin* in one moment in time, fits with the tannaitic and amoraic record on combining rituals over one cup of wine. Since *erusin* and *nisuin* are not two aspects of the same thing—as are kiddush and birkat hamazon on Shabbat—it would be permissible to recite them over one cup.

However, as we saw, the editorial level of the sugya took things in a different direction, allowing rituals to be combined over one cup only when they are חדא מילתא, which many read as meaning that the two rituals are essentially the same. Since *erusin* and *nisuin* are plainly different, this would argue for maintaining two cups of wine, even when they are performed consecutively. In a sense, using two cups of wine is conservative, as it maintains the original distinctiveness of *erusin* and *nisuin*. But it is also very odd to say a blessing over the wine twice in a row over two different cups when drinking them at such a short interval from one another.[17] Indeed, Rashi is said to have instituted the reading of the ketubah between *erusin* and *nisuin* so as to make it more plausible that two blessings over wine should be said, in keeping with the notion that a new blessing is required whenever one's focus has been diverted elsewhere. It is clear that the editorial voice of our sugya played a significant role in pushing some authorities to insist on two cups in what they felt was a "two things" case. R. Tam and the communities he influenced in France staunchly defended this custom[18] and it eventually became dominant and standard.[19]

Finally, the redaction of this sugya had a deep effect on the mechanics of the *sheva berakhot* recited at the end of birkat hamazon for the first week

---

[15] Sefer Hayashar, Responsa, 47:7.

[16] Beit Habehirah Pesahim 102b.

[17] R. Meshullam argues that the entire amoraic debate around the proper order of a combined kiddush and havdalah in the case of a Yom Tov that begins on Saturday night is in fact based on an assumption that it would be forbidden to split these in two, for fear of saying an unnecessary blessing over two cups of wine! An additional unnecessary blessing—known as a ברכה שאינה צריכה—is a potentially serious offense of taking God's name in vain.

[18] Sefer Hayashar, Responsa, 48:8; Tosafot Pesahim 102b s.v. שאין. Note that Meiri is aware of this practice and says it is unnecessary.

[19] See Shulhan Arukh EH 62:9, at the end.

after the wedding. It is quite clear that the original, dominant practice was to say birkat hamazon, to follow it with the six distinctive blessings of *sheva berakhot* and to conclude with a blessing over one cup of wine that would double for *sheva berakhot* and birkat hamazon.[20] According to the original meaning of the core sources in our sugya, this makes perfect sense: These two rituals are different and combining them should be no different than combining havdalah and birkat hamazon, an accepted practice in tannaitic and amoraic settings.

But the redactional layer of our sugya again pushed some interpreters to insist that, just as birkat hamazon and kiddush are described as "two things," meaning two distinct rituals requiring two cups of wine, so, too, are birkat hamazon and *sheva berakhot*. Barring the unusual case where only one cup of wine was available, the two blessings would require separate cups of wine. A second cup would thus be set aside for the distinctive six blessings of *sheva berakhot*, whereas birkat hamazon and the blessing over the wine at its end would be said over the first cup.[21]

In the Shulhan Arukh (Even HaEzer 62:9), R. Yosef Karo notes that some require two cups but that widespread practice is to use one. R. Moshe Isserless glosses this by saying that the practice in Ashkenazi lands is to use two cups, a practice that was subsequently adapted by many non-Ashkenazim as well. This practice is ultimately the triumph of the editorial creativity of the redactors of this sugya. Every time two cups of wine are used at the end of a celebratory wedding meal, it is the halakhic real-world manifestation of the literary creativity of the Talmud's editors. The origin of double cups of wine at Jewish wedding celebrations is an example of the deep relationship between historical readings of Talmudic texts and the later development of halakhah. They are two things, as distinct as kiddush and birkat hamazon, but as is often the case, we can only fully understand one by fully understanding the other.

---

[20] See Tosafot Pesahim 102b s.v. שאין, who report that R. Meshullam defended this practice, by arguing that birkat hamazon and *sheva berakhot* should be considered חדא מילתא, since the *sheva berakhot* are said only on account of birkat hamazon. This seems to be a use of the legal language of the redactional layer of the sugya to defend a practice that reflects the pre-redactional material.

[21] This position is described as the practice of some by the Tosafot ("יש נוהגין") and the Meiri ("נהגו בקצת מקומות"). See Tosafot Pesahim 102b s.v. שאין and Beit Habehirah Pesahim 102b.

CHAPTER FIVE

WOMEN AT THE RABBINIC TABLE: BIRKAT HAMAZON

BERAKHOT 20B

Introduction

The rabbis of the Mishnah derived the commandment to recite birkat hamazon, the blessing over food, from a verse in Deuteronomy: "And you shall eat, and you shall be satisfied and you shall bless." (8:10). This commandment seems to apply to both men and women, as indeed Mishnah Berakhot 3:3 states explicitly. Yet as we shall see in this chapter, the question of women's obligation in birkat hamazon was no simple matter. In exploring this question, we employ most of the critical methodologies that we emphasize throughout this book, including comparison of the Mishnah with the Tosefta, examination of manuscript traditions of the Tosefta, comparison of the Yerushalmi with the Bavli, comparison of baraitot in the Bavli with their toseftan parallels, and separation of chronological levels within the Bavli. We again see the impact that stammaitic conceptualization had on halakhah. The stammaim create rules by which to unite disparate fields of halakhah, and by doing so, they deeply impact subsequent developments in halakhah.

However, beyond the usual textual techniques, this chapter also includes some cultural analysis. The question of women's participation in banquets and banquet rituals was a source of great contention in the Greco-Roman world, and rabbinic literature from the tannaitic period must be considered in the context of this broader discourse. Finally, the subject of women's participation in Jewish ritual serves as a springboard for our discussion of feminist/gender analysis of rabbinic literature, an issue we address in an appendix to this chapter.

The Tannaitic Texts

Mishnah Berakhot 3:3 states clearly and unambiguously that women are obligated to recite birkat hamazon:

נשים ועבדים וקטנים	Women, slaves and minors are exempt
פטורין מקריאת שמע ומן	from the recitation of the Shema and
התפילין וחייבין בתפלה	from tefillin. And they are obligated in te-
ובמזוזה ובברכת המזון.	fillah, mezuzah and birkat hamazon.

This ruling is even explained as "obvious" in a passage from the Bavli, based on the following mishnah from Kiddushin which provides a general principle as to when women are obligated or exempt from certain commandments:

משנה קידושין א:ז	**Mishnah Kiddushin 1:7**
וכל מצות עשה שהזמן	All positive, time bound commandments—
גרמה—האנשים חייבין,	men are obligated and women are exempt;
והנשים פטורות; וכל	and all positive non- timebound command-
מצות עשה שלא הזמן	ments, both men and women are obligated.
גרמה—אחד אנשים	
ואחד נשים, חייבין.	

If the mishnah in Kiddushin had already stated that women are obligated to perform non-timebound positive commandments and birkat hamazon is non-timebound, then why, the Talmud in Berakhot asks, does the mishnah in Berakhot need to restate the same halakhah:

בבלי ברכות כ ע"ב	**Bavli Berakhot 20b**
ובברכת המזון פשיטא!	And [they are obligated] in birkat hamazon.
מהו דתימא: הואיל	This is obvious! What might you have said?
וכתיב בתת ה' לכם בערב	Since it is written, In God's giving to you in
בשר לאכל ולחם בבקר	the evening meat to eat, and in the morning
לשבע (שמות טז:ח),	bread to your satisfaction (Exodus 16:8) [you
כמצות עשה שהזמן גרמא	might have thought] that this is like a positive
דמי - קמשמע לן.	timebound commandment. Therefore [the mish-
	nah] teaches us [that women are obligated].

This passage offers a reason why one might have thought that women should be exempt from birkat hamazon: perhaps it could be considered a positive timebound commandment from which women are exempt. But the comment nevertheless affirms what the mishnah states—women, as well as slaves and minors,[1] are in the end obligated in birkat hamazon. Indeed, despite the "what might you have said" statement found here, it is obvious that birkat hamazon is not a positive timebound commandment. The entire sugya, which is full of "what might you have said" comments, serves the rhetorical purpose of supporting the necessity of the laws of this mishnah. There does not really seem to be any serious consideration of the possibility that birkat hamazon is indeed time bound. Tosefta Kiddushin 1:10 lists sukkah, lulav and tefillin as paradigms of positive timebound commandments. These are timebound because there are days on which they cannot be fulfilled. Birkat hamazon can be fulfilled any day, any time of day. It is clearly not time bound.

The Yerushalmi, in a comment placed directly on the Berakhot mishnah, also affirms that women are obligated in birkat hamazon:

ירושלמי ברכות ג:ו, ו ע"ג	**Yerushalmi Berakhot 3:6, 6b**
ונשים מניין?...	How do we know that women [are obligated]?...
וברכת המזון דכתיב:	And [they are obligated] in birkat hamazon as it
ואכלת ושבעת וברכת את	is written: *and you shall eat and be satisfied and*
ה' אלהיך (דברים ח:י).	*bless the Lord your God* (Deuteronomy 8:10).

The point is clear: whoever eats must bless. Since women eat, obviously they must bless God for the food they have received.

The picture begins to get a bit more complicated in Tosefta Berakhot 5:17. There is a significant difference between the manuscript traditions of this halakhah, and therefore we have included both versions in parallel columns:

---

[1] Concerning the obligation of minors to perform commandments see Yitzhak Gilat, *Perakim Behishtalshelut Hahalakhah* (Ramat Gan: Bar Ilan University Press, 2001), 19–31. Gilat demonstrates that there was no blanket exemption from mitzvot for minors in the mishnaic period. The concept that a minor became fully obligated at the age of 13 was a Talmudic and post-Talmudic development.

Erfurt manuscript	Vienna manuscript and printed edition
נשים ועבדים וקטנים אין מוציאין את הרבים ידי חובתן.	נשים ועבדים וקטנים פטורין ואין מוציאין את הרבים ידי חובתן.
באמת אמרו אשה מברכת לבעלה בן מברך לאביו עבד מברך לרבו.	באמת אמרו אשה מברכת לבעלה בן מברך לאביו עבד מברך לרבו.
Women, slaves and children cannot aid the multitude (רבים) in fulfilling their obligation.	Women, slaves and children are exempt [from birkat hamazon] and they cannot aid the multitude (רבים) in fulfilling their obligation.
In truth they said, a woman can bless for her husband, a son for his father and a slave for his master.	In truth they said, a woman can bless for her husband, a son for his father and a slave for his master.

The difference between these two versions is really only one word but it is critical. According to the Vienna manuscript and printed edition (on the right), women are exempt from birkat hamazon, whereas the Erfurt manuscript (on the left) does not say that they are exempt, but merely that they cannot aid "the multitudes" (רבים)—a term we will deal with below—in fulfilling their obligation.

According to Lieberman, the Erfurt manuscript is the correct and original version of the Tosefta.[2] There are two main criteria he employs to support this preference. First of all, this version does not contradict the Mishnah, which obligates women to say birkat hamazon. Second, the two halves of the halakhah make more sense—a woman is obligated (section one) and therefore she can aid her husband in fulfilling his obligation (section two). In contrast, the Vienna manuscript and printed version, in which women are exempt and yet can aid their husbands in fulfilling their obligation, is

---

[2] Saul Lieberman, *Tosefta Kifshuta: Zeraim* (New York: Jewish Theological Seminary, 1956), 83–84. Lieberman notes that the version preserved in Erfurt was known to some rishonim and that it is unlikely to be a result of scribal emendation. Scribes wishing to "fix" the Tosefta to match the Mishnah would not have simply erased the word "פטורים" but would have added the word "חייבין," which is found in the Mishnah.

⬡ **Tosefta Manuscripts** The Tosefta text has survived in three manuscripts: Vienna, Erfurt, and London. The Vienna manuscript is nearly complete, while Erfurt contains the first four orders and London includes only Moed. In his critical edition of the Tosefta, Saul Lieberman chose MS Vienna as the base text for his work because the manuscript is the closest to the original textual tradition. The Erfurt version was often revised and harmonized with the Talmudim. See Lieberman, *Tosefta Kifshuta: Moed* (New York: Jewish Theological Seminary, 1962), Introduction, 13–14.

difficult because there is a general halakhic principle that only one who is obligated in a mitzvah can aid others in fulfilling their obligation (Mishnah Rosh Hashanah 3:8).

Of course, an obvious difficulty still remains with the version found in Erfurt—if a woman cannot aid the רבים, which usually means "any others," in fulfilling their obligation (section one) how can she bless on behalf of her husband (section two)? Lieberman answers this by reading the phrase in an unusual fashion. While the phrase usually means, as we shall demonstrate below, that the woman under discussion is not obligated in the particular mitzvah being discussed and therefore cannot discharge the duties any other person has to perform that mitzvah, here it refers to a *public* recitation of birkat hamazon. A woman cannot fulfill the obligation for the public because the rabbis of this period considered it disgraceful for a woman to have this type of public role, especially in connection with a meal. This understanding of the word רבים prevents the first half of the halakhah from contradicting the second half. The second half of the halakhah, "In truth they said" serves as a specific contrast with the first half.[3] Women are allowed to fulfill their husband's obligation because this is a private act, one probably performed in the home. Their husbands and other members of the household are not included in the רבים mentioned in the first half.

We should note that the same formula that Lieberman believes is secondary in Tosefta Berakhot, the one that appears in the Vienna manuscript and printed edition of Tosefta Berakhot, does appear in all manuscript traditions in two other places in the Tosefta.

---

[3] This is the typical function of "באמת אמרו" in tannaitic texts. See, for instance, Mishnah Terumot 2:1.

תוספתא ראש השנה ב:ה	**Tosefta Rosh Hashanah 2:5**
נשים ועבדים וקטנים	Women, slaves and children are exempt [from
פטורין ואין מוציאין	the shofar] and they can't aid the multi-
את הרבים ידי חובתן.	tudes (רבים) in fulfilling their obligation.
תוספתא מגילה ב:ז	**Tosefta Megillah 2:7**
נשים ועבדים וקטנים	Women, slaves and children are exempt [from
פטורין ואין מוציאין	reading the megillah] and they can't aid the
את הרבים ידי חובתן.	multitudes (רבים) in fulfilling their obligation.

In both of these cases the word רבים, which literally translates as "multitudes," is synonymous with "others"—it means that women cannot exempt *anybody* from their obligation because they themselves are not obligated. As both sources state explicitly, women are exempt from hearing the shofar or the reading of the megillah. Any person who is not obligated in a given mitzvah cannot fulfill the mitzvah on behalf of others (Mishnah Rosh Hashanah 3:8). Thus Lieberman's reading of the word in Tosefta Berakhot is admittedly against the grain. Nevertheless, the evidence does seem to support this reading. It is the reading found in the Erfurt manuscript of Tosefta Berakhot, it prevents the Tosefta from blatantly disagreeing with the Mishnah, and it prevents the two halves of the Tosefta (that she cannot exempt the multitudes, and that she can exempt her husband) from disagreeing with each other.[4]

The Tosefta teaches, therefore, that as a human being who has eaten food, a woman has a personal obligation to bless God. In contrast, she is not supposed to take a public role in aiding others in fulfilling their obligation. These same notions also emerge from another mishnah which deals with women's role vis-a-vis birkat hamazon:

משנה ברכות ז:ב	**Mishnah Berakhot 7:2**
נשים ועבדים וקטנים	Women, slaves and minors are not part of
אין מזמנין עליהם.	the invitation [to recite birkat hamazon].

---

4 Lieberman does not surmise why the word פטורים entered into the tradition preserved in Vienna and the printed edition. The most likely possibility is that this tradition was influenced by the phrase as it appears in Tosefta Rosh Hashanah and Megillah.

This mishnah refers to an important element of the recitation of birkat hamazon—the *zimmun*, or invitation. Beyond an individual's obligation to recite birkat hamazon, when a group of at least three people eat together, one is to invite the others to bless. The entire seventh chapter of Mishnah Berakhot deals with this institution, testifying to its centrality. Since the *zimmun* is a public institution, women, slaves and minors are excluded. But this does not have any implication as to their obligation to recite birkat hamazon, a personal blessing acknowledging God as the source of all sustenance.

The Role of Women in the Greco-Roman and Rabbinic Banquet

Before we proceed with our analysis of the Bavli, it would be helpful to take a broader look at the perception of a woman's role in the formal meal of the rabbinic period. What emerges from the tannaitic literature concerning birkat hamazon is a dichotomy between a woman's personal obligation and her public role. This dichotomy seems to reflect the social mores of the times—a woman was not meant to have a public role at a formal meal, one in which the רבים would be participating, but she did have a personal obligation to recite birkat hamazon, and she could take a role in reciting birkat hamazon on behalf of others in a more casual dining setting with her husband and family. The reluctance to allow women to participate actively in the rituals of formal, public dining or in the specific types of banquets frequently discussed by the rabbis, the *haburah* meal[5] and the Pesah seder, is implicated in many sources and reflects Greco-Roman norms as well. Below we will investigate some of the salient rabbinic texts, as well as touch upon a few such texts from contemporaneous non-Jewish sources which deal specifically with the issues of women reclining and drinking wine at the formal meal.

---

5 *Haburah* is a word used in tannaitic literature to refer to a group of people who are formally eating a meal together. See for instance Mishnah Eruvin 6:6. It is mentioned frequently in connection with a group of people gathered together to eat the Pesah sacrifice. See note 12 below.

Reclining

In the ancient world the position in which a person dined—reclining, sitting or standing—was reflective of his/her social status—the higher the status, the more horizontal the position. As Dennis Smith summarizes, "the act of reclining in itself was a mark of one's rank in society: only free citizens were allowed to recline."[6] In rabbinic literature, diners are usually described as reclining (see for instance Tosefta Berakhot 5:5). Mishnah Pesahim 10:1 mandates that all participants at a seder recline as a way of emphasizing their celebration of freedom. While tannaitic texts do not mention whether a woman is to recline, this concern is raised by the amoraim. In Yerushalmi Pesahim 10:1, 37b, an amora asks whether a woman must recline at the seder when in front of her husband:

רבי יוסי בעא קומי רבי	R. Yose asked in front of R. Simon: Even a slave
סימון: אפילו עבד לפני רבו	in front of his master and even a woman in
אפילו אשה לפני בעלה?	front of her husband [is obligated to recline]?

While in the Yerushalmi the question is not answered, the following source in the Bavli offers an ambivalent answer:

בבלי פסחים קח ע"א	**Bavli Pesahim 108a**
אשה אצל בעלה -	A woman who is with her husband—
לא בעיא הסיבה.	she is not required to recline.
ואם אשה חשובה היא	But if she is an important wom-
- צריכה הסיבה.	an, she must recline.

The Bavli leaves room for situational decisions. In general, women are excluded from reclining, but there are situations in which such exclusion would not be appropriate.

Rabbinic concerns about these phenomena are clearly reflections of the broader society in which the rabbis found themselves. The connection between a person's social status and his/her posture was so significant in the Greco-Roman world that there has developed a rich scholarly literature

---

[6] Dennis Smith, *From Symposium to Eucharist: The Banquet in the Early Christian World* (Minneapolis: Augsberg Fortress, 2003), 11.

concerning the question. Matthew B. Roller has dedicated a full book to the topic, with an entire section devoted to the issue of women.[7] Here we offer just a few examples of Greco-Roman texts he cites which give voice to the anxiety surrounding women's dining posture.

The following source, composed by Isidore of Seville in the seventh century, quotes Varro, a first century B.C.E. Roman scholar:[8]

> Sedes [seats—i.e. places on the dining couches] are so called because among the old Romans there was no practice of reclining, for which reason they were also said to 'take a seat.' Afterward, as Varro says in his work, *On the Life of the Roman People*, men began to recline and women sat, because the reclining posture was deemed shameful in a woman.

While this source gives the impression that it was standard for men to recline and women to sit, a source from Valerius Maximus (first century C.E.) portrays a more nuanced picture of the contemporary situation, as well as the author's attitude towards it:[9]

> [Concerning 'old Roman custom']. Women ordinarily dined sitting next to men who reclined, a custom that passed from human dining practice to the gods: for at the feast of Jupiter he himself was invited to dine on a couch, and Juno and Minerva on chairs…Our own age cultivates this type of discipline more assiduously on the Capitol [the location of the feast of Jupiter] than in our own homes, evidently because it is of greater consequence to the commonwealth to ensure the orderly conduct of goddesses than of women.

In the beginning of this quote Valerius refers to a religious festival celebration "in which images of these three divinities were placed on the specified items of furniture."[10] Jupiter reclined while the goddesses Juno and Minerva sat on

---

[7] *Dining Posture in Ancient Rome: Bodies, Values and Status* (Princeton: Princeton University Press, 2006).

[8] Cited in Roller, 2.

[9] Cited in Roller, 96.

[10] Roller, 96.

chairs. Valerius then contrasts this archaic practice with contemporary times, where women recline when dining in their own homes. Roller summarizes the tension in Valerius's words, "Valerius clearly implies two things: first, that by his day women were likely to be found reclining in convivia…; and second, that this postural shift marks a moral decline."[11] Women's behavior was not simply a matter of custom or whim; it was an issue fraught with moral implications, in Greco-Roman literature and rabbinic literature as well.

Drinking Wine

The second issue we examine concerns the question of whether women should drink wine, specifically at a banquet, a context in which wine generally played a key role. In describing a holiday meal, Tosefta Pesahim 10:4 states:

מצוה על אדם לשמח	A man is commanded to make his chil-
בניו ובני ביתו ברגל.	dren and his wife happy on the festival.
במה משמחן?	With what does he make them happy?
ביין דכתיב: ויין ישמח לבב	With wine, as it is written: *and wine glad-*
אנוש (תהילים קד:טו).	*dens the human heart* (Psalms 104:15).
ר' יהודה אומר: נשים	R. Yehudah says: Women with what
בראוי להם וקטנים	is appropriate for them, and children
בראוי להם.	with what is appropriate for them.

Wine, according to R. Yehudah, is not appropriate for women. Other sources seem to imply that wine was appropriate for rich women (see Tosefta Ketubot 5:7; Yerushalmi Ketubot 5:11, 30b; Bavli Ketubot 64b–65a) or for women who were eating with their husbands. But regardless, it seems clear that the rabbis felt the need to limit the contexts in which it was permissible for women to drink. Since wine was emblematic of formal dining, these discussions hint at the discomfort that rabbis felt with regard to women's full and equal participation at such meals. One who did not drink wine at the meal would not have been seen as a full participant.

---

[11] Ibid.

As was the case with the issue of women reclining, rabbinic concerns and anxieties echo those that arise in Greco-Roman literature.[12] Here we cite one example of such a text, again from Valerius Maximus, this time in his work, *Memorable Deeds and Sayings* 6.3.9. He writes:

> Egnatius Metellus ... took a cudgel [heavy stick] and beat his wife to death because she had drunk some wine. Not only did no one charge him with a crime, but no one even blamed him. Everyone considered this an excellent example of one who had justly paid the penalty for violating the laws of sobriety [seriousness]. Indeed, any woman who excessively seeks the use of wine closes the door on all virtues and opens it to vices.

The violence of this source seems to be an expression of the severity of the perceived threat and perhaps of the pervasiveness of the phenomenon as well. These texts concerning women reclining and drinking wine reflect precisely the types of anxieties we would expect to exist in a world in which women's roles at formal meals were the subject of debate. Anxiety is felt most acutely when customs are changing. In a world in which women were either completely banned from the formal meal and never drank wine or in which their participation in such social rituals was completely unremarkable, there would be little reason for the impassioned debate we find in both rabbinic and Greco-Roman sources. Presumably, then, these debates developed against the background of a society in flux.[13]

---

[12] See Nicholas Purcell, "Women and Wine in Ancient Rome," *Gender, Drink and Drugs*, ed. Maryon, McDonald (London: Berg, 1994), 191–208; Matthew Dickie, *Magic and Magicians in the Greco-Roman World* (London: Routledge, 2001), 178–180; Bruce W. Winter, *Roman Wives, Roman Widows*, (Grand Rapids, MI: W. M. Eerdmans, 2003), 151–153.

[13] Besides reclining and drinking wine there is another issue in rabbinic literature which demonstrates rabbinic hesitancies as to women's participation in banquet meals—the *haburah*, or company of people who eat the Pesah sacrifice together. Mishnah Pesahim 8:7 states: "One does not make a *haburah* of women, slaves or minors." This mishnah is best interpreted as meaning that at least some adult men must be present in the *haburah*. One should not have a *haburah* consisting completely of women, slaves or minors so that, as Bar Kapara states in Yerushalmi Pesahim 8:7, 36a, "they should not bring the sacrifices to a state of disgrace."

Finally, when we consider the question of whether these sources reflect actual historical practice, we must exercise extreme caution. These are mostly prescriptive sources, not descriptions, and they were composed by a few men living in specific times and places. There is ample evidence that women did recline and did drink wine.[14] But how Jews, Greeks and Romans actually ate their meals cannot be gleaned from a few literary sources of this nature. What we can glean from these sources is the pervasive anxiety that men of this period felt concerning women's roles, which was played out undeniably at formal meals. The meal was an important social occasion in both rabbinic and Greco-Roman culture (as it is in most cultures), and the meal dictated and reinforced the social hierarchy. How a woman acted at a meal was reflective of her role vis a vis her husband, her family and the public. A woman reclining and drinking wine with men may have implied that she had attained equal social standing to her husband, a message that the male diner may or may not have wanted to convey to others.

The above texts serve as an important backdrop for our understanding of the passages concerning women and birkat hamazon. The rabbis understood that women would, at least on occasion, be present at formal banquets, but they dictated that in public they should play a less prominent role than their male counterparts. While our sugya in Berakhot is not about reclining or drinking wine together with men, the issue of a woman leading men in birkat hamazon or fulfilling the obligation on their behalf is closely related. What lies behind all of these issues is not women's presence at a meal—that seems to be taken for granted. The issue is her place in the social hierarchy vis a vis the men at the table. Does she recline in their presence, an act which would imply social equality? Does she drink wine as they do? Does she count in the number of diners required for a *zimmun*, which would again imply

---

[14] Most scholars today realize that in actual Roman practice women probably did recline. As Matthew Roller, *Dining Posture*, 98, writes: "the standard view that women changed their dining posture from sitting to reclining at one or another historically specifiable time is untenable, for it cannot be shown (contra Valerius and Varro) that women of any status ever dined seated as a matter of course." Similarly, Susan Treggiari, *Roman Marriage* (Oxford: Clarendon Press, 1991), 423 writes: "Women by the late Republic reclined at dinner and seem normally to have shared a couch with their husbands." See also Dennis Smith, *From Symposium to Eucharist*, 43, who writes: "By the first century C.E. there is evidence that respectable women of the Roman aristocratic class were increasingly to be found at banquets and would often recline."

social equality? Can she fulfill the obligation of birkat hamazon on behalf of men, a function which might imply religious and social equality? These are the questions that men, including the rabbis, seem to have been asking and debating throughout the ancient world.

Bavli Berakhot 20b

As seen above, the mishnah ruled simply that women were personally obligated to recite birkat hamazon. This is true even if they are not supposed to take a role in the public performance of birkat hamazon. Surprisingly, the nature of this unequivocal ruling is questioned in the Bavli. The Bavli begins with a short discussion of women's obligation to recite kiddush on Shabbat and on festivals. Despite the fact that this section is not directly relevant to the issue of birkat hamazon, it sets the tone for what follows and it will help us demonstrate the thought processes of some of the amoraim. Therefore, we will begin with this section of the sugya.

Section One

(1) אמר רב אדא בר אהבה: נשים חייבות בקדוש היום דבר תורה.	(1) R. Ada bar Ahava said: Women are obligated by the Torah in the sanctification of the day.
(2) אמאי? מצות עשה שהזמן גרמא הוא, וכל מצות עשה שהזמן גרמא נשים פטורות!	(2) Why? This is a positive time bound commandment, and women are exempt from all positive time bound commandments.
(3) אמר אביי: מדרבנן.	(3) Abaye said: [They are obligated] by the rabbis.
(4) אמר ליה רבא: והא דבר תורה קאמר! ועוד, כל מצות עשה נחייבינהו מדרבנן!	(4) Rava said to him: But he said "by the Torah!" And furthermore, we should obligate them rabbinically for all positive timebound commandments!

(5) אלא אמר רבא: אמר
קרא זכור (שמות כ:ז) ושמור
(דברים ה:יא) - כל שישנו
בשמירה ישנו בזכירה,
והני נשי, הואיל ואיתנהו
בשמירה - איתנהו בזכירה.

(5) Rather Rava said: Scripture states, Remember (Exodus 20:7) and Observe
(Deuteronomy 5:11): Anyone obligated to
observe [by not transgressing the negative
commandments] is obligated to remember. And women, since they are obligate to
observe, are also obligated to remember.

The passage begins with R. Ada bar Ahava stating that women are obligated
in "the sanctification of the day (קידוש היום)," despite the fact that this does
seem to fall into the category of a positive timebound commandment, from
which women are supposed to be exempt (see above, Mishnah Kiddushin
1:7). We should note that this is not the only case of an amora stating that
a woman is obligated to perform a positive timebound commandment.
There are three places in the Bavli where the amora R. Yehoshua ben Levi
states that women are obligated to perform this type of commandment: (1)
lighting Hannukah candles (Shabbat 23a); (2) drinking four cups of wine
on Pesah (Pesahim 108a); (3) reading Megillat Esther (Megillah 4a).[15] It
does not seem that these amoraim considered the mishnah from Kiddushin,
which exempts women from positive timebound commandments, to be
fully encompassing. They allowed for certain mitzvot to fall outside of its
parameters.

Abaye (section three), who lived a generation after R. Ada bar Ahavah,
seems to have a different response to the mishnah from Kiddushin. This
mishnah is now in his eyes fully prescriptive—women are not obligated
in *any* positive timebound commandments. Therefore, he interprets their
obligation for *kiddush hayom* to be only "*derabbanan*" of rabbinic and not
biblical status. This is an invention of Abaye's, meant to preserve the func-
tionality of R. Ada bar Ahavah's ruling and yet to harmonize it with the
mishnah in Kiddushin. Note that according to this interpretation, Abaye

---

[15] The obligation for women to read (or at least hear) the megillah is also found in
Yerushalmi Megillah 2:5, 73b. It is likely that this is the original context of his statement and that the Babylonian editors moved it from the context of Megillah to Shabbat candles and the four cups at the seder. We should note that these passages obligate
women to hear the megillah even though Tosefta Megillah 2:7 specifically exempts
them (see above).

is not reflective of a change in women's status, neither in his eyes nor in any sort of reality he is trying to describe. That is to say, he does not have some personal agenda to demote women's obligation, nor is he commenting that in his world women do not participate in *kiddush hayom*. Rather, he engages in the usual activity of amoraim—harmonizing one literary source with another.

Rava raises two challenges against Abaye (section four). First, there is no such category as obligated *"derabbanan"* when it comes to women's performance of commandments. Second, R. Ada bar Ahavah specifically states "from the Torah." Rava (section five) therefore defends the notion that women are obligated by the Torah for *kiddush hayom* by creating his own midrash. This midrash seems, at least in Rava's eyes, to mitigate the contradiction between R. Ada bar Ahavah's statement and the mishnah from Kiddushin. Women are generally exempt from positive timebound commandments unless there is some specific text or perhaps reason for them to be obligated (as there was in the cases of megillah, Shabbat candles and the four cups of wine, see citations above).

For the issue of birkat hamazon, to which we are about to return, the importance of this section is that it introduces the notion of women being rabbinically obligated in the performance of a mitzvah. Despite the fact that Abaye's position was rejected, the very possibility that a woman would be obligated to perform a mitzvah, but that her obligation would be less than that of a man, is the basis for the question that opens the second part of the sugya.

Section Two

QUESTION

(1) אמר ליה רבינא	(1) Ravina said to Rava : Women's ob-
לרבא: נשים בברכת המזון,	ligation in birkat hamazon—is it from
דאורייתא או דרבנן?	the Torah or from the rabbis?

Tannaitic Source	Amoraic Source	Stammaitic Source

EXPLANATION

(2) למאי נפקא מינה -
לאפוקי רבים ידי חובתן.
אי אמרת דאורייתא
- אתי דאורייתא ומפיק
דאורייתא, ואי אמרת
דרבנן - הוי שאינו מחוייב
בדבר, וכל שאינו מחוייב
בדבר - אינו מוציא את
הרבים ידי חובתן. מai?

(2) What is the practical difference? To exempt others from their obligation. If you say that it is from the Torah, then her biblical obligation can exempt another biblical obligation. But if you say it is from the rabbis, then she is not obligated in the matter, and anyone not obligated in a matter cannot fulfill the obligation for others. What [is the ruling]?

ANSWER

(3) תא שמע, באמת
אמרו: בן מברך לאביו,
ועבד מברך לרבו, ואשה
מברכת לבעלה; אבל אמרו
חכמים: תבא מארה לאדם
שאשתו ובניו מברכין לו.

(3) Come and learn: In truth they have said, a son may bless for his father and a slave may bless for his master, and a woman may bless for her husband. But the sages have said: Let a curse be brought upon a man whose wife and children bless for him.

STAMMAITIC EXPLANATION

(4) אי אמרת בשלמא
דאורייתא - אתי דאורייתא
ומפיק דאורייתא, אלא
אי אמרת דרבנן - אתי
דרבנן ומפיק דאורייתא?

(4) It goes well if you say that her obligation is from the Torah, her biblical obligation can exempt another biblical obligation. But if you say her obligation is from the rabbis, can one with a rabbinic obligation fulfill the obligation for one with a biblical obligation?

DIFFICULTY

(5) ולטעמיך, קטן
בר חיובא הוא?

(5) And according to your reasoning—is a minor obligated?

| Tannaitic Source | Amoraic Source | Stammaitic Source |

186

STAMMAITIC EXPLANATION

(6) אלא, הכא במאי
עסקינן - כגון שאכל
שיעורא דרבנן, דאתי
דרבנן ומפיק דרבנן.

(6) Rather what are we dealing with here? For instance he ate only an amount that would make him obligated in birkat hamazon from the rabbis, and the one with a rabbinic obligation could fulfill the obligation for one with a rabbanic obligation.

AMORAIC MIDRASH

(7) דרש רב עוירא, זמנין
אמר לה משמיה דרבי אמי
וזמנין אמר לה משמיה
דרבי אסי: אמרו מלאכי
השרת לפני הקדוש ברוך
הוא: רבונו של עולם, כתוב
בתורתך: אשר לא ישא
פנים ולא יקח שחד (דברים
י':יז) והלא אתה נושא פנים
לישראל, דכתיב: ישא ה'
פניו אליך (במדבר ו:כו).
אמר להם: וכי לא אשא
פנים לישראל? שכתבתי
להם בתורה: ואכלת ושבעת
וברכת את ה' אלהיך (דברים
ח:י), והם מדקדקים [על]
עצמם עד כזית ועד כביצה.

(7) R. Avira expounded, sometimes he said it in the name of R. Ami and sometimes in the name of R. Asi: the ministering angels said in front of the Holy One, blessed be He: Master of the Universe, it says in your Torah, Who does not show favorites and does not take bribes (Deuteronomy 10:17). But do you not show favor to Israel, as it says, May God show His favor to you (Numbers 6:26). He said to them: Why should I not show favor to Israel? For I have written in the Torah, And you shall eat, and you shall be satisfied and you shall bless the Lord your God (Deuteronomy 8:10). And they are stringent upon themselves and bless even when they only eat the amount of an olive or an egg.

Tannaitic Source	Amoraic Source	Stammaitic Source

The sugya opens with Ravina's question as to whether birkat hamazon for women is considered "*derabbanan,*" of rabbinic status, or "*deorayta,*" of biblical status. The question itself is surprising for several reasons. First of all, as Rava said above, the obligations set forth for women in the mishnah were all understood to be equal to those of men. While much later halakhic authorities begin to claim that women's obligation for prayer is different from that of men, nowhere else do we hear of such a claim in classic rabbinic literature.[16] Why should birkat hamazon be any different? Second, earlier in the sugya it was "obvious" that women are obligated in birkat hamazon. Why should the level of their obligation be questioned now?

There are three points that serve as the background for Ravina's question. The first is Abaye's comment above. Ravina lived slightly later than Abaye and, as can be seen here, was one of Rava's students. Abaye and subsequently Ravina seem to be open to the lack of equality between a man and a woman's obligation in the performance of certain mitzvot. Second, in general amoraim, and especially later amoraim, increasingly categorize mitzvot as rabbinic or biblical.[17] In an earlier period, while there is some such categorization, there is more of an emphasis on whether or not one is obligated to perform a given commandment.[18] In the amoraic period, there is a greater emphasis on determining whether a mitzvah that is to be performed is done so out of rabbinic command or because of a biblical mitzvah. Finally, Ravina's question may arise specifically with regard to birkat hamazon due to general anxieties about a woman's role at a meal, an issue we explored above.

If this last explanation is correct, then the stammaitic comment (section four) that follows is an accurate reflection of Ravina's intent. The point of Ravina's asking whether or not a woman's obligation is rabbinic is to question her ability to recite the blessing on behalf of men, who are certainly obligated biblically. A woman will recite birkat hamazon no matter the level of her obligation. But if her obligation is lesser in status than that of men, then she will not be able to fulfill the blessing for men.

More specifically, the stam in section two posits that what lies behind Ravina's question is a woman's ability to discharge the obligation of the רבים.

---

[16] See Judith Hauptman, "Women and Prayer: An Attempt to Dispel Some Fallacies," *Judaism* 42:1 (1993) 94–103.

[17] See Benjamin De Vries, *Toldot Hahalakhah Hatalmudit* (Tel Aviv: Abraham Zioni Publishing House, 1966), 69–95.

[18] The obligation to eat bitter herbs on Pesah is a good example. The Mekhilta de-Rabbi Ishmael Pisha 6 establishes that one is obligated to eat marror even without the Pesah sacrifice, meaning even after the destruction of the Temple. It says nothing about the level of obligation. Bavli Pesahim 120a says that without a Pesah sacrifice the obligation for marror is rabbinic.

Above we saw that in the Tosefta, as explained by Lieberman, the word רבים was not synonymous with אחרים, any others. Rather it was specific—a woman cannot exempt the *multitudes*, i.e. the public, from their obligation, even though she can exempt her husband. In consequence, Lieberman notes that word as it used in the Bavli here (section two) is not precise; the Bavli means to say אחרים, and indeed this is the version preserved in the commentary of R. Asher.

The key to this shift in meaning is found in the fact that the version of the baraita quoted by Rava in section three in order to answer Ravina's question does not contain the line found in the Tosefta, "Women, slaves and children cannot aid the multitudes (רבים) in fulfilling their obligation" but does contain the second line, that a woman can bless for her husband. Taken together these two lines in the Tosefta demonstrate the distinction between the רבים, whose obligation she cannot fulfill, and her husband, whose obligation she can fulfill. In the Bavli, which does not contain this first line of the baraita, the distinction does not exist. To Rava and to the stam, either a woman is obligated to say birkat hamazon and she can bless for *any* man, or she is not obligated and she cannot bless for *any* man (unless he, too, is not obligated, as we shall see below). Rava uses this version of the baraita to prove that women are obligated to say birkat hamazon, since they can exempt any other person. Thus the original amoraic core of the sugya would have consisted of Ravina's opening question followed by Rava's response from the abbreviated baraita found in section three. The stam explained Ravina's question in section two and Rava's answer in section four.

The other difference between the baraita in the Tosefta and the version in the Bavli is that in the Bavli there is an additional line: "let a curse come upon a man whose wife or children bless for him." The origin of this line is found in Mishnah Sukkah 3:10 which reads:

מי שהיה עבד או אשה או קטן מקרין אותו עונה אחריהן מה שהן אומרין, ותהי לו מאירה.	One who has a slave, a woman, or a minor read [the Hallel] to him, he must repeat after them what they say, and a curse be upon him.

This line has a slightly different meaning in the context of Hallel in Mishnah Sukkah.[19] It is easier to understand why a husband whose wife must recite Hallel for him is cursed than why a husband whose wife must recite birkat hamazon for him his cursed because of two key differences between these prayers. First, Hallel is probably (although not necessarily) recited in the synagogue and thus it is a more public affair. In ancient times it would have been perceived as exceedingly shameful for a husband (or for any man) to require a woman to read for him in such a setting. In contrast, birkat hamazon can be (but is not always) more of a private affair, as explained above. While a man whose wife must recite birkat hamazon for him might feel ignorant, shame is usually a publicly experienced emotion and thus would not be as powerful when experienced in the home. Second, Hallel is written Scripture. The verb used in the Mishnah is "read for him", which can mean that she is reading a text that her husband simply cannot read. That is not to say that written scripture was so readily available that Hallel would have always or even normally been read from a scroll. But at least the possibility exists. Furthermore, the biblical text of Hallel was more widely-known than a rabbinic text such as birkat hamazon would have been. A woman reading Hallel for her husband implies that he cannot even read the familiar text of Hallel. In contrast, blessings were transmitted only orally. Thus the woman *recites* for her husband. While this does imply that she knows how to recite birkat hamazon and is more learned than him, at least there is no implication that he is completely illiterate.

---

[19] In Yerushalmi Berakhot 3:6, 6b, this mishnah from Sukkah is cited in juxtaposition with the baraita concerning women and children blessing birkat hamazon for others but only in the Bavli is the curse also applied to a woman who recites birkat hamazon for her husband. Further evidence as to the origin of this line can be found in the fact that the same baraita concerning birkat hamazon is quoted in Bavli Sukkah 38a, immediately following the mishnah concerning Hallel. It is not commented upon there by any amoraim, and thus it seems likely that the editors in Sukkah brought it from Berakhot due to the already existent similarity. Thus the curse line originated in Mishnah Sukkah in the context of Hallel, in Yerushalmi Berakhot Mishnah Sukkah was quoted in the context of a baraita concerning women and birkat hamazon, and in Bavli Berakhot the curse line was added to the baraita itself. From there, the baraita concerning birkat hamazon was cited but not commented upon in Bavli Sukkah.

As is almost always the case in these situations, we cannot know who added this line to the baraita or when it was added, but it does seem to have been added before Rava, a mid-fourth century amora. Rava cites the baraita as concrete proof that a woman does have a biblical obligation to recite birkat hamazon because, as the stam notes in section four, if her obligation were only of rabbinic origin, she would not be able to aid a man in fulfilling his obligation.

Sections five and six contain a refutation of the proof that Rava cites in section three. The language and terms indicate that the provenance of these lines is stammaitic. The stam seems to agree with Abaye from the previous section of the sugya, that women's obligation for these commandments is rabbinic. The stammaitic strategy is to compare the obligation of a woman to that of a minor, whose obligation is clearly not biblical (again, according to the stam, similar to the Yerushalmi cited below). Since the baraita allows a minor to bless for his father, the stam must assume that the man being described himself has only a rabbinic obligation to recite birkat hamazon. And if so, the woman's obligation may be rabbinic as well. Importantly, nowhere else in the entire corpus of rabbinic literature do we directly learn that there is such a thing as a *rabbinic* obligation for a man to recite birkat hamazon, i.e. an obligation to recite birkat hamazon when a biblical obligation does not exist. The stam invents such a notion by drawing on R. Avira's statement, found in section seven.

The original context of R. Avira's statement is clearly an explanation of Mishnah Berakhot 7:2 (the same mishnah that discusses women and the *zimmun*):

עד כמה מזמנין? עד כזית.	How much [must one have eaten] in order for
ר' יהודה אומר עד כביצה.	them to recite an invitation? As much as an olive. Rabbi Judah says: as much as an egg.

R. Avira praises Israel for offering such a strict interpretation of the phrase "and you shall be satisfied" from Deuteronomy 8:10. His statement has nothing to do with categorizing men's obligation as biblical or rabbinic. This is the stammaitic interpretation of his statement, one which the rishonim found exceedingly problematic and controversial. But this is the nature of the stammaim, as we have seen throughout our analysis of Babylonian sugyot.

The stam is willing to create a new halakhic category, in this case a rabbinic obligation for men to recite birkat hamazon, as long as through that category a difficulty can be solved—how can women recite birkat hamazon for their husbands if the former have a rabbinic obligation and the latter's obligation is biblical?

Finally, we might also be able to detect a stammaitic halakhic "agenda" in this resolution. Yerushalmi Berakhot also asks how a minor can bless for his father.

ירושלמי ברכות ג:ג, ו ע״ג	**Yerushalmi Berakhot 3:3, 6b**
וקטן לאביו?	And a son [can recite birkat hamazon] for his father?
לא כן א״ר אחא בשם ר' יוסי ביר' נהוראי: כל שאמרו בקטן כדי לחנכו.	Did not R. Aha say in the name of R. Yose son of R. Nehorai: Anything said about a minor's [obligation] is only in order to educate him.
תיפטר בעונה אחריהן אמן.	You can solve this by saying that he (the father) answers amen after him.
כיי דתנינן תמן: מי שהיה עבד או אשה או קטן מקרין אותו עונה אחריהן מה שהן אומרים ותהא לו מאירה. אבל אמרו תבוא מאירה לבן עשרים שצריך לבן עשר.	Like that which is taught there: The one whose slave or wife or son reads for him [the Hallel] must answer after them whatever they say. And a curse be upon him. But they (the sages) said a curse should be upon the twenty year old who needs a ten year old.

We cannot be certain whether the traditions found in the Yerushalmi were known in Babylonia.[20] But if they were, it is significant that the stam does not choose to accept the Yerushalmi's answer as to how a minor could bless for his father—that his father repeats the words after him. Had the stam answered his own question, "can a minor be obligated" (section five) in this manner, then Rava's answer to

---

[20] For a review of the scholarly debate see Alyssa Gray, *A Talmud in Exile: the Influence of Yerushalmi Avodah Zarah on the Formation of Bavli Avodah Zarah* (Providence: Brown Judaic Studies, 2005), 9–15.

the original question could have stood. A child, whose obligation can only be rabbinic, could recite the birkat hamazon with his father repeating the words after him, and the simple meaning of the baraita with regard to a woman could have been retained—a woman is obligated biblically to recite birkat hamazon and therefore she can aid her husband in his fulfillment of the mitzvah. Thus the stam goes one step further than the transmitter of the baraita, who added the line "let a curse be brought upon a man..." This transmitter, who seems to have preceded Rava, believed, assumedly, that it was not respectable for a husband to have his wife recite the birkat hamazon for him, but that she was legally empowered to do so. Rava, who quoted the baraita, answered that a woman is indeed obligated by the Torah to recite birkat hamazon. In contrast, the stam believes that in general this is not even possible. The only case in which a wife could recite birkat hamazon on behalf of her husband is when his obligation is only rabbinic and therefore matches hers. And even then—"let a curse be brought upon a man whose wife and children bless for him."

The Impact of the Stam on Halakhah

The stammaitic resolution found in section six had substantial impact on two areas of halakhah. First, as we just stated, had the sugya ended with Rava's answer to Ravina's question (section three), the halakhah would have clearly been that women are obligated by the Torah to recite birkat hamazon. They would have been able to aid anyone in discharging their obligation.

Second, this is the only sugya in which we learn that someone who has not eaten to satisfaction is obligated to say birkat hamazon only from rabbinic authority. Indeed, as the rishonim point out, there are other places in the Talmud in which it is clear that as long as one ate an olive's worth of food, he is obligated and can bless for others who ate to their satisfaction.[21] To solve this problem most rishonim reluctantly answer that even if the man's obligation is only rabbinic because he did not eat to his satisfaction, he can fulfill the obligation of any man, even one who did eat to his satisfaction. In other words, while most rishonim do accept the halakhah embedded in this stammaitic comment—men who eat more than an olive's worth of food but

---

[21] See the discussion of the Baal HaMeor and the Ramban on the Rif.

do not eat to satisfaction are required to recite birkat hamazon only from rabbinic authority—they utterly reject any implications this has on a man's behavior. The only implication it has is for a woman's and a child's behavior.[22] Women can bless for their husbands and minors can bless for their fathers only if the adult male ate to less than satisfaction.

Finally, this sugya is a case in which R. Yitzhak Alfasi (11th century, North Africa), known more famously as the Rif, simply ignores the stammaitic sections of the sugya and rules according to what he perceives to be the simple meaning of the texts, specifically the mishnah and the baraita. This is a common phenomenon with the Rif's rulings[23] and in this case he is supported by the Raavad (12th century Provence) and Nachmanides[24] (12th century, northern Spain) as well. All three rule that women are simply obligated to recite birkat hamazon without qualification. In contrast, Maimonides (12th century, Spain and Egypt) adds that we are not sure whether this obligation is biblical or rabbinic, thereby restoring the stam's comments to the sugya. Since this is also Rabbenu Asher's (13th century, Germany and then Spain) ruling, as well as that of the Tosafot and many other rishonim, the eventual halakhah as encoded in the Shulkan Arukh is made to fit the stammaitic comments in section six. In this case, as in many others, the stam's comments end up having a decisive influence on halakhic history.

Conclusion

The topic of women's obligation in birkat hamazon showcases the variety of critical techniques available to the modern Talmudic scholar. Textual analysis allowed us to tease out a tension that existed in the tannaitic period between

---

[22] Later halakhic authorities (see Mishnah Berurah Orah Hayyim 184:15) apply this issue to the case of one who is not sure whether he recited birkat hamazon. If birkat hamazon is rabbinic because the person ate to less than his satisfaction, then he would not be obligated to recite birkat hamazon. However, the rishonim rule that if one is not sure if he recited birkat hamazon, he must go back and recite it. See Rambam, Laws of Blessings 2:14.

[23] See Israel Ta-Shma, *Hasifrut Haparshanit Latalmud* (Jerusalem: Hebrew University Magnes Press, 1999), 1:145–146.

[24] See their comments on the Rif in *Hasagot HaRaavad* and *Milhemet Hashem*.

women's personal obligation to recite birkat hamazon and the rabbinic reluctance to allow them to play a public role in banquet ritual. We showed that this tension was very much reflective of the Greco-Roman period in which the rabbis lived. We find in rabbinic literature some of the same conversations recorded in Greek literature—should women recline in the presence of men? Should they drink wine? Should they be counted among the active participants in the formal banquet? Understanding the historical context allowed for a richer understanding of why these questions arose with such intensity in tannaitic literature.

Moving on to the talmudic period, we saw how the harmonistic tendencies of the amoraim came into play with this question. How can one source exclude women from public ritual (Mishnah Kiddushin) yet other sources obligate them (R. Ada b. Ahavah)? Thus Abaye and Ravina invented the notion that women might be obligated to perform certain mitzvot (sanctification of the day and birkat hamazon), but that their obligation could be less than that of men. The stammaim applied this distinction with greater fervor, and their demotion of women to a lower level of obligation left an indelible impact on halakhah. Thus textual analysis and cultural comparison come together to provide a rich opportunity to understand the history of this particular halakhah.

FEMINIST/GENDER INTERPRETATION OF RABBINIC LITERATURE

ALIEZA SALZBERG

The chapter on women's obligation to recite birkat hamazon provides an opportunity to explore some of the techniques that scholars in the fields of feminist and gender studies have applied to the study of rabbinic literature. As we concluded, originally women had a personal obligation to thank God for the food they had eaten, but the sages were anxious about women's overt participation in public banquets and legislated accordingly. Although our analysis focused on the development of the texts and halakhot, source analysis also allowed for the recovery of viewpoints that would not have been otherwise available had the Bavli's sugya and the stam's voice overshadowed all other sources and voices. This is a common technique among modern feminist scholars, many of whom are trained in the field of source criticism, or use the work of critical scholars as the basis for their own analysis.[25] Along with the search for fissures in the text, feminist thinkers have been fascinated by knowledgeable and dynamic women, mostly wives and daughters of sages, who occasionally appear in the Talmud. What can these characters teach us about women's roles in the usually male-dominated arenas of Torah study and ritual? Answers to these questions have been complicated by modern scholars of aggadah (rabbinic legend) who have called into question our ability to recover even a kernel of historical truth from this literary genre.[26] Stories concerning learned women such as Beruriah the wife of Rabbi Meir or Yalta the wife of Rav Nahman are not simple recordings of the lives of these women and the role they actually played in the world of the men with whom they are described as interacting.

---

[25] See Tal Ilan, "Feminist Interpretations of Rabbinic Literature: Two Views," *Nashim* 4 (2001), 11–13.

[26] See Jeffrey Rubenstein, *Talmud Stories: Narrative Art, Composition, and Culture* (Baltimore: Johns Hopkins University Press, 1999), 3–15.

However, rejection of the historicity of the Talmudic record engenders questions which may be even more illuminating: If Talmudic legends are not historical records or even echoes thereof, then what are they? One answer that scholars have given is that these literary creations provide the rabbis with the opportunity to imagine the impact that their exclusionary halakhot have on women. Through the actions and voices of women in these stories, rabbis can express anxieties about their own systematic exclusion of women from the realms of Torah study and other mitzvot, without rocking the foundations of their own religious lives by directly critiquing their own halakhic system. In addition, by imputing certain dangerous or more extreme claims to women, the rabbis create space for these more countercultural voices within the Talmud.[27] Thus while scholars no longer believe that accurate history can be gleaned from aggadah, these texts have become a rich source of the intellectual history of those who composed them.[28]

Turning our attention beyond stories of women to the broader picture of rabbinic culture, feminist scholars recognize that this culture was at its core male centered—privileging the power of men, scholars, fathers, kings, male images of God, etc. Previous generations of feminist scholars tended to either "apologize" for the overall character of rabbinic literature, or attack the male dominated rabbinic culture.[29] In contrast, many modern feminist scholars find themselves somewhere in between—admitting that rabbinic culture generally excluded women,

---

[27] Scholars have noted that this technique is used with other marginal figures throughout rabbinic literature. Such marginal figures are allowed to ask the dangerous questions that rabbis would have found risky to even voice. See Christine Hayes, "Displaced Self-Perceptions: The Deployment of Minim and Romans in b. Sanhedrin 90b–91a," *Religious and Ethnic Communities in Later Roman Palestine*, ed. Hayim Lapin (Bethesda: University Press of Maryland, 1998), 249–289; Richard Kalmin, *Jewish Babylonia between Persia and Roman Palestine* (New York: Oxford University Press, 2006), 110–116.

[28] See our chapter on R. Pinhas b. Yair.

[29] Judith Hauptman, *Rereading the Rabbis: A Woman's Voice* (Boulder: Westview Press, 1998); Judith Romney Wegner, *Chattel or Person? The Status of Women in the Mishnah* (New York: Oxford University Press, 1988).

but also searching for evidence of women's presence and their voices, a task that Ilana Pardes calls "excavation."[30] Textual analysis can reveal hidden layers of meaning that have been embedded in the texts, both intentionally and unintentionally. Sometimes we discover an alternate opinion the authors were trying to silence, a counter-voice that pushes against the majority.[31] On other occasions, behind the veil of the text we can discern the worries and anxieties that male rabbis were trying to work through concerning the role of women in their world.[32]

Importantly, feminist readers are not neutral, dispassionate literary archaeologists, chipping away at the ancient world. Rather, alongside the literary and academic tools at their disposal, they use their passion and political concern as guides for their literary excavation of these male-dominant texts. As Charlotte Fonrobert, a contemporary scholar at the forefront of source-critical Talmudic feminist criticism, writes, "The most powerful claim brought forth by feminist thinking in the Jewish context has perhaps been the claim that these texts belong to women also, that they are part of women's heritage, religious commitments and aesthetic pleasures...This claim and the related emergence of women scholars of Talmud already has begun to change the 'face'

---

[30] Ilana Pardes uses the word "excavation" to describe a feminist reading strategy for the Bible, though it applies to Talmud scholarship as well. See her cogent methodological overview in *Countertraditions in the Bible: A Feminist Approach* (Cambridge: Harvard University Press, 1992), 1–13.

[31] Daniel Boyarin devotes a chapter of his groundbreaking work *Carnal Israel* to teasing out a counter voice to the absolute rabbinic exclusion of women from Torah study. See *Carnal Israel: Reading Sex in Talmudic Culture* (Berkeley: University of California Press, 1993), 167–196.

[32] An excellent example can be found in Ishay Rosen-Zvi's analysis of the mishnaic Sotah ritual. He demonstrates that the Mishnaic description reimagines the biblical test of the sotah in a manner which emphasizes her sexuality and presumes her guilt. The Mishnah does not reflect a historical portrayal of the second Temple but instead serves the ideological purpose of controlling the invisible power of women's sexuality. See *The Mishnaic Sotah Ritual: Temple Gender and Midrash* (Leiden: Brill, 2012).

of the text, as women move from being spectators in the talmudic beit midrash to being participants in it."[33]

As an example of the feminist study of rabbinic sources, we will examine the character of Yalta, one of the most famous and oft-studied women in rabbinic literature.[34] A story in tractate Berakhot deals with her exclusion from partaking in the ritual cup of wine at the conclusion of birkat hamazon. Our analysis of this story will not just demonstrate feminist reading strategies, but will also deepen our understanding of the focus of the previous sugya, namely women's relationship to birkat hamazon.

Bavli Berakhot 51b

Bavli Berakhot 51b records a baraita that lists ten requirements pertaining to the cup of wine used during birkat hamazon and then adds an eleventh: "Some say, He [also] sends it—the cup—to the members of his household…as a present so that his wife may be blessed." The following story appears after the baraita:

(1) עולא אקלע	(1) Ulla was once at the house of
לבי רב נחמן. כריך	R. Nahman. He (Ulla) ate bread and
ריפתא בריך ברכת	said birkat hamazon. He handed the
מזונא.יהב ליה כסא	cup of blessing to R. Nahman.
דברכתא לרב נחמן.	

---

[33] "Feminist Interpretations of Rabbinic Literature: Two Views," *Nashim* 4 (2001), 10.

[34] See Rachel Adler, *Engendering Judaism* (Philadelphia: Jewish Publication Society, 1998), 21–60; Tal Ilan, *Mine and Yours are Hers: Retrieving Women's History From Rabbinic Literature* (Leiden: Brill, 1997), 121–130; Judith Baskin, *Midrashic Women: Formations of the Feminine in Rabbinic Literature* (Hanover: Brandeis University Press, 2002), 83–87; Tamara Or, *Massekhet Betsa: A Feminist Commentary on The Babylonian Talmud* (Tubingen: Mohr Siebeck, 2010), 122–134.

(2) אמר ליה רב נחמן: לישדר מר כסא דברכתא לילתא.

(2) R. Nahman said to him: Send the cup of blessing to Yalta.

(3) אמר ליה הכי אמר ר' יוחנן: אין פרי בטנה של אשה מתברך אלא מפרי בטנו של איש, שנאמר: וברך פרי בטנך (דברים ז: יג), פרי בטנה לא נאמר, אלא פרי בטנך.

(3) He [Ulla] said to him: R. Yohanan said the following: The fruit of a woman's belly is blessed only from the fruit of a man's belly, as it says: *He will also bless the fruit of your belly* (Deuteronomy 7:13). It does not say the fruit of her belly, but the fruit of your (masc.) belly.

(4) תניא נמי הכי: ר' נתן אומר: מנין שאין פרי בטנה של אשה מתברך אלא מפרי בטנו של איש? שנאמר: וברך פרי בטנך. פרי בטנה לא נאמר, אלא פרי בטנך.

(4) It was also taught in a baraita: Rav Natan said: From where do we know that the fruit of a woman's belly is only blessed from the fruit of a man's belly? Because it says: *He will also bless the fruit of your belly.* It does not say the fruit of her belly, but the fruit of your (masc.) belly.

(5) אדהכי שמעה ילתא קמה בזיהרא, ועלתה לבי חמרא, ותברא ד' מאה דני דחמרא.

(5) Meanwhile Yalta heard, she rose in anger and went to the wine house and broke four hundred jugs of wine.

(6) אמר ליה רב נחמן: נשדר לה מר כסא אחרינא.

(6) R. Nahman said to him: Let the Master send her another cup.

(7) שלח לה: כל האי נבגא דברכתא היא.

(7) He sent her [a message]: All that [wine can be counted as] the cup for [making] the blessing.

(8) שלחה ליה: (8) She sent to him: Gossip comes
ממהדורי מילי   from peddlers and vermin from rags.
ומסמרטוטי כלמי.

This story opens with Ulla passing the cup to his host, Rav Nahman, ignoring the baraita's instruction to pass the cup of blessing after birkat hamazon to the wife. R. Nahman gently but forthrightly rebukes his colleague, telling him to pass the cup to his wife Yalta. Ulla's justification for his refusal to pass the cup to Yalta reveals that the technical dispute concerning the ritual reflects a deeper debate about women's fertility and God's blessings. Ulla's (overly) literal and ideological reading of Deuteronomy 7:13 is based on the fact that "your belly" is in the masculine in the original Hebrew. To Ulla, this implies that fertility is solely a male blessing. God's relationship with a woman's fertility is mediated through her husband, and it is for this reason that he, not she, should drink the wine. R. Nahman clearly disagrees with the midrash, since he sends her the cup of blessing. We can also assume that he disagrees with its theological implications as well—a woman's fertility is blessed directly through God and thus she should drink the wine to symbolically receive the blessing.

At this point in the story, rather than remain a passive participant who receives or does not receive the cup of wine from the male diners, Yalta forcefully takes action. In a dramatic demonstration of her discontent, she rises from the table (section five) and destroys 400 jugs of wine, symbolically rebelling against the male co-option of fertility and the rituals symbolizing it.[35] She will not remain seated at the table while two men debate her fertility, whether she is blessed directly or indirectly through God. While her anger is most directly pointed at Ulla, she does

---

[35] Bavli Eruvin 54a describes Beruria in a similar manner, lacking control over her emotions and violently lashing out in anger. See Shulamit Valler, "Women's Talk - Men's Talk: Babylonian Talmud Erubin 53a–54a" *Revue des Etudes Juives*, 162 (2003), 421–445.

not participate in the halakhic debate, as does her husband. Instead of engaging the two men at the table, she chooses to take action.

R. Nahman attempts to ease the tension by suggesting that Ulla send her another cup (section six). Notably the more measured and civil response is ascribed to the calm rabbi, who has less at stake than his wife. Ulla ignores R. Nahman's request because he believes it does not matter whether Yalta drinks the wine or spills it, for God's blessing of fertility does not flow through the woman. Instead he sends a message down to Yalta in the wine cellar (section seven), "All that [wine can be counted as] the cup for [making] the blessing." Ulla uses the Middle Persian loan word נבגא, umixed wine, to refer to the wine that has spilled on the floor from the smashed barrels.[36] He is in essence saying that a woman drinking the cup of blessing is akin to spilling wine on the floor—there is no value to such an act, and it is just a waste of wine.

However we understand R. Nahman's silence or Ulla's cool remark, neither rabbi responds with anger or violence. Only Yalta acts with rage at the obtuseness of her rabbinic fellow diners. It is as though she were saying—do not sit there and calmly debate my fertility as if this is one of your theoretical/philosophical/midrashic debates. The cup of blessing may be a ritual, but a woman's relationship to fertility is real and consequential. Call me simply a vessel, she implies, a vessel for a man's blessed seed. But if that vessel is broken your precious seed will end up worthless, spilled all over the floor, just like I did to your wine.

Yalta does engage in speech following Ulla's comment, but this speech is not the cool voice of dispassionate halakhic discourse. Rather, she counters Ulla's message with an insult, "Gossip comes from peddlers and vermin from rags." In a scathing verbal attack on the source of her anger, she deems Ulla a peddler who spreads rumors, as filthy as the vermin spread from a dirty rag. Tal Ilan cleverly suggests that Yalta's proverb is a subversive reading of Ben Sira 42:13: "From a garment

---

[36] Shaul Shaked, "Between Iranian and Aramaic: Iranian Words Concerning Food in Jewish Babylonian Aramaic," *Irano-Judaica V*, ed. Shaul Shaked and Amnon Netzer (Jerusalem: Ben-Zvi Institute, 2003), 128.

comes a moth, and from a woman the wickedness of women."[37] Ben Sira poetically claims that wickedness is spontaneously generated from women just as moths were believed to be spontaneously generated from garments. Yalta takes the misogynist verse and applies it to Ulla, a rabbi who "peddles" his worthless rabbinic aphorisms. The "Torah" that Ulla believes he is spreading, considered the domain of men throughout rabbinic literature, is described as "gossip," a realm generally associated with women.[38] Ulla, believing himself to be the "man" associated with Torah and with the blessing of fertility, is demoted to the role of peddler, a gossipmonger trading in worthless and even dangerous words. Ulla tried to usurp the woman's role by rendering fertility a male blessing;[39] Yalta turns the table, converting the male role, the valued art of spreading Torah, into the lowly female-associated art of gossip.

It is worth paying attention, too, to the symbols invoked in this story, as feminist scholars have noted. It is no accident that Yalta signals her rebellion against the male co-option of fertility and rituals by breaking jugs of wine. Wine jugs are used elsewhere in the Talmud to represent the female body, fertility, and women's sexuality. Elsewhere, the Talmud records the custom of dancing with a sealed cask of wine at the wedding of a virgin and an open cask of wine at the wedding of a widow or divorcee (B. Ketubot 16a). The closed cask represents the virgin's sealed virginity and the well-kept potential of her fertility. In another passage, (B. Ketubot 10b), a woman's virginity is examined by passing her over a vat of wine. A virgin is a closed cask, exuding

---

[37] See *Integrating Women into Second Temple History* (Tubingen: Mohr Siebeck, 1999), 171–174.

[38] See Mishnah Sotah 6:1; Bavli Kiddushin 49b.

[39] Anthropologists suggest that while both men and women are needed to conceive, the visibility of childbearing and the subsequent relationship between mother and baby threatens male power. Hence culture has sought to limit women's role to a natural process, distancing them from religious, familial and national meaning. See Sherry B. Ortner, "Is Female to Male as Nature Is to Culture?" *Feminist Studies* 1 (1974), 5–31.

no smell, whereas a non-virgin is an open cask, whose smell flows out of her mouth. And so in destroying her husband's precious store of wine out of anger at being excluded from the blessing of fertility, Yalta symbolically destroys his ability to control her fertility. The breaking of the jugs signifies that she is destroying the boundaries that contain her sexuality and fertility, breaking free of male control.

Again, we should emphasize that this is not "Yalta's" unmediated voice speaking through the text. After all, Talmduic texts were written by men for a male audience, and the women they depict are—at least in part—male creations. The pure, unmediated voice of an actual Talmudic woman is sadly irrecoverable. The best the feminist scholar can hope for is to gain insight into how the rabbis imagined that a woman of Yalta's social and intellectual standing might react to her exclusion from the blessing of fertility and its attendant ritual. Nevertheless, this is an important "fissure" in the general rabbinic exclusion of women that comprises the bedrock of halakhah. It is a moment when rabbis realize that their usurping of women's fertility may backfire, causing "all that wine to be spilled." [40]

---

[40] Charlotte Fonrobert offers similar reflections on her analysis of the Yalta story from Niddah 20b. Yalta is portrayed as questioning the rabbis' authority to determine whether a woman's blood is menstrual. Fonrobert outlines two different feminist approaches to the text. The first reads Yalta as a "protofeminist hero of protest, whose lonely voice somehow made it into the canon of rabbinic literature." The second approach perceives "her story as an index of a more systematic problem in the rabbinic science of women's blood." While Fonrobert defends both approaches, she adopts the latter, as we have in the analysis of the Yalta birkat hamazon story. See *Menstrual Purity: Rabbinic and Christian Reconstructions of Biblical Gender* (Stanford: Stanford University Press, 2000), 118–127.

Chapter Six

From Eretz Yisrael to Bavel: The Interruption of Mourning by a Festival

Moed Katan 20a

Introduction

The Jewish laws of mourning are often praised as an effective means by which to allow the individual a chance to express his/her grief publicly, to accept comfort from the community, and then to be reintegrated gradually into his/her routine. The mourner ceases his normal activity for a week: He does not work, shave or cut his hair, or change his clothes etc. Instead he stays at home and members of the community visit to offer consolation for his loss. After the week has been completed, he resumes some of these activities; depending upon his relationship with the deceased, some of them are not resumed until later. Eventually he returns fully to normal life.

However, one aspect of these laws seems to work against this goal, and that is the ruling that if a person buries a dead relative immediately before a festival, the festival annuls the shivah, the seven day period of mourning. Thus R. Yosef Karo writes (Shulkhan Arukh, Orah Hayyim, 548:7): "One who buries his dead before the festival...and observed even one hour's worth of mourning, [the festival] interrupts the mourning and annuls from him the decree of the seven days of mourning." In this chapter we will see how this aberrance in the Jewish mourning laws developed from the tannaitic period through the amoraic period. We will also attempt to explain how the Bavli's laws of mourning may have been influenced by the surrounding Babylonian culture.

Tannaitic Literature

The vast majority of Jewish mourning laws and customs are found in the final chapter of Moed Katan. Mishnah Moed Katan 3:5 states quite clearly that if one buries one of his dead relatives *three days* before a festival, he need not complete the seven days of mourning after the festival.

הקובר את מתו שלשה ימים קודם לרגל בטלה הימנו גזרת שבעה.	One who buries his dead three days be- fore the festival, the decree of seven [days of mourning] is annulled from him.

Tosefta Moed Katan 2:6 demonstrates the same rule by discussing a related case, where the person dies two days before the festival:

הקובר את מתו שני ימים קודם הרגל מפסיק את הרגל ומונה חמשה אחר הרגל.	One who buries his dead two days before the festival, the festival interrupts [his seven days of mourning] and he counts five days [of mourning] after the festival.

Both tannaitic halakhot require at least three days of mourning before the festival. If fewer days are observed, full mourning resumes when the festival is concluded. The reason for the three day minimum is illustrated in the following aggadah in the Yerushalmi:

ירושלמי מועד קטן ג:ה, פב ע"ב דבר קפרא אמר: אין תוקפו של אבל אלא עד שלשה ימים. ר' אבא בריה דרבי פפי ר' יהושע דסיכנין בשם רבי לוי: כל תלתא יומין נפשא טייסא על גופא, סבירה דהיא חזרה לגביה.	**Yerushalmi Moed Katan 3:5, 82b[1]** For Bar Kapara said: the full power of mourning is only up until three days. R. Abba the son of R. Papi, R. Yehoshua of Sikhnin in the name of R. Levi: For all three days the soul circles over the body, thinking that it will return [to the body].

---

[1] There is a parallel in Leviticus Rabbah 18. There the stomach's expelling its contents is connected either to Ecclesiastes 12:6 or to Malachi 2:3.

כיון דהיא חמייא דאישתני זיוייהון	Once it sees that the appearance of the
דאפוי, היא שבקא ליה ואזלה	face has changed, it leaves and goes
לה. לאחר שלשה ימים הכרס	away. After three days the stomach bursts
נבקעת על פניו ואומרת לו: הא	open onto its face and says to it: "Here
לך מה שגזלתה וחמסתה ונתת בי.	is what you stole and gave to me."

רבי חגיי בשם רבי יאשיה	R. Haggai in the name of R. Yoshaya
מייתי לה מן הכא: וזריתי	brings proof from the following verse: *And*
פרש על פניכם ואפילו פרש	*I will strew dung upon your faces, the dung*
חגיכם (מלאכי ב:ג).	*of your festival sacrifices* (Malachi 2:3).

באותה השעה: אך בשרו	At that moment: *He feels only*
עליו יכאב ונפשו עליו	*the pain in his flesh, and his spir-*
תאבל (איוב יד:כב).	*it mourns in him* (Job 14:22).

Various passages in rabbinic literature demonstrate that the rabbis believed that the dead body remained sentient and that the soul mourned the loss of the body.[2] According to R. Levi three days is the period during which the soul remains attracted to the body because for three days the body retains its "divine image," a notion that we shall see later in another statement attributed to Bar Kapara. As long as the face is recognizable, the soul retains its connection to the body. Once the soul has abandoned the body, the essential power of the mourning process is diminished. Therefore, there are certain leniencies that can be taken after three days of mourning have already been observed.

The distinction between the first three days of mourning and the subsequent days is also anchored in other baraitot in the Bavli. For instance:

Bavli Moed Katan 21a

בבלי מועד קטן כא ע"ב	
תנו רבנן: אבל, שלשה ימים	Our rabbis taught: a mourner for the first
הראשונים אסור במלאכה,	three days is forbidden to perform work,
ואפילו עני המתפרנס מן	[and this includes] even a poor person who
הצדקה. מכאן ואילך - עושה	is sustained by charity. Henceforth he can
בצינעא בתוך ביתו, והאשה	work privately in his own home, and a
טווה בפלך בתוך ביתה.	woman can spin on the spindle in her home.

---

[2] See for instance Bavli Shabbat 152a–b; Berakhot 18b.

תנו רבנן: אבל, שלשה ימים הראשונים - אינו הולך לבית האבל, מכאן ואילך - הולך, ואינו יושב במקום המנחמין אלא במקום המתנחמין.	Our rabbis taught: A mourner for the first three days does not go to the house of another mourner. Henceforth he can go, but he does not sit in the place of the comforters but rather in the place of those being comforted.
תנו רבנן: אבל, שלשה ימים הראשונים - אסור בשאילת שלום, משלשה ועד שבעה - משיב ואינו שואל, מכאן ואילך - שואל ומשיב כדרכו.	Our rabbis taught: A mourner for the first three days is forbidden to greet others with shalom. From three to seven days, he can respond but not greet. Henceforth he can greet and respond in a normal manner.

We shall now turn our attention to the Babylonian sugya which seems to be the glaring exception to the three-day rule. As we shall see, this exception is responsible for the strange halakhah whereby the festival cuts off mourning after only one hour.

Bavli Moed Katan 20a

BARAITA

(1) תנו רבנן: קיים כפיית המטה שלשה ימים קודם הרגל אינו צריך לכפותה אחר הרגל דברי רבי אליעזר. וחכמים אומרים אפילו יום אחד ואפילו שעה אחת.	(1) Our Rabbis taught: If one fulfilled overturning the bed for three days before the festival, he need not overturn it after the festival, the words of R. Eliezer. But the sages say: Even if he had [done so] only for one day or even for one hour.
אמר ר' אלעזר בר' שמעון: הן הן דברי בית שמאי הן הן דברי בית הלל, שבית שמאי אומרים: שלשה ימים, ובית הלל אומרים: אפילו יום אחד.	R. Elazar son of R. Shimon said: Those are the very words of Beit Shammai and the very words of Beit Hillel, for Beit Shammai say: For three days, and Beit Hillel say: Even for one day.

Tannaitic Source	Amoraic Source	Stammaitic Source

208

FIRST AMORAIC RULING

(2) אמר רב הונא: אמר ר' חייא
בר אבא אמר ר' יוחנן ואמרי
לה אמר ר' יוחנן לר' חייא
בר אבא ולרב הונא: אפילו
יום אחד אפילו שעה אחת.

(2) R. Huna said: R. Hiyya b. Abba said in the name of R. Yohanan and some say R. Yohanan said to R. Hiyya bar Abba and R. Huna: Even if he had [overturned the bed] for one day; even for one hour.

SECOND AMORAIC RULING

(3) רבא אמר: הלכה כתנא
דידן דאמר שלשה.

(3) Rava said that the halakhah is according to our tanna [of the mishnah] who said three days.

THIRD AMORAIC RULING

(4) רבינא איקלע לסורא דפרת.
אמר ליה רב חביבא לרבינא:
הלכתא מאי? אמר ליה אפילו
יום אחד ואפילו שעה אחת.

(4) Ravina once came to Sura on the Euphrates. R. Haviva said to Ravina: What is the law? He replied: Even [if he had overturned the bed] for one day and even for one hour.

| Tannaitic Source | Amoraic Source | Stammaitic Source |

The sugya opens with a baraita whose source is Tosefta Moed Katan 2:9.[3] R. Eliezer opens the baraita by ruling that if one observes the mourning custom of "overturning the bed," a custom that we will describe below, for three days before the festival, he need not overturn the bed after the festival. In the continuation of the baraita, R. Shimon ben Elazar identifies the anonymous opinion with Beit Shammai. The sages, following Beit Hillel, rule more leniently—as long as he overturned the bed for at least one day, or (according to the sages) even one hour, he need not overturn the bed after the festival.

Before we analyze how the amoraim understood this baraita, we need to analyze it in the context in which it originally appeared in the Tosefta. First of all, this is the only mourning custom in which the Tosefta specifically states, "If one fulfilled performing X before the festival, one need not do so after the festival." The normative way of phrasing these halakhot is

---

[3] The differences between the two are minor and only stylistic.

as cited above: "One who *buries* his dead two days before the festival" or in the Mishnah "one who *buries* his dead three days before the festival." The question we must ask is—of all the mourning rituals, why does this halakhah specify this ritual? Second, as we have seen, the Mishnah states and the Tosefta implies that if one has buried his dead at least *three* days before the festival, he does not resume his mourning after the festival. How is this possible when Beit Hillel rule that overturning the bed for one day before the festival is sufficient? Do the Mishnah and Tosefta instead follow Beit Shammai, who holds that one must overturn the bed for at least three days in order not to resume doing so after the festival? Or is overturning the bed different—i.e. according to Beit Hillel this custom need not be continued after the festival, but other mourning customs are to be resumed? In order to answer this question, we must first examine sources concerning this particular ritual of "overturning the bed."

Overturning the Bed: Shabbat and the Festival

Overturning the bed is mentioned in the baraita from the Tosefta quoted in section one of our sugya, and in a more subtle fashion in the Mishnah:

משנה מועד קטן ג:ז	**Mishnah Moed Katan 3:7**
ואין מברין אלא	The meal for mourners is given [on
על מטה זקופה.	hol hamoed] on an upright bed.

This mishnah refers to a situation in which a burial takes place on hol hamoed, the intermediate days of the festival. The special meal eaten immediately after the burial is usually eaten while sitting on an overturned bed.[4] If burial takes place on hol hamoed, however, when many of the laws of mourning are suspended, this meal is eaten on an upright bed, one that has not been overturned. Similarly, Tosefta Moed Katan 2:9 (below; see also Shmuel's opinion in Bavli 24) mandates that a mourner keep his bed upright on

---

[4] See the biblical precedent for this meal in II Samuel 3:35 where the people come to feed David after his son died.

Shabbat because an overturned bed is considered a public sign of mourning and public mourning is prohibited on Shabbat.[5]

There is some disagreement in the sources about whether someone who has put the bed upright before Shabbat must overturn it after Shabbat for the remaining days of shivah. Tosefta Moed Katan 2:9 states the following:

ובערב שבת זוקף את	On Friday eve he uprights his bed and on
מטתו ובמוצאי שבת כופה	Saturday night he overturns it, even if there
אפילו לא נשתייר לו	is only one day [of mourning] remaining.
אלא יום אחד בלבד.	

This toseftan halakhah is unequivocal—only on Shabbat is the bed uprighted. After Shabbat the bed must be overturned again, even if only one day of shivah remains. This source disagrees with a more lenient position that appears in the Yerushalmi:

ירושלמי מועד קטן	**Yerushalmi Moed Katan**
ג:ה, פג ע"א	**3:5, 83a**
(1) חד תלמיד מן דרבי	(1) A student of R. Mana instructed one of
מנא הורי לחד מן קריבוי	the relatives of the patriarch's house [say-
דנשייא: משהוא זוקפה	ing]: Once you have made [the bed] upright,
שוב אינו כופה.	you do not need to overturn it again.
(2) כמה ימים היה לו?	(2) How many days [had he already overturned it]?
(3) רבי יעקב בר	(3) R. Yaakov b. Aha in the name of
אחא בשם רבי יסא:	R. Yasa: he had observed two days.
שני ימים היה לו.	

---

[5] Amoraim debate whether or not mourning is permitted on Shabbat. See Bavli Moed Katan 23b and 24a. See also Yerushalmi Moed Katan 3:5, 83a and the discussion of Joshua Kulp, *A Virgin is Wedded on Wednesday: A Commentary of Bavli Ketubot Chapter 1* (Dissertation; Bar Ilan University, 2002), 133–137. The sources that we analyze in this chapter clearly take a stand that at least the public aspects of mourning are forbidden on Shabbat.

רבי בא רבי אמי (4)	(4) R. Ba, R. Ami, R. Yaakov bar Zavdi
רבי יעקב בר זבדי בשם	in the name of R. Yitzhak: three days.
רבי יצחק: שלשה.	
רבי חיננא בר פפא (5)	(5) R. Hanina bar Papa instructed him
הורי לכפותה [=לא	not to overturn it [again][6] even if he
לכפותה[6]] אפילו יום אחד.	[had overturned it] for only one day.
ואיתחמי ליה: יען כי (6)	(6) And they looked at him [as if to say]:
מריתה (מלכים א יג:כא).	*Behold for you have rebelled* (1 Kings 13:21).

In this story, R. Mana's student (section one) rules directly against the Tosefta. As long as one has overturned the bed even once, it is not mandated to do so again after Shabbat. This source seems to take Beit Hillel's ruling in the Tosefta (and section one in the Bavli) with regard to the festival and apply it to Shabbat. Just as the festival interrupts overturning the bed and one need not resume this observance during the remaining days, so, too, does Shabbat. This is also the ruling of R. Hanina bar Papa in section five. Section six describes his lenient ruling as an act of rebellion because he rules against the explicit ruling in the Tosefta. The rabbis in section three rule slightly more strictly, requiring two days of observance in order to exempt the mourner from having to again overturn his bed. The opinion of the amoraim in section four brings this halakhah in line with the ruling we saw earlier regarding the festival—only if one observed mourning customs for three days prior to the festival they are not to be resumed.

Lieberman summarizes this passage as follows:

> It is clear that they ruled leniently when it comes to overturning the bed and that there were those who thought that even Shabbat, which counts as part of the shivah, interrupts the practice of overturning the bed. And even though this is not the halakhah [that if one overturns the bed before Shabbat one does not overturn it after Shabbat], it is not surprising that when it comes to the festival they say that if he

---

[6] See Saul Lieberman, *Tosefta Kifshuta: Moed* (New York: Jewish Theological Seminary, 1962), 1255.

fulfilled 'overturning the bed' for one hour…, the festival interrupts even though three days since the burial have not passed.

The fact that the rules are more lenient for "overturning the bed" than for other mourning rituals leads Lieberman to the conclusion that when Tosefta MK 2:9 (the parallel to the baraita in the Bavli) says that if one has overturned the bed for one day or one hour before the festival, he need not overturn the bed after the festival (according to Beit Hillel), this refers *only to overturning the bed.* In other words, the normal rituals of mourning are to be resumed after the conclusion of the festival. Only the bed is not overturned again, for the laws with regard to this specific act are generally lenient. Thus tannaitic law, as well as the Yerushalmi's interpretation of it, did not recognize the notion that if one observed *any form of mourning* for one hour before the festival, the shivah is terminated by the festival. This is an innovative Babylonian reading of the baraita, which we will discuss below.

Overturning the Bed: A Unique Mourning Ritual

Before we turn our attention to the Bavli, we must ask why the festival and Shabbat (according to some Eretz-Yisraeli amoraim) end the practice of overturning the bed but do not end the other shivah customs if they have not been observed for three days. What is unique about overturning the bed? A potential answer can be found in the justification for this custom attributed to Bar Kappara in the two Talmuds:[7]

---

[7] There are two other reasons given in Yerushalmi Moed Katan 3:5, 83a for overturning the bed. R. Krispa refers to Job 2:13, "And they sat toward the ground with him." He reads this as meaning that Job's friends sat on an overturned bed. R. Shimon ben Lakish says that the overturned bed causes the mourner discomfort; he should wake up at night and remember he is a mourner. Note that these two amoraim assume that one sits or sleeps on the overturned bed. However, it is not at all clear whether the original function of overturning the bed was so that one would sit on it. It may be that the custom to sit on the ground (see Mishnah Sanhedrin 2:1–2) was originally distinct from the custom to overturn the bed.

ירושלמי מועד קטן
ג:ה, פג ע"א
בר קפרא אמר: איקונין
אחת טובה היתה לי בתוך
ביתך וגרמתני לכפותה.
אף את כפה מיטתך.

Yerushalmi Moed Katan
3:5, 83a
Bar Kapara said: I had a beautiful image (icon)
in your house and you caused me to overturn
it. So, too, you should overturn your bed.

ואית דמפקין לישנא:
יכפה הסרסור.

Some say this with the following language: Let the agent be overturned.

בבלי מועד קטן טו ע"א
אבל חייב בכפיית המטה,
דתני בר קפרא: דמות
דיוקני[8] נתתי בהן,
ובעונותיהם הפכתיה –
כפו מטותיהן עליה.

Bavli Moed Katan 15a
A mourner is obligated to overturn the bed
as Bar Kapara taught: I placed an image[8]
within them and through their sins I overturned it. [Now] overturn your beds.

Both Talmuds explain death as a result of sin, although it is not clear exactly
whose sin it is—the mourners or the deceased. In any case, Bar Kapara's
teaching describes the act of overturning the bed as a measure-for-measure
response to death. God describes the death of a human being as the overturning of His "icon."[9] Just as God overturns the icon of the dead, so, too,
should the mourners perform an act of overturning. The bed is chosen as a
symbol because that is where life both begins and ends. As Yair Lorberbaum
points out in his book-length study of the rabbinic understanding of the
concept of creation in the divine image, it is at these two points, procreation

---

[8] The doubling of the word for image is a result of a translation of the Greek word for
icon which appears in the Yerushalmi. The readers of the Bavli would not have understood the Greek so the Hebrew translation דמות was appended to the Greek, forming
the phrase found throughout the Bavli: דמות דיוקני or just דיוקן. See David Rosenthal,
"Mesorot Eretz Yisraeliot ve-Darkan le-Bavel" *Katedra* 92 (1999), 13.

[9] The imagery alludes to the practice in ancient Rome of overturning or defacing stat-
ues and coins that contain the depictions of deposed emperors. See Yair Furstenburg,
"The Rabbinic View of Idolatry and the Roman Political Conception of Divinity,"
Journal of Religion, 90, 3 (2010), 335–366.

and death, that we most often find the rabbis employing the language of the body as "icon."[10] Bar Kapara understands overturning the bed as a symbolic act that undoes the procreative act. This sage employs the notion of human beings created in the image of God to create the contrast between the upright bed, "the agent," where the image was originally formed at the moment of conception, and the overturned bed, which symbolizes the diminishing of the image at the moment of death.

The unique halakhic status of overturning the bed may relate to the fact that this is the only mourning custom that is purely symbolic. The main mourning rituals as observed in the tannaitic period are performed on the body or by the body of the mourner himself. These include not washing, not laundering one's clothing, not cutting one's hair or shaving, not working, not greeting others, not having sexual relations, not wearing shoes, not studying Torah, not wearing tefillin, and covering one's head with special mourner's headwear (עטיפת הראש). While these actions might be construed as representations of the person's mourning, they are not merely symbols. Rather the physical acts themselves serve a specific purpose, whether it be denying the mourner the pleasures of the world or separating him from his community and his normal routine. These denials could be construed as symbolic, but they are better understood as acts of asceticism which have an effect on the mourner or on his place within society. In contrast, "overturning the bed," at least as understood by Bar Kappara, is a *purely symbolic action*—one overturns the bed to symbolize that the body which was conceived on a bed has been overturned by death. By overturning the bed, *perhaps even once*, one has demonstrated this symbolism, and so perhaps it need not be performed again. Thus the reason for being lenient solely with regard to overturning the bed could be connected to the symbolic nature of this ritual.

This understanding also helps explain a challenge to Lieberman's theory that was raised by Eric Zimmer.[11] Zimmer noted that overturning the bed is used as the symbol *sine qua non* for mourning. For instance we read in the following baraita:

---

[10] Yair Lorberbaum, *Tzelem Elohim* (Jerusalem: Schocken, 2004).

[11] Eric Zimmer, "Kefiyat Hamitah Beavelut Vegilgulei Toldotav," *Sinai* 73 (1973), 129 n. 7.

בבלי מועד קטן כז ע"א

תנו רבנן: מאימתי כופין
את המטות? משיצא מפתח
ביתו, דברי רבי אליעזר.
רבי יהושע אומר: משיסתם
הגולל. מעשה שמת רבן
גמליאל הזקן, כיון שיצא
מפתח ביתו אמר להם רבי
אליעזר: כפו מטותיכם.
וכיון שנסתם הגולל,
אמר להם רבי יהושע:
כפו מטותיכם. אמרו לו:
כבר כפינו על פי זקן.

Bavli Moed Katan 27a

Our rabbis taught: From when do they over-turn the bed? From the time [the body] goes out the front door, the words of R. Eliezer. R. Joshua says: from the time the stone is put over [the grave]. It happened that R. Gam-liel the elder died. Once [the body] went out the door R. Eliezer said to them: Overturn your beds. And when the stone was put over the grave, R. Joshua said to them: Overturn your beds. They said to him: We already over-turned them based on the words of the elder.

How, Zimmer asks, can Lieberman say that the sages were lenient specifi-cally with regard to overturning the bed and that they did not require its resumption after the festival, when we can see that overturning the bed was considered the prime signal that mourning had begun? We can answer this question when we realize that overturning the bed is different from other aspects of mourning. First of all, overturning the bed can be understood as a symbolic act that, when performed once and then undone (by uprighting the bed due to Shabbat or the festival), need not be performed again. The point is not to have the bed overturned for a specific duration of time, but simply the act of overturning it. Second, it makes sense for the sages to use "overturning the bed" as the focal point of when mourning begins (as in the above source) for it is a symbolic act that will immediately signify the assumption of mourning. The prohibitions on washing, shaving etc. will not be noticeable until later. Finally, overturning the bed is not connected specifically to the mourners, unlike most other mourning customs. The beds in the house must be overturned, regardless of whether they belong to the mourner or the deceased, as the Talmud explicitly states:

בבלי מועד קטן כז ע"א	**Bavli Moed Katan 27a**

בבלי מועד קטן כז ע"א

תנו רבנן: הכופה מטתו, לא
מטתו בלבד הוא כופה, אלא
כל מטות שיש לו בתוך ביתו
הוא כופה. ואפילו יש לו
עשר מטות בעשרה מקומות
כופה את כולן, ואפילו חמשה
אחין ומת אחד – כולן כופין.

Bavli Moed Katan 27a

Our rabbis taught: one who overturns his
bed, he overturns not only his own bed but
all the beds that he has in house. And even
if he has ten beds in ten different places, he
overturns them all. And even five brothers
and one dead relative, they all overturn.

All beds must be overturned because all beds are a symbol of potential life and their overturning is symbolic of death. Nevertheless, it is possible that once this commandment has been fulfilled and then the bed is uprighted because of the festival or Shabbat, it need not be overturned again. In other words, it is not difficult to understand how the halakhah could be adamant and stringent in general with regard to overturning the bed, and yet not demand that the bed be overturned again after Shabbat or the festival.

However we understand overturning the bed, it is clear that Lieberman is correct that nowhere in the Yerushalmi do we find the ruling that if *any* form of mourning has been observed for one day or one hour before the festival, then no shivah rituals are resumed after the festival. In the Yerushalmi, mourning must be observed for *three days* in order for the festival to annul the shivah. We shall see further evidence of this below when we compare our Babylonian sugya with the Yerushalmi's parallel. The strongest evidence is, as Lieberman notes, that this three-day minimum continued to be Eretz Yisraeli practice in the post-Talmudic period, as the following source attests:

ספר החילוקים בין בני
מזרח ומערב סימן ה
אנשי מזרח פוטרין
את האבל לפני הרגל
אפילו שעה אחת.

The Book of Differences Between the People of the East and West, Section Five

The people of the east (Babylonia) exempt the mourner [from continuing mourning] if he [buried his dead] even an hour [before the festival.]

ובני ארץ ישראל עד	And the people of Eretz Yisrael only if he [has
שיהיו לו ג' ימים לפני	observed] three days before the festival. From
הרגל. מן הדא: הקובר את	here: one who buries his dead three days before
מתו ג' ימים קודם הרגל	the festival, the decree of shivah is annulled.
בטלה ממנו גזרת שבעה.	

The people of Eretz Yisrael followed the Mishnah—shivah is annulled only if three days of mourning are observed before the festival. We shall now explore the Babylonian custom of annulling shivah if any amount of mourning was observed before the festival. To do so, we return to our sugya in Bavli Moed Katan 20a quoted above.

The Transformation in the Bavli

The entire sugya in the Bavli consists of the baraita followed by three amoraic rulings. According to traditional commentators, the three opinions debate whether one who buries his dead one day or even one hour before the festival must continue with shivah after the festival. According to this understanding, R. Huna (section 2) rules that one day or one hour is sufficient. Rava (3) rules against the baraita and in favor of the mishnah, that one must observe three days. The sugya concludes with Ravina's ruling (4) in favor of R. Huna, and Beit Hillel from the baraita. According to this reading of the sugya, all three opinions understand "overturning the bed" in the baraita as paradigmatic of all mourning customs—just as one need not overturn the bed if one did so for even one day/hour before the festival (according to Beit Hillel), so, too, one need not resume any of the other customs of shivah.

However, if we read carefully, we can see that it is actually Rava who initiates this understanding of the baraita. The first statement, attributed to mostly Eretz-Yisraeli amoraim, could be read as merely ruling that *with regard to the custom of overturning the bed* the halakhah is according to Beit Hillel. The remaining mourning customs must be observed after the festival if one did not observe them for three days before the festival, as the Mishnah states.

Rava is the first amora who reads *the Mishnah and Tosefta as being opposing texts*. Rava reads "overturning the bed" as one paradigmatic aspect of

> ⚫ **The Book of Differences Between the People of the East and West**
> This anonymous work is a list of approximately fifty differences in customs between Babylonia and the land of Israel. The list is not exhaustive and the author's intent in including those specific examples remains unclear. Furthermore, his own origins remain obscure due to his lack of consistency in the few cases where he reveals his preference in custom. The only information which can be stated with certainty is that this work was composed after the Muslim conquest in the 650s and before the first half of tenth century. For more see Robert Brody, *The Geonim of Babylonia and the Shaping of Medieval Jewish Culture* (New Haven: Yale University Press, 1998), 112–113.

shivah. According to Rava, the baraita therefore rules that just as the bed is not overturned after the festival, so, too, no mourning customs are resumed. However, we should emphasize that Rava does not initiate any change in halakhah, for by saying that the halakhah is like the Mishnah he maintains the earlier halakhah that one must observe three days of mourning for the festival to annul the shivah. His innovation is his reading of the baraita. He implies that according to the baraita one must observe only one day or one hour of mourning for the entire shivah to be annulled. According to his reading of the baraita, overturning the bed is paradigmatic of all mourning activities—just as it is not resumed after the festival, so, too, all of the shivah customs are not resumed. In other words, while he does not change the Eretz Yisraeli halakhah, he understands the baraita in a distinctly non-Eretz Yisraeli manner. He does not recognize the unique nature of the custom of overturning the bed and simply reads it as representative of all mourning practices.

Ravina's statement to R. Haviva must be interpreted in light of Rava's earlier statement. In other words, when R. Haviva asks Ravina what the halakhah is, he means to say: if one observes *any aspect* of mourning for one hour before the festival must he resume *any form of mourning* after the festival? To this, Ravina replies in the negative. Here the later, Babylonian halakhah is created—as long as the burial took place before the festival, there is no resumption of shivah after.

As to why Ravina disagrees with Rava, it is possible that this is a result of his wish not to rule according to Bet Shammai. Rava maintains the halakhah of the Mishnah even though, according to his reading, the halakhah accords with Bet Shammai from the baraita. Thus in a case where there is tension between maintaining the normative halakhah (three days) and observing the norm of ruling according to Bet Hillel, Rava maintains the halakhah.[12] However, Ravina may have had a different opinion on this matter, preferring to rule in favor of Bet Hillel even at the cost of changing the halakhic norm. We might even sense this tension in the question he is asked by R. Haviva: what is the halakhah? Can we rule as does Rava, even though this contradicts Bet Hillel from the baraita?

That this is the correct interpretation of Ravina's ruling is proven from a parallel passage found on 24b:

(1) דרש רבי עניני בר ששון אפיתחא דבי נשיאה: יום אחד לפני עצרת ועצרת - הרי כאן ארבעה עשר.	(1) R. Anani bar Sasson expounded at the door of the house of the Patriarch: One day [of mourning] before Atzeret [Shavuot] together with [one day of] Atzeret count as fourteen days [out of the thirty].
שמע רבי אמי ואיקפד. אמר: אטו דידיה היא? דרבי אלעזר אמר רבי אושעיא היא!	R. Ami heard of this and got upset, saying: Is that his own view? That is what R. Elazar [b. Pedat] said in the name of R. Oshaya.
(2) דרש רבי יצחק נפחא אקילעא דריש גלותא: יום אחד לפני עצרת, ועצרת - הרי כאן ארבעה עשר.	(2) R. Isaac the smith expounded in the chamber of the Exilarch: One day [of mourning] before Atzeret together with [one day of] Atzeret, count as fourteen days [out of the thirty].
שמע רב ששת איקפד, אמר: אטו דידיה היא? דרבי אלעזר אמר רבי אושעיא היא.	R. Sheshet heard of this and got upset, saying: Is that his own view? That is what R. Elazar said in the name of R. Oshaya!

---

[12] On the decision to follow Beit Hillel see Shmuel Safrai, "Halakha" *The Literature of the Sages: First Part*, ed. Shmuel Safrai (Philadelphia: Fortress Press, 1987), 194–200.

דאמר רבי אלעזר אמר רבי אושעיא: מנין לעצרת שיש לה תשלומין כל שבעה - שנאמר בחג המצות ובחג השבועות (דברים טז:טז) מה חג המצות יש לה תשלומין כל שבעה - אף חג השבועות יש לה תשלומין כל שבעה.

For R. Elazar said in the name of R. Oshaya: From where do we know that Atzeret has a supplementary period of seven days? From what is said: *On the Festival of Matzot and on the Festival of Weeks* (Deuteronomy 16:16). Just as the Festival of Matzot has a supplementary [period] of seven days, so, too, the Festival of Weeks has a supplementary period of seven days.

(3) אדבריה רב פפא לרב אויא סבא, ודרש: יום אחד לפני ראש השנה, וראש השנה - הרי כאן ארבעה עשר.

(3) R. Papa took R. Avia the elder and he expounded: One day [of mourning] before Rosh Hashanah and Rosh Hashanah [together] count as fourteen days [out of the thirty].

אמר רבינא: הלכך, יום אחד לפני החג, וחג, ושמיני שלו - הרי כאן עשרים ואחד יום.

Ravina said: Therefore one day [of mourning] before the festival [of Sukkot] together with [seven days of the] festival and its eighth day count as twenty-one days [out of the thirty days of mourning].

(4) רבינא איקלע לסורא דפרת, אמר ליה רב חביבא מסורא דפרת לרבינא: אמר מר יום אחד לפני ראש השנה וראש השנה הרי כאן ארבעה עשר?

(4) Ravina came to Sura-on-the- Euphrates. R. Habiba of Sura-on-the Euphrates asked him: Did the master say that one day before Rosh Hashanah and Rosh Hashanah [together] count for fourteen [out of the thirty days]?

אמר ליה: אנא מסתברא כרבן גמליאל הוא דאמינא.

He replied: I hold like Rabban Gamliel.

The topic of this sugya is Mishnah Moed Katan 3:6, which discusses whether Shavuot (which the rabbis call Atzeret),[13] Rosh Hashanah and Yom Kippur

---

[13] The sages refer to Shavuot as the gathering (עצרת) and celebration which marks the conclusion of Pesah and the counting of the Omer.

function vis-a-vis mourning as do the other festivals. The question arises because Rosh Hashanah and Yom Kippur are not pilgrimage festivals, and because Shavuot is only one day. The amoraic commentary on this mishnah demonstrates that later Babylonian amoraim, including Ravina (section four), rule that if one observes *one day of mourning* before any festival, including Shavuot, Rosh Hashanah and Yom Kippur, one need not continue shivah after the festival. For instance, in sections one and two, R. Anani b. Sasson and R. Yitzchak Nafha rule that if one observed one day of mourning before Shavuot (Atzeret), that one day counts as an entire period of shivah, as does the one day of Shavuot, and he is credited with fourteen days towards the longer period of thirty days (*sheloshim*). R. Ami's and R. Sheshet's anger at both of these amoraim is illuminating. These two amoraim are upset not because they disagree with the opinions expounded. Rather they are upset because these sages present these rulings as their own, whereas R. Ami and R. Sheshet believe they originate with R. Oshaya, an Eretz-Yisraeli amora. However, when we examine the Eretz-Yisraeli statement itself, we can see that R. Oshaya's teaching was made in an entirely different context. His midrash teaches that should a worshiper miss bringing his pilgrimage sacrifice on Shavuot, which lasts only one day, he may offer the sacrifice on one of the subsequent six days, just as he would be allowed to do on the seven day festival of Sukkot. His statement was not related to mourning rituals and has no bearing on whether or not the one day observed before the festival is sufficient for shivah to be annulled. In other words, we have here Babylonian amoraim (R. Ami and R. Sheshet) quoting an Eretz-Yisraeli amora but interpreting him in a quintessentially Babylonian manner.

In section three, R. Papa continues the trend, ruling the same way concerning Rosh Hashanah. Ravina extends this further in section four, ruling that even Shemini Atzeret can count as an entire week, such that if one buries his dead before Sukkot, he is credited with twenty-one days of mourning! Finally, section four contains another story of R. Haviva asking a question of Ravina in Sura on the Euphrates. Here it is clear—R. Haviva assumes that Ravina holds that mourning for one hour before the festival annuls the entire shivah. The only question R. Haviva even has is whether Ravina rules like Rabban Gamaliel, who treats Rosh Hashanah and Yom Kippur like the festivals. Thus it is clear that in the sugya on 20a Ravina rules that if one overturns the bed and thereby observes even one hour of mourning before the festival, all the remaining days of shivah are annulled.

We can see just how "Babylonian" this sugya is when we compare it with the parallel in the Yerushalmi:

ירושלמי מועד קטן פרק ג:ו פג ע"א	**Yerushalmi Moed Katan** **3:6, 83a**
(1) דבית רבי יניי אמרי: עצרת עולה שבעה כרגלים.	(1) Those of the House of Yannai say: Atzeret counts as seven like the [other] festivals.
(2) בעון קומי רבי יוסה: שלשה לפני העצרת, ועצרת שבעה הרי עשרה? אלא שלשה לפני עצרת שבעה ועצרת שבעה הרי ארבעה עשר?	(2) They asked in front of R. Yose: three days [of mourning] before Atzeret, and Atzeret which counts as seven, add up to ten? Or three days before Atzeret which count as seven, and Atzeret which counts as seven, add up to fourteen?
(3) אמר רבי יוסי בי רבי: וכיני יום אחד לפני עצרת מונה חמשה לאחר העצרת. שנים מונה ארבעה. שלשה בטלו ממנו גזירות שבעה.	(3) R. Yose son of Rabbi said: so it is. For if he observes one day before Atzeret, he counts five days after Atzeret. Two days [he counts] four days. Three days and the decrees of shivah are annulled.

The sugya begins with a determination that Shavuot (Atzeret) counts as seven days towards *sheloshim,* as do the other festivals. The follow-up question in section two is what concerns us here: Do the three days of mourning observed before shivah was annulled by the festival count as three days, or as seven? However one explains R. Yose's answer to the question, it is clear that one must observe *three days* of mourning, not just one as is assumed in the parallel in the Bavli. This is stated with even greater clarity by R. Yose in section three. The shivah is annulled only if he observes *three days* of mourning.

The Babylonian Leniency Concerning Mourning

It is possible that the Babylonian ruling that even one hour of mourning before the festival is sufficient to annul the shivah is the result of a simple misreading of the baraita. While the original meaning was restricted to overturning the

223

bed, as we explained above, later Babylonian amoraim did not understand that there was a reason not to resume observance of this custom *alone* while resuming all other mourning practices. Therefore, these amoraim understood overturning the bed as being paradigmatic of all mourning customs. Once they understood the baraita in this manner, they coupled it with their tendency to rule like Beit Hillel and ruled against Rava. The problem with this interpretation is that it is hard to imagine that mourning customs, which are so central in people's actual lives, could change so radically as a result of a misreading of a baraita. Indeed, Rava, while he does misread the baraita, does not allow the halakhah to change accordingly. Rather he rules like the Mishnah, even though this opposes Beit Hillel.

It seems more likely that the ruling of Ravina and the other amoraim—that the festival annuls mourning even if only one hour is observed beforehand—is part of a larger Babylonian tendency to rule leniently in matters concerning mourning, and occasionally even to abolish or at least curtail many mourning customs. This tendency is summarized in the amoraic statement attributed to Shmuel, "the halakhah is like the lenient position in mourning."[14] We find this tendency throughout the final chapter of Bavli Moed Katan, where Shmuel's statement is cited often.

Below, Shai Secunda, an expert on the Iranian background to the Babylonian Talmud, will provide some cultural background as to why the Babylonian rabbis may have ruled leniently on matters of mourning ritual.

---

[14] Moed Katan 18a, 19b, 22a, 26b. A direct link between this principle and our sugya is found in the geonic work *She'iltot*, Genesis no. 15.

THE ZOROASTRIAN CONTEXT

SHAI SECUNDA

In recent years, Talmudists have paid increasing attention to the Iranian context of the Babylonian Talmud.[15] This area of scholarly research has helped account for some of the Bavli's unexpected halakhic developments. For the current discussion, it may be significant that according to contemporary critical scholars and present-day Zoroastrian believers alike, Zoroastrianism—the ancient Iranian religion practiced by the Babylonian rabbis' Persian neighbors and overlords—opposes excessive mourning. It is possible that such opposition was not merely limited to Zoroastrians, but was rather part of a broader cultural norm with which other Sasanian communities, including Babylonian Jews, identified. This norm may have influenced the halakhic development that occurred in Babylonian mourning practice, as traced in this chapter. However, before making such a claim, we need to survey the relevant Zoroastrian material.

A number of Zoroastrian texts from the Sasanian era—the period from the third to the seventh centuries CE during which the amoraim and their anonymous successors flourished and the Bavli took shape—strongly encourage people not to lament their deceased relatives excessively. One passage from a Middle Persian work known as Ardā Wirāz Nāmag ("The Book of the Righteous Wirāz") describes the metaphysical effects of excessive mourning on the deceased. As we often find in this text, the narrator Wirāz inquires of his heavenly

---

[15] For a description of the field known by some scholars as "Irano-Talmudica", and a survey of its history, see Shai Secunda, *The Iranian Talmud: Reading the Bavli in its Sasanian Context* (Philadelphia: University of Pennsylvania Press, 2014).

guides, Srōš and Ādur, about the meaning of the many strange and frightening sights that he encounters in the next world:[16]

> I came to a place and I saw a big mighty river, dark as hell, in which there were many souls and *fravaši*-spirits, some of whom were not able to cross, and some who were crossing with great difficulty, and some who were crossing easily. And I asked: What is this river and who are these people who are thus troubled?

> Srōš the pious and the god Ādur said: This river is the many tears which men shed from their eyes after the departed. And they mourn, lament, and cry, they shed tears illicitly, and it increases this river. Those who are not able to cross are those for whom after their passing much mourning, lamenting and crying was made. And those (who cross) more easily are those who are less (lamented). And tell those in the world: When (you are) in the world, do not illicitly mourn, lament, and cry, for the souls of your departed shall receive that much harm and difficulty.

This particularly vivid text is but one of a number of passages in Middle Persian wisdom literature that depict mourning in an entirely negative light,[17] and even equate it with sin.[18]

---

[16] Ardā Wirāz Nāmag 17.7. Text and translation have been adapted from Faridun Vahman, *Arda Wiraz Namag: The Iranian "Divina Commedia"* (London and Malmo: Curzon Press, 1986), with some significant changes.

[17] See for example Dēnkard, Book VI B14.17: "Love, possession of a warm heart and compassion are goodness, and mourning and lament are their adversary." Adapted from Shaul Shaked, *The Wisdom of the Sasanian Sages (Dēnkard VI)* (Persian Heritage Series; Boulder, Colo.: Westview Press, 1979), 138–9, with some changes.

[18] Dēnkard Book VI, 275: "They held this too, when idol worship is annihilated a little of the faith of the spiritual world departs with it. When schism (?) and disobedience are smitten, a little joy departs from them. When mourning is smitten, a little love departs with it. It is (however) after all better when these three sins are taken out of the world as soon as possible (based on Shaked, *Wisdom*, 108–9, with some changes)."

To be sure, Zoroastrianism has its prescribed mourning practices. One of these is a prohibition against consuming meat or wine for three days after a relative has died. This practice constitutes a normative display of mourning that is still practiced by some Zoroastrians to this day. The prohibition against eating certain foods within three days after a relative has died is not stated explicitly in the Avesta—Zoroastrianism's ancient "scriptures"[19]—but is derived by Sasanian Zoroastrian interpreters via inference.[20] As for expressions of lament, here, too, the Avesta itself does not explicitly state that excessive mourning is problematic. Rather, Zoroastrianism's ethos against excessive mourning seems to have emerged through the protracted and complex processes involved in scriptural exegesis. This is true, too, of Zoroastrian wisdom literature. A passage preserved in the Mēnōy ī Xrad ('Spirit of Wisdom'), a Middle Persian wisdom text, discusses the ten places in which the earth is most unhappy. The tenth place

---

[19] Based on linguistic differences, scholars divide the Avesta into two parts; namely, a core of ancient songs known as the Gathas that were composed in Old Avestan as early as the second millennium BCE, and the majority of the texts which survive in Young Avestan and were apparently composed in the first half of the first millennium BCE.

[20] The relevant "scriptural" passage is from an Avestan work known as the Videvdad ('The Law Discarding the Demons'), and reads as follows:

> After that (i.e. three days and a ritual purification ceremony) let the Mazdayasnians (worshippers of the Zoroastrian supreme god, Ahura Mazda, i.e. 'Zoroastrians') at will go forth, [as well as] small and large domestic animals, men and women, and the fire, son of Ahura Mazdā, and the barsom spread out in orderly fashion. After that let the Mazdayasnians place *myazd* (the ritual meal) in this house, full of meat and wine. It will be clean, producing no sin, just like before (Videvdad 3.11).

The Pahlavi Videvdad, a Middle Persian (the language spoke by the rabbis' Persian neighbors) translation and commentary on the Avestan Videvdad that was composed during the Talmudic period, comments on this passage: "…This demonstrates that within three days and nights, meat of the frying pan should not be put to use."

is where "they make mourning and lament." This passage bears a relationship to a section of the Avestan Videvdad that refers to the *five* places in which the earth is least happy. In the Videvdad's scheme, Ahura Mazdā—the supreme Zoroastrian deity –describes the fifth and last location of earthly unhappiness as:

> Wherever the man, sustainer of Order, O Spitama Zarathustra, and (his) woman and child are dragged captive along the road *raising a plaintive voice with mouths full of dust, with dry mouths.*

In the Middle Persian rendition, the final line is translated and then glossed as follows:[21]

> 'They will cry out laments in dust and dryness'—the meaning is this: when they all go into captivity, dust and dryness will be theirs.

> There is one who says the meaning is this: dry and dusty mouths are from it.

The late antique interpreters puzzle over what it means to "cry out laments in dust and dryness." The first opinion stays relatively close to the plain, contextual meaning of the Avestan source, and suggests that the earth is unhappy wherever the oppressed cry out about their plight in a dry and dusty captivity. The second view is far less clear. This approach seems to read the phrase causatively—a dusty and dry mouth comes from (too much?) lamenting. In light of the parallel passage at Mēnōy ī Xrad, this interpretation seems to stray from the plain sense of the Avestan original and refer to a kind of punishment for excessive mourning. Perhaps Middle Persian exegetical literature reflects the development of late antique Zoroastrian views of mourning that on the one hand prohibited meat and wine for three days,

---

[21] PV 3.11 (ed. Jamasp, p. 63).

yet at the same time advanced a view that was strongly opposed to *excessive* lament.

Another Middle Persian exegetical text tries to derive condemnation of excessive mourning from an Avestan passage—in this case from one of the oldest and most sacred hymns in the tradition. The original, written in Old Avestan—an archaic and difficult language that is subject to much debate among philologists—has been rendered by P. Oktor Skjærvø as follows:[22]

> Of the things that have been thought, spoken, or performed
> both here and elsewhere [at this time and at other times?]
> both those that are being thought, spoken, or performed and those that have
> been thought, spoken, or performed, we are the singers of songs of welcome
> *—we are not blamers*—in our effort to obtain good things.

In the final line of this passage, the poet refers to himself as one of a group who are "not blamers"—where "blame" retains a critical, almost technical meaning in Avestan and Indo-European poetics. A Middle Persian exegetical collection that interprets and epitomizes the ancient sacred hymns of which this selection is a part, offers the following reading of the passage:[23]

> (The ancient liturgical poem, Yasna Haptanghaiti is also) about the advice not to mourn and lament over the departed, after everything has passed, not to increase lamentation in your mind. And (about) the harm done also to the Spirit of the House from mourning the departed. And this too, that the *frawahr*-spirits of the righteous are on the search after their own sacrifice and the blessings righteous men, not mourning and lamentations.

---

[22] Yasna 35.2. Italics are mine.
[23] Dēnkard IX, 12.20–21.

In other words, one of the Middle Persian interpretations of this ancient text is that the poet is referring to the fact that he is not an excessive lamenter. This is used as an opportunity to convey the idea that mourning and lamenting are harmful—they harm the "spirit of the house" and also the divine *frawahr*-spirits[24] who prefer sacrifices and blessings to mourning and lament. Here again, the fact that Zoroastrian exegetes locate the idea that mourning is detrimental in an ancient and foundational Zoroastrian text highlights how they were attempting to convey this important cultural value and ground it in ancient tradition.

It is interesting to note that Zoroastrians may not have been the only community neighboring the Babylonian rabbis to strongly discourage excessive mourning. The Mandaeans—a 'Gnostic' religious group that lived in late antique Mesopotamia and spoke a dialect of Aramaic that was quite close to that of the rabbis– seem to have shared this value with Zoroastrians and even its accompanying metaphysics. The Mandaean sacred book, the Ginza, views mourning as negative, as we find in one myth in the Ginza Raba where the complex divine character, Ruha, tempts Hawa (i.e. Eve) into excessively mourning over Adam. Centuries later, in the first half of the twentieth century, British anthropologist Lady E.S. Drower offered the following description of the Mandaean community:

> Weeping is forbidden. Mandean women must not scatter dust over their heads, nor tear garments and hair, nor beat their breasts and leap in funeral dances like their neighbours, for Moslems, Jews, and Christians of the humble classes all manifest grief in these ways. Tears become a river which the soul of the departed must ford, and torn

---

[24] This is a complicated supernatural entity which underwent a shift from earlier times— where it seems to have referred to a powerful divine force—to a later period where it was deemed part of the human soul that exists after the death of the body.

hair forms entanglements about his feet, say the Subba ("baptizers," a common designation for Mandaeans).

As Drower points out, and as we saw previously, the idea of tears forming a river that acts as an obstacle for the passage of the deceased is shared with Zoroastrianism.

In sum, a number of Middle Persian texts strongly oppose excessive mourning, and Zoroastrian exegetes attempted to derive this idea from their scriptural heritage. Moreover, the same cultural value was shared with another Sasanian religious community—the Mandaeans. This background might help account for the Bavli's ruling that one hour of mourning prior to a festival annuls the requirement to mourn after the festival, as well as for Shmuel's principle that the law is decided in favor of the lenient opinion in the rules of mourning. While there certainly may be some internal textual factors at work in the development of this lenient approach, perhaps the evolution of the Bavli's approach to mourning can be linked, at least in part, to a broader cultural conception of mourning as something to be limited and curtailed.

CHAPTER SEVEN

INTERPRETATIONS AND THEIR IMPLICATIONS: THE STOLEN LULAV

SUKKAH 29B–30A

Introduction

The opening sugya in the third chapter of Bavli Sukkah discusses the case of the stolen lulav, which the Mishnah disqualifies for use on Sukkot. The Bavli gives two reasons why a stolen lulav is invalid, both of which we will explore in this chapter.

The first reason for the disqualification of a stolen lulav is that it is considered a מצווה הבאה בעבירה—a commandment performed through a transgression. One who performs a commandment in this manner has not, according to the sugya, discharged his duty to perform the commandment. The second reason that a stolen lulav is invalid is that it does not belong to its owner. The rabbis base the notion that a person must own his lulav on a midrash on the word "for yourself" (לכם) found in Leviticus 23:40: "And you shall take for yourself on the first day (ולקחתם לכם ביום הראשון) the product of *hadar* trees, branches of palm trees, boughs of leafy trees, and willows of the brook; and you shall rejoice before the Lord your God seven days." This midrash would disqualify not only a stolen lulav, but a borrowed lulav as well, a halakhah which is indeed found in other mishnayot. In that sense it is a broader explanation than a commandment performed through a transgression. However, the rabbis limited the rule that the lulav must belong to its bearer to the first day of the festival. On subsequent days, one can use a borrowed lulav. In this sense, the reason is more limited and would allow for the use of stolen lulav on subsequent days.

These two reasons for the disqualification of the stolen lulav appear in tannaitic literature and resurface in the Eretz Yisraeli amoraic midrash on

233

Leviticus known as Vayikra Rabbah, in the Yerushalmi and in the Bavli. In Eretz Yisraeli literature, these two reasons for the disqualification of the stolen lulav remain distinct from one another. In the Bavli, however, their different ramifications and applications are compared and contrasted. The Bavli advances the discussion of the stolen lulav by noting how these two reasons lead to different halakhic results. This sugya thus serves as an excellent example of how the Bavli can be better understood and appreciated when we have a deeper understanding of the sources it includes.

Finally, at the end of this chapter we shall examine how the creation of a named halakhic category can and did have impact upon post-Talmudic halakhah. In tannaitic and early amoraic times, while there may have been a notion that one could not use a stolen item to perform a ritual act (such as sacrifice or lulav) there was no general principle stating that a mitzvah may not be performed through a transgression. This notion was crystallized and formulated in the Bavli, and from there it was applied to a variety of other situations. This is a common occurrence in halakhic development and is further demonstration of the deep halakhic impact of the stam on Jewish history.

The Stolen Lulav

The beginning of chapter three of Mishnah Sukkah lists attributes which render a lulav unfit for ritual use, including the following:

לולב הגזול והיבש פסול.   A stolen or dried-up lulav is invalid.

While the Mishnah itself does not explain why either lulav is invalid, other rabbinic sources offer different explanations for the halakhah. The Bavli (cited below) explains that the dried up lulav is invalid because it does not fulfill the biblical criterion of being beautiful—הדר. As for the stolen lulav, we find two distinct explanations. One appears in the tannaitic midrash on Leviticus, Sifra or Torat Kohanim:

ספרא: אמור, יב, ג	**Sifra: Emor, 12, 3**
ולקחתם לכם (ויקרא	*And you shall take for yourself* (Leviticus
כג:מ): כל אחד ואחד.	23:40): Each and every one of you.

"לכם": משלכם, לא הגזול.

For yourself: From your own,
not one that is stolen.

מיכן אמרו: "אין אדם
יוצא ידי חובתו ביום טוב
הראשון שלחג בלולבו
שלחבירו" (=משנה סוכה
ג,יג): אילא אם רצה,
נותנו מתנה לחבירו וחבירו
לחבירו אפילו הן מאה.

From here they have said: "One cannot fulfill
his obligation on the first day of the festival
with another person's lulav (=Mishnah Sukkah 3:13)." Rather, if he wants, he can give
it to another person as a gift, and another to
another, even if there are one hundred.

The midrash explains the term "for yourself" as indicating that one must
own the lulav he uses to fulfill his obligation. The author of the midrash
uses the example of the stolen lulav as one which would be invalid because
it does not belong to him. This teaching is followed by the phrase מיכן אמרו,
a technical term indicating a later addition by the editor of the midrash of a
related mishnah or tosefta.[1] The mishnah cited teaches that on the *first day*
of the festival one cannot fulfill his obligation with a *borrowed* lulav. This
halakhah is based on the continuation of the verse in Leviticus 23:40, "on
the first day (ביום הראשון)," which is read as limiting the requirement of לכם,
that the lulav must belong to its bearer, to the first day. The midrash implies
that on the remaining days of sukkot the worshipper would be able to fulfill
his obligation with any lulav that does not belong to him, borrowed or stolen.

We should note that there is a certain amount of dissonance in this midrash.
The word משלכם seems to disqualify any lulav that does not belong to him,
borrowed or stolen. The following words, ולא הגזול, might be read as limiting
the disqualification to a stolen lulav, a sub-category of the broader category
of lulavim that do not belong to him. The midrash then quotes a mishnah
which disqualifies a borrowed lulav, again invoking the broader category. It
seems likely that in citing the example of the stolen lulav the author of the
midrash is alluding to the mishnah at the beginning of the third chapter of

---

[1] See David Weiss Halivni, *Midrash, Mishnah, and Gemara* (Cambridge: Harvard University Press, 1986), 135 n. 48.

Sukkah, quoted above.[2] In this manner, he may be offering his interpretation of that mishnah—the stolen lulav is invalid because it does not belong to its bearer. However, this leads to a significant implication—just as it would be permissible to use a borrowed lulav after the first day of the festival because there is no requirement for it to belong to the user, so, too, would it be permitted to use a stolen lulav subsequent to the first day. This qualification is not hinted to at all by mishnah 3:1, which simply disqualifies a stolen lulav without any qualification or limitation on the rule.

An alternative explanation for the disqualification of a stolen lulav is found in a parable that appears in both Vayikra Rabbah (30:6) and Pesikta deRav Kahana (piska 27), both Eretz-Yisraeli midrashim composed during the amoraic period.[3] This parable leads to the invalidation of the lulav for all seven days, a more straightforward understanding of mishnah 3:1:

ויקרא רבה ל:ו	**Vayikra Rabbah 30:6**
ולקחתם (ויקרא כג:מ). תני ר' חייא. שתהא לקיחה לכל אחד ואחד מכם. "לכם": משלכם ולא הגזול.	*And you shall take* (Leviticus 23:40): R. Hiyya taught: That there should be a taking for each and every one of you. For yourself: From your own and not one that is stolen.
אמר ר' לוי: מי שהוא לוקח לולב גזול למה הוא דומה? ללסטים שהיה יושב בפרשת דרכים והיה מקפיח העוברים והשבים.	R. Levi taught: Anyone who uses a stolen lulav—to whom may he be likened? To a highwayman who sat at a crossroads, robbing all those who came and went.
חד זמן עבר עילויה חד ליגיון בעי לימגבי דימוסיא דההיא מדינתא.	Once, a legionary passed him on his way to collect the tax of a certain province.

---

[2] In an effort to resolve the contradiction in terms, the Vilna Gaon emends the midrash to read לא את השאול ולא את הגזול-neither the borrowed nor the stolen lulav. He bases this change on the version of the midrash found in Bavli Sukkah 43a.

[3] The cited midrash is found in one of the five chapters which appear in both compositions. There is an intense scholarly debate as to the original source text of the common material. See Anat Reizel, *Mavo LeMidrashim* (Alon Shevut: Mikhlelet Herzog, 2011), 228–229.

קם קדמיה וקפחיה ונסב
כל מה דהוה בידיה.

The highwayman arose before him and robbed him, taking all [the legionary] had with him.

בתר יומין איתצייד
ההוא ליסטיא ואיחבש
בפילקי. שמע ההוא
ליגיונא ואתא לגביה.

After a time the highwayman was captured and thrown into prison. When the legionary heard [the news], he went to him.

אמר ליה: הב לי כל מה
דקפחתני ואנא מילף
עלך זכו קדם מלכא.

He said to him: "Give me all that you robbed from me, and I shall plead for you before the king."

אמר ליה: כל מה דקפחית
ומן כל מה דנסבית לית
ליה לההוא גברא מיניה
אלא להדין טפיטא
דתחותי דהוא מן דידך.

He [the highwayman] said to him: "Of all that a certain person (I) robbed and took away from you there is nothing left except this rug beneath me which belongs to you."

אמר ליה: הב יתיה לי ואנא
מליף עלך זכו קדם מלכא.

He [the legionary] said to him: "Give it to me, and I shall plead for you before the king."

אמר ליה: ניסבה.

He said to him: "Take it."

אמר ליה: תהא ידע דאת
עליל למחר לדינא קדם
מלכא, והוא שאיל לך ואמר
לך: אית לך בר אנש מילף
עלך זכו? ואת אמר ליה:
אית לי ליגיון פלן מילף עלי.
והוא משלח וקרי לי, ואנא
אתי ומליף עלך זכו קדמוי.

He [the legionary] said: "Know that tomorrow you will enter before the king for judgment, and when he asks you and says to you, 'Is there any man that will plead for you?' you should say, 'I have such and such a legionary who will plead for me.' [Thereupon] he will send [a messenger] summoning me, and I will plead on your behalf before him."

למחר אוקמוהי לדינה קדם
מלכא. שאל ליה מלכא ואמר
ליה, אית לך בר נש מלף
עלך זכו? אמר ליה אית לי
ליגיון פלן מליף עלי זכו.
שלח מלכא קרא ליה.

The next day they stood him in judgment before the king. The king asked him: "Have you a man to plead for you?" He [the highwayman] said to him: "I have such and such a legionary who will plead for me." The king then sent for the legionary and summoned him

אמר ליה: מה את חכם מילף
על הדין גברא זכו? אמר ליה:
חכם אנא כד שלחתני למיגבי
דימוסיא דההיא מדינתא
קם קדמי וקפחי ונסב כל
מה דהוה עמי והדין טפיטא
דהוא מדידי מסהיד עילויה.

He asked: "Do you know how to plead for this man?" He said to him: "I know, when you sent me to levy the tax of a certain province, he arose before me and robbed me, and took all that I had with me. And this rug which belongs to me is witness to what he did."

התחילו כל העם צווחין
ואמרין: אוי לו לזה
שנעשה סניגורו קטיגורו!

Whereupon everyone cried out, saying: "Woe to the man whose advocate turns accuser!"

כך אדם לוקח לולב לזכות
בו, ואם היה גזול צווח
לפני הקב"ה ואומר: גזול
אני! חמוס אני! ומלאכי
השרת אומרין: אוי לו לזה
שנעשה סניגורו קטיגורו!

So, too,, a person takes a lulav in order to gain God's favor through it. If it was stolen, the lulav itself cries out before the Holy One, blessed be He and says: "I am stolen! I was attained by violence!" And the ministering angels exclaim: "Woe to this one whose advocate became his accuser!"

While the verses in Leviticus do not provide any clue as to the symbolic/theological purpose of the lulav, it is clear that at least by rabbinic times, and perhaps earlier, the "four species"—the lulav and the accompanying etrog, myrtle and willow—were considered a supplication for rain. Yerushalmi Ta'anit 1:1, 63c makes this connection explicit:

על ידי שארבעת מינין הללו
גדילים על המים, לפיכך
הן באין פרקליטין למים.

Because these four species grow near water; therefore they serve as advocates for water.

238

Understanding the lulav as a symbolic means by which Jews petition God for rain, R. Levi uses a parable to demonstrate how counterproductive it would be to use a stolen lulav. The essence of R. Levi's parable is that the very item which is meant to advocate before God becomes the object which testifies against its bearer.

We should emphasize that the parable is independent of the לכם משלכם midrash that immediately precedes it. This line, attributed by the midrash to R. Hiyya, is identical to that found in the Sifra. It seems likely that Vayikra Rabbah is simply quoting the tannaitic midrash, without the מיכן אמרו reference to the borrowed lulav. Thus this midrash is actually the earliest juxtaposition of both reasons for the disqualification of the stolen lulav—(1) it does not belong to its bearer; (2) a stolen object cannot be used for a ritual purpose because it defeats the very purpose of that ritual. The לכם משלכם midrash would limit the disqualification to the first day, while R. Levi's interpretation would extend the prohibition to all of the days; any use of a stolen lulav, no matter the day, would turn the advocate into an accuser. Nevertheless, the authors of Vayikra Rabbah do not in any way delve into the ramifications of these differences.

Performing a Commandment with the Product of a Transgression

Before we turn our attention to the Bavli, we will first analyze a Tosefta and two sugyot in the Yerushalmi that serve as background. While the phrase מצווה הבאה בעבירה appears only in the Bavli, there are statements in the Tosefta and Yerushalmi that refer to a similar concept. Each of the sources below refers to a situation in which an item was stolen and then used to perform a ritual act. The following passage from Tosefta Sanhedrin 1:2 appears among a group of midrashim on Psalms 10:3:

ר' אליעזר בן יעקב או'.	R. Eliezer b. Yaakov says: What is the
מה תלמוד לומר: ובוצע	meaning of *The robber pronounces a ben-*
ברך ניאץ ה' (תהילים	*ediction [but in fact] condemns the Lord*
י:ג). משלו משל.	(Psalms 10:3). They composed a parable.

למה הדבר דומה? לאחד	What is this like? [Like] one who stole a *se'ah* of
שגנב סאה של חטין. טחנן	wheat, ground it, baked it, set aside a portion of
אפאן והפריש מהן חלה	it as *hallah,* and fed it to his children. How can
והאכיל לבניו. היאך זה	he make a blessing? Rather he is blaspheming.
מברך. אינו אלא מנאץ. על	About him it is said: The robber pronounces a
זה נאמ' ובוצע ברך נאץ ה'.	benediction [but in fact] condemns the Lord.

The word בוצע, which appears in the Biblical verse, is properly translated as the noun "robber," and it serves as the subject of the verb ברך, bless.[4] R. Eliezer b. Yaakov, however, understands the "robber" to be the unwritten subject of the verb, freeing up the word בוצע to serve as a verb, signifying the cutting or slicing of bread, a common meaning of this word in rabbinic Hebrew.[5] This allows him to interpret the verse as referring to a robber who steals the bread, then breaks it, makes a blessing (ברך), and in doing so blasphemes (נאץ) God. In a manner similar to the teaching of R. Levi cited above, a ritual act performed with stolen goods produces the opposite of the intended outcome. One who blesses on stolen bread ends up blaspheming God.

A similar midrash on Psalms 10:3 appears in Yerushalmi Shabbat 13:3 (14a), which is the source whose concepts and language are closest to what the Bavli terms מצווה הבאה בעבירה. The mishnah from Shabbat upon which this passage is based states that one who tears an item of clothing on Shabbat out of anger or as a sign of mourning is not liable for having transgressed Shabbat. While the mishnah exempts him from bringing a sin-offering for transgressing Shabbat, it is not clear if, in the case of a mourner, his actions fulfill the halakhic obligation to rend one's clothes following the death of a relative.[6] In a passage not quoted below, R. Yose concludes that if he tore his clothes, he fulfilled his halakhic obligation. Below R. Yose's colleagues question the implication of his ruling by invoking a source about a mitzvah performed with stolen goods:

---

[4] Francis Brown, S. R. Driver, Charles A. Briggs, Edward Robinson, Wilhelm Gesenius, and James Strong, *The Brown, Driver, Briggs Hebrew and English Lexicon* (Peabody, Mass: Hendrickson Publishers, 2001), 371.

[5] See Mishnah Shabbat 7:2; Sifra Emor 13:2; Bavli Shabbat 39b.

[6] See Yerushalmi Moed Katan 3:7 (83b–c); Bavli Moed Katan 20b–21a

משנה: הקורע בחמתו ועל מתו, וכל המקלקלין, פטורין.

Mishnah: One who tears out of anger or for his dead, and anyone who destroys, is exempt.

(1a) חברייא בעון קומי ר' יוסה: לא כן אמ' ר' יוחנן בשם ר' שמעון בן יוצדק: מצה גזולה אינו יוצא בה ידי חובתו בפסח.

(1a) R. Yose's colleagues asked him: Did not R. Yohanan say in the name of R. Shimon b. Yotzadak: One does not fulfill his obligation on Passover with stolen matzah.

(1b) אמר לון. תמן גופה עבירה, ברם הכא הוא עבר עבירה. כך אנו אומרים הוציא מצה מרשות היחיד לרשות הרבים אינו יוצא בה ידי חובתו בפסח.

(1b) He said to them: There [in the case of the matzah] it itself is [the product of] a sin. But here [in the case of tearing] he is transgressing. Do we say that one who transfers matzah from the private to the public domain [on Shabbat] does not fulfill his obligation?!

(2a) תני: מצה גזולה אסור לברך עליה.

(2a) It was taught: It is forbidden to bless over stolen matzah.

(2b) אמר רב הושעיה: על שם "ובוצע ברך נאץ ה'" (תהילים י:ג).

(2b) R. Hoshaya said: Because [Scripture states]: The robber pronounces a benediction [but in fact] condemns the Lord (Psalms 10:3).

(2c) אמר ר' יונה: הדא דאת אמר בתחילה, אבל בסוף לא דמים הוא חייב לו.

(2c) R. Yonah said: That which you say [refers to] before [eating] but at the end does he not owe him money?!

(3a) ר' יונה אמר: אין עבירה מצוה.

(3a) R. Yonah said: A transgression cannot become a commandment.

(3b) ר' יוסה אמר: אין מצוה עבירה.

(3b) R. Yose said: A commandment cannot become a transgression.

241

(3c) אמר ר' אילא: אלה
המצות (ויקרא כז:לד): אם
עשיתן כמצוותן הן מצות,
ואם לאו אינן מצות.

(3c) R. Ila said: *These are the commandments* (Leviticus 27:34): If you did them as they were commanded, they are commandments, and if not, they are not commandments.

R. Yose's colleagues object to his assertion that if a mourner tears his clothes on Shabbat he would fulfill his halakhic obligation. Based on the example of stolen matzah which cannot be used to fulfill one's obligation, his colleagues imply that in all situations it should be categorically impossible to fulfill a ritual obligation through the performance of a transgression. R. Yose resolves (1b) this difficulty by stating that in the case of the stolen matzah the ritual object is itself the product of a transgression, whereas in the case of rending clothing on Shabbat it is the person's actions that constitute the transgression. There is nothing inherently wrong with the clothing that served as the object of the ritual. Therefore, one has fulfilled his obligation to rend his clothing as a sign of mourning, even if he does so on Shabbat. In contrast, the stolen matzah came into the possession of the one who eats it through a transgression. Therefore, it cannot be used to fulfill his obligation. R. Yose cites support for his interpretation from the case of matzah which was carried from one domain to another on Shabbat. Similar to tearing one's clothes, the transgression is the action performed with the object and not the acquisition of the object itself. The performance of a ritual is invalidated only when the very object of that ritual was attained by a transgression.

The sugya continues with an examination of the case of stolen matzah. A baraita (2a) states that it is forbidden to make a blessing over stolen matzah. R. Hoshaya (2b) cites the same verse from Psalms found in the tosefta passage above as proof for the prohibition. R. Yonah (2c) clarifies the ruling and states that the prohibition exists only before the matzah has been consumed. Once the bread has been consumed, there is nothing more to offend God and the thief is obligated to recite the blessing after the meal.

The sugya concludes with an amoraic debate on the general relationship between performing transgressions and commandments and shifts the focus back to the mishnah. R. Yonah declares—אין עבירה מצווה—a transgression cannot become a commandment. If one commits a sin in the performance of a mitzvah, then he has not fulfilled his obligation, even if he is not liable for having transgressed, as is the case in the mishnah.[7] This provides a negative answer to the question asked above about the situation referred to in the mishnah—when he rends his clothes on Shabbat he has not fulfilled his obligation. R. Yose (3b) reverses the wording found in R. Yonah's statement, saying—אין מצווה עבירה—an action which is done in order to fulfill a commandment cannot be also considered a transgression. Like R. Yonah, R. Yose also relates to the mishnah, but in a different manner. One who tears his clothes as a sign of mourning on Shabbat has not transgressed because he was performing a mitzvah. If we wish to harmonize R. Yose's statement in this section with his statement in the section above (1b), we have to posit that R. Yose holds that since there is nothing inherently wrong with the clothing which he tore, he has fulfilled his mitzvah (as he stated above). Thus while both amoraim may agree with the mishnah's exemption of the one who tore on Shabbat, they disagree as to the implications of this exemption. The sugya concludes with R. Ila's midrash that presumably supports R. Yonah, who holds that if while performing a mitzvah one also transgresses, he does not receive credit for the mitzvah.[8]

We should also note that these statements, especially R. Yonah's, are the closest that the Yerushalmi gets to a generally formulated rule. The leap from אין עבירה מצווה to מצווה הבאה בעבירה is not large. However, in our analysis R. Yonah was referring to a slightly different situation from the case of the stolen object. The mishnah in Shabbat referred to a case in which the very same act is both a transgression and a mitzvah. The passage that we omitted

---

[7] In the above section that we have not quoted, the exemption is attributed to R. Shimon, who exempts anyone who performs a forbidden act on Shabbat for a reason other than its primary creative purpose. In the mishnah he is exempt from bringing a sin-offering because tearing in order to sew is the prohibited act, for it is has a creative purpose; one who rends as a sign of mourning did not have creative intent. In the Yerushalmi this is termed עד שיהא לו צורך בגופו של דבר. In the Bavli it is termed מלאכה שאינה צריכה לגופה.

[8] However, if we were to accept a lack of harmony between R. Yose's statement in section three and his statement in section one, there is a possibility that despite the reversal in words, there is no halakhic disagreement between them. According to this explanation, R. Yona and R. Yose's explanations are complementary—R. Yona explains that since he performed a transgression (one for which he is not liable, as is stated in the mishnah), he does not receive credit for performing a mitzvah. R. Yose explains the converse: since he has performed a mitzvah (albeit one for which he does not get credit), he has not transgressed (as is stated in the mishnah).

deals with another such situation—one who slaughters a sin-offering on Shabbat. In both this case and the case of one who tears on Shabbat, we have a transgression that is also a commandment. This differs from the case of the stolen lulav (or matzah or sukkah), which are ritual items that "come to his hand" through a transgression—literally a "mitzvah that came to his hand through a transgression." Thus it is significant that while general rules are formulated on a similar matter in the Yerushalmi, they still differ from the legal formulation that appears only in the Bavli.

Performing a Commandment with Stolen Goods

While the amoraim in Yerushalmi Shabbat disqualify the use of an object which is the product of a transgression in order to fulfill a commandment, the anonymous voice in Yerushalmi Sukkah on Mishnah Sukkah 3:1 (53c) suggests an entirely different line of reasoning, one which we have already encountered in the Sifra—the stolen object cannot be used because it does not belong to its bearer. As we shall see, this allows for the stolen item to be used once it has been legally acquired by the thief.

(1) תני ר' חייה: ולקחתם
לכם (ויקרא כג:מ):
משלכם, ולא הגזול.

(1) Rabbi Hiyya taught: *And you shall take for yourselves* (Leviticus 23:40) From your own, not one that is stolen.

(2) אמר ר' לוי: זה שהוא
נוטל לולב גזול למה הוא
דומה? לאחד שכיבד את
השלטון תמחוי אחד ונמצא
משלו. אמרו: אי לו לזה
שנעשה סניגורו קטיגורו...⁹

(2) R. Levi said: This one who takes a stolen lulav to what can he be compared? To one who honored the ruler with a [gift of a] plate and it turned out to be his [the ruler's]. They said: Woe to this one whose advocate became his accuser...[9]

(3a) גזל לולב מיכן והדס
מיכן וערבה מיכן ואגדן.
נישמעינה מן הדא:

(3a) One who stole a lulav from here, a myrtle from here, and a willow from here and tied them together. [What is the ruling?] Infer from this [teaching]:

(3b) סוכה גזולה: אית תניי תני כשירה. אית תניי תני פסולה.	(3b) A stolen sukkah: There is a tanna who teaches that it is valid and a tanna who teaches that it is invalid.
(3c) ר' סימון בשם ר' יהושע בן לוי: מאן דאמר כשירה בשגזל קרקע. מאן דאמר פסולה בשגזל פסל.	(3c) R. Simon in the name of R. Yehoshua b. Levi [said]: He who said it is valid [refers to a case] where he stole the land. He who said it is invalid [refers to a case] where he stole *skhakh*.
(3d) ואיפשר שלא ייקשר? במייישב מלמעלן.	(3d) And is it possible for him not to tie them? [It is a case] where he rests them from above.
(3e) רבנן דקיסרין בשם ר' יוחנן: בין זה ובין זה פסולה.	(3e) The rabbis of Caesarea [said] in the name of R. Yohanan: In either case it is invalid.
(4a) אי זו היא גזולה פסולה? כל שהוא נכנס בתוך סוכתו של חבירו שלא מדעתו.	(4a) What type [of sukkah] is stolen and invalid? One who enters his neighbor's sukkah without permission.
(4b) כהדא גמליאל זוגא עבד ליה מטלא גו שוקא עבר רבי שמעון בן לקיש. אמר ליה: מאן שרא לך.	(4b) As [in the incident of] Gamaliel Zuga who erected a sukkah in the marketplace. R. Shimon b. Lakish walked past. He said to him, "who gave you permission?"

The Yerushalmi passage begins with the לכם משלכם midrash and an abridged version of the parable of R. Levi, which were both discussed above. The anonymous voice of the Yerushalmi continues (3a) by questioning the status of a lulav made up of stolen parts and subsequently bound together. We should immediately note that the question itself relates a certain understanding of why stolen items cannot be used to perform a mitzvah. The anonymous voice clearly believes that their invalidity is a result of their not belonging to the bearer, and is not related to the fact that the item was acquired by a transgression. This accords with the reasoning found in section one of this sugya, לכם משלכם, but does not seem to follow R. Levi's parable or R. Yose's argument in the sugya in Shabbat.

The mechanism for transfer of ownership that underlies the Yerushalmi's question is based upon a tannaitic halakhah (Mishnah Bava Kamma 9:1) according to which a physical modification to a stolen object effects a change in ownership. The idea of this halakhah is that when a thief modifies the object he has stolen, he must return the value of the object but not the object itself, which he now owns. In the Bavli (Bava Kamma 66a) this principle is known as "a change transfers ownership" (שינוי מעשה קונה). Tying the lulav bundle together, although not a permanent change, may constitute an alteration which would effect a change in ownership, thereby allowing the thief to own the lulav and use it to fulfill his mitzvah. Does it?

To answer this question, the Yerushalmi compares this situation with the case of a stolen sukkah, concerning which there are differing tannaitic opinions (3b). The conflicting positions of the tannaim are harmonized by R. Simon in the name of R. Yehoshua b. Levi (3c). The tanna who permits the use of a stolen sukkah refers to a case in which the land beneath the sukkah was stolen, while the one who forbids it refers to a case in which the *skhakh* was stolen. While R. Yehoshua b. Levi does not explicitly explain why the stolen *skhakh* would be problematic, it is likely that he prohibits it for the same reasons explored above in Yerushalmi Shabbat regarding stolen matzah. The essential element in fulfilling the commandment of sukkah is the *skhakh,* and one cannot fulfill his obligation with the product of a transgression.

As far as why R. Yehoshua b. Levi permits the case of the stolen land, there are two possible reasons. First, the land is not a necessary element of the fulfillment of the mitzvah of sukkah, and therefore the fact that it is stolen is not relevant to the use of the sukkah. A second explanation for the leniency regarding stolen land is that there is a halakhic principle that land cannot be stolen.[9] Therefore, when an individual builds a sukkah on land that does not belong to him, there is no actual theft taking place.[10]

The anonymous voice objects to the second half of R. Yehoshua b. Levi's statement, that all tannaim agree that stolen *skhakh* invalidates the sukkah

---

[9] See Yerushalmi Kilayim 7:6; Orlah 2:1 and Bavli Bava Kamma 117b, as well as the Bavli sugya which will be discussed below.

[10] A parallel to this discussion appears in Bavli Sukkah 31a, but a full analysis is beyond the scope of this chapter.

(3d). According to the stam of the Yerushalmi, just as bundling the lulav would render a change in ownership, so, too, tying the *skhakh* down to the top of the sukkah should be considered a change sufficient such that the stolen sukkah belongs to the thief, and he could use it to fulfill his mitzvah. Unlike the amoraim who seem to disqualify the stolen *skhakh* because it is a product of a transgression, the anonymous voice reasons that stolen *skhakh* is invalid for use in a sukkah because it does not belong to its owner. As a consequence, legal change in ownership would validate use of the *skhakh* because it would now belong to the thief. Thus we can see that while the amoraim disqualified the stolen *skhakh* for a categorical reason (it was involved in a transgression), the stam of the Yerushalmi mitigates the disqualification by offering a more tentative explanation—it does not belong to the owner.

The resolution to the difficulty in essence maintains the stam's understanding of why stolen *skhakh* is invalid. The *skhakh* is invalid only if the one who stole the material for the *skhakh* did not tie it down, for in such a case there was no physical change wrought upon the stolen goods. Therefore the sukkah remains stolen and invalid. This line of questioning by the stam of the Yerushalmi (sections 3a and 3d) is significant because it is the first time that the principle of "a change transfers ownership" is applied to the case of a stolen lulav. Whereas the editor of the Sifra seems to have posited that the stolen lulav is invalid because it does not belong to the bearer, the Yerushalmi takes this one step further and posits that the issue of ownership of stolen objects can be remedied.

The discussion concludes with the statement of R. Yohanan (3e), who rules that in both cases, stolen land and stolen *skhakh,* the sukkah is invalid. He, like R. Yehoshua b. Levi, does not provide any explanation for his reasoning. We can assume that R. Yohanan continues to disqualify the use of stolen items in the performance of a mitzvah for the same reason as did the other amoraim—the object was acquired through a transgression. This is true even if R. Yohanan thinks that land technically cannot be stolen. It is invalid because he still built this sukkah through a transgression—by using someone else's property without their permission. Since he has taken possession of the land through an illicit act, he cannot fulfill his obligation. In other words, R. Yohanan disagrees with R. Yehoshua ben Levi about whether the fact that, legally speaking, land cannot be stolen means that one can use stolen land to build a sukkah.

The sugya concludes with a clarification regarding the situation in which a stolen sukkah is invalid. Tosefta Sukkah 1:4 includes the stolen sukkah among a list of sukkot which are invalid:

סוכת הרועין סוכת הקייצין	The shepherd's sukkah, the fig harvester's
וסוכה גזולה פסולה.	sukkah and the stolen sukkah are invalid.

The first two cases are invalid because they are sukkot –and here it might be more apt to translate the term as booths—which are built for the purpose of providing shade during the year, and not for the intent of fulfilling the mitzvah. It seems that the Tosefta groups these three sukkot together because they were all constructed correctly with regard to the laws of sukkah—materially they are valid sukkot for use on the festival—but they are nevertheless invalid. The Yerushalmi (4a) explains that a stolen sukkah would include a case in which one uses his neighbor's sukkah without permission. When one sits in one's neighbor's sukkah without permission, it is simply considered theft. He uses something which does not belong to him and thereby transgresses. There is no halakhic difference between someone who uses a sukkah without asking and one who steals *skhakh* to put in his own sukkah.

The Yerushalmi (4b) then connects the case of a stolen sukkah with a story which describes a sukkah built in the public domain. In this story R. Shimon b. Lakish chastises Gamaliel Zuga for building his sukkah in the marketplace. We should note that R. Shimon ben Lakish does not explicitly state that the sukkah is invalid. Rather he simply rebukes Gamaliel Zuga for building his sukkah in an area he is not supposed to use. The issue of building a sukkah in the public domain is mentioned in Tosefta Bava Kamma 6:28:

אילו מסככין על פתחי	Those who place *skhakh* over the entrance
חנויותיהן ברשות הרבים	to their shops in the public domain, even
בחג אף על פי שיש להן	though they have permission [to do so], if
רשות ובא אחר והוזק	one came and was injured by it, he [the
בהן הרי זה חייב.	shopkeeper] is liable [for damages].

The Tosefta allows store owners to make use of the area immediately in front of their shops to build their sukkot. It does not allow any individual to build a sukkah anywhere in the marketplace he so desires. Thus it seems that the story in the Yerushalmi accords well with the Tosefta's halakhah.[11] R. Shimon b. Lakish rebukes Gamaliel Zuga for building a sukkah in an area of the public domain where the building of sukkot is not allowed. The editor of the sugya connects this story to the case of the "stolen sukkah," implying that building a sukkah on the public domain is also a transgression. Whether or not the editor believes that Gamaliel Zuga had fulfilled his obligation is difficult to determine.

In conclusion, the amoraim in this passage from the Yerushalmi (3c, 3e) seem to maintain, as they do in the passage from Yerushalmi Shabbat, that a product of transgression can never be used to fulfill a commandment. Once something has been involved in a transgression, one can never use it to perform a mitzvah. This is extended from the lulav to the sukkah, although there remain some situations in which a stolen sukkah can be used. The shift in this sugya occurs with the anonymous voice, who has a different understanding of why stolen objects cannot be used in the performance of ritual acts—they do not belong to the bearer. Thus, if the thief has performed an act with the lulav that would legally transfer ownership to him, he may use it to perform the mitzvah. To nuance the discussion, the stam opens (3a) with a question concerning a thief who bound the species together—is this a sufficient alteration to render a change in ownership? In section 3d he limits the amoraic ruling that stolen *skhakh* cannot be used in a situation where the thief has not tied the *skhakh* to the sukkah. The implication is that if the thief has tied it down, the *skhakh* now belongs to him and he can use it to fulfill his mitzvah. While these stammaitic halakhot may remedy the problem of מושלכם mentioned in section one, they do not seem to remedy the problem raised in R. Levi's parable in section two. The advocate, though changed, has still become the accuser.

In sum, both the Tosefta and the Yerushalmi sources demonstrate that many Eretz Yisraeli sages held that a stolen object could never be used in the performance of a mitzvah. This approach is reflected in R. Levi's parable, which is specific to the case of the lulav, and R. Yehoshua b. Levi and R. Yohanan's categorical invalidation of the stolen *skhakh*. In contrast, the לכם מושלכם midrash found in the Sifra and in the anonymous voice of the Yerushalmi Sukkah sugya approach the issue from an entirely different perspective. There is no concern for the fact that the goods were once stolen or were obtained

---

[11] See Yehezkel Abramsky, *Tosefta: Im Perush Hazon Yehezkel, Bava Kamma* (Jerusalem, 1948), 74.

through theft. Instead, the focus is solely on current ownership of the object. The Yerushalmi clarifies this point by noting that if the thief performed an act which would legally transfer the item into his possession, he could subsequently use it to perform a mitzvah.

Bavli Sukkah 29b–30a

We can frame our sugya in Sukkah chapter three of the Bavli as having a rough correspondence to these two Eretz Yisraeli understandings of why the stolen lulav is invalid: (1) it was acquired through a transgression; (2) the lulav does not belong to its bearer. The Bavli focuses on comparing the halakhic ramifications of these two different reasons. If the stolen lulav is disqualified because it does not belong to its owner (the לכם משלכם midrash and sections 3a and 3d of Yerushalmi Sukkah), then it can be changed—perhaps bundled—and used by the thief or, alternatively, used after the first day. If, however, the problem with the stolen lulav is that it was acquired through a transgression—as argued by R. Levi and implied by the amoraim in the Yerushalmi—then a stolen lulav is disqualified from use for the entire festival.

(1a) קא פסיק ותני, לא
שנא ביום טוב ראשון ולא
שנא ביום טוב שני.

(1a) The tanna definitively teaches [that the stolen lulav is invalid]. It does not matter [if it is to be used] on the first day of the festival or on the second day.

(1b) בשלמא יבש - הדר
בעינן, וליכא. אלא גזול,
בשלמא יום טוב ראשון -
דכתיב לכם - משלכם, אלא
ביום טוב שני אמאי לא?

(1b) [The prohibition on the second day concerning] a dry [lulav] is understandable, [since] we require beautiful (Leviticus 23:40) and this is not. But with regard to a stolen lulav, [the prohibition] is understandable on the first day, since it is written, for yourself (Leviticus 23:40)—from your own, but why should it not be allowed on the second day?

Tannaitic Source	Amoraic Source	Stammaitic Source

AMORAIC STATEMENT IN THE NAME OF A TANNA

(1c) אמר רבי יוחנן משום רבי
שמעון בן יוחי: משום דהוה
ליה מצוה הבאה בעבירה.
שנאמר והבאתם גזול ואת
הפסח ואת החולה (מלאכי
א:יג), גזול דומיא דפסח, מה
פסח לית ליה תקנתא - אף
גזול לית ליה תקנתא.

(1c) R. Yohanan said in the name of R. Shimon bar Yohai: Because it would be a commandment performed through a transgression, as it is said *And you bring the stolen, the lame and the sick* (Mal 1:13). The stolen is similar to the lame; just as the lame can never be rectified, so that which is stolen can never be rectified.

CLARIFICATION

(1d) לא שנא לפני יאוש
ולא שנא לאחר יאוש.

(1d) [This is so] irrespective of whether [the stolen thing is used] before [the owner has] despair [of recovery] or after despair.

QUESTION

(1e) בשלמא לפני יאוש -
אדם כי יקריב מכם (ויקרא
א:ב) אמר רחמנא, ולאו
דידיה הוא. אלא לאחר
יאוש - הא קנייה ביאוש!

(1e) This is all understandable before despair, for God has said: *A person, when he offers from his own* (Leviticus 1:2) and this is not his, but [why should the law apply] after despair, seeing [that the robber] has acquired it by [virtue of that] despair?

ANSWER

(1f) אלא לאו - משום דהוה
ליה מצוה הבאה בעבירה.

(1f) The reason must then be that it is a commandment fulfilled through a transgression.

RELATED MIDRASH

(2) ואמר רבי יוחנן משום רבי
שמעון בן יוחי: מאי דכתיב:
כי אני ה' אהב משפט שונא
גזל בעולה (ישעיהו סא:ח).
משל למלך בשר ודם שהיה
עובר על בית המכס, אמר
לעבדיו: תנו מכס למוכסים.

(2) And R. Yohanan said in the name of R. Shimon b. Yohai: What is the meaning of that which is written: *For I the Lord love justice, I hate robbery with a burnt offering* (Isa 61:8)? This may be compared to a human king who passed through his custom-house and said to his attendants, "pay the tax to the tax-collectors."

Tannaitic Source   Amoraic Source   Stammaitic Source

אמרו לו: והלא כל המכס כולו
שלך הוא! אמר להם: ממני
ילמדו כל עוברי דרכים, ולא
יבריחו עצמן מן המכס. אף
הקדוש ברוך הוא אמר: אני ה'
שונא גזל בעולה, ממני ילמדו
בני ויבריחו עצמן מן הגזל.

They said to him, "But the whole tax belongs to you!" He answered them, "All travelers will learn from me not to evade their payments of tax." So the Holy One, blessed be He, said, I the Lord hate robbery with a burnt-offering; let My children learn from Me and keep away from robbery.

EXPLANATION OF THE MISHNAH

(3a) אתמר נמי, אמר רבי
אמי: יבש פסול מפני שאין
הדר (ויקרא כג:ד). גזול
פסול משום דהוה ליה
מצוה הבאה בעבירה.

(3a) It was also stated: R. Ami said: A dry [lulav] is invalid because it is not beautiful (Leviticus 23:4). A stolen one is invalid because it is a commandment performed through a transgression.

DISSENTING OPINION

(3b) ופליגא דרבי יצחק.
דאמר רבי יצחק בר נחמני
אמר שמואל: לא שנו אלא
ביום טוב ראשון, אבל ביום
טוב שני, מתוך שיוצא
בשאול - יוצא נמי בגזול.

(3b) And this disagrees with R. Yitzhak, since R. Yitzhak b. Nahmani said in the name of Shmuel: This was taught only with regard to the first day of the festival, but on the second day, since one fulfills his obligation with a borrowed [lulav] he also fulfils it with a stolen one.

OBJECTION

(3c) מתיב רב נחמן בר יצחק:
לולב הגזול והיבש פסול, הא
שאול - כשר. אימת? אילימא
ביום טוב ראשון - הא כתיב,
לכם - משלכם, והאי לאו
דידיה הוא. אלא לאו - ביום
טוב שני, וקתני גזול פסול!

(3c) R. Nahman b. Yitzhak objected: "a stolen or dry lulav is invalid," this implies that a borrowed one is valid. When is this so? If you say, on the first day of the festival, is it not written "for yourself"' implying that it should be your own, and this one is not his! Rather, [it must be] on the second day of the festival, and yet it teaches that a stolen one is invalid.

Tannaitic Source   Amoraic Source   Stammaitic Source

AMORAIC EXPLANATION

(3d) אמר רב אשי: לעולם ביום טוב ראשון, ולא מיבעיא קאמר: לא מיבעיא שאול - דלאו דידיה הוא. אבל גזול, אימא סתם גזילה יאוש בעלים הוא, וכדידיה דמי - קא משמע לן.	(3d) Rav Ashi replied: Indeed [the mishnah] refers to the first day of the festival but [the mishnah] is stated in the form of 'it is not required': It is not required to state that a borrowed one is invalid since it is not his; but in the case of a stolen one, of which I might say that normally a robbery [implies immediate] despair by its owner and that it is like his own, therefore he informs us [that even a stolen one is invalid].

Tannaitic Source   Amoraic Source   Stammaitic Source

We will begin our analysis of the Bavli by presenting the traditional reading of the sugya, comparing the positions of the sages represented to those found in the Eretz Yisraeli sources. Based on our findings, we will reconstruct the development of the Bavli sugya.

The sugya begins (1a) by positing that the mishnah invalidates a stolen lulav not only on the first day of the festival but on the remaining days as well. It then analyzes why this should be the case. The לכם משלכם midrash disqualifies the stolen lulav only on the first day. What are the grounds, the stam asks, to disqualify a stolen lulav on subsequent days? R. Yohanan in the name of R. Shimon b. Yohai (1c) answers that such an act would be considered a מצווה הבאה בעבירה, a commandment fulfilled through a transgression. Subsequently (section two), the Talmud cites a related midrash of R. Yohanan also transmitted in the name of R. Shimon b. Yohai concerning God's hatred of stolen sacrifices.

The passage continues with amoraic statements concerning the interpretation and scope of the mishnah. R. Ami (3a) explains that a dried-up lulav is invalid because it is not הדר—"beautiful"—and a stolen lulav is forbidden because it is a מצווה הבאה בעבירה. The stam (3b) indicates that Shmuel disagrees with this interpretation of the mishnah because Shmuel permits the use of a stolen lulav after the first day of the festival, when the rule that the lulav belong to its bearer no longer applies. The fact that Shmuel allows a stolen lulav after the first day indicates, to the stam, that Shmuel does not subscribe to the principle of מצווה הבאה בעבירה. R. Nahman b. Yitzhak (3c) objects to Shmuel based on an inference from the mishnah's invalidation of the stolen lulav, which implies that a borrowed one is valid. This indicates that the mishnah refers to the days after the first day of the festival, for on the first day even a borrowed lulav would be invalid. Rav Ashi (3d) responds to the objection by rejecting the inference made by R. Nahman b. Yitzhak. The mishnah's rule is indeed limited to the first day of the festival. On subsequent days, just as a borrowed lulav may be used, so, too, may a stolen one. R. Ashi explains that the mishnah specified the stolen lulav because the principle of "despair" (explained below) may lead one to think that a stolen lulav immediately becomes the property of the thief, and therefore could be used to perform the mitzvah even on the first day. By citing the example of a stolen lulav, the mishnah teaches that stolen objects do not immediately become the property of thieves. A stolen lulav cannot be used on the first day of the festival because it is like a borrowed lulav—it does not belong to the thief. It was so obvious to the mishnah that a borrowed lulav is invalid (on the first day) that it did not even need to say so.

The Bavli sugya presents the same explanations for the prohibition of the stolen lulav found in both Vayikra Rabbah and the Yerushalmi. Although the exact named category of מצווה הבאה בעבירה does not exist in the earlier sources, a similar such notion is found in Yerushalmi Shabbat, in R. Levi's parable in Vayikra Rabbah (and in an abbreviated format in Yerushalmi Sukkah), and in the amoraic statements in Yerushalmi Sukkah. And although Shmuel (section 3b) does not explicitly mention the לכם משלכם midrash, his statement is clearly based upon it. His position correlates, to a certain extent, with the Sifra and the opinion of the stam of Yerushalmi Sukkah. What distinguishes the Bavli from the earlier compositions is its intense interest in comparing the ramifications of each interpretation. There are two ways in which this is achieved. First, Shmuel's statement itself hints at the difference between the לכם משלכם interpretation and the מצווה הבאה בעבירה interpretation. Shmuel explicitly states that the stolen lulav is invalid only on the first day. While this may have been alluded to in the Sifra's reference to the borrowed lulav, it was not stated explicitly there. Second, the comparison of the two interpretations of the mishnah is also realized in the term ופליגא ד' which opens section 3b. This technical term was added by the Babylonian redactor in order to highlight the incompatibility of the two interpretations. The redactor contrasts Shmuel with R. Ami and posits that Shmuel, who allows for the use of a stolen lulav after the first day, rejects the entire concept of מצווה הבאה בעבירה. The lulav is prohibited because it does not belong to the thief. On subsequent days, when there is no longer the requirement of לכם משלכם, the stolen lulav would be suitable. Alternatively, if a change were to be made to the lulav such that it could no longer be considered the property of the original owner, it would be suitable as well.

Shmuel's position that the stolen lulav is invalid because it does not belong to its owner is consistent with two other Babylonian amoraim who explicitly permit the use of stolen objects in the performance of a commandment after a change has been made to them. On Sukkah 30b Rav Huna issues the following statement to a group of merchants: "When you buy myrtles from a non-Jew do not cut them yourselves; rather have them cut them and give them to you." Rav Huna is concerned about the ownership of the myrtles because he assumes they were grown on land stolen by the non-Jew. To avoid this problem he demands that the non-Jew cut the myrtle branches off their tree before selling them to the Jewish merchants in order to ensure there is a change in ownership before the myrtle arrives in the hands of the eventual Jewish buyer.

On Sukkah 31a the Bavli records the following incident involving R. Nahman. While the topic of this story is the sukkah and not the lulav, it demonstrates that R. Nahman does not subscribe to a halakhah that invalidates any mitzvah performed through a transgression.

ההיא סבתא דאתאי לקמיה דרב נחמן.	A certain old woman came before R. Nahman.
אמרה ליה: ריש גלותא וכולהו רבנן דבי ריש גלותא בסוכה גזולה הוו יתבי.	She said to him: The Exilarch and all of the sages of the house of the Exilarch are sitting in a stolen sukkah.
צווחה ולא אשגח בה רב נחמן.	She was shouting but R. Nahman paid her no heed.
אמרה ליה: איתתא דהוה ליה לאבוהא תלת מאה ותמני סרי עבדי צווחא קמייכו ולא אשגחיתו בה.	She said to him: A woman whose father has three hundred and eighteen slaves is shouting before you and you pay her no heed.

אמר להו רב נחמן: He said to them [the sages sitting with
פעיתא היא דא ואין לה   him]: She is a quarrelsome women and only
אלא דמי עצים בלבד.   has [a right] to the value of the wood.

The woman comes to R. Nahman claiming that the *skhakh* used to build the Exilarch's sukkah was made from wood stolen from her property. R. Nahman is not concerned about the use of stolen goods in the performance of the commandment. His only concern is that the *skhakh* must belong to the person using it. Since a change in state took place when the wood was made into *skhakh*, the wood no longer technically belongs to the woman. While she can make a claim for the value of the wood, the sukkah is not hers.

Analysis of all these sources demonstrates how the rabbinic discourse unfolds over the centuries. The earliest texts, the Sifra, Vayikra Rabbah and the Yerushalmi, contain two distinct reasons as to why a stolen lulav is invalid, but we do not know if those who hold one position disagree with the other. The stam of the Yerushalmi offers the earliest suggestion that the invalidity of the stolen lulav can be remedied by the legal transfer of ownership over the lulav to the thief. But only the Bavli creates a straightforward and direct dispute between the two positions. Those who disqualify the lulav because it does not belong to the bearer do not subscribe to any concept whatsoever of מצווה הבאה בעבירה. And as such, they would allow the use of a stolen lulav after the first day, when ownership of the lulav is unnecessary. Likewise, those who disqualify the stolen lulav because it was acquired through a transgression would continue to invalidate the lulav even after "despair," when it belongs to the thief.

R. Yohanan's First Statement: Part Two

We will begin our source-analysis of this section with the second half of R. Yohanan's statement (1c), which provides the midrashic source for מצווה הבאה בעבירה, and return below to the first half. We note that R. Yohanan's statement contains a mixture of Hebrew and Aramaic (in bold below). The combination of the two languages raises doubts as to whether the second half of the statement was actually uttered by R. Yohanan, let alone by R. Shimon b. Yohai, a tanna.[12]

In order to clarify the textual history of this statement, we need to note the existence of a very close parallel in Bava Kamma 67a:

Bavli Sukkah 30a	**Bavli Bava Kamma 67a**
אמר ר' יוחנן משום רבי שמעון בן יוחי: משום דהוה ליה מצוה הבאה בעבירה, שנאמר: והבאתם גזול ואת הפסח ואת החולה (מלאכי א:יג). גזול דומיא דפסח; מה פסח לית ליה תקנתא, אף גזול לית ליה תקנתא. לא שנא לפני יאוש ולא שנא אחר יאוש.	אמר עולא: מנין ליאוש שאינו קונה? שנאמר: והבאתם גזול ואת הפסח ואת החולה (מלאכי א:יג). גזול דומיא דפסח וחולה; מה פסח דלית ליה תקנה כלל אף גזול נמי דלית ליה תקנה כלל. לא שנא לפני יאוש ולא שנא אחר יאוש.
R. Yohanan said in the name of R. Shimon bar Yohai: Because it would be a commandment fulfilled through a transgression, as it is said: *And you bring the stolen, the lame and the sick* (Malachi 1:13), the stolen is similar to the lame; just as the lame can never be rectified, so that which is stolen can never be rectified. [This is so] irrespective of whether the stolen thing is used before [the owner has] despair [of recovery] or after despair.	Ulla said: From where do we know that despair does not transfer ownership? As it is said: *And you bring the stolen, the lame and the sick* (Malachi 1:13), the stolen is similar to the lame and the sick; just as the lame can never be rectified, so that which is stolen can never be rectified. [This is so] irrespective of whether the stolen thing is used before [the owner has] despair [of recovery] or after despair.

In Bava Kamma, the amora Ulla uses the verse from Malachi as a basis for the halakhah that even if an owner gives up hope of recovering a stolen object (he has "ייאוש"), he still retains legal ownership over the item. In rabbinic law, the concept of despair, ייאוש, plays a role in determining ownership over an item that has either been lost or stolen. In the case of a lost object, a finder who can assume that the original owner of the lost object has abandoned all

---

[12] See our discussion of using changes in language to differentiate between the strata of the Talmud in this book's introduction pp. 36 ff.

hope of recovery may keep the object.[13] In the case of a stolen object, however, Ulla maintains that despair does not cause transfer of ownership to the thief. He proves his position with a midrashic reading of the verse in Malachi. In the biblical context, Malachi chastises the Israelites for their disingenuous behavior and declares that God will not accept their sacrifices. The midrash, as it often does, ignores the context and focuses on the particulars of the verse to posit a general legal principle. Stolen and lame animals are lumped together in order to teach that just as there is nothing which can be done to change the status of a lame animal, so, too, nothing can be done to change the status of a stolen object; title over it will never be transferred to the thief.

In contrast, the statement of R. Yohanan in the name of R. Shimon b. Yohai in Sukkah ignores the comparison between the lame and sick animals and shifts the focus back to its biblical context.[14] In Sukkah, the stolen sacrifice mentioned by Malachi itself serves as a paradigm for a מצווה הבאה בעבירה. Indeed, the Aramaic words could be removed completely without impairing at all the meaning of his statement, a clear indication that they were a later addition.[15]

Thus it is clear that at a minimum the Aramaic words of this section were transferred from their original setting in Bava Kamma to Sukkah. The redactor imported the line לא שנא לפני יאוש לא שנא לאחר יאוש (section 1d) to introduce the concept of despair into the sugya and to directly emphasize the difference between the מצווה הבאה בעבירה explanation for the mishnah and the לכם משלכם interpretation (sections 1e–f).[16] This is an additional point in the sugya where we can sense the Bavli's tendency to compare different interpretations of the Mishnah and, most importantly, to highlight how these differences manifest themselves in halakhah. Note that these sections completely change the thrust of the original midrash in Bava Kamma. According to Ulla, a thief *does not* acquire a stolen object through the despair of its original owner. A stolen object has no rectification—it will never belong to the thief. In Sukkah, the

---

[13] See Tosefta Bava Metzia 2:2.

[14] Rashi (s.v. שנאמר והבאתם) resolves the difficulty by bypassing the midrash and linking the concept directly to the verse.

[15] See Hyman Klein, "Gemara and Sebara," *The Jewish Quarterly Review* 38:1 (1947), 75.

[16] Tosafot s.v. הא קנייה ביאוש point out the difficulty with the inclusion of this line of reasoning because elsewhere in the Bavli R. Yohanan rejects the transfer of ownership of stolen goods through despair.

stam completely changes the meaning of the line "can never be rectified."[17] Instead of meaning that the stolen item does not belong to the thief because despair does not affect transfer of ownership, it now means that *even when the animal does belong to the thief because he acquired it through despair* (section 1e), he still cannot use it for a sacrifice because it is a commandment performed through a transgression (section 1f).

Having established that at least the Aramaic words were brought to this sugya from another context, we can turn our attention to the first half of R. Yohanan's statement. However, in order to analyze this half, we need to first consider the second statement also issued by R. Yohanan in the name of the tanna R. Shimon b. Yohai.

The Parable of God and the Tax-Collector

Section two of the Bavli contains another midrash which also mentions the use of stolen sacrifices. The verse cited from Isaiah clearly expresses God's abhorrence of stolen sacrifice. R. Shimon b. Yohai supplements this verse with a parable which we are meant to understand as illustrating the same general concept. According to Rashi, despite the fact that the entire world belongs to God, God still despises stolen sacrifices offered to him. Its context in this sugya leads us to interpret the message of the parable as another example of מצווה הבאה בעבירה—God hates stolen sacrifices because they are a commandment performed through a transgression. However, since these precise words are actually absent from the statement, we need to analyze this midrash and parable carefully, independent of their context in the sugya.

The detail that stands out most in the parable is the character of the tax-collector. Had R. Shimon b. Yohai simply been teaching about the prohibition of offering stolen sacrifices, why would the verse from Isaiah not have been sufficient? Furthermore, what is the function of the tax-collector in the parable? Jonathan Klawans, in his book on sacrifice and the Temple, suggests that this parable is at the heart of a first-century debate over the status of the yearly half-shekel Temple tax levied on all Israelite males. Jesus argued that Israelites should be exempt from the tax, while his opponents maintained

---

17 See Ritva ad loc. s.v. אלא לאחר יאוש.

that every male over the age of twenty was required to pay it. The position of Jesus is articulated in Matthew 17:24–26:

> After Jesus and his disciples arrived in Capernaum, the collectors of the two-drachma tax came to Peter and asked, "Doesn't your teacher pay the temple tax?" "Yes, he does," he replied. When Peter came into the house, Jesus was the first to speak. "What do you think, Simon?" he asked. "From whom do the kings of the earth collect duty and taxes—from their own sons or from others?" "From others," Peter answered. "Then the sons are exempt," Jesus said to him. "But so that we may not offend them, go to the lake and throw out your line. Take the first fish you catch; open its mouth and you will find a four-drachma coin. Take it and give it to them for my tax and yours."

This parable suggests that God does not require the contribution of his own sons, that is, Israel. R. Shimon b. Yohai employs virtually the same parable but draws an opposite lesson. In the rabbinic parable the king exempts no one, not even himself, from the tax. The rabbis disagree with the exemption that Jesus assumes to be the right of the Jews, whom he considers the sons of God. In rabbinic law, the half-shekel was meant to be used to finance communal sacrifices offered on behalf of the entire community of Israel. Even though God does not need the money/sacrifices, the collection of the half-shekel is an act which aids in cementing the relationship of the Jew with God. If Jews are exempted from paying the tax, they would be excluded from the communal aspects of Temple worship, thereby weakening their connection to God.[18]

In its original context, the midrashic parable presented by R. Shimon b. Yohai was in no way connected to the concept of מצווה הבאה בעבירה; it was related to the positive rabbinic appraisal of the obligation to pay the yearly Temple tax. Likely influenced by the verse and by the general topic of using stolen items in the performance of a ritual, the redactor of the Babylonian sugya placed R. Shimon b. Yohai's parable in a new context, thereby muting its connection to the Temple tax. In this new context, it is the verse which

---

[18] See Jonathan Klawans, *Purity, Sacrifice, and the Temple: Symbolism and Supersessionism in the Study of Ancient Judaism* (New York: Oxford University Press, 2005), 222–245.

speaks of stolen sacrifice that best illustrates the category of a commandment performed through a transgression; the parable becomes an afterthought.

R. Yohanan's First Statement: Part One

Having established that the second half of R. Yohanan's first statement in the name of R. Shimon b. Yohai was certainly transferred to Sukkah from Bava Kamma and that the second statement was originally made in the context of the Temple tax, we now turn our attention to the Hebrew portion of the first statement. While the Tosefta, Yerushalmi, and midrashim had a notion of the concept מצווה הבאה בעבירה, the precise categorical term appears only in the Bavli. It is of course possible that the Bavli preserves an authentic statement of R. Yohanan in the name of R. Shimon b. Yohai and that the redactor appended the Aramaic words from Bava Kamma to the original Hebrew statement. But this seems unlikely for several reasons. First of all, the strong similarity of the first half of the statement here with Ulla's statement in Bava Kamma makes it likely that the entire statement was transferred, not just the Aramaic portions. Second, had R. Yohanan actually created the broad conceptual category of מצווה הבאה בעבירה, we would have expected to see a reflection of this in the Yerushalmi, where R. Yohanan figures prominently. Instead in both sugyot in the Yerushalmi, while R. Yohanan does prohibit the use of stolen objects to perform a commandment, he never provides a generalized conceptualization such as מצווה הבאה בעבירה. Furthermore, the Yerushalmi's amoraic dispute concerning the relationship between commandments and transgressions (Yerushalmi Shabbat, section three) occurs between sages who lived two generations after R. Yohanan. For all these reason, it seems more likely that R. Yohanan's statement is not historical but was attributed to him by the redactor.[19]

We can even speculate as to why the redactor might have acted in this manner. The cornerstone of the sugya in Sukkah is the redactor's juxtaposition of the amoraic explanations for the prohibition of the stolen lulav: מצווה הבאה בעבירה for R. Ami and לכם משלכם for Shmuel. The redactors may have

---

[19] See Shamma Friedman, *Talmud Arukh: Hanusah* (Jerusalem: Jewish Theological Seminary of America, 1996), 16–18.

felt a need to provide textual support for the concept of מצווה הבאה בעבירה in order to balance R. Ami's statement with Shmuel's, which was already supported by the לכם משלכם midrash. Furthermore, R. Ami's own statement lacks literary balance: the disqualification of a dried-up lulav is based on the midrash on the word הדר while the broad concept of מצווה הבאה בעבירה was not accompanied by any midrash.

To provide balance, the redactor presumably took two steps. One was to import the parable concerning the Temple tax into the sugya about the stolen lulav. It is likely that the trigger for this was not the parable, which as we have shown does not really fit the context, but the verse from Isaiah which mentions God's hatred of stolen sacrifices. In any case, once the source was brought to Sukkah, the connection to the Temple tax was lost and a new connection was created between the verse and the concept of מצווה הבאה בעבירה. The same tell-tale sign of transfer of material which we saw for the first statement exists here. It is the verse that seems to have most bearing on the concept of מצווה הבאה בעבירה and not the parable itself.[20] Only the context of the sugya implies that this section has any relationship with the concept whatsoever.

The other step was the creation of the midrash (section 1c), which does explicitly mention the notion of מצווה הבאה בעבירה. As is typical, the redactor did not create this midrash ex nihilo, but rather borrowed the language virtually whole cloth, as detailed above, from Bava Kamma 67a.

We should also note that there may be yet another earlier source which impacted the creation of the midrash in section 1c. Bereshit Rabbah 54 contains a midrash which is similar in form and content and is attributed to R. Shimon b. Yohai:

אי זהו גזלן? ר' לעזר בר קפרא זה שגוזל בפרהסיא... ר' שמעון בן יוחי מייתי לה מהכא והבאתם גזול את הפסח וגו' (מלאכי א:יג) מה פסח מום שבגלוי אף גזלן בגלוי.	Who is a גזלן? R. Eliezer Bar Kappara says: One who steals in public...R. Shimon b. Yohai brought proof from here: And you bring the stolen (גזול), the lame and the sick. Just as the lame and the sick are overt blemishes, so, too, a thief (גזלן) is one who acts overtly.

---

[20] A sign of this is that R. Hananel connects מצווה הבאה בעבירה directly to the verse, ignoring the parable altogether.

Like the midrash in Bava Kamma, this midrash also compares the lame with the stolen but to an entirely different end, using Malachi's juxtaposition to offer a precise definition of the crime of גזלנות. Just as a physical injury to an animal can be seen, so, too, גזלנות is a type of stealing that occurs in public. The existence of this parallel makes it virtually impossible to be certain whether the redactor of the sugya in Sukkah created the entire R. Yohanan in the name of R. Shimon b. Yohai statement (Hebrew and Aramaic sections) by drawing material from Bava Kamma or whether he fashioned this statement by reworking material from Bereshit Rabbah, preserving the attribution, the verse and even the midrashic comparison of the lame to the stolen, and then appending the Aramaic lines taken from Bava Kamma. Such precision is often not possible in Talmudic source-criticism. But more importantly, the existence of both of these parallels does lead to greater clarity (albeit still not certainty) in one matter: The statement issued in section 1c was probably not uttered by R. Yohanan, let alone by R. Shimon b. Yohai, but was a creation of the stammaitic redactors.

A Late Talmudic Expansion of the Category and Its Impact on Halakhah

Bavli Berakhot 47b expands the category of מצווה הבאה בעבירה from the narrow use of the term found in the passages above, where it refers specifically to stolen items used to perform a ritual. This sugya suggests that when *any transgression* is committed as part of the process of performing a mitzvah, it may be considered a מצווה הבאה בעבירה. The Bavli relates the story of R. Eliezer who freed his slave in order to complete a minyan of ten for prayers. The anonymous voice of the Talmud objects to his action on the grounds that it would be considered a מצווה הבאה בעבירה since Shmuel rules that it is forbidden to free one's slave. The stam's objection dramatically expands the category beyond the other sources which almost entirely restricted it to cases of theft.

Comparing the passage in Berakhot to a parallel found in Gittin 38b reveals that the objection which expands the category of מצווה הבאה בעבירה was itself a later addition to the Berakhot sugya:

גיטין לח ע"ב	ברכות מז ע"ב
(1) אמר רב יהודה אמר שמואל: כל המשחרר עבדו עובר בעשה, שנאמר: לעולם בהם תעבודו (ויקרא כה:מו).	(1) ואמר ריב"ל תשעה ועבד מצטרפין.
(2) מיתיבי: מעשה בר' אליעזר שנכנס בבית הכנסת ולא מצא עשרה, ושחרר עבדו והשלימו לעשרה.	(2) מיתיבי: מעשה ברבי אליעזר שנכנס לבית הכנסת ולא מצא עשרה ושחרר עבדו והשלימו לעשרה. שחרר אין לא שחרר לא.
(3) מצוה שאני.	(3) תרי אצטריכו, שחרר חד ונפיק בחד.
	(4) והיכי עביד הכי? והאמר רב יהודה כל המשחרר עבדו עובר בעשה שנאמר: (ויקרא כה, מו) לעולם בהם תעבודו. לדבר מצוה שאני. מצוה הבאה בעבירה היא! מצוה דרבים שאני.

Gittin 38b

(1) R. Yehudah said in the name of Shmuel: Whoever frees his slave transgresses a positive commandment, as it says: *they shall be your slaves forever* (Leviticus 25:46)

(2) They objected: Once R. Eliezer entered the synagogue and did not find ten so he freed his slave and used him to complete the ten.

(3) If it is for a commandment it is different.

Berakhot 47b

(1) R. Yehoshua b. Levi said: Nine and a slave may be [counted] together [to form a quorum of ten].

(2) They objected: Once R. Eliezer entered the synagogue and did not find ten so he freed his slave and used him to complete the ten. This was because he freed him, otherwise he could not have done so.

(3) He needed two. He freed one and fulfilled the obligation with one.

(4) But how could do this? Did not R.
Yehudah say: Whoever frees his slave
transgresses a positive commandment,
as it says: *they shall be your slaves forever* (Leviticus 25:46)?
If it is for a commandment. It is different. **But this is a commandment
performed through a transgression?**
A commandment which affects the
masses is different.

Both of these sugyot cite the statement of R. Yehudah (section one in Gittin,
section four in Berakhot) that forbids the releasing of a slave and the incident
involving R. Eliezer who frees his slave (section two in both sugyot). Section
four in Berakhot was clearly imported from Gittin, the original context of
R. Yehudah's statement. The story of R. Eliezer seems to have served as a
trigger—R. Eliezer frees his slave, prompting the stam to remind the reader
that while it is generally prohibited to free slaves, because he freed the slave
as part of a mitzvah, the act was permitted. It was only after this material
was transferred from Gittin to Berakhot that the מצווה הבאה בעבירה objection
was added to the sugya in the late stammaitic (or perhaps post-Talmudic)
period. If it had been indigenous to the sugya, the question should also have
been asked by the stam in Gittin as well.[21]

This late question which appears only here in Berakhot is significant because
it demonstrates the far-reaching influence of the Bavli's crystallization of the
concept of מצווה הבאה בעבירה. Originally this concept did not have an abstract
formulation and was related only to the concrete cases of theft. When the Bavli
created an abstract formulation of the concept, it allowed for its expansion
into situations in which any type of transgression was committed as part of
the performance of a mitzvah. Despite the rejection of the suggestion that

---

[21] The מצוה הבאה בעבירה objection does not appear in Genizah fragment (T-S F1 (1) 113)
and MS Paris of Berakhot but it is likely that this is a result of a homeoteleuton (a
mistake due to similar words appearing in close proximity) in which the copyist erroneously omitted the text between the two appearances of the word שאני.

R. Eliezer's action was a מצווה הבאה בעבירה, the Bavli opened the door for the possibility that other types of cases may also be judged according to this rubric.

The use of the concept in post-Talmudic literature reflects this expanded interpretation. An interesting example is found in Sefer Hasidim, the 13th century Ashkenaz ethical treatise, on the subject of wedding attendance:

ספר חסידים אות שצ"ג	**Sefer Hasidim no. 393**
כל מצוה הבאה בעבירה	Any commandment which is performed through
על ידה, מוטב שלא יעשה	a transgression, it is better for that command-
המצוה, כמו מצוה לשמח	ment not to have been performed. For example,
החתן, שאם יש שם פריצים	it is a commandment to rejoice before a groom,
ויודע שבלא פריצות	but if there are promiscuous people there and
לא יהיה, או אינו יכול	he knows that it will not be without promis-
להיות בלא הרהור, או	cuity, or if he cannot be there without having
אינו יכול להיות מלראות	inappropriate thoughts, or he cannot be there
בנשים, אל יהיה שם.	without seeing women, he should not attend.

The above passage is an excellent illustration of the expansion of the category of מצווה הבאה בעבירה. The ruling which prohibits attendance at a "promiscuous" wedding based on the problem of מצווה הבאה בעבירה would not have been possible were it not for the creation of the abstract category in Bavli Sukkah and the subsequent expansion of that category in Bavli Berakhot.

CHAPTER EIGHT

REVEALING MANUSCRIPTS:
THE BLESSINGS OVER TORAH STUDY

BERAKHOT 11B

Included among the various morning blessings found in the siddur (*birkot hashahar*, etc) are blessings recited over personal study of Torah. While blessings over the public reading of the Torah are mentioned in tannaitic literature (Mishnah Megillah 4:1; Mekhilta de-Rabbi Yishmael Pisha 16), the requirement for an individual to bless over personal, non-public study of Torah first appears in the two Talmuds. The Bavli sugya, which will be the focus of this chapter, begins with the statement of the Babylonian amora Shmuel, who requires a blessing only if one studies Torah before reciting the morning Shema. According to Shmuel, one who has already recited the Shema and its blessings is exempt from reciting a blessing over Torah study. Both Talmuds discuss which genre of Torah study mandates a blessing. Additionally, the Bavli includes three amoraic formulations of these blessings. Essentially, with some minor modifications which we address below, these are the blessings found in siddurim to this day.

Our main emphasis in analysing this sugya is to illustrate the contribution of manuscripts to the study of Talmud. The version of the sugya that appears in the Vilna printed edition of the Bavli is an extremely late version of the text, one which does not reflect the state of this text during the Talmudic period. The Vilna's version of the text includes numerous intentional emendations and errors in transmission. Studying this version without consulting manuscripts distorts the original meaning of the text. This is one sugya that simply cannot be properly understood without analysis of earlier manuscript traditions. The sugya also provides an example of the difficulty of determining appropriate Talmudic readings for liturgical sources, which were often altered by copyists and printers in order to correspond to the tradition with which they were familiar. This particular passage is well-known for the large number of discrepancies between the manuscript traditions and the printed edition, as previously analyzed in depth by both Avraham Rosenthal and Moshe Benovitz.[1] Our analysis is based on their conclusions.

Studying Torah Before Reciting Shema

Both Talmuds attribute the requirement to recite a blessing over personal Torah study to the Babylonian amora Shmuel:

ירושלמי ברכות א:ח, ג ע״ג שמואל אמר: השכים לשנות קודם קריאת שמע צריך לברך, לאחר קריאת שמע אינו צריך לברך.	**Yerushalmi Berakhot** **1:8, 3c** Shmuel said: If one rose early to recite [Torah] before he [had said] the Shema, he must bless. After the recitation of the Shema, he need not bless.
בבלי ברכות יא ע״ב אמר רב יהודה אמר שמואל: השכים לשנות עד שלא קרא קריאת שמע, צריך לברך.	**Bavli Berakhot 11b** Rav Yehudah said in the name of Shmuel: One who rose early to recite [Torah] before he read the Shema, he must bless.
משקרא קריאת שמע אינו צריך לברך, שכבר נפטר באהבה רבה.	After he had read the Shema, he need not bless, because he has already fulfilled his obligation with *Ahavah Rabbah*.

---

[1] Avraham Rosenthal, "Torah Shebeal Peh veTorah miSinai," *Mehkerei Talmud II: Talmudic Studies Dedicated to the Memory of Professor Eliezer Shimshon Rosenthal*, ed. M. Bar-Asher and D. Rosenthal (Jerusalem: Hebrew University Magnes Press, 1993), 448–87; Moshe Benovitz, *Talmud Ha-Igud: BT Berakhot Chapter 1* (Jerusalem: The Society for the Interpretation of the Talmud, 2006), 529–544.

Shmuel rules that a blessing over Torah study is necessary only when one studies prior to the recitation of the Shema. Before analyzing the content of Shmuel's teaching, it is important to highlight the technical terms he uses, for these terms demonstrate some essential aspects of the nature of Torah study in the rabbinic period. Shmuel uses the verb קרא, to read, when referring to the Shema; he uses the verb שנה, to recite, when referring to Torah study (see also Tosefta Berakhot 5:12 cited below). This difference is significant because it reflects the fact that Bible was read from a written text while rabbinic material, also known as the Oral Torah (תורה שבעל פה), was studied orally. In fact, the verb קרא, when used in the context of Torah study, refers exclusively to the study of the Bible.[2] Thus the person to whom Shmuel refers rose early to *recite* texts from the oral Torah, before he *read* the Shema, which is part of the written Torah.

It is difficult to determine if the innovation in Shmuel's teaching is the requirement to bless, the fact that the Shema obviates the need for such a blessing, or both.[3] According to the Bavli's version of the statement, Shmuel rules that the second blessing before the Shema *(Ahavah Rabbah)*,[4] which praises Torah and its study—"instill in our hearts to understand and elucidate, to listen, learn, teach, etc..."—is in its essence a blessing over the act of Torah study, and thus exempts one from reciting a subsequent blessing. The Yerushalmi does not include this explanation. Rather, it seems that in the Yerushalmi there is no requirement for a formalized blessing over the study of Torah—the recitation of the Shema itself is sufficient to exempt one from reciting a formal blessing over Torah study. Perhaps the reason that the Yerushalmi does not mention the blessing that immediately preedes the Shema is because many Eretz Yisraeli versions of this blessing *(Ahavat Olam* in this tradition) do not even mention Torah study. Such versions

---

[2] Yaakov Sussman, "Torah SheBe'al Peh: Pshutah Kemashma'ah," *Mehkerei Talmud III: Talmudic Studies Dedicated to the Memory of Professor Ephraim E. Urbach,* ed. Y. Sussman and D. Rosenthal (Jerusalem: Hebrew University Magnes Press, 2005), 251–254.

[3] Louis Ginzberg, *A Commentary on the Palestinian Talmud* (New York: Jewish Theological Seminary of America, 1941), 1:171; Benovitz, 532.

[4] The previous sugya presents a debate about whether the second blessing begins *Ahavah Rabbah* or *Ahavat Olam*. All manuscripts of our sugya, however, record *Ahavah Rabbah* in Shmuel's statement.

could therefore not possibly be understood as a blessing over Torah study. For example, the following version appears in a Cairo geniza fragment published by Jacob Mann:[5]

ומאהבתך אלוהינו הרבה
והעצומה שאהבתנו מקדם
בגלל אבתינו אשר בטחו בך,
לארח משפטך נקוה לשמך
ולזכרך הטוב תתאוה נפשינו
ניחד ונחכה לעד כי אתה
מעולם אבינו שמך עלינו
נקרא. אנא אלוהינו אל
תניחנו משוך עלינו לחסדך
להודיע אהבתך בנו לעיני
כל היצרוים ככתוב: ואהבת
עולם אהבתיך על כן משכתיך
חסד (ירמיהו לא:ג). ברוך
אתה ה' אוהב עמו ישראל.

And by Your great and abundant love, our God, with which You loved us from aforetime because of our fathers who trusted in You, we will hope for the ways of Your justice, our souls will yearn for Your good, we will unite and wait forever because You have always been our Father, we will call Your name upon us. Please, our God, do not abandon us, continue Your grace to us, declare Your love for us before the eyes of all creations as it is written: Eternal love I conceived for you then; Therefore I continue My grace to you (Jeremiah 31:3). Blessed are You, Who loves His nation Israel.

While this is clearly a version of the *Ahavah Rabbah/Ahavat Olam* blessing and is found in this ancient siddur immediately preceding the Shema, the theme of Torah study does not appear. And so instead of referencing a blessing preceding the Shema, the Yerushalmi simply states that recitation of the Shema alone is sufficient to frame subsequent study of Torah as the fulfillment of God's commandment, without the need to recite an additional formal blessing.

What is Considered Torah Study?

In both Talmuds, Shmuel's statement is followed by an amoraic debate over the genre of Torah study which necessitates a blessing. Due to the significant

---

[5] Jacob Mann, "Genizah Fragments of the Palestinian Order of Service," *Hebrew Union College Annual* 2 (1925), 308.

discrepancies between the passages we will first analyze the Yerushalmi and Bavli independently and only then compare the two.

Yerushalmi

ירושלמי ברכות א:ח, ג ע"ג	Yerushalmi Berakhot 1:8, 3c
(1) ר' חונא אמר: נראין הדברים מדרש צריך לברך, הלכות אינו צריך לברך.	(1) R. Huna said: The following seems to be [correct]: midrash requires a blessing, halakhot do not require a blessing.
(2) ר' סימון בשם ר' יהושע בן לוי: בין מדרש בין הלכות צריך לברך.	(2) R. Simon in the name of R. Yehoshua b. Levi: both midrash and halakhot require a blessing.
(3) אמר רב חייא בר אשי: נהגין הוינן ויתבין קומוי רב בין מדרש בין הלכות זקיקינן למיברכה.	(3) R. Hiyya b. Ashi said: [when] we used to sit before Rav, he would require us to bless both for halakhot and midrash.

In this passage the term halakhot refers to apodictic statements of law which are transmitted without scriptural prooftexts, similar to the statements found in the Mishnah.[6] Midrash, on the other hand, refers to laws and statements derived from Scripture and which retain their literary connection to the Bible. R. Huna requires a blessing only for midrash, whereas R. Yehoshua b. Levi requires a blessing for halakhot as well. R. Hiyya b. Ashi supports the position of R. Yehoshua b. Levi with his testimony that Rav would require a blessing even over halakhot.

Avraham Rosenthal explains that the source of the amoraic disagreement lies in their definition of the type of study that fulfills the biblical requirement to study Torah.[7] R. Huna holds that the study of halakhot does not fulfill the commandment to study Torah because halakhot were not revealed at Sinai and do not explicitly reference Scripture. Since midrash is still connected to the Biblical verses from which it is derived, it deserves a blessing, as does the public recitation of Torah.

---

6 For a similar use, see Bavli Kiddushin 49a.

7 Rosenthal, 466–467.

R. Yehoshua ben Levi represents a different ideology, one which rejects the distinction between laws attached to the Torah and those separate from it, and even the distinction between written law (the Torah) and oral law (the teachings of the rabbis). This ideology is expressed in the following statement attributed to him:

Yerushalmi Peah 2:6 (17a)	**ירושלמי פאה ב:ו (יז, א)**
R. Yehoshua b. Levi said:…Scripture,	רבי יהושע בן לוי אמר:
mishnah, talmud, aggadah, and even that	… מקרא, משנה, תלמוד,
which a venerable student will say before	ואגדה, אפילו מה שתלמיד
his master, were all said to Moses at Sinai.	ותיק עתיד להורות לפני
What is the reason? *Sometimes there is a*	רבו כבר נאמר למשה בסיני,
phenomenon of which they say, "Look, this one	מה טעם? יש דבר שיאמר
is new." His friend responds and says to him: "It	ראה זה חדש הוא וגו' (קהלת
occurred long since" (Ecclesiastes 1:10).	א:י). משיבו חבירו ואומר לו:
	כבר היה לעולמים (שם).

In this statement, R. Yehoshua b. Levi expands the revelation at Sinai to include all future rabbinic statements. Any interpretation offered by the rabbis, new and innovative though it may seem, is not, according to this ideology, in actuality new, because it was already revealed to Moses at Sinai. Thus the line separating halakhot and midrash does not exist according to R. Yehoshua ben Levi—all was revealed at Sinai. One must bless before any type of study. Below we will see that these two ideological stances also lie at the core of the Bavli, although their borders have been obfuscated by both the Talmudic redaction of that sugya and emendations wrought upon the text after its conversion into writing.

Bavli

As mentioned in the introduction, one of the central methodological techniques demonstrated in this chapter is the use of manuscript traditions to determine the precise meaning of the Bavli. To that end, we begin by quoting the version of the sugya which appears in the Vilna printed edition, the edition of the Talmud still used to this day. This will provide us with a baseline for evaluating the numerous textual variants.

Bavli Berakhot 11b,
Vilna Edition

בבלי ברכות יא ע"ב,
דפוס וילנא

(1) R. Huna said: For Scripture it is necessary to bless, but for midrash it is not necessary to bless.

(1) אמר רב הונא: למקרא צריך לברך, ולמדרש אינו צריך לברך.

(2) And R. Elazar said: For both Scripture and midrash it is necessary to bless, but for mishnah it is not necessary to bless.

(2) ורבי אלעזר אמר: למקרא ולמדרש צריך לברך, למשנה אינו צריך לברך.

(3) And R. Yohanan said: Even for mishnah it is necessary to bless, but for talmud it is not necessary to bless.

(3) ורבי יוחנן אמר: אף למשנה נמי צריך לברך אבל לתלמוד אינו צריך לברך.

(4) And Rava said: Even for talmud it is necessary to bless.

(4) ורבא אמר: אף לתלמוד צריך לברך.

(5) As R. Hiyya b. Ashi said: Many times I stood before Rav to recite our section of the "Sifra of the School of Rav," and he would first wash his hands and say a blessing, and then teach us our section.

(5) דאמר רב חייא בר אשי: זימנין סגיאין הוה קאימנא קמיה דרב לתנויי פרקין בספרא דבי רב - הוה מקדים וקא משי ידיה ובריך ומתני לן פרקין.

This version of the Bavli contains four distinct amoraic opinions concerning which texts require a blessing before their study, a debate that is similar, yet crucially different, from that in the Yerushalmi. In the Yerushalmi the debate is clear—do "halakhot" which are purely Oral Torah without any overt connection to Scripture require a blessing? Or is a blessing required only for midrash, rabbinic teachings explicitly derived from Scripture? In the Vilna's version of the Bavli, what distinguishes texts that require a blessing from those that do not has become murkier, for the dichotomy between Torah that is attached to Scripture and Torah that is separated from it has been blurred. The fact that all amoraim agree that a blessing is required for Scripture may echo the agreement in the Yerushalmi concerning the requirement to bless before midrash, texts which are attached to Scripture. But from this point onward the Yerushalmi's simple dichotomy breaks down—R. Huna (in the Bavli) requires a blessing for Scripture but not for midrash, despite the latter's connection to the former. As opposed to the dichotomy found in the Yerushalmi, the order found in this version of the Bavli seems to reflect a hierarchy based on the relationship of the given text to the written Torah. Midrash is closest to Torah because it contains citations of verses. Mishnah is derived from the Torah but is no longer attached to it. Talmud, which Rashi defines as explanations and analysis of the Mishnah, is an additional step removed from the Torah and therefore only one amora rules that it requires a blessing.[8]

The key to unlocking this sugya and allowing us to describe in detail its development from the original version still found in some manuscripts to the version found in the Vilna edition lies in the interpretation of the word "talmud." It is obvious that the amoraim are not referring to what we call Talmud because "the Talmud" did not yet exist. Once we have engaged in a close reading of the manuscript traditions along with a comparison of the parallel found in the Yerushalmi, we will be able to interpret the word "talmud" in light of its meaning in parallel traditions. We will then have a better understanding of this sugya and its development.

Textual Traditions

The textual variants in this sugya are significant enough that they caused Raphael N. N. Rabbinovicz, author of *Dikdukei Soferim,* to write, "the versions of this sugya vary greatly…they each vary from the other in such a way that there is not a single one which is the same as another."[9] Below is a chart including several of these manuscripts in order to emphasize the astounding number of differences between them. The manuscripts are identified below by the geographic location of the library where they are housed and the approximate date when they were written, but those identifiers can be misleading. The city names attached to the manuscripts do not reflect the original location of composition and the

---

[8] Rashi consistently uses this definition throughout his commentary on the Bavli to explain the world תלמוד. See Hanokh Albeck, *Mavo LeTalmudim* (Tel Aviv: Dvir, 1969), 3–4.

[9] Raphael N. N. Rabbinovicz, *Dikdukei Soferim: Berakhot* (Jerusalem: Or Hehokhmah, 2002), 25 n. 4

> ⚫ **Dikdukei Soferim** is a fifteen volume work containing a comprehensive comparison of the Munich manuscript of the Babylonian Talmud with other manuscripts, early printed editions and evidence gleaned from the writing of the rishonim. Rabbinovicz, originally from Kovno, began his work on the massive project in 1863 after hearing of the existence of the fourteenth-century manuscript during a visit to Vienna. He describes in the introduction to his work that he spent almost four years at the Royal Library of Munich transcribing the manuscript before he began publication of the variants.

dates indicate the year that the specific copy was written down, not the year the source was composed. Thus the date of a manuscript is what's known as its "terminus ad quem"—the latest date in which it might have been composed. But it is not its "terminus a quo"—the earliest date it might have been composed.

The transition from oral to written study of the Babylonian Talmud began at some point in the eighth century, but very little material evidence remains of the earliest written texts of the Bavli.[10] The extant manuscripts of the Bavli are copies of those earlier versions which are themselves often hundreds of years removed from the original source.[11]

	FLORENCE (1177)
א' רב הונא: למקרא מדרש צריך לברך, לתלמוד אין צריך לברך. ר' אלעזר אמר: לתלמוד למדרש צריך לברך, למשנה נמי צריך לברך. רבא א': אף למשנה אין צריך לברך.	

	OXFORD (13TH CENT)
אמר רב הונא: למקרא ולתלמוד צריך לברך, למדרש אין צריך לברך. ר' אליעזר אומ': אף למדרש צריך לברך.	

---

[10] One of the earliest written fragments of the Bavli was examined in great depth by Shamma Friedman, "An Ancient Scroll Fragment (B. Hullin 101a–105a) and the Rediscovery of the Babylonian Branch of Tannaitic Hebrew," *Jewish Quarterly Review* 88, 1–2 (1995), 9–50.

[11] The word מקרא was added into the manuscript between the lines.

[12] The Munich manuscript is the only extant complete manuscript of the Bavli. See Michael Krupp, "Manuscripts of the Babylonian Talmud," *The Literature of the Sages: First Part*, ed. Shmuel Safrai (Philadelphia: Fortress Press, 1987), 346–366.

	ר' יוחנן אמ': אפי' לתלמוד נמי צריך לברך.	ר' אלעזר אור': אף למדרש נמי צריך לברך, לתלמוד אינו צריך לברך.	אמ' רב הונא: [למקרא][11] צריך לברך למשנה, ולמדרש אינו צריך לברך.	MUNICH[12] (1342)
רב' אמ': אף למדרש צריך לברך.	ר' יוחנן א': אף לתלמוד צריך לברך, למדרש אין צריך לברך.	ר' אלעזר א': אף למשנ' צרי' לברך, לתלמוד אין צריך לברך.	א' רב הונא: למקרא צריך לברך, למשנה אין צריך לברך.	MUNICH MARGIN[13]
	ור' יוחנן אמר: בתלמוד צריך לברך.	ור' אלעזר אמר: אף למשנה צריך לברך, לתלמוד אין צריך לברך.	אמר רב הונא: למקרא צריך לברך, למשנה אין צריך לברך.	PARIS (15TH CENT)
	ור' יוחנן אמר: אף למשנה צריך לברך.	ור' אלעזר אמר: למקרא ולתלמוד צריך לברך, למשנה אין צריך לברך.	אמר רב הונא: למקרא צריך לברך, ולמדרש לתלמוד אין צריך לברך.	SONCINO[14] (1484)
ורבא אמר: אף לתלמוד צריך לברך, אבל לתלמוד אינו צריך לברך.	ורבי יוחנן אמר: אף למשנה נמי צריך לברך, אבל לתלמוד אינו צריך לברך.	ורבי אלעזר אמר: למקרא ולמדרש צריך לברך.	אמר רב הונא: למקרא צריך לברך, ולמדרש אינו צריך לברך.	VILNA (1859)

With the exception of the Oxford manuscript, all of these versions include statements attributed to at least three amoraim and mention three sources which may or may not require a blessing: מקרא, משנה, תלמוד—Scripture, mishnah and talmud. Avraham Rosenthal narrowed down the numerous variations between these manuscripts into two archetypes which he identified as the base of all the variants: the Paris and the Florence manuscripts.[16]

---

[13] There is another version of the sugya which appears in the margin of the Munich manuscript. This is the version that is common to most of the Rishonim.

[14] This is a printed version of the Bavli, the first Jewish book printed by the Soncino family.

[15] This is the familiar printed edition that has served as the basis of the printing of the Talmud since 1859.

[16] Rosenthal, 468; Benovitz, 538.

Paris (15th Century)	Florence (1177)
(1) אמר רב הונא: למקרא צריך לברך, למשנה אין צריך לברך.	(1) א' רב הונא: למקרא (מדרש)[17] צריך לברך, לתלמוד אין צריך לברך.
(1) R. Huna said: For Scripture it is necessary to bless, for mishnah it is not necessary to bless.	(1) R. Huna said: For Scripture (midrash)[17] it is necessary to bless, for talmud it is not necessary to bless.
(2) ור' אלעזר אמר: אף למשנה צריך לברך, לתלמוד אין צריך לברך.	(2) ר' אלעזר אמר: לתלמוד (למדרש) צריך לברך, למשנה אין צריך לברך.
(2) And R. Elazar said: even for mishnah it is necessary to bless, for talmud it is not necessary to bless.	(2) R. Elazar said: For talmud (midrash) it is necessary to bless, for mishnah it is not necessary to bless.
(3) ור' יוחנן אמר: בתלמוד צריך לברך.	(3) רבא אמר: אף למש־נה נמי צריך לברך.
(3) And R. Yohanan said: for talmud it is necessary to bless.	(3) Rava said: It is even necessary to bless for mishnah.

(4) דאמר רב חייא בר אשי: זימנין סגיאין הוה קאימנא קמיה דרב לתנויי פר־
קין בספרא דבי רב - הוה מקדים וקא משי ידיה ובריך ומתני לן פרקין.

(4) As R. Hiyya b. Ashi said: Many times I stood before Rav to recite our section of the "Sifra of the School of Rav," and he would first wash his hands and say a blessing, and then teach us our section.

---

[17] The Florence MS contains redundancies: Rav Huna speaks of "Scripture midrash" and Rabbi Elazar speaks of "Talmud midrash." The inclusion of the word midrash is clearly out of place as the pattern of each statement is to include one source and exclude a different source. Furthermore, were one to argue that two can be listed it does not make sense for midrash to be listed both with Scripture and with talmud. As our analysis above will demonstrate, the word midrash is included due to confusion surrounding the term talmud. We will therefore read the Florence text ignoring the inclusion of the word midrash.

While the genres of Scripture and mishnah are easily identifiable, the term "talmud" as used by amoraim is more difficult to interpret. Rosenthal has shown that originally, before the creation of the text that we know of as "the Talmud," the term talmud was synonymous with the genre of rabbinic literature known as midrash.[18] A clear and representative example of this use of the word is found in Bavli Bava Kamma 104b:

אימתי הוא משלם קרן על גזל אביו? בזמן שנשבע הוא ואביו: אביו ולא הוא, הוא ולא אביו, לא הוא ולא אביו מנין? תלמוד לומר: גזילה ועושק אבידה ופקדון (ויקרא ה:כג)—יש תלמוד.	When does he [the son] pay the principal for a robbery committed by his father? When both he and his father took oaths. When his father did and he did not, or he did and his father did not, or neither he nor his father [took oaths], how do we know this? Scripture teaches: *[That which he got through] robbery, fraud, or the deposit that was entrusted to him, or the lost thing that he found* (Leviticus 5:23)—yesh talmud [i.e. there is a midrashic basis for it].
ויתיב רב הונא וקאמר להא שמעתא, אמר ליה רבה בריה: יש תלמוד קאמר מר, או ישתלמו קאמר מר? אמר ליה: יש תלמוד קאמינא, ומריבויא דקראי אמרי.	And when R. Huna was sitting and said this teaching, his son Rabbah said to him: Did the Master say yesh talmud [i.e. there is a midrashic basis] or did the Master say yishtalmu [the heirs should have to pay]? He replied to him: I said yesh talmud [i.e. there is a midrashic basis] which can be derived by the ribuy hermeneutic.

The details of this passage and the midrash it refers to are not relevant for our analysis, but we can immediately see that Rav Huna uses the phrase *yesh talmud* to mean that there is a midrashic basis for his teaching. Even the frequently used technical term תלמוד לומר—the exegesis of Scripture teaches—found so often in midrashim, demonstrates that the word talmud was used in the tannaitic and amoraic periods to refer to midrash.

The interchangeability of talmud and midrash is also noticeable if we compare a baraita on Berakhot 22a with its parallel in Tosefta Berakhot 2:12,

---

[18] Rosenthal, 463 n. 48. See also Benovitz, 538.

both of which deal with the halakhic permissibility of Torah study for ritually impure individuals:

תוספתא ברכות ב:יב	בבלי, ברכות כב ע"א, דפוס שונצינו
...מותרין לקרות בתורה בנביאים וביכתובים ולשנות במשנה במדרש בהלכות ובאגדות.	...מותרין לקרות בתורה ובנביאים ובכתובים לשנות במשנה ובתלמוד ובהלכות ובאגדות.
Tosefta Berakhot 2:12	**Bavli Berakhot 22a** **Soncino Printed Edition (1484)**
...They are permitted to read Torah, Prophets, and Writings, and to recite mishnah, midrash, halakhot, and legends.	...They are permitted to read Torah, Prophets, and Writings, and to recite mishnah, talmud, halakhot, and legends.

While the Tosefta uses the term "midrash," the Bavli's version of the baraita uses the term "talmud." Despite the difference in terminology both refer to the same genre of study.

The More Difficult Reading is Stronger

Returning to the two archetypes of our sugya (MSS Florence and Paris), we will evaluate them using the principle of *lectio difficilior potior*—"the more difficult reading is the stronger." According to this principle when textual traditions diverge, the more difficult reading is more likely to be the original one. The rationale for this theory is that a later copyist or editor is more likely to change a text that he finds problematic or difficult than one that he finds to be more straightforward. Thus if there are two readings, it is more likely that the difficult reading was changed into the simpler reading. In our case, the more difficult reading is found in MS Florence. The tradition preserved here creates the problem that the actions of Rav in section four are supposed to be an illustration of the principle articulated in section three. This was what we saw in the Yeushalmi, where Rav's action in section three supported Rabbi Yeshoshua ben Levi's statement in section two. But this is not the case

⊛ **Talmud and Gemara** The Vilna edition reads גמרא instead of תלמוד as is found in the Soncino printing. The text of the Vilna edition is, in part, based on the Talmud printed in Basel in 1578. The history behind this particular edition is fascinating and complex. In brief, beginning in the 1550s there was a revival of anti-Talmud sentiment, especially in Italy, leading to various incidents of burning and outright banning of the Talmud. In 1563 the Council of Trent classified the Talmud among other books that were, "prohibited only provisionally until they had been expurgated." This declaration led to a 1578 contract between a Frankfurt Jew and Christian printers in Basel to publish a censored edition of the Talmud. The contract stipulated that Marco Morino, the papal inquisitor of Venice, was to serve as the censor of the text. Among the changes he made to the text was the systematic replacement of the word "talmud" with the word "gemara."

in the Bavli: Rav's act of blessing before teaching Sifra (a midrashic collection) does not support Rava's principle that it is necessary to bless before mishnah. Why would the fact that Rav recited a blessing before teaching midrash prove that a blessing is necessary for the study of mishnah? In MS Paris this is not a problem because R. Yohanan rules, "for talmud a blessing is necessary." Since, as stated above, talmud is synonymous with midrash, the story of Rav teaching Sifra does indeed support R. Yohanan. It seems likely that the version preserved in MS Paris was created in order to resolve this very problem. A scribe or scholar emended R. Yohanan's statement from "mishnah" to "talmud" and thereby resolved the overt problem of the lack of correspondence between R. Yohanan's statement (section three) and the story about Rav (section four).

Having emended R. Yohanan's statement from "mishnah" to "talmud," he was also forced to emend R. Elazar (section two) from "talmud" to "mishnah," such that each amora would add to his predecessor. Once this secondary emendation had been performed, R. Elazar now states that for mishnah one does need to bless, but not for talmud. But this change has created a new, less explicit, problem in the order or hierarchy of the sources. Why would R. Elazar require a blessing for mishnah, a genre which does not reference Scripture, but not require one for midrash/talmud, which originally did mean a genre which referenced Scripture? As we have seen in the Yerushalmi passage above, the original amoraic debate was between requiring a blessing for all Oral Torah (mishnah/halakhah and midrash/talmud) or only for the

genre of oral law which includes references to the written law, i.e. midrash/
talmud but not mishnah/halakhah.

All of these emendations do not appear in MS Florence, which reflects the
original progression of genres: R. Huna requires a blessing only for the study
of the written Torah. R. Elazar also requires a blessing for the study of talmud/
midrash because it is a combination of both the oral and written law. His
position corresponds with R. Huna in the Yerushalmi. R. Yohanan[19] (section
three), corresponding to R. Yehoshua b. Levi in the Yerushalmi, requires a
blessing even for the study of mishnah, despite its significant distance from
Scripture. This parallel with the Yerushalmi can easily be seen when we line
them up in parallel columns:

Bavli – MS Florence	**Yerushalmi**
(1) א' רב הונא: למקרא צריך לברך, לתלמוד אין צריך לברך.	
(2) ר' אלעזר אמר: לתלמוד צריך לברך, למשנה אין צריך לברך.	(1) ר' חונא אמר: נראין הדברים מדרש צריך לברך, הלכות אינו צריך לברך.
(3) ר' יוחנן[20] אמר: אף למשנה נמי צריך לברך.	(2) ר' סימון בשם ר' יהושע בן לוי: בין מדרש בין הלכות צריך לברך.

(1) R. Huna said: For Scripture it is
necessary to bless, for talmud
it is not necessary to bless.

(2) R. Elazar said: For talmud it
is necessary to bless, for mishnah
it is not necessary to bless.

(1) R. Huna said: The following
seems to [be correct]: midrash
requires a blessing, halakhot
do not require a blessing.

(3) R. Yohanan[20] said: It is even
necessary to bless for mishnah.

(2) R. Simon in the name of R.
Yehoshua b. Levi: both midrash
and halakhot require a blessing.

---

[19] Emended from Rava, see below.

As explained above, the term halakhot in the Yerushalmi is synonymous with mishnah. The amoraim disagree about the status of sources which do not cite Scripture. In contrast, the progression in the Paris manuscript is far removed from the original amoraic debate found in the Yerushalmi, another reason to discount its originality.

Now that we have established that MS Florence preserves the original version of the sugya, we must answer how R. Hiyya b. Ashi's statement originally functioned within the sugya. The immediately preceding amoraic position required the blessing over the study of *mishnah*, a text not connected to Scripture, yet the text studied by Rav in the testimony of R. Hiyya b. Ashi is *midrash*, a text connected to Scripture. In our reconstruction of the original amoraic debate these are opposite positions, and yet in the Bavli one seems to support the other.

To answer this difficulty we must delve into a deeper level of analysis of the Bavli. If above we dealt with what is usually termed "lower criticism"—the study of the variants preserved in post-compositional manuscripts—here we reach the level of "higher criticism"—a study of the redaction of the original text before it was set as a written composition. Avraham Rosenthal explains that the key to resolving the difficulty is geographically mapping the amoraim involved in this dispute. The section opens with a statement made by R. Huna, a second-generation Babylonian amora. It continues with R. Elazar, a third-generation Eretz Yisraeli amora and then with a statement by his teacher R. Yohanan. It concludes by returning to R. Hiyya b. Ashi, R. Huna's contemporary in Babylonia. Understanding this mapping clarifies the fact that the Bavli actually contains two independent debates over what requires a blessing.

Babylonian Amoraim	Eretz Yisraeli Amoraim (As Transmitted in the Bavli)
R. Huna said: For Scripture it is necessary to bless, but for midrash it is not necessary to bless.	R. Elazar said: For talmud it is necessary to bless, for mishnah it is not necessary to bless.

---

[20] MS Florence is the only manuscript which attributes the opinion in section 3 to Rava rather than Rabbi Yohanan. Therefore, we accept R. Yohanan as the valid attribution of the statement, and have emended the text accordingly.

R. Hiyya b. Ashi said: Many times I stood before Rav to recite our section of the "Sifra of the School of Rav," and he would first wash his hands and say a blessing, and then teach us our section.	R. Yohanan said: It is even necessary to bless for mishnah.

In the debate between Babylonian amoraim, R. Hiyya b. Ashi responds to and rejects R. Huna's ruling, which requires a blessing only over the study of the written Torah. This also corresponds with the Bavli's version of Shmuel's statement. If one already recited the blessing over Shema (Scripture) one need not recite another blessing later, because only Scripture requires a blessing and he has already recited such a blessing. R. Hiyya b. Ashi objects by invoking the report of Rav's practice of blessing even before the teaching of midrash, which is part of the Oral Torah. Neither Babylonian amora addresses the question of blessing before mishnah, Oral Torah, which does not include citations of Scripture.

The Eretz Yisraeli debate, which mirrors the opinions found in the Yerushalmi, is between R. Elazar and his teacher R. Yohanan. R. Elazar requires a blessing to be made only over Oral Torah which is attached to Scripture, i.e. talmud/midrash, while R. Yohanan necessitates a blessing for any study of the Oral Torah, even mishnah, which is independent of Scripture.

The Babylonian sugya's redactor received both of these debates, but instead of preserving them as two separate literary sources, he inserted the independent Eretz Yisraeli debate into the Babylonian debate, which caused the original intention of R. Hiyya b. Ashi's rejection of R. Huna to become obfuscated.[21] The redactor seems to have wished to preserve the Eretz Yisraeli debate in order to ensure that all three genres of sources—Scripture, midrash, and mishnah—would be addressed. Without the Eretz Yisraeli debate there would have been no explicit ruling on the status of mishnah/halakhot, sources not attached to Scripture. Although the insertion of the debate severed the connection between R. Huna and the story of Rav, the redactor chose to place the opinions of R. Elazar and R. Yohanan before the story because their literary structure is parallel to R.

---

[21] Rosenthal, 472; Benovitz, 540–541.

Huna's statement—"for X it is necessary to bless, for Y it is not necessary to bless." This also sets up a hierarchy between the sources, transitioning from Scripture to midrash to mishnah without interruption. Once the Babylonian debate was interrupted, the redactor added the word "as" (ד) before the statement of R. Hiyya b. Ashi to create a smoother transition between sections three and four and thereby link what seemed to have been independent debates. We should also note that the redactor inserted the Eretz Yisraeli dispute into the Babylonian amoraic dispute without emending the texts themselves. This left the difficult text that still remains in the Florence edition, as we demonstrated above.

From Florence to Vilna

Now that we have utilized both lower and higher criticism to uncover the amoraic debates in their original form, we are still left with the task of explaining how the text preserved in the Vilna printed edition came to be formed. In the following explanation we will refer to versions of our sugya by the name of the manuscript or printed edition in which they appear. The appearance of a particular version in a given manuscript does not indicate the moment in history in which the textual content was formed. In fact, it is likely that many, if not all, of the emendations to our sugya were made not long after the formation of the Talmud. This is true even of the versions that appear only as late as the printed edition. Despite their appearance at such a late date, such versions may have existed hundreds of years earlier, even before Rashi. And manuscripts that were written at a later date may preserve versions that were created before the versions preserved in manuscripts written at an earlier date.

As detailed above, the original form of our sugya, preserved in MS Florence, orders the genres of study from Scripture to talmud to mishnah. Talmud was originally a synonym for midrash. Mishnah is the genre of study least likely to necessitate a blessing because it is the furthest removed from Scripture. MS Paris reorders the sources to conclude with talmud (Scripture, mishnah, talmud) in order to strengthen the connection with the story of Rav blessing over Sifra, which appears at the end of the sugya. In this reading "talmud" is still synonymous with "midrash."

However, later copyists began to understand the term "talmud" in the same way that Rashi[22] understood it—explanations of the Mishnah which were later complied to form "the Talmud." This understanding might have even emerged from this version of the text which prioritizes "Mishnah," the earlier more fundamental text, over "Talmud," the explanations of the Mishnah. However, there remained two problems with this version. First of all, the problem addressed by MS Paris reemerged: How does the story of Rav blessing over midrash support the amoraic ruling which directly precedes it that one must bless over talmud? Second, this version makes no direct mention of midrash. To address both of these problems, an additional change was made to the text by appending a fourth amoraic opinion which requires blessing over midrash. As is usually the case, it is impossible to determine precisely when this version was created and there is no extant manuscript which preserves the reading. It is, however, found in the commentaries of most rishonim (see for instance Rabbenu Hananel; Rif; Ritva) and was written in the margins of the Munich manuscript.[23] The additional words which do not appear in MS Paris are italicized below:

> (1) R. Huna said: For Scripture it is necessary to bless, for mishnah it is not necessary bless.
>
> (2) R. Elazar said: it is even necessary to bless for mishnah, for talmud it is not necessary to bless.
>
> (3) R. Yohanan said: it is even necessary to bless for talmud, *for midrash it is not necessary to bless.*
>
> *(4) Rav said: it is even necessary to bless for midrash.*

The creator of this version attributed the opinion in section four to Rav since Rav is the amora who blesses over the Sifra, a midrashic text, at the end of the sugya. In order to transition from R. Yohanan's opinion in section three

---

[22] See Rashi s.v. אַף לגמרא.

[23] In other words, whoever wrote these lines on the margins of the manuscript had in his hands a different manuscript which he compared with the text found in Munich. Upon noticing such a significant discrepancy between the tradition preserved in Munich and that in the other manuscript, he copied one tradition in the margins of the other. The manuscript from which he copied has not survived.

into Rav's opinion in section four, he also was forced to add the words, "for midrash it is not necessary to bless" into section three.

The difficulty with the reading found in this tradition is twofold: (1) it places the amoraim out of chronological order (Rav is earlier than the other amoraim) and (2) there is no logical explanation for R. Yohanan's position. Why would a blessing be required for talmud and not for midrash? If anything, the opposite should be true, as midrash is closer to the written Torah than talmud.

These two difficulties led a later copyist to make even more changes to the text. First, the problem of chronology was resolved with the simple addition of an aleph to Rav's name, thereby attributing the final position to Rava, a later Babylonian amora. The other change was rearranging the genres among the four amoraim. Since the term "talmud" was understood as explanations of the Mishnah, a progression was created among the sources from Scripture, to midrash, to Mishnah, and concluding with Talmud. These changes created the reading found in the Vilna edition.[24] Ultimately, the text which appears before us greatly distorts the original amoraic debate.

And so by combining higher and lower criticisms we can reconstruct a history of the sugya from its formulation by the redactors to the drastically altered form found in the Vilna printed edition. At the core of our sugya lie two distinct amoraic debates over the requirement to make a blessing before studying the oral law, one stemming from Babylonia (Scripture vs. midrash) and one from Eretz Yisrael (midrash/talmud vs. mishnah/halakhah). The redactor of the sugya combined the Babylonian and Eretz Yisraeli disagreements into a single source represented by MS Florence (Scripture, talmud, mishnah). In doing so he created a difficulty whereby the story of Rav blessing over midrash does not support the immediately preceding amoraic position which requires blessing over mishnah. The copyist of the tradition preserved in MS Paris resolved the problem by rearranging the opinions so that R. Yohanan requires a blessing over talmud and Rav's story illustrates his position (Scripture, mishnah, talmud). The Paris source still proved vexing for readers who understood "talmud"

---

[24] While it cannot be determined with certainty if Rashi had an identical version to the one preserved in the Vilna edition, he already distinguishes between the genres of midrash and talmud and comments on them in that order.

to mean "the Talmud." The creator of the tradition found in the margins of MS Munich and in the commentaries of many rishonim addressed the issue by adding a fourth amoraic opinion (Scripture, mishnah, talmud, midrash). The final step in the process was made by an even later copyist who still found the version preserved in the Munich margin to be difficult. This copyist again rearranged the genres (Scripture, midrash, mishnah, talmud) and changed the last attribution from Rav to Rava. This final version is preserved in the Vilna printed edition (although as stated above, it may have existed in a much earlier period, perhaps even as early as Rashi). Four or more steps removed from the original version, this is the canonical version of the text that has been studied by students of the Talmud for the past several hundred years.

The Formulation of the Blessing

Following the debate over what texts require a blessing, the Bavli continues with an amoraic debate concerning the formulation of the blessing over Torah study. As we shall see, this section also requires analysis of manuscript traditions in order to uncover its original form and meaning. Furthermore, this passage demonstrates an important phenomenon regarding the textual transmission of liturgical texts embedded in rabbinic literature: a copyist or printer will frequently emend the text to reflect a ritual practice with which he is familiar. We will again begin with the version found in the Vilna printed edition:

בבלי ברכות יא ע"ב	**Bavli Berakhot 11b**
מאי מברך?	What does he bless?
(1) אמר רב יהודה	(1) R. Yehudah said in the name of
אמר שמואל: אשר	Shmuel: Who has sanctified us with
קדשנו במצותיו וצונו	His commandments, and command-
לעסוק בדברי תורה.	ed us to engage in the study of Torah.

(2) ורבי יוחנן מסיים בה
הכי: הערב נא ה' אלהינו
את דברי תורתך בפינו
ובפיפיות עמך בית ישראל
ונהיה אנחנו וצאצאינו
וצאצאי עמך בית ישראל
כלנו יודעי שמך ועוסקי
תורתך ברוך אתה ה'
המלמד תורה לעמו ישראל.

(2) R. Yohanan used to conclude as follows: Please, Lord our God, make pleasant the words of Your Torah in our mouths and in the mouths of Your people the House of Israel. May we and our offspring, and the offspring of Your people the House of Israel all know Your Name and study Your Torah. Blessed are You, O Lord, who teaches Torah to His people Israel.

(3) ורב המנונא אמר:
אשר בחר בנו מכל העמים
ונתן לנו את תורתו ברוך
אתה ה' נותן התורה.

(3) And R. Himnuna said: Who selected us from all the nations and gave us His Torah. Blessed are You, O Lord, Giver of the Torah.

(4) אמר רב המנונא: זו
היא מעולה שבברכות.

(4) R. Himnuna said: This is the finest of the blessings.

(5) הלכך לימרינהו לכולהו.

(5) Therefore let us say all of them.

In the Vilna edition the first blessing reads: לעסוק בדברי תורה—"to engage in the study of Torah." In contrast, all manuscripts read: על דברי תורה—"regarding the words of Torah." The only manuscript in which the phrase לעסוק בדברי תורה appears is in the margin of the Munich manuscript. In this case, a reader of the Munich text wrote in the margins of the manuscript the formulation of the blessing which reflected his personal practice. Clearly על דברי תורה is the original version.

The change in practice originated as a result of the medieval Ashkenazi authorities' attempt to create a standard rubric for differentiating between blessings which begin with על and those which begin with ל.[25] Bavli Pesahim 7a–b presents a lengthy discussion of various blessings made before the performance of commandments without arriving at any conclusion as to why a particular formulation is chosen for a particular blessing. R. Eliezer ben Natan of Mainz (1090–1170) suggested that blessings using על should be recited

---

[25] The contemporary Sefardic practice is to recite על דברי תורה.

before commandments which are performed and completed immediately. For example, one recites על נטילת לולב before taking the four species because he fulfills his obligation immediately upon lifting the species together. Blessings which use the infinitive (ל) should be recited before commandments which continue over an extended period of time. Therefore one recites לישב בסוכה for the commandment of sitting in the sukkah which lasts for all seven days of Sukkot.[26] Later authorities then applied his distinction to the blessing over Torah study. Since Torah study continues over an extended period of time, it was concluded by Ashkenazi authorities that the blessing should be in the infinitive—לעסוק—and not על.[27] Both the gloss in the margin of the Munich manuscript and the printed editions reflect the change that took place in Ashkenazi circles.

The text continues with R. Yohanan's formula for the blessing. According to printed editions, R. Yohanan's blessing is intended to complete that of Shmuel: מסיים בה הכי—"used to conclude." However, none of the manuscript traditions include these three words in the body of the text. In these versions, the statement of R. Yohanan reads, "R. Yohanan *said*," indicating that he offers an alternate version of the blessing, one which was intended to replace that of Shmuel.[28] The words מסיים בה הכי entered the printed editions from a marginal gloss found in the Florence and Munich manuscripts. This gloss was created due to the halakhic ruling of Rabennu Tam (1100–1171) that all blessings must open with the form "Blessed are you," unless they immediately follow another blessing, such as the second blessing before the Shema and the second blessing of birkat hamazon.[29] Were R. Yohanan's version of the blessing an independent formula meant to replace that of Shmuel, it would have to open with "Blessed are you." Therefore, the phrase מסיים בה הכי was inserted into the talmudic text, transforming R. Yohanan's independent formula to one intended to conclude Shmuel's version. It did not need to open with "Blessed are you" because it was the second blessing in the formula. The rishonim from Sefarad, on the other hand, do not follow the rulings of

---

[26] See *Teshuvot Ra'avan* no. 35.

[27] The actual formulation of the blessing as לעסוק first appears in the works of French halakhic authorities. See Rabbenu Tam, *Sefer HaYashar*, no. 308 and *Mahzor Vitry*, 102.

[28] Yerushalmi Berakhot 4:1 (7d) attributes a different personal prayer to R. Yohanan.

[29] Tosafot Pesahim 104b s.v. חוץ.

Rabbenu Tam and preserve the independent status of R. Yohanan's blessings. The difference in approaches can be clearly seen in their disagreement over the number of blessings that make up the blessings over Torah study. Rashi and Tosafot (Berakhot 46a s.v. כל הברכות), who understand R. Yohanan's blessing to be a conclusion of Shmuel's, argue that there are only two blessings and that R. Yohanan's blessing should be read with a vav (והערב) to indicate that it is connected to the opening blessing. Maimonides (*Tefillah* 7:10) believes that there are three separate blessings, which explains his formulation without the vav (הערב).

The conclusion to Rabbi Yohanan's blessing in the Vilna, המלמד תורה לעמו ישראל, is also the result of an emendation. Originally, the formula attributed to R. Yohanan concluded with Psalms 119:12, "Blessed are You O Lord; train me in Your laws—ברוך אתה ה' למדני חקיך" This reading is preserved only in the Oxford manuscript. Rashi objected to this formula on the grounds that it is not a blessing but rather a request—"train me." Both he and the Tosafot emend the text to the version which appears in the Vilna edition.

The final version of the blessing, suggested by R. Himnuna, is the same blessing recited over the public reading of the Torah. In MSS Oxford and Florence and the printed editions, R. Himnuna's suggestion is then followed by another statement attributed to him, "This is the finest of blessings." This reading, however, seems problematic. Why would R. Himnuna describe his own blessing as "the finest of blessings"? Surely he would not have suggested it in the first place if he did not think that it was the most appropriate version. MS Munich and the text preserved by the majority of rishonim rectify the problem by making the second statement anonymous ("this is the finest of blessings"). This creates the impression that it is actually an editorial comment made by the anonymous voice of the Talmud.[30] MS Paris and a Cairo Genizah fragment (JTS ENA 2068.9–11) remove the difficulty by attributing the formulation of the blessing to R. Huna, a name which appears earlier in the sugya and could easily have been mixed up with Himnuna. Again, assuming *lectio difficilior potior*, we must look for an explanation that preserves the difficult reading which attributes *both statements* to R. Himnuna. Moshe Benovitz explains that unlike the other

---

[30] See *Dikdukei Soferim,* 1:51 n. 10.

blessings suggested, R. Himnuna did not create the formulation of the blessing. His comment, "this is the finest of blessings" is meant to indicate his belief that the blessing said over the public reading of Torah is the most appropriate to be recited before personal Torah study.[31]

The Vilna edition's version of the concluding statement of the sugya, "therefore let us say all of them" also contains an error in transmission. All manuscripts read, "Rav Papa said: Therefore let us say all of them," but this attribution mistakenly dropped out of the printed text, where the statement is transmitted anonymously.[32] In fact, this is a statement attributed to Rav Papa six other times in the Bavli (Berakhot 59a, 59b, 60b; Megillah 21b; Ta'anit 6a; Sotah 40a). In each of those cases, Rav Papa advocates combining a group of blessings into a single blessing. For example, Berakhot 59a records two different opinions regarding the appropriate formulation of the blessing recited upon seeing a rainbow: (1) Who remembers the covenant and (2) Who is trustworthy in His covenant, and fulfills His word. Rav Papa suggests combining them: "Who remembers the covenant, is trustworthy in His covenant, and fulfils His word." In our sugya, however, Rav Papa seems to be suggesting that all three distinct blessings should be recited and not combined into a single blessing. The unusual use of this formula may indicate that the statement of Rav Papa was taken from another location and added later to our sugya. In sum, by using lower criticism, we are able to identify that the proper reading of the sugya is with the attribution to Rav Papa, as it is found in manuscripts. Higher critical techniques, namely the fact that the same exact statement appears elsewhere, where it has other meanings, allows us to conclude that Rav Papa's statement was transferred from another location in order to serve as a conclusion to our sugya. R. Papa himself did not recite or rule that one should recite all three blessings—this was the opinion of the redactor. Ultimately, later halakhic authorities accepted the redactor's work as authoritative, leading to the post-talmudic practice of reciting all three blessings before personal Torah study. Here too, the redactor's influence on halakhic history was determinative.

---

[31] Benovitz, 543.

[32] Rabbenu Tam, who combines Shmuel and R. Yohanan's blessing into one, maintains that the proper reading of Rav Papa's statement is consistent with the majority of the other appearances which state: "therefore let him say *both* of them."

Conclusion

The hands of numerous post-amoraic talmudic editors, medieval scribes and even modern printers had a profound impact on the final form of this sugya. The Babylonian redactor combined two separate debates over which sources require a blessing for Torah study into a single sugya, creating the three part hierarchy of Scripture, midrash, and mishnah. Scribes and eventually printers continued to offer massive emendations to the details of this section, changing the order of the sources, their content and their attributions. The second half of the sugya originally consisted of independent amoraic suggestions for the appropriate language of the blessing. The late Babylonian redactor imported R. Papa's statement into the conclusion of the sugya. Medieval scribes changed the language of the amoraic blessings in order to conform to certain halakhic rulings of the Tosafists on the proper formulation of blessings. Contemporary halakhic practice reflects these editorial combinations and scribal emendations. R. Yaakov b. Asher, the author of the fourteenth century halakhic compilation known as the Tur (Orah Hayyim, 47), rules that all three blessings are recited according to their emended readings and a blessing must be made over the study of Scripture, midrash, Mishnah, and Talmud.

CHAPTER NINE

THE JOURNEY OF A TALMUDIC LEGEND: R. PINHAS B. YAIR AND HIS RIGHTEOUS DONKEY

HULLIN 7A–7B

Introduction

In this chapter we analyze a long aggadic passage about the legendary figure of R. Pinhas ben Yair, a sage famous for his wondrous deeds and his halakhically observant donkey. The passage (Hullin 5b–7b) begins with three stories describing the infallibility of various sages, each of which concludes with the statement, "If the Holy One, blessed be He, does not allow the beast of the righteous to stumble, all the more so the righteous themselves." The mention of the "beast of the righteous" leads to the centerpiece of the passage—the story of R. Pinhas b. Yair and his donkey. The Bavli tells the tale of the righteous R. Pinhas b. Yair, who never derived benefit from another human being, and the miracles he wrought and encountered on his journey to redeem a captive. The Yerushalmi, in a passage we will also analyze, preserves an earlier version of the R. Pinhas b. Yair traditions in the form of eight distinct incidents describing various wonders he performed.

Our analysis focuses primarily on two specific aspects of the rich literature surrounding R. Pinhas b. Yair. By comparing the Bavli with the Yerushalmi and highlighting their similar and divergent themes, we will demonstrate how the Babylonian storytellers reworked the disjointed earlier material to create a single narrative about R. Pinhas b. Yair. At the same time we will highlight the transformation of the character of R. Pinhas b. Yair from the miracle worker found in the Yerushalmi into a more normative rabbinic authority presented in the Bavli. This chapter provides an example of the literary creativity of Babylonian storytellers and the various techniques they use in reworking earlier material to create legends and stories which portray their priorities, concerns, anxieties, and way of life. The methodological foundations of this chapter are greatly based on the work of Jeffrey Rubenstein, who has published three books demonstrating how the same comparative, analytical methods that guide the academic study of halakhic sugyot are effective in studying aggadic passages.[1]

The Holy One Does Not Allow the Righteous To Stumble

Hulin 5b–7b consists of a collection of stories in which sages are portrayed as either eating foods that might actually be forbidden or unwittingly eating food that is certainly forbidden. The unit appears following a lengthy halakhic discussion concerning the permissibility of animals slaughtered by Samaritans or apostates. The discussion concludes with the amoraic assertion that R. Gamaliel, the son of R. Yehudah HaNasi (Rebbi), and his court forbade eating meat slaughtered by a Samaritan. This declaration is followed by the first of three stories in which a sage eats halakhically questionable food and another sage reacts in astonishment.

Story One[2]

חולין ה ע"ב	Hullin 5b
(1a) אמר ר' חנן אמר ר' יעקב בר אידי אמר ר' יהושע בן לוי משום בר קפרא: רבן גמליאל ובית דינו נמנו על שחיטת כותי ואסרוה...	(1a) R. Hanan said in the name of R. Yaakov b. Idi, R. Yehoshua b. Levi said in the name of Bar Kapara: Rabban Gamaliel and his court voted on animals slaughtered by a Samaritan and forbade them...

---

[1] *Talmudic Stories: Narrative Art, Composition and Culture*, (Baltimore: Johns Hopkins University Press, 1999); The *Culture of the Babylonian Talmud*, (Baltimore: Johns Hopkins University Press, 2003); *Stories of the Babylonian Talmud*. (Baltimore: Johns Hopkins University Press, 2010).

[2] We will cite and analyze only the parts of the passages relevant to our discussion.

(1b) ...אמר ר' נחמן בר
יצחק אמר ר' אסי: אני
ראיתי את רבי יוחנן שאכל
משחיטת כותי, אף רבי
אסי אכל משחיטת כותי.

(1b) ...R. Nahman b. Yitzhak said in the name of R. Assi: I saw R. Yohanan eating an animal slaughtered by a Samaritan. R. Assi also ate an animal slaughtered by a Samaritan.

(1c) ותהי בה רבי זירא: לא
שמיעא להו, דאי הוה שמיעא
להו הוו מקבלי לה, או דלמא
שמיע להו ולא קבלוה?

(1c) And R. Zera was astonished: Did they [these sages] not hear [the ruling of Rabban Gamaliel], and if they had heard it would they have accepted it, or perhaps they heard and did not accept it?

(1d) הדר פשיט לנפשיה,
מסתברא דשמיע להו ולא
קבלוה, דאי סלקא דעתך לא
שמיע להו, ואי הוה שמיע
להו הוו מקבלי לה, היכי
מסתייעא מילתא למיכל
איסורא? השתא בהמתן של
צדיקים אין הקדוש ברוך
הוא מביא תקלה על ידן,
צדיקים עצמן לא כל שכן!

(1d) He later concluded for himself: It stands to reason that they heard it and did not accept it, for if you think they did not hear it and if they had heard it they would have accepted it, how could they have successfully eaten something forbidden? Now, if the Holy One, blessed be He, does not allow the beast of the righteous to stumble, all the more so the righteous themselves!

Seeming to contradict the ruling of R. Gamaliel's court, R. Assi declares that he saw R. Yohanan eat meat slaughtered by a Samaritan. This is followed by a related statement that R. Assi himself ate meat of the same halakhic status. R. Zera, aware of the prohibition issued by R. Gamaliel, reacts with surprise that R. Yohanan and R. Assi had either not even heard of this ruling or that alternatively they rejected it. R. Zera (1d) reasons that they must have rejected the ruling because otherwise we would have to conclude that sages accidentally consumed forbidden meat. R. Zera then emphatically rejects the fallibility of the sages, exclaiming "if the Holy One, blessed be He, does not allow the beast of the righteous to stumble, all the more so the righteous themselves."[3] R. Zera argues that it is impossible that rabbis would have sinned by eating forbidden meat and references what seems to be a well-known saying concerning R. Pinhas ben Yair's donkey (as we shall see below) which God prevented from ever committing a transgression.[4] According to R. Zera, God does not allow even the animals of the righteous to err. Since they could not have sinned, R. Zera argues that one must conclude that R. Yohanan and R. Asi rejected R. Gamaliel's ruling. It is important to note that R. Zera uses the allusion to R. Pinhas b. Yair's donkey to answer the halakhic question which stands at the heart of the sugya. R. Zera is so sure of God's protection of the righteous that he can use this assumption as a rhetorical means through which to determine R. Yohanan and R. Assi's ruling as to the permissibility of an animal slaughtered by a Samaritan. Based on his assumption, R. Zera concludes that it indeed must be permitted to eat meat from an animal slaughtered by a Samaritan.

Story Two

חולין ו ע"א	Hullin 6a
(2a) רבי זירא ורב אסי איקלעו לפונדקא דיאי, אייתו לקמייהו ביצים המצומקות ביין, רבי זירא לא אכל ורב אסי אכל,	(2a) R. Zera and R. Assi came to the inn of Yai. They brought before them eggs roasted in wine. R. Zera did not eat them and R. Assi ate them.
(2b) אמר ליה רבי זירא לרב אסי: ולא חייש מר לתערובת דמאי? אמר ליה: לאו אדעתאי.	(2b) R. Zera said to R. Assi: Is the master not concerned about a mixture containing demai? He [R. Assi] said to him [R. Zera]: I was unaware.

---

[3] For a detailed analysis of the statement and its attribution to R. Zera see Leib Moscovitz, "The Holy One Blessed be He...Does Not Permit the Righteous to Stumble," *Creation and Composition*, ed. Jeffrey Rubenstein (Tuebingen: Mohr-Siebeck, 2005), 125–179. Moscovitz compares the doctrine of rabbinic infallibility espoused by our sugya to other statements about the righteous being protected from error. He concludes that despite the seeming attribution to R. Zera, the statement is actually a stammaitic inversion of the passage in the Yerushalmi which we will examine in detail below.

[4] The phrase appears six times in the Bavli.

(2c) אמר ר' זירא: אפשר
גזרו על התערובת דמאי,
ומסתייעא מילתא דרב אסי
למיכל איסורא? השתא בהמתן
של צדיקים אין הקדוש ברוך
הוא מביא תקלה על ידן,
צדיקים עצמן לא כל שכן!

(2c) R. Zera said: Is it possible that they [the rabbis] decreed against eating a mixture containing demai and R. Assi would succeed in eating something forbidden? Now, if the Holy One, blessed be He, does not allow the beast of the righteous to stumble, all the more so the righteous themselves!

(2d) נפק רבי זירא דק ואשכח,
דתנן: הלוקח יין לתת לתוך
המורייס או לתוך האלונתית,
כרשינין לעשות מהן טחינין,
עדשים לעשות מהן רסיסין -
חייב משום דמאי, ואין צריך
לומר משום ודאי, והן עצמן
מותרין מפני שהן תערובת.

(2d) R. Zera went out and investigated and found that it was taught: If one purchased wine to put into brine or into aluntit, vetches (animal food) to make into grist, lentils to make into groats, it is subject to demai and certainly [must be tithed] if it is known to be untithed, but they themselves are permitted because they are mixtures.

In this story, R. Zera and R. Assi arrive at an inn where R. Assi eats eggs roasted in wine which contain *demai*. The rabbis placed an added stringency on produce purchased from an *am haaretz*, a Jew who is suspected of not tithing properly. Such produce has the status of *demai* (lit. "what is it" in Aramaic), and must be tithed by the purchaser in case the owner did not tithe. R. Zera points out the transgression to R. Assi, and R. Assi admits that he did not know that what he was eating was forbidden. R. Zera, however, responds with the same declaration found in the previous story—it is simply impossible that a righteous person such as R. Assi could have made a mistake and eaten forbidden food. R. Zera investigates and discovers that it was he who was mistaken and that the particular mixture consumed by R. Assi was in fact permitted. The baraita he quotes distinguishes between purchasing ingredients for a mixture from a person suspected of not tithing and purchasing the mixture itself. If the prepared mixture was purchased it is not necessary to tithe, as was the case when R. Assi ate the eggs roasted in wine. The main point here is that even if R. Assi had intended to eat forbidden food, God simply would not have allowed a sage to transgress.

Story Three

חולין ו ע״ב - ז ע״א	Hullin 6b–7a
(3a) העיד רבי יהושע בן זרוז בן חמיו של רבי מאיר לפני רבי על ר״מ שאכל עלה של ירק בבית שאן, והתיר רבי את בית שאן כולה על ידו...	(3a) R. Yehoshua b. Zaruz, the son of R. Meir's father-in-law, testified before Rebbi that R. Meir ate the leaf of a vegetable in Bet She'an, and Rebbi permitted all of [the produce of] Beit She'an [to be eaten without tithing] because of his [action]...
(3b) אמר ליה ר' ירמיה לרבי זירא: והא ר' מאיר עלה בעלמא הוא דאכיל!	(3b) R. Yirmiyah said to R. Zera: But R. Meir merely ate a leaf [which is always exempt from tithes].
אמר ליה: מאגודה אכליה, ותנן: ירק הנאגד, משיאגד.	He [R. Zera] said to him [R. Yirmiyah]: He [R. Meir] ate it from a bundle and it was taught [in a mishnah]: Vegetables tied in a bundle [are liable for tithing] once they are tied.
(3c) ודלמא לאו אדעתיה!	(3c) Perhaps he was unaware [that it needed to be tithed]?
(3d) השתא בהמתן של צדיקים אין הקדוש ברוך הוא מביא תקלה על ידן, צדיקים עצמן לא כל שכן.	(3d) Now, if the Holy One, blessed be He, does not allow the beast of the righteous to stumble, all the more so the righteous themselves!

The final story in the group recounts the incident of R. Meir eating an untithed leaf of a vegetable in Beit She'an. Rabbi Yehudah HaNasi (Rebbi) assumes that by eating this leaf R. Meir was demonstratively teaching that vegetables grown in Beit She'an are exempt from tithes. As a result, Rebbi declares all of Beit She'an exempt from tithing, presumably because it is not considered part of the land of Israel. R. Yirmiyah and R. Zera then debate the actual amount that R. Meir consumed. R. Yirmiyah suggests that perhaps R. Meir ate only a leaf, which would be exempt from tithing in any case because it is not considered a sufficient amount to be liable for tithes. R. Zera responds that R. Meir ate an entire bundle. R. Zera's statement is followed by the anonymous suggestion that perhaps R. Meir did not realize that the leaf was not tithed. This possibility is met with the same declaration found in the previous stories, "Now, if the Holy One, blessed be He, does not allow the beast of the righteous to stumble, all the more so the righteous themselves." It is not possible that R. Meir could have mistakenly eaten forbidden food, and therefore the vegetables of Beit She'an must indeed be exempt from tithes. As in the first story, the allusion that God protects the righteous serves as the legal justification for Rebbi's lenient ruling. In other words, God would protect R. Meir from an unwitting sin; hence he must have intentionally eaten the bundle of vegetables in order to demonstrate that produce from Bet She'an is not liable to tithes.

The above stories have their own unique textual histories.[5] We have summarized them briefly here because of the important role they play in setting the stage for the central story of R. Pinhas b. Yair. Context plays an important role in the interpretation of aggadic passages.[6] Therefore, we must read our narrative in light of the preceding stories concerning the infallibility of the sages.

R. Pinhas b. Yair and his Donkey

These three stories concerning the infallibility of the rabbinic sages all refer to a certain beast belonging to the righteous that God did not allow to stumble. The Bavli now begins a story-cycle in which this beast is identified as the righteous R. Pinhas ben Yair's donkey, which became legendary for its avoidance of sin.

חולין ז ע״א-ע״ב	Hullin 7a–7b
מאי בהמתן של צדיקים?	What is the beast of the righteous?
(1a) דרבי פנחס בן יאיר	(1a) R. Pinhas b. Yair was going to redeem
הוה קאזיל לפדיון שבויין	captives. He encountered the Ginai river.
פגע ביה בגינאי נהרא.	

---

5 See Moscovitz, 125–137.

6 Jeffrey Rubenstein, *Talmudic Stories*, 11–15.

אמר ליה: גינאי, חלוק
לי מימך ואעבור בך.

He said to it: Ginai, split your wa-
ters so that I may cross you.

אמר ליה: אתה הולך
לעשות רצון קונך ואני
הולך לעשות רצון
קוני, אתה ספק עושה
ספק אי אתה עושה,
אני ודאי עושה.

It said to him: You are going to do the will
of your Maker and I am going to do the
will of my Maker. It is possible that you
will succeed and possible that you will not
succeed, but I will definitely succeed.

אמר ליה: אם אי אתה
חולק, גוזרני עליך
שלא יעברו בך מים
לעולם. חלק ליה.

He said to it: If you do not split, I decree that water will never pass through
you again. It split for him.

(1b) הוה ההוא גברא
דהוה דארי חיטי לפיסחא.

(1b) There was a man who was carrying wheat for Passover,

אמר ליה: חלוק ליה
נמי להאי דבמצוה
עסיק. חלק ליה.

He [RPBY] said to it: Split for this one too because he is engaged in a mitzvah. It split for him.

(1c) הוה ההוא טייעא
דלווה בהדייהו. אמר
ליה: חלוק ליה נמי להאי,
דלא לימא: כך עושים
לבני לויה? חלק ליה.

(1c) There was an Arab accompanying
him [RPBY]. He said to it: Split for this
one too, so [people] will not say: This is
what you do to escorts? It split for him.

(1d) אמר רב יוסף:
כמה נפיש גברא ממשה
ושתין רבוון, דאילו
התם חד זימנא, והכא
תלתא זימנין. ודלמא
הכא נמי חדא זימנא!

(1d) Rav Yosef said: How much greater is
this man than Moses and the 600,000 [Isra-
elites], for there it [split] once and here three
times. Perhaps here too it was only once!

אלא כמשה ושתין רבוון.

Rather, [say he is] like Moses and the 600,000.

300

(2a) אקלע לההוא
אושפיזא. רמו ליה שערי
לחמריה לא אכל. חבטינהו
לא אכל. נקרינהו לא אכל.

(2a) He went to a certain inn. They placed barley before his donkey and she did not eat. They beat [the barley] and she did not eat. They sifted it and she did not eat.

אמר להו: דלמא לא
מעשרן? עשרינהו ואכל.

He said to them: perhaps it is not tithed? They tithed it and the donkey ate.

אמר: ענייה זו הולכת
לעשות רצון קונה ואתם
מאכילין אותה טבלים.

He said: This poor thing is going to do the will of its Maker and you are feeding her untithed produce?

(2b) ומי מיחייבא?

(2b) But does [such produce] need to be tithed?

והתנן: הלוקח לזרע
ולבהמה, וקמח לעורות,
ושמן לנר, ושמן
לסוך בו את הכלים
- פטור מהדמאי.

But did it not teach: One who purchases [grain to use] for seed or for an animal, or flour for [use in processing] hides, or oil for a lamp or oil for greasing utensils, is exempt from demai.

(2c) התם הא אתמר
עלה, אמר רבי יוחנן: לא
שנו אלא שלקחן מתחלה
לבהמה, אבל לקחן מתחלה
לאדם ונמלך עליהם
לבהמה, חייב לעשר.

(2c) There it has been stated about this: R. Yohanan said: They only taught this if he bought the grain from the outset for animal consumption; but if he bought it from the outset for human consumption and later decided to give it to animals, it must be tithed.

(2d) והתניא: הלוקח
פירות מן השוק לאכילה,
ונמלך עליהן לבהמה -
הרי זה לא יתן לא לפני
בהמתו ולא לפני בהמת
חברו אלא אם כן עישר.

(2d) And so it has been taught in a baraita: One who buys produce in the market for eating and decides later to use it for animals, behold he may not give it either to his own animal or to his neighbor's animal without first tithing it.

(3a) שמע רבי
נפק לאפיה.

(3a) When Rebbi heard [of the arrival of RPBY], he went out to meet him.

אמר ליה: רצונך
סעוד אצלי.

He said to him: Will you please dine with me?

אמר לו: הן.

He [RPBY] responded: Yes.

צהבו פניו של רבי.

Rebbi's face brightened with joy.

אמר לו: כמדומה אתה
שמודר הנאה מישראל
אני? ישראל קדושים הן.
יש רוצה ואין לו ויש שיש
לו ואינו רוצה, וכתיב: אל
תלחם [את] לחם רע עין
ואל תתאו למטעמותיו כי
כמו שער בנפשו כן הוא
אכול ושתה יאמר לך ולבו
בל עמך (משלי כג:ו-ז).
ואתה רוצה ויש לך.
מיהא השתא מסרהיבנא,
דבמלתא דמצוה קא
טרחנא, כי הדרנא
אתינא עיילנא לגבך.

He [RPBY] said to him: Do you imagine that I am forbidden by vow from deriving any benefit from an Israelite? The people of Israel are holy. Yet there are some who desire [to give to others] but have not the means; while others have the means but have not the desire, and it is written: *Do not eat of a stingy man's food. Do not crave for his dainties. He is like one who keeps accounts. Eat and drink he says to you, but he does not really mean it* (Proverbs 23:6–7). But you have the desire and also the means. However, right now I am in a hurry for I am occupied with a mitzvah. When I return I will come and visit you.

(3b) כי אתא, איתרמי על
בההוא פיתחא דהוו קיימין
ביה כודנייתא חוורתא.
אמר: מלאך המות בביתו
של זה ואני אסעוד אצלו?

(3b) When he arrived, he happened to enter by a gate near which were some white mules. At this he exclaimed: The angel of death is in this house and I shall dine with him?

שמע רבי נפק לאפיה.
אמר ליה: מזבנינא להו.

When Rebbi heard of this, he went out to meet him.
He [Rebbi] said: I will sell the mules.

אמר ליה: ולפני עור לא תתן מכשול (ויקרא יט:יד).	R. Pinhas replied: *You shall not put a stumbling block before the blind* (Leviticus 19:14).
מפקרנא להו.	I will abandon them.
מפשת היזקא.	You would increase their danger.
עקרנא להו.	I will hamstring them.
איכא צער בעלי חיים.	You would be causing suffering to animals.
קטילנא להו.	I will kill them.
איכא בל תשחית.	There is the prohibition against needless destruction.
הוה קא מבתש ביה טובא. גבה טורא ביניי הו.	Rebbi was contending with him persistently. A mountain rose up between them.
בכה רבי ואמר: מה בחייהן כך, במיתתן על אחת כמה וכמה.	Rebbi wept and said. If this is [the power of the righteous] in their lifetime, how great must it be after their death!
(3c) דאמר ר' חמא בר חנינא: גדולים צדיקים במיתתן יותר מבחייהן, שנאמר: ויהי הם קוברים איש והנה ראו [את] הגדוד וישליכו את האיש בקבר אלישע וילך ויגע האיש בעצמות אלישע ויחי ויקם על רגליו (מלכים ב יג:כא)	(3c) For R. Hanina b. Hama said: The righteous are more powerful after their death than in their lifetime, for it is written: *Once a man was being buried, when the people caught sight of such a band; so they threw the corpse into Elisha's grave and made off. When the dead man came into contact with Elisha's bones, he came to life and stood up* (2 Kings 13:21).

303

אמר ליה רב פפא לאביי:
ודילמא לקיומי ביה
ברכתא דאליהו, דכתיב:
ויהי נא פי שנים ברוחך
אלי (מלכים ב ב:ט).

R. Papa said to Abaye: Perhaps [the restoration to life was] to fulfill Elijah's blessing, as it is written: *Let a double portion of your spirit be upon me* (2 Kings 2:9).

אמר ליה: אי הכי,
היינו דתניא: על רגליו
עמד ולביתו לא הלך?
אלא במה איקיים?

He replied: If so, that is was has been taught: He stood upon his feet but he did not walk to his home? How then was Elijah's blessing fulfilled?

כדאמר ר' יוחנן: שריפא
צרעת נעמן שהיא שקולה
כמת, שנאמר: אל נא תהי
כמת (במדבר יב:יב).

As R. Yohanan said: He healed the leprosy of Na'aman, which is the equivalent of death, as it is written: *Let her not, I pray, be as one dead* (Numbers 12:12).

(3d) אמר ר' יהושע
בן לוי: למה נקרא
שמן ימים? שאימתם
מוטלת על הבריות.

(3d) R. Yehoshua ben Levi said: Why are they [mules] called yemim? Because the fear of them is upon people.

דאמר ר' חנינא: מימי
לא שאלני אדם על מכת
פרדה לבנה וחיה.

For R. Hanina has said: My entire life no one has ever consulted me for a case of a wound from a white mule and has lived.

והא קחזינא דחיי?

But do we not see people recovering from it?

אימא וחיית.

Say: And has healed.

והא קחזינא דמיתסי?

But do we not see cases where the wound has healed?

דחיוורן ריש כרעייהו
קא אמרינן.

I was speaking about [a case where] the tips of their legs are white.

(4a) אין עוד מלבדו
(דברים ד:לה): אמר רבי
חנינא: ואפילו כשפים.

(4a) *There is none else beside Him* (Deuteronomy 4:35): R. Hanina said: Even sorcery.

ההיא איתתא דהות קא
מהדרא למישקל עפרא
מתותיה כרעיה דרבי
חנינא. אמר לה: שקולי,
לא מסתייעא מילתיך,
אין עוד מלבדו כתיב.

There once was a woman who tried to take earth from under R. Hanina's feet. He said to her: Take it, it will not help you, for it is written: *There is none else beside Him.*

והאמר ר' יוחנן: למה נקרא
שמן כשפים? שמכחישין
פמליא של מעלה! שאני ר'
חנינא, דנפישא זכותיה.

But did not R. Yohanan say: Why is sorcery called keshafim? Because it overrules [the decree of] the heavenly council? R. Hanina is different for his merits are abundant.

(4b) ואמר ר' חנינא: אין
אדם נוקף אצבעו מלמטה
אלא אם כן מכריזין עליו
מלמעלה, שנאמר: מה'
מצעדי גבר כוננו (תהלים
לז:כג), ואדם מה יבין
דרכו (משלי כ:כד).

(4b) And R. Hanina said: No man bruises his finger here on earth unless it was so decreed against him in heaven, for it is written: *It is of the Lord that a man's steps are determined* (Psalms 37:23), *How then can a man understand his path?* (Proverbs 20:24).

אמר ר' אלעזר: דם ניקוף
מרצה כדם עולה.

R. Elazar said: The blood of a bruise atones like the blood of a burnt-offering.

אמר רבא: בגודל ימין
ובניקוף שני, והוא
דקאזיל לדבר מצוה.

Rava said: They taught that only about the second bruising of the thumb of the right hand, and then only if it happened to one who was on his way to perform a mitzvah.

(5) אמרו עליו על ר' פנחס
בן יאיר: מימיו לא בצע
על פרוסה שאינה שלו,
ומיום שעמד על דעתו
לא נהנה מסעודת אביו.

(5) They said of R. Pinhas ben Yair: Never in his life did he say a blessing over a piece of bread which was not his own and from the day he reached years of discretion he derived no benefit from his father's table.

The Bavli's story of R. Pinhas b. Yair (RPBY) can be divided into three scenes. The story begins with RPBY on a mission to redeem captives. The Ginai river stands in his way and he commands the river to part so that he may continue on his path. The river acquiesces to his command, interrupting the natural order of the world for RPBY and two others. The second scene (section two) takes place in an inn. RPBY's donkey refuses to eat and it becomes clear that the reason is because the food has not been properly tithed. The final scene (section three) describes an encounter between Rabbi Yehudah HaNasi (Rebbi) and R. Pinhas b. Yair. Rebbi invites RPBY to dine with him. After initially accepting the invitation, RPBY refuses to eat with Rebbi because he sees that Rebbi owns white mules. White mules are considered to be extremely dangerous and RPBY will not break bread with someone who has "the angel of death" in his home. After a lengthy halakhic discourse in which Rebbi tries to appease RPBY by ridding himself of the mules, a mountain rises between them, forever separating the two sages. The storyteller does not yet reveal entirely why RPBY's original acceptance of the meal was so extraordinary, but from Rebbi's reaction of overwhelming joy it is clear that the event was extremely significant to Rebbi. Upon realizing that RPBY will not end up sharing a meal with him, Rebbi laments the fact that he has forever lost his opportunity of being honored by RPBY's presence. Section 3c provides midrashic evidence for Rebbi's despair that he will never have the opportunity to get close to RPBY. Like the prophet Elisha, who was more powerful in death than in life, the gap between the two sages will only increase after RPBY's death.

This section concludes (3d) with two statements clarifying the danger surrounding the mules. R. Yehoshua b. Levi's midrash on the etymology of the name *yemim* refers to Genesis 36:24:

ואלה בני-צבעון, ואיה	The sons of Zibeon were these: Aiah and
וענה; הוא ענה, אשר מצא	Anah—that was Anah who discovered the
את-הימם במדבר, ברעתו	*yemim* in the wilderness while pasturing
את-החמרים, לצבעון אביו.	the asses of his father Zibeon.

The exact meaning of the *yemim*, a word which appears only here in the Bible, is unclear, but rabbinic tradition understands it to refer to mules apparently as a result of its similarity to the Greek *hemionos*.[7] In Hullin, this midrash supports RPBY's decision to decline Rebbi's invitation. The Bavli then connects this statement with R. Hanina's declaration that he has never seen someone survive the blow of a white mule.[8]

After the story, the sugya digresses (section four) into a discussion of magic. R. Hanina explains that while it might seem as if magic can alter the course of nature, in truth "there is none beside Him." The magician cannot act without the sanction of God. R. Hanina's belief is illustrated by an accompanying story in which a woman approaches R. Hanina trying to take dirt from beneath his feet. The woman intends to use the dirt in order to perform an act of sorcery against R. Hanina. R. Hanina is unafraid of her actions because of God's control over the universe. If he is righteous, God will protect him, and if not he deserves to be harmed and the spell will succeed. Gideon Bohak highlights the unusual nature of R. Hanina's lack of reaction.[9] In a similar scene in Apuleius' *The Golden Ass* (second century C.E.), a barber takes proactive steps to prevent a witch from gathering hair-clippings from his client in order to cast an erotic spell. In contrast with the barber who is clearly concerned with the spell's efficacy, R. Hanina remains unfazed by the woman's actions. Her magical acts are futile, so he believes, in the face of Divine Providence. However, while R. Hanina is unfazed, the anonymous voice of the Talmud is not. The stam is surprised at R. Hanina's lack of concern about the effects of magic, quoting R. Yohanan who teaches that magic "overrules [the decree of] the heavenly council." In light of R. Yohanan's statement, how

---

[7] Nahum Sarna, *Genesis: The Traditional Hebrew Text with the New JPS Translation* (Philadelphia: Jewish Publication Society, 1989), 251.

[8] Genesis Rabbah 82:24 explains that the dangerous temperament of mules is a direct result of being a product of a forbidden mixture of animals unsanctioned by God.

[9] *Ancient Jewish Magic: A History* (New York: Cambridge University Press, 2008), 55–57.

could R. Hanina have been so sure that he was immune from the sorceress's attack? The stam resolves the contradiction by explaining that R. Hanina's extraordinary righteousness protects him. As Bohak writes, "ordinary Jews cannot blindly trust God's Providence to make them magic-proof, and when they see a witch collecting the dust from underneath them they better react just like Apuleius' barber."

The final statement of R. Hanina (4b) teaches that God controls even the most minor aspect of each individual's life. While the connection to the prooftext is not entirely clear, the verse is used to teach that nothing as insignificant as a bruised finger occurs without having been previously determined by heaven.[10] His statement is followed by a related teaching which suggests that accidental bruises atone for sin.

The cycle of stories closes by returning to R. Pinhas b. Yair and his famous piety. RPBY was so hesitant to derive benefit from others that from the time he was able to provide for himself, he would not eat even from his own father's table. This comment serves as an epitaph for R. Pinhas b. Yair, emphasizing that behind the miracles wrought by this sage is a character of extraordinary integrity. RPBY's righteousness, and with it his unique protection from sin, is a result of his exceptional piety.

Structure and Language

Rabbinic aggadot are literary creations and not historical records.[11] Therefore it is necessary to analyze this extended sugya and aggadic compilation by focusing on the ways in which the storytellers, editors and redactors drew from earlier material, employed rhetorical devices and imposed literary structures onto the narrative in order to create a cycle of stories that fit their pedagogical and literary goals.

The intensive literary crafting of the sugya can be detected in the storyteller's creation of numeric, thematic, and linguistic links which tie its various

---

[10] The Hamburg manuscript reads: "A man does not injure *his leg*." It seems likely that this is a later emendation trying to solve how a verse dealing with man's steps (legs) can have anything to do with a statement concerning fingers.

[11] Yonah Fraenkel, "She'elot Hermenutiyot Beheker Ha'aggadah," *Tarbiz* 47 (1978), 139–172; Jeffrey Rubenstein, *Talmudic Stories*, 8–10.

elements together. First and foremost, we can see that the redactor consistently employs tri-partite structures.[12] There are three stories of sages allegedly erring in the introduction, three episodes in R. Pinhas b. Yair's story (the river, the inn, and Rebbi's house), the three individuals permitted to cross the Ginai, and three statements issued by R. Hanina (3d, 4a, 4b).

Another technique through which these stories are unified is the frequent appearance of the concept of engaging in the performance of a mitzvah. The river splits for RPBY who is on his way to redeem captives. The second man to cross the river is carrying wheat to be used in the performance of the mitzvah of eating matzah. RPBY initially declines Rebbi's invitation because he is engaged in the performance of a mitzvah (3a), and the editor appends to the end of the sugya Rava's interpretation that the blood from a blow only acts as repentance if it comes while performing a mitzvah (section 4b).

There are also phrases that appear repeatedly and serve to connect the stories. The phrase שמע רבי ונפק appears twice in the passage (3a, 3b). The phrase מסתייעא מילתא is found both in the introductory stories and the encounter between R. Hanina and the sorceress (4a). The concept of will/desire is repeated multiple times (sections 1a, 2a, 3a רצון קונו, רצונך סעוד). Additionally, the Aramaic word for feet (כרעא) appears in the stammaitic explanation that R. Hanina refers to mules with white tipped legs (3d) and in the story which immediately follows of the woman taking the dirt from the feet of R. Haninah (4a).

Above all, the storyteller's hand is evident in his adoption and reworking of sources from which he drew to embellish and expand upon the RPBY cycle. One example is his reworking of an earlier source to create the midrash of R. Yehoshua b. Levi about the danger of white mules (section 3d). In its original context in Genesis Rabbah 26:7 this midrash had nothing to do with mules:

חולין ז ע"ב	בראשית רבה פרשה כו
אמר ר' יהושע בן לוי: למה נקרא שמן ימים? שאימתם מוטלת על הבריות.	הנפילים היו בארץ—שבעה שמות נקראו להם: נפילים, אימים, רפאים, גיבורים, זמזומים, ענקים, עוים. אימים: שאימתן נופלת על הכל.

---

[12] This structure is a common feature of rabbinic aggadot. See Yonah Fraenkel, *Darkhei Ha'aggadah Vehamidrash* (Masada: Yad Letalmud, 1991), 261–268.

Bavli Hullin 7b

R. Yehoshua ben Levi said: Why are they [mules] called yemim? Because the fear of them is upon people.

Genesis Rabbah 26:7

The Nephilim were on the land—
They are given seven names: Nephilim, Emim, Refaim, Giborim, Zamzumim, Anakim, and Evim.
Emim: That the fear (eimah)
of them is upon everyone.

Genesis 6:4 describes the origins of the *Nephilim*, legendary giants which inhabited the world. The midrash from Genesis Rabbah lists the various names used to refer to these giants throughout the Bible and provides a midrashic/etymological explanation for each. Deuteronomy 2:11 records that the Moabites referred to the indigenous giants as Emim. The midrash connects the name of these creatures with the similar Hebrew word for fear—אימה. The extreme similarity between the Hebrew words אימים and ימים allows the original midrash in Genesis Rabbah to be adopted in the Bavli to explain a different word altogether. The dangerous nature of mules is referred to in other rabbinic sources (Genesis Rabbah 82:24, Bavli Pesahim 54a) and is attributed to their being the product of a forbidden mixture unsanctioned by God. Those sources, however, do not connect the name of the mules to the danger they present. The storyteller may have chosen to rework this specific midrash in order to maintain linguistic consistency in the passage. When refashioning the midrash, he provided it with the same formulation—"why is it called"—found in R. Yohanan's statement about magic in section four, creating a linguistic link between the conclusion of the RPBY chain of events and the subsequent discussion of magic.

The storyteller's hand is most recognized, however, in his reworking of the stories of RPBY and his donkey. These characters are also the subject of several tales in the Yerushalmi. We shall now focus our lens on these stories and compare them with the Bavli.

"If They Were the Children of Men, We are Donkeys"

The Yerushalmi presents an extraordinarily rich parallel to our sugya which contains a significantly different and almost certainly earlier cycle of stories

310

concerning R. Pinhas ben Yair and his famous donkey. These stories are taught in connection with a mishnah which rules that food that is meant for animal consumption is exempt from *demai*. This collection of aggadot is linked directly to this mishnah through the second story in the cycle in which R. Pinhas b. Yair's donkey refuses to eat food from which *demai* was not taken. Additionally, the theme of tithing appears in the stories found in sections two, four and six.

We shall first briefly explain these stories as they appear in the Yerushalmi. Following that brief exposition we will turn our attention to our main interest—how we can analyze the Yerushalmi to better understand the Bavli.

ירושלמי דמאי א:ג, כא ע״ד	Yerushalmi Demai 1:3, 21d
(1a) ר' ירמיה שלח לר' זעירא חדא מסאנא דתאניה דלא מתקנא.	(1a) R. Yirmiyah sent a basket of untithed figs to R. Zera.
והוה ר' ירמיה סבר מימר: מה רבי זעירא מיכול דלא מתקנא?	R. Yirmiyah thought: Would R. Zera eat [something] which was not tithed?
והוה ר' זעירא סבר מימר: מה איפשר דר' ירמיה משלחה לי מילא דלא מתקנא?	And R. Zera thought: Is it possible that R. Yirmiyah would send me something that was not tithed?
מה בין דין לדין, איתכלת טבל.	Between the two of them, untithed produce was eaten.
(1b) למחר קם עימיה. אמר ליה: ההיא מסנתא דשלחת לי אתמל מתקנא הות?	(1b) The next day he met him. He [R. Zera] said to him [R. Yirmiyah]: Was the basket that you sent me yesterday tithed?
אמר ליה: אמרית מה רבי זעירא מיכול מילה דלא מיתקנה?	He [R. Yirmiyah] said to him: I said [to myself]: Would R. Zera eat something which was not tithed?

אמר ליה: אוף אנא אמרית
כן, הוה ר׳ ירמיה משלח
לי מילה דלא מתקנה?

He [R. Zera] said to him: I too said [to myself]: Would R. Yirmiyah send me something which was not tithed?

(1c) רבי אבא בר זבינא בשם
ר׳ זעירא אמר: אין הוון קדמאי
בני מלאכים אנן בני נש ואין
הוון בני נש אנן חמרין!

(1c) R. Aba b. Z'vina in the name of R. Zera said: If our predecessors were the children of angels, we are the children of men; and if they were the children of men, we are donkeys!

א״ר מנא: בההיא שעתא
אמרין אפילו לחמרתיה דרבי
פינחס בן יאיר לא אידמינן.

R. Mana said: At that moment they said: We are not even comparable to the donkey of R. Pinhas b. Yair.

(2a) חמרתיה דר׳ פינחס בן
יאיר גנבונה ליטסיי בלילייא.
עבדת טמורה גבון תלתא
יומין דלא טעמא כלום.

(2a) The donkey of R. Pinhas b. Yair was stolen by robbers at night. It stayed hidden [in a cave] for three days during which it did not eat anything.

בתר תלתה יומין איתמלכון
מחזרתה למרה.

After three days they decided to return her to her master.

אמרין: נישלחינה למרה דלא
לימות לגבן ותיסרי מערתא.

They said: We will send her to her master so that she will not die here and make the cave stink.

(2b) אפקונה אזלת וקמת
על תורעת דמרה.
שוריית מנהקה.

(2b) They brought her out and she went and stood at her master's gateway. She began to bray.

אמר לון: פותחון להדא
עליבתא דאית לה תלתא
יומין דלא טעימת כלום.

He [RPBY] said: Open [the gate] for that unfortunate one for it has been three days since she has eaten.

פתחון לה ועלת לה.

They opened the gate and she entered.

אמר לון: יהבון לה כלום תיכול.

He [RPBY] said: Give her something to eat.

יהבון קומה שערין ולא בעית מיכול.	They put barley in front of her and she did not want to eat.
(2c) אמרו ליה: רבי, לא בעית מיכול.	(2c) They said: Master, she does not want to eat.
אמר לון: מתקנן אינון?	He said to them: Is it [the barley] tithed?
אמרו ליה: אין.	They said: Yes.
אמר לון: ואריםיתון דמיין?	He said to them: Did you take out demai?
אמרו ליה: ולא כן אילפן ר', הלוקח לזרע לבהמה קמח לעורו שמן לנר שמן לסוך בו את הכלים פטור מן הדמאי.	They said to him: Did the master not teach us: One who purchases [grain to use] for seed or for an animal, or flour to use [in processing] hides, or oil for a lamp or oil for greasing utensils, is exempt from demai.
אמר לון: מה ניעביד להדא עליבתא דהיא מחמרה על גרמה סגין.	He said to them: What can we do for this un- fortunate one for she is very strict with herself?
ואריםון דמיין ואכלת.	They took out demai and she ate.
(3) תרין מסכינין אפקדון תרין סאין דשערין גבי רבי פינחס בן יאיר.	(3) Two poor people deposited two *seahs* of barley with R. Pinhas b. Yair.
זרעון וחצדון.	He sowed them and reaped them.
ואעלון בעיין מיסב שעריהון.	They came wanting to take their barley.
אמר לון: אייתון גמליא וחמריא וסבון שעריהון.	He said to them: Bring a camel and a donkey and they took their barley.

(4) רבי פינחס בן יאיר אזל לחד אתר. אתון לגביה, אמרו ליה: עכבריא אכל עיבורן.	(4) R. Pinhas b. Yair went to a certain place. They [the townspeople] came to him and said: Mice ate our grain.
גזר עליהון וצמתון, שרון מצפצפין.	He decreed upon them [the mice] and they gathered together. They began to squeak.
אמר לון: ידעין אתון מה אינון אמרין?	He said to them [the townspeople]: Do you know what they [the mice] are saying?
אמרו ליה: לא.	They said: No.
אמר לון: אמרן דלא מתקנא.	He said to them: They said that it is not tithed.
אמרו ליה: עורבן.	They [the townspeople] said to him: Pledge to us [that the mice will stop if we tithe].
וערבון ולא אנכון.	He pledged to them and they were not harmed [by the mice].[13]
(5) מרגלי מן דמלכא סרקיא נפלת ובלעת חד עכבר.	(5) The pearl of an Arab king fell and was swallowed by a mouse.
אתא לגבי רבי פינחס בן יאיר.	He [the king] came before R. Pinhas b. Yair.
אמר ליה: מן אנא חבר?	He [RPBY] said to him [the king]: What am I, a sorcerer?
אמר ליה: לשמך טבא אתית.	He [the king] said to him: I have come for your good name.
גזר עליהון וצמתון.	He [RPBY] decreed upon them and they gathered together.

[13] The word used for harm comes from the root נ.כ.י. , whose primary meaning is to deduct. See Michael Sokoloff, *Dictionary of Jewish Palestinian Aramaic* (Ramat Gan: Bar Ilan University Press, 2002), 350.

חמא חד מגבע ואתי, אמר: גבי ההן ניהו.	He saw one [mouse] walking like a hunch-back, he said: It is with that one.
וגזר עלוי ופלטה.	He decreed upon it and it spit it [the pearl] out.
(6) רבי פינחס בן יאיר אזל לחד אתר.	(6) RPBY went to a certain place.
אתון לגביה אמרון ליה: לית מבועין מספק לן.	They [the townspeople] came to him and said: Our spring does not supply us [with water].
אמר לון: דילמא לא אתון מתקנן.	He said to them: Perhaps you are not tithing.
אמרו ליה: עורבן.	They said to him: Pledge to us.
וערבון ואספק להון.	He pledged to them and it [the spring] supplied them [with water].
(7) רבי פינחס בן יאיר הוה אזיל לבית ווعד והוה גיניי גביר.	(7) RPBY was going to the academy and the Ginai [river] was swollen.
אמר ליה: גיניי גיניי מה את מנע לי מן בית ווعדה, ופלג קומוי ועבר.	He said: Ginai, Ginai why do you hold me back from the academy? And it split before him and he crossed.
אמרו ליה תלמידיו: יכלין אנן עברין?	His students said to him: Are we able to cross?
אמר לון: מאן דידע בנפשיה דלא אקיל לבר נש מן ישראל מן יומוי יעבור ולא מנכה.	He said to them: One who knows of himself that he never treated a Jew im-properly will cross and not be harmed.

(8a) רבי בעא מישרי שמיטתא. סלק רבי פינחס בן יאיר לגביה.	(8a) Rebbi wanted to annul the sabbatical year. RPBY went to him [to protest].
אמר ליה: מה עיבוריא עבידין?	He [Rebbi] said to him [RPBY]: How are the crops doing?
אמר ליה: עולשין יפות.	He [RPBY] said to him [Rebbi]: Endives are good.[14]
מה עיבוריא עבידין?	[Rebbi said to RPBY]: How are the crops doing?
אמר ליה: עולשין יפות.	He [RPBY] said to him [Rebbi]: Endives are good.
וידע רבי דלית הוא מסכמא עימיה.	And Rebbi knew that he did not agree with him.
(8b) אמר ליה: מישגח רבי מיכול עימן ציבחד פטל יומא דין.	(8b) He [Rebbi] said to him [RPBY]: Would the master mind eating with us a small amount of food[15] today?
אמר לון: אין.	He [RPBY] said to him [Rebbi]: Yes.
מי נחית חמא מולוותא דרבי קיימין.	When he went he saw Rebbi's mules standing.
אמר: כל אילין יהודאי זנין?	He said: Do the Jews support all of these?
איפשר דלא חמי סבר אפוי מן כדון.	It is possible he will never see my face again.

---

[14] By asking about the crops, Rebbi was hinting that it was a particularly difficult year for farmers and due to the crisis the Sabbatical year should be canceled, thereby allowing them to plant for the next year. RPBY disagrees with Rebbi and explains that endives, which grow without planting, are sufficient to sustain the people during the sabbatical year.

(8c) אזלון ואמרון לרבי.	(8c) They went and told Rebbi.
שלח רבי בעי מפייסתיה.	Rebbi sent [messengers] to appease him.
מטון ביה גבי קרתיה.	They caught up with him in his town.
אמר: בני קרתיה קורבין לי. ונחתו בני קרתא ואקפון עלוי.	He [RPBY] said: Townspeople come near me. And his townspeople descended and surrounded him.
אמר לון: רבי בעי מפייסתיה.	They [the messengers] said to them [the towns-people]: Rebbi wants to appease him [RPBY].
שבקוניה ואזול לון.	They left him [RPBY] and went away.
אמר: בני דידי קורבין לי. נחתת אישתא מן שמיא ואקפת עלוי.	He [RPBY] said: My children come near me. A fire descended from the heavens and surrounded him.
אזלון אמרון לרבי.	They [the messengers] went away and told Rebbi.
אמר: הואיל ולא זכנינן נישבע מיניה בעלמא הדין ניזכי נישבע מיניה בעלמא דאתי.	He [Rebbi] said: Since I did not merit to gain satisfaction from him in this world, may I merit to gain satisfaction from him in the world to come.
(9) רבי חגיי בשם רבי שמואל בר נחמן: מעשה בחסיד אחד שהיה חופר בורות שיחין ומערות לעוברים ולשבים.	(9) R. Haggai in the name of R. Shmuel b. Nahman: There was a righteous man who was digging cisterns, ditches and caves for travelers.
פעם אחת היתה בתו עוברת לינשא ושטפה נהר.	Once, his daughter was going to get married and she was washed away by the river.

---

15 The exact meaning of the word פטל is unclear. See Sokoloff, *Palestinian Aramaic*, 429.

והוון כל עמא עללין לגביה בעיין מנחמתיה ולא קביל עלוי מתנחמה.	Everyone came wishing to console him, but he refused to be consoled.
עאל רבי פינחס בן יאיר לגביה בעי מנחמתיה ולא קביל עלוי מתנחמה.	RPBY came to console him and he refused to be consoled.
אמר לון: דין הוא חסידכון.	He [RBPY] said to them [the townspeople]: This is your righteous man?
אמרו ליה: רבי כך וכך היה עושה כך וכך אירעו.	They said to him: Master, this is what happened, this is what befell him.
אמר: איפשר שהיה מכבד את בוראו במים והוא מקפחו במים?	He [RPBY] said: Is it possible that he was honoring his Maker with water and He deprived him with water?
מיד נפלה הברה בעיר: "באת בתו של אותו האיש".	Immediately an echo was heard in the city: "The daughter of that man has come."
אית דאמרי בסיכתא איתעריית, ואית דאמרי מלאך ירד בדמות רבי פינחס בן יאיר והצילה.	There are those who say she was caught on a branch and there are those who say an angel in the image of RPBY descended and saved her.

The Yerushalmi's cycle of stories is far less thematically coherent than its Babylonian counterpart. These stories are more loosely strewn together and there are fewer linguistic features and themes which serve to connect one to the other or to highlight some central purpose. Most importantly, there is no sequence imposed upon them.

The sugya begins with the story of R. Yirmiyah, who sent a basket of untithed figs to R. Zera. Both sages assumed that the other had tithed/ would tithe the produce, and as a result R. Zera mistakenly ate forbidden produce. In response to their error, R. Zera exclaims that their actions demonstrate that they are "donkeys" in comparison with their predecessors. Indeed, he continues, they are not even comparable to donkeys, at least not to the donkey of R. Pinhas b. Yair. R. Zera and R. Yirmiyah should have acted more cautiously. In a case of uncertainty both the sender and the receiver should have tithed, and thereby R. Zera would have been saved from transgression.

To highlight the transgressions of these sages and to explain R. Zera's reference, the Yerushalmi now brings the story of RPBY's donkey. The most important aspect of the story is that this donkey is exceedingly stringent with itself[16] and will not eat food from which *demai* had not been removed, even if animals are in actuality allowed to eat such food. Indeed, even when practically starving after three days of not eating, the donkey refuses to eat until not only tithes have been removed but *demai* as well. This contrasts sharply with the rabbis who should have acted more stringently and tithed their food.

Following the introduction there is a cycle of seven stories which paint a vivid picture of RPBY as a righteous miracle worker. He miraculously increases the crop yield (three and six), he is able to communicate with mice for the benefit of human beings (four and five), the river parts before him because he has never mistreated his fellow Jew (seven), he causes fire to descend from the heavens in order to protect himself (eight), and he may even revive the daughter of a ditch digger (nine). These episodes place RPBY in the group of tannaitic sages described elsewhere as the early pious men (חסידים ראשונים) or men of acts (אנשי מעשה), such as Honi the Circle-Drawer and Hanina Ben Dosa.[17] The parallel between R. Pinhas b. Yair and R. Hanina Ben Dosa is particularly salient because rabbinic sources attribute the same miracles to each.[18]

---

[16] Note the word play of the Hebrew for donkey חמור and stringent מחמיר.

[17] For more on the "men of acts" see Galit Hasan-Rokem, "Did Rabbinic Culture Conceive of the Category of Folk Narrative," *European Journal of Jewish Studies* 3, 1 (2009), 19–55.

[18] According to Bavli Yevamot 121b it is R. Hanina Ben Dosa who saves the ditch digger's daughter and Avot De Rabbi Natan 1:8 attributes the donkey story to Ben Dosa. See also Bavli Shabbat 112b: "Rebbi Zera said in the name of Rava Bar Zimuna: If the early ones were sons of angels, we are sons of men, and if the early ones were sons of men, we are like donkeys, and not like the donkey of R. Hanina b. Dosa and of R. Pinhas b. Yair, but like all other donkeys." There is, however, no tradition preserved in the Bavli about R. Hanina Ben Dosa's donkey. See Moscovitz, "The Holy One...," 139 n. 43.

RPBY's own emphasis on piety can be found in the baraita appended to the end of Mishnah Sotah:[19]

ר' פנחס בן יאיר אומר: זריזות
מביאה לידי נקיות, ונקיות מביאה
לידי טהרה, וטהרה מביאה לידי
פרישות, ופרישות מביאה לידי
קדושה, וקדושה מביאה לידי
ענוה, וענוה מביאה לידי יראת
חטא, ויראת חטא מביאה לידי
חסידות, וחסידות מביאה לידי רוח
הקדש, ורוח הקדש מביאה לידי
תחיית המתים, ותחיית המתים בא
על ידי אליהו זכור לטוב אמן.

Rabbi Pinhas ben Yair says: Heedfulness leads to cleanliness, cleanliness leads to purity, purity leads to separation, separation leads to holiness, holiness leads to modesty, modesty leads to fear of sin, fear of sin leads to piety, piety leads to the Holy Spirit, the Holy Spirit leads to the resurrection of the dead, and the resurrection of the dead comes from Elijah, blessed be his memory, Amen.

RPBY lists piety as an essential step which will bring about the resurrection of the dead. The various stories throughout rabbinic literature which describe the wonders of the "men of acts" often connect their ability to perform miracles with their extreme piety. The connection is explicit in story seven, in which RPBY explains that the Ginai river parts before him because he has never mistreated his fellow Jew. Furthermore, story nine seems to suggest that he himself even played a part in resurrecting the dead.

Miracles, Magic, or Divine Justice?

The cycle of stories in the Yerushalmi expresses a tension between the depiction of RPBY as a miracle worker and the possibility that miracles are not breaches in the natural order of the world because the world is predicated entirely upon divine justice. The Ginai river miraculously parts before RPBY (seven), but he understands the miracle as a sign of righteousness, claiming that anyone who has never mistreated his fellow Jew would experience the

---

[19] On the additions to the Mishnah at the conclusion of tractates see Yaakov Nahum Epstein, *Mavo Lenusah Hamishna* (Jerusalem: Hebrew University Magnes Press, 1949), 974–979.

same effect. While RPBY does seem to have magical powers in the story of the mice (four, five) and the spring (six), the original state is restored not due to his performance of wonders but because the people promise to tithe their produce properly. RPBY's ability is expressed only in discerning the righteous acts that need to be performed. Indeed, RPBY himself explicitly rejects the possibility that he is a miracle worker when he responds to the Arab king's request (five) saying, "What am I? A sorcerer?" His use of the term חבר, one of the magic acts explicitly prohibited in Deuteronomy 18:10, indicates that he finds the very implication that he in any way alters the natural order of the world to be insulting.

However, while RPBY might resist the label of miracle worker, the reader/listener, like the Arab king, is left with the impression that RPBY does indeed have miraculous powers. The mere fact that he is in possession of the poor men's barley produces the abundant yield (three). Furthermore, there is no moral justification for the mouse having eaten the pearl (five) and the king makes no promises about his behavior in the future. RPBY's decree upon the mouse is reminiscent of an act of exorcism. Similarly, he interrupts the natural order of the world when he calls out and brings fire down from the heavens (8c).

The dual ending of the story of the ditch digger's daughter that concludes this passage effectively expresses the ambivalence which exists in the cycle of stories. The first ending describes the incident as a simple misunderstanding. God would not possibly punish the righteous ditch digger in such a cruel manner. Indeed, the daughter did not drown; she was caught on a tree branch and no one found her until later. Salvation came through natural and not supernatural means. The second ending describes the daughter as having been saved by a miraculous event involving an angel in the image of RPBY. Rather than commit to one version of the story the Yerushalmi provides both, leaving the reader with an unresolved picture of RPBY. Does he (or an angel in his image) actually perform a miracle, or was there never a need for a miracle in the first place?

As we compare the Yerushalmi's version of the story to the Bavli's below it will become evident that the Bavli takes steps to further temper RPBY's portrayal as miracle maker, and yet like the Yerushalmi, the Bavli still acknowledges the efficacy of magic in the world.

Comparing the Bavli to the Yerushalmi

We will now turn our attention to the methodological question of how one can better understand the Bavli, its editing, the themes it wishes to highlight and its pedagogical message by comparing the Bavli's version of the stories to those that likely served as its raw material—those found in the Yerushalmi. As Shamma Friedman explains, "Much of the narrative Aggadah in the Babylonian Talmud is of Palestinian origin. The literary sources used by the Babylonian Talmud have generally not survived, but many parallels exist in the Palestinian Talmud and Midrashim."[20] By comparing and contrasting the earlier versions of the stories found in the Eretz Yisraeli literature with the Bavli we are able to better appreciate the composition of the Babylonian storytellers.

The analysis will focus on two main aspects of the creation of the Babylonian R. Pinhas b. Yair story: (1) literary—how the Babylonian storyteller reworked the eight distinct stories found in the Yerushalmi into a single narrative, (2) thematic—how the storyteller shaped and supplemented the Yerushalmi in order to transform R. Pinhas b. Yair into a more normative rabbi. As we shall see, the Babylonian storyteller emphasizes dedication to Torah study, scholarly aptitude, and performance of commandments rather than the wonders and moral and ethical virtues which are highlighted in the Yerushalmi.[21] Additionally, the Bavli tempers the efficacy of magic and wonder working which plays a more overt role in the earlier version of the stories.[22]

The Fallibility of Sages and Donkeys

We will begin by analyzing R. Zera's own statement, which both Talmuds understand as a reference to R. Pinhas ben Yair's donkey.

---

[20] Shamma Friedman, "Literary Development and Historicity in the Aggadic Narrative," *Community and Culture: Essays in Jewish History in Honor of the Ninetieth Anniversary of the Founding of Gratz College*, ed. N.M. Waldman (Philadelphia: Gratz College, 1987), 67–80.

[21] See Jeffrey Rubenstein, *The Culture of the Babylonian Talmud*, 39–53.

[22] See Joshua Levinson, "Enchanting Rabbis: Contest Narratives Between Rabbis and Magicians in Late Antiquity," *Jewish Quarterly Review*, 100,1 (2010), 54–94.

Bavli

Now, if the Holy One, blessed be He, does not allow the beast of the righteous to stumble, all the more so the righteous themselves... What is the beast of the righteous?

Yerushalmi

R. Aba b. Z'vina in the name of R. Zera said: If our predecessors were the children of angels, we are the children of men; and if they were the children of men, we are donkeys! R. Mana said: At that moment they said: We are not even comparable to the donkey of R. Pinhas b. Yair.

The introductions to the story of R. Pinhas b. Yair in the Yerushalmi and the Bavli are exact opposites. In the Yerushalmi, R. Zera admits that he was negligent in his actions and thereby came to consume forbidden produce. He makes the self-deprecating declaration that such behavior likens him to an animal when compared to the previous generations of sages. In fact, he cannot even compare himself to the donkey of RPBY, who was appropriately stringent upon itself. Sages are more fallible than donkeys! In contrast, the Bavli begins with a collection of stories which demonstrate the infallibility of the sages and God's intervention in their lives. In each of the stories, even when it seemed as if a sage transgressed a prohibition by consuming forbidden food, further investigation reveals that he did not actually transgress. Simply put, God does not allow the righteous to make mistakes.[23]

We should note that in both Talmuds the donkey refrains from eating untithed food, but in the Yerushalmi this is simply due to the donkey's stringency with itself. The donkey is righteous, more righteous than the rabbis. In the Bavli, the donkey loses its independent will and is instead protected from sin by virtue of its belonging to a righteous sage. The sages' infallibility is due to their righteousness, and such righteousness rubs off even on their beasts. In short, in both Talmuds the donkey is the yardstick for the sage, but only in the Yerushalmi does the sage come out lacking.

---

[23] It is significant that the Bavli describes the sages as righteous without providing evidence of their righteous deeds. The reader is left to assume that the sages are worthy of the title of "righteous" due to the very thing which classifies them as sages in the first place—their dedication to Torah study.

As we proceed in our analysis of the Bavli, we shall see that this shift in the stories and in the saying is emblematic of how the Bavli's storyteller shifted the themes of the earlier stories. Already in these early stories the Bavli establishes its central theological theme—God controls the world and protects the righteous and their animals from sin. In contrast, the Yerushalmi does not present an overarching theme which persists throughout the entire passage. Rather, the stories appear as a group in the Yerushalmi because they all involve RPBY. There are minor themes, described above, which are found in two or more of the stories, but the Yerushalmi has not undergone anywhere near the same amount of editing as the Bavli.

Crossing the Ginai

Bavli – Section One	**Yerushalmi – Section Seven**
RPBY was going to redeem captives. He encountered the Ginai river. He said to it: Ginai, split your waters so that I may cross you. It said to him: You are going to do the will of your Maker and I am going to do the will of my Maker, it is possible that you will succeed and possible that you will not succeed, but I will definitely succeed. He said to it: If you do not split, I decree that water will never pass through you again.	RPBY was going to the academy and the Ginai [river] was swollen. He said: Ginai, Ginai why do you hold me back from the academy.
It split for him. There was a man who was carrying wheat for Passover, He [RPBY] said to it: Split for this one too because he is engaged in a mitzvah. It split for him. There was an Arab accompanying him [RPBY], he said to it: Split for this one too, so [people] will not say: this is what you do to escorts? It split for him.	And it split before him and he crossed.

Rav Yosef said: How much greater is this man than Moses and the 600,000 [Israelites], for there it [split] once and here three times. Perhaps here too it was only once! Rather [say] like Moses and the 600,000.

His students said to him: Are we able to cross? He said to them: One who knows of himself that he never treated a Jew improperly will cross and not be harmed.

The Yerushalmi's version portrays R. Pinhas b. Yair on his way to the study house when the Ginai river impedes the path to his destination. He asks the river, "Why do you hold me back from the academy?" whereupon the river splits and he crosses. He explains to his students who are accompanying him that only one who is certain that he has not treated another Jew improperly will not be harmed when crossing. All of the students are on their way to study Torah, but only RPBY is worthy of having the river split, on account of his extreme piety. It is the way that R. Pinhas b. Yair treats other human beings, and not his dedication to Torah study, that causes the Ginai to part before him.

In contrast, in the Bavli RPBY is on his way to redeem captives. The change in mission aids the Bavli storyteller in multiple ways. First, it allows the storyteller to further develop the character of RPBY. The Yerushalmi describes him as not having mistreated his fellow Jew; the Bavli provides a concrete example of him performing a selfless act to save the life of another. The change also creates a sense of urgency to the story not found in the Yerushalmi and raises the stakes of RPBY's mission. It serves as a thread which unites the different parts of the story because in each encounter RPBY relates that he is performing an urgent mitzvah and must not be delayed. Furthermore, in the Bavli the raw material of the RPBY story cycle has been formed into one continuous episode. Thus, instead of immediately beginning with the story of the unerring donkey, the Bavli uses R. Pinhas b. Yair's encounter with the Ginai river, found towards the end of the Yerushalmi collection, as a back story to a larger episode. Assuming that he had the Yerushalmi material before him, the Babylonian storyteller chose from among the eight distinct stories to create a complete narrative with a beginning, middle, and end.

The actual encounter with the river also differs between the two Talmuds. In the Yerushalmi, RPBY asks the river why it stands in his way and the river responds by splitting. The Babylonian storyteller elaborates upon this simple story by creating a tense exchange between the two. As RPBY approaches, he demands that the river split. The river responds that it is simply fulfilling the will of its Maker and is certain to succeed, while RPBY is on a mission that is not certain to succeed. The dialogue added into the Bavli highlights the overall theme of the passage—everything in the world performs God's will. The river expresses the doubts that a reader might share; it in a sense stands in for the reader of the story. But the river's voice is opposed by the viewpoint advocated by the storyteller himself. While the river suggests that RPBY may fail, in reality there is no doubt that he will succeed because God always acts to protect the righteous.

The Bavli also embellishes the miracle by having the river split three times for three different people. In the Yerushalmi only RPBY is allowed to cross, for only he is sufficiently pious. In contrast, the Bavli emphasizes that the river splits for anyone, even for one of lesser stature, who is on his way to perform a mitzvah; it splits for RPBY, it splits for the man who performs the mitzvah of carrying wheat for Pesah, and it even splits for a non-Jew who aids in the performance of a mitzvah.

By recounting the splitting of the Ginai, the Babylonian storyteller is immediately confronted with the challenge of explaining the magical element behind RPBY's wonder working. He surreptitiously couches his defense of RPBY in what seems to be R. Yosef's statement of astonishment. The image of Moses and the splitting of the Sea of Reeds conjures up an event which might have been interpreted as within the realm of the magical but is clearly understood in the Torah and in tradition as divine intervention into the natural world. Moses is a prophet who serves as a conduit for performing God's miracles; he is never explicitly described as a magician.[24] Rav Yosef's comparison of RPBY to Moses serves to temper the desire to ascribe the title of magician to RPBY. He, like Moses, simply benefits from God's intervention in the world.

---

[24] On Moses as a magician see Levinson, "Enchanting Rabbis," 61–64.

R. Pinhas b. Yair's Righteous Donkey

Bavli – Section Two

Yerushalmi – Section Two

The donkey of R. Pinhas b. Yair was stolen by robbers at night. It stayed hidden [in a cave] for three days during which it did not eat anything. After three days they decided to return her to her master. They said: We will send her to her master so that she won't die here and make the cave stink.

They brought her out and she went and stood at her master's gateway. She began to bray. He [RPBY] said: Open [the gate] for that unfortunate one for it has been three days since she has eaten. They opened the gate and she entered.

He went to a certain inn, they placed barley before his donkey and she did not eat, they beat it [the barley] and she did not eat, they sifted it and she did not eat. He said to them: Perhaps it is not tithed? They tithed it and the donkey ate. He said: This poor thing is going to do the will of its Maker and you are feeding her untithed produce? But does it need to be tithed?

He [RPBY] said: Give her something to eat. They put barley in front of her and she did not want to eat. They said: Master, she does not want to eat. He said to them: Is it [the barley] tithed? They said: Yes. He said to them: Did you take out demai?

But did it not teach: One who purchases [grain to use] for seed or for an animal, or flour to use [in processing] hides, or oil for a lamp or oil for greasing utensils, is exempt from *demai*. There it has been stated about this: R. Yohanan said they only taught this if he bought the grain from the outset for animals; but if he bought it from the outset for human consumption and later decided to give it to animals, it must be tithed. And so it has been taught in a baraita: One who buys fruit in the market for eating and decides later to use it for animals, behold he may not give it either to his own animal or to his neighbor's animal without first tithing it.

They said to him: Did the master not teach us: One who purchases [grain to use] for seed or for an animal, or flour to use [in processing] hides, or oil for a lamp or oil for greasing utensils, is exempt from *demai*. He said to them: What can we do for this unfortunate one for she is very strict with herself? They took out *demai* and she ate.

As was the case with the previous story, these two stories are clearly parallels, but again the Bavli has completely modified the circumstances. In the Bavli, in order to continue the chain of events from the previous section, the incident takes place at an inn while RPBY is on his way to redeem the captives. As a consequence, the element of the donkey having been stolen has been removed. The innkeeper gives the donkey food but she refuses to eat. RPBY realizes the donkey will not eat because the food offered to her has not been properly tithed. He rebukes the innkeeper exclaiming: "This poor thing is going to do the will of her Maker and you are feeding her untithed produce?" His language mirrors the same claim that the Ginai river brought against RPBY. This strengthens the link between the two stories as it becomes clear that the donkey is carrying RPBY on his mission to redeem the captives. It also emphasizes again the connection between divine intervention in the natural order and the performance of the "will of the Maker." The donkey, which is aiding in the performance of a mitzvah, does not deserve to be fed untithed produce.

The major change in the Bavli sugya comes in the halakhic discussion which appears at the end of the incident. Both Talmuds present the story of RPBY's donkey as the paradigmatic example of God protecting the righteous and his beasts from error. But Mishnah Demai, which is cited in both Talmuds, does not actually require produce given to animals to have *demai* taken from it. The Yerushalmi explains that the donkey's refusal to eat *demai* was an act of stringency—meritorious but not halakhically necessary. The Yerushalmi's resolution does not fit the Bavli's pedagogical aims because the donkey's refusal must serve as an example of the protection of the righteous. All of the stories in the Bavli which lead up to the donkey episode declare that if God protects the animal of the righteous from sin, He certainly protects the righteous themselves. If the donkey's refusal is unnecessarily stringent, what sin has God protected it from? Were the Bavli to accept the Yerushalmi's description of the episode, the Bavli would lose the basis for the argument that God protects the righteous. Therefore, the storyteller provides a different resolution to the seeming contradiction between the donkey's behavior and the mishnah in Demai. To transform the donkey's refusal into an act of God's protection, the storyteller brings in the halakhic statement of R. Yohanan. We learn that the food had originally been intended for human consumption; this triggered the requirement to separate *demai* from it. The change creates a situation in which the donkey acts in accordance with actual rabbinic law. God controls the donkey in order to prevent it, and by extension RPBY, from inadvertently sinning. Thus, according to the Bavli, the story is not an anecdote about an unnecessarily stringent donkey, but rather about God's indispensable protection of the righteous.

Dining with Rebbi and the Danger of the Mules

Bavli – Section Three	Yerushalmi – Section Eight
	Rebbi wanted to annul the sabbatical year. RPBY went to him [to protest]. He [Rebbi] said to him [RPBY]: How are the crops doing? He [RPBY] said to him [Rebbi]: Endives are good. [Rebbi said to RPBY]: How are the crops doing? He [RPBY] said to him [Rebbi]: Endives are good. And Rebbi knew that he did not agree with him.

When Rebbi heard [of the arrival of RPBY], he went out to meet him. He said to him: Will you please dine with me? [RPBY] responded: Yes. Rebbi's face brightened with joy. [RPBY] said to him: Do you imagine that I am forbidden by vow from deriving any benefit from an Israelite. The people of Israel are holy. Yet there are some who desire [to give to others] but have not the means; while others have the means but have not the desire, and it is written:

Do not eat of a stingy man's food. Do not crave for his dainties. He is like one who keeps accounts. Eat and drink he says to you, but he does not really mean it (Proverbs 23:6–7). But you have the desire and also the means. However, right now I am in a hurry for I am occupied with a mitzvah. When I return I will come and visit you.

He [Rebbi] said to him [RPBY]: Would the master mind eating with us a small amount of food today? He [RPBY] said to him [Rebbi]: Yes.

When he arrived, he happened to enter by a gate near which were some white mules. At this he exclaimed: The angel of death is in this house and I shall dine with him? When Rebbi heard of this, he went out to meet him. He [Rebbi] said: I will sell the mules. R. Pinhas replied: *You shall not put a stumbling block before the blind* (Leviticus 19:14). I will abandon them. You would increase their danger. I will hamstring them. You would be causing suffering to animals.

When he went he saw Rebbi's mules standing. He said: Do the Jews support all of these? It is possible he will never see my face again. They went and told Rebbi. Rebbi sent [messengers] to appease him. They caught up with him in his town. He [RPBY] said: Townspeople come near me. And his townspeople descended and surrounded him. He [the messengers] said to them [the townspeople]: Rebbi wants to appease him [RPBY].

I will kill them.

There is the prohibition against needless destruction.

Rebbi was contending with him persistently. A mountain rose up between them.

Rebbi wept and said: If this is [the power of the righteous] in their lifetime, how great must it be after their death!

They left him [RPBY] and went away. He [RPBY] said: My children come near me. A fire descended from the heavens and surrounded him. They [the messengers] went away and told Rebbi.

He [Rebbi] said: Since I did not merit to gain satisfaction from him in this world, may I merit to gain satisfaction from him in the world to come.

Both the Bavli and Yerushalmi include an account of Rebbi and RPBY planning to dine together and RPBY refusing to attend because he sees that Rebbi owns mules. As in the previous stories, the Bavli changes many elements of the Yerushalmi passage in order to fit the story to its larger context and themes. In the Yerushalmi the background to Rebbi's meal invitation is his abrogation of the sabbatical year. Rebbi wishes to cancel *shemittah* following the destruction of the Temple.[25] RPBY approaches him, presumably to express his belief that these laws remain in force after the destruction. The two have a cryptic exchange through which Rebbi realizes that RPBY does not support his initiative. RPBY's suggestion that people can survive on endives, which do not require cultivation, indicates to Rebbi that RPBY believes that the *shemittah* laws continue to retain their force after the destruction. The exchange in the Yerushalmi is followed by Rebbi's invitation to RPBY to dine with him.

The Bavli removes this context entirely for two important reasons. First, the storyteller wishes to connect this incident to the chain of events which preceded it. Therefore, in the Bavli's setting, Rebbi hears that RPBY is in town after he has spent the night in the inn and invites him for a meal. Second, the storyteller wants to shift the focus from Rebbi's attempt to annul *shemittah* to the unique character of RPBY. In the Yerushalmi, the tension surrounding

---

[25] Numerous rabbinic sources indicate that Rebbi, following the destruction, was lenient with various commandments tied to the land. In an effort to ease the economic burden he sought to abrogate many of the agricultural laws. See Albert Baumgarten, "Rabbi Judah I and His Opponents," *Journal for the Study of Judaism* 12,2 (1981), 161–170.

the invitation is a result of the halakhic dispute between the sages. In the Bavli such a halakhic dispute might distract from the main theme and would not serve any larger purpose. In lieu of the halakhic debate concerning *shemittah*, the storyteller builds social tension between the sages surrounding the shared meal. This allows him to flesh out the characters in the episode and establish the power relationship between them.

The Yerushalmi depicts Rebbi in the position of authority. He makes his halakhic decision without consulting RPBY but still maintains deference to him by calling him master, as is required within the social structure of the rabbinic world. RPBY avoids direct confrontation with him both when he cryptically responds to Rebbi's desire to annul *shemittah* and when he retreats upon discovering the white mules. Even when Rebbi sends messengers to approach him, he surrounds himself with a wall of people or fire to avoid the confrontation. RPBY is sufficiently authoritative to disagree with Rebbi, but not explicitly and not to his face, suggesting that Rebbi is the more dominant figure.

In contrast, the Bavli portrays Rebbi as the subordinate character who is overly excited about the prospect of becoming close to RPBY. RPBY's acceptance of the invitation is an extraordinary event and Rebbi is overwhelmed with joy because he believes he is the only person whose invitation RPBY has ever accepted. Immediately, RPBY explains, based on the verse from Proverbs, why he has never before accepted an invitation. It is not as if he has taken an oath not to derive benefit from any Jew, an oath which would have been frowned upon by the rabbis. Rather, RPBY was able to accept Rebbi's invitation because Rebbi represents the unique blend of someone who can afford to invite others and someone who has the true desire to do so. The Babylonian storyteller strengthens the link between this incident and the previous events by having RPBY relate that he cannot immediately accept the invitation because he is in the process of performing a mitzvah, the redemption of captives.

Upon his return from redeeming captives, RPBY rebukes Rebbi for owning white mules: "The angel of death is in this house and I shall dine with him?" RPBY's attack on Rebbi heightens the contrast between the two main characters. RPBY uses his donkey to redeem a captive and save a life, while Rebbi's white mules—"angels of death"—only endanger lives. RPBY uses one of God's creations in order to perform God's will and fulfill His commandments. Rebbi owns the byproduct of an unsanctioned mixture which only serves to destroy the world; white mules are neither righteous animals nor the animals of the righteous.

In the Yerushalmi, the story concludes with Rebbi's failed attempt to appease RPBY. After the townspeople allow Rebbi's men to approach RPBY, the latter calls out "my children," causing fire to descend from the heavens, sealing off any possible approach. The Yerushalmi portrays RPBY as having supernatural powers; he is the father of fire. RPBY uses these powers to prevent Rebbi from coming near. Rebbi consoles himself with the thought that he may have an opportunity to have his "fill of him" in the world to come. The events which transpired prove to Rebbi that he is not on the same level as RPBY, a man who has the ability to perform wonders. With that realization, Rebbi offers a personal prayer that while they are not equals in this world, perhaps he will be closer to RPBY's status in the world to come.

In contrast, the Bavli creates a dramatic face to face confrontation between the two sages. RPBY, instead of retreating behind a wall, directly confronts Rebbi. RPBY bests Rebbi in a dialectical spar in which he rejects each of Rebbi's suggestions to rid himself of the mules. RPBY draws upon an abstract halakhic concept to reject every proposal Rebbi has to offer. Unlike the Yerushalmi, where Rebbi cannot match RPBY's wonderworking, in the Bavli, Rebbi cannot stand up to RPBY's halakhic prowess. RPBY's supernatural abilities are replaced with his extraordinary grasp of rabbinic concepts. The debate ends with a mountain rising up between them. The change from fire descending from heaven to a mountain arising from the earth may temper some of the overt magic found in the Yerushalmi. RPBY does not call out to heaven bringing down the fire to protect him; rather the mountain simply rises up, as if of its own accord. Instead of RPBY magically preventing himself from dining with Rebbi, God has intervened on his behalf.

Rebbi's response to the situation in the Bavli is the opposite of that found in the Yerushalmi. Whereas in the Yerushalmi he is hopeful that at least in the world to come he will be able to benefit from RPBY, in the Bavli he finds no comfort. He reasons that if he was unable to come close to RPBY in this world by sharing a meal with him, he certainly will not be able to do so in the world to come. The Bavli intensifies the emotions in the exchange between the two main characters. The stakes are much higher because RPBY has never before accepted an invitation, and Rebbi's extreme excitement and honor are justified because sharing the meal would indicate that he is the only person who is on par with RPBY. The storyteller appropriately modifies Rebbi's reaction to correspond to the uniqueness of the circumstances. Rebbi feels like his one and only chance to be on par with RPBY has been lost forever.

Conclusion

The context of the Bavli's RPBY narrative plays an important role in shaping the portrayal of RPBY. As we have demonstrated above, the Babylonian storyteller emends the Yerushalmi's stories of wonder in an effort to depict RPBY as a normative, albeit exceedingly pious, rabbi. The placement of the RPBY narrative between the stories of God's protection of the righteous (stories 1–3) and the discussion questioning the efficacy of magic (section four) serves to support this portrayal. The miracles which occur are not a result of RPBY's wonder working abilities; rather, they are additional demonstrations of God's protection of the righteous. Just as God protects the rabbis in the first three stories which open the passage, He protects RPBY from the pitfalls which he encounters.

The storyteller, however, makes a significant choice to continue the sugya after the narrative section is complete. Rather than simply conclude with the epitaph (section five) he includes the material in section four, whose main theme is a broader discourse about the role of magic in a world controlled by a single divine power. The storyteller imports part of an extensive discussion of magic and magicians found in Masekhet Sanhedrin in order to explore the same tension between miracles, magic, and divine justice that is present in the Yerushalmi. The amoraic statements serve to highlight the differing approaches to the complex theology which rests at the foundation of the sugya. R. Hanina's midrash on Deuteronomy 4:35 opens with a claim that magic is completely ineffectual because God is in control of the entire universe. He substantiates his belief by standing up to the woman who attempts to cast a spell on him, certain it will not succeed. R. Yohanan disagrees with R. Hanina's position, arguing that he has indeed seen magic performed effectively. The stam resolves the contradiction by explaining that God protects those "with merits." The stam uses R. Yohanan's opposing belief to subjugate R. Hanina to the theme that God protects the righteous. It is not that magic is subject to God, but rather that divine protection of the righteous trumps any efficacy that magic may have.

The lengthy sugya concludes similar to the way it began. The sugya opened with the declaration that God does not allow the righteous to make a mistake which would cause them to sin. It concludes with R. Hanina's statement, "No man bruises his finger here on earth unless it was so decreed against him in heaven"—God is directly involved in the lives of every individual, even in their mistakes. R. Hanina's statement expands on the theme of the sugya by suggesting that God controls the steps and missteps of both the righteous and ordinary individuals. The editor, however, adds a subtle caveat to R. Hanina in order to limit his expansion on the theme. By adding the statement of R. Eliezer together with Rava's limitation, "only if it happened to one who was on his way to perform a mitzvah," the pendulum swings back in the other direction. Divine intervention into the life of the individual and the reward which accompanies it is limited to those who are righteous, or at the very least are engaged in righteousness.

The thematic, literary, and linguistic choices of the Babylonian storyteller generate a portrait of RBPY dramatically different from his more explicit portrayal as a miracle worker in the Yerushalmi. The Yerushalmi recounts numerous episodes extolling him for the various wonders he performs in order to help others. Although the possibility exists that the seemingly miraculous events are actually the result of divine justice, there is a strong voice in the Yerushalmi which indentifies RPBY as a miracle worker. In contrast, the Bavil's creation of a continuous narrative and its tempering of the role of magic in RPBY's wonders paints a different picture. RPBY is celebrated for his halakhic prowess, his tenacious commitment to performing the commandment of redeeming captives, and his strict refusal to derive benefit from others. He fits all of the definitions of a righteous sage, and as such, God protects him, just as God always protects the righteous and performs miracles on their behalf.

Jewish Magic in Rabbinic Literature

Avigail Manekin-Bamberger

The story of R. Pinhas ben Yair concludes with the tale of Rabbi Hanina's encounter with a sorceress, which offers us an occasion to consider both the rabbinic relationship with magic as well as the scholarly assessment of this relationship. The Talmud's discussion of this incident clearly articulates the tension in rabbinic culture between divine providence and the magical forces that might undermine it. Furthermore, the rabbis were of course aware that magic is explicitly prohibited by the Torah (Deuteronomy 18:10–12). Still, rabbinic literature is filled with references to spells, amulets, curses, the evil eye, contest narratives between rabbis and magicians, encounters with demons and other magical tales. What, then, are we to make of all this material?

Early academic research on the subject was often clouded by a negative attitude towards the Jewish practice of magic. To rational academic Jewish scholars, it was simply inconceivable that the great rabbinic thinkers would waste their time dabbling in what they considered nonsense and charlatanism. As a result, academic scholars often approached these texts apologetically in an attempt to "purify" the rabbis of their belief in popular magic.[26] For example, Ephraim E. Urbach argued that the rabbis, especially those of Babylonia, could not ignore the practice of sorcery because "broad masses of the people believed in and made use of these practices." Therefore, they "sought to find a compromise" by including only a modified form of magical material in rabbinic literature although they themselves did not believe in these practices.[27]

---

[26] For a comprehensive survey of academic research on Jewish magic see Yuval Harari, *Hakishuf Hayehudi Hakadum* (Jerusalem: Mossad Bialik, 2010), 67–90.

[27] Ephraim E. Urbach, *The Sages: Their Concepts and Beliefs*, translated from the Hebrew by Israel Abrahams (Jerusalem: Hebrew University Magnes Press, 1975), 101.

Saul Lieberman was more willing to acknowledge the active participation of the rabbis in the world of magic. He wrote: "The rabbis did their utmost to combat the superstitions which smacked of idolatry, but they had to accept those charms which were sanctioned by the 'scientist' of that time."[28] Lieberman legitimized the "scientific" medicinal magic practiced by the rabbis themselves yet retained the scholarly bias of his time that magic was "external" to the rabbis and that they battled against its foreign influence.

In the last two decades scholars of ancient Jewish magic, most notably Gideon Bohak and Yuval Harari, have rejected these apologetic tendencies and have recognized the central role that magic played in the rabbinic world.[29] Furthermore, they have worked to remove the subjectivity from the study of magic by clearly defining the parameters of the discipline. The discovery of Jewish incantation bowls from Babylonia in modern day Iraq, amulets in the land of Israel, and magical recipe books which, although found in the Cairo Genizah, often reflect earlier traditions, have contributed significantly to our understanding of the ancient Jewish practice of magic. Modern scholars have analyzed these material sources in light of discussions of magic in literary sources, including rabbinic literature. Likewise, archaeological sources have deepened our understanding of the Talmud and provided us with a better appreciation of the world of the sages in general.

In this chapter we will consider two examples from Aramaic incantation bowls that demonstrate how artifacts enhance our understanding of certain Talmudic passages relating to magic. The texts written upon these bowls are of considerable importance to rabbinic studies, as they constitute the only Jewish epigraphic material that exists from

---

[28] Saul Lieberman, *Greek in Jewish Palestine: Studies in the Life and Manners of Jewish Palestine in II–IV Centuries C. E.* (New York: Jewish Theological Seminary of America, 1942), 110.

[29] Yuval Harari above n. 26; Gideon Bohak, *Ancient Jewish Magic: A History* (Cambridge: Cambridge University Press, 2008).

the Talmudic era in Babylonia. The incantation bowls were usually designated to protect one's household by expelling demons. In order to do so, they employed various magical practices including writing divine names, curses and incantation formulae. Together with these magical formulae, the incantation bowls also contain legal formulae primarily used in oaths, vows, pronouncements of excommunication and divorce documents.

Cursing Demons

In this first example we will see how an incantation bowl can be used to decipher a puzzling passage in the Bavli and confirm the authenticity of the magical formulae quoted there. Bavli Shabbat 67a lists incantations which can be recited to counteract various illnesses and dangerous situations. The following formula is said to protect against demons:

לשידא לימא הכי: הוית	For a demon say as follows: you were cursed
ליט דפקוק דפקוק הוית	dafkuk dafkuk[29] you were cursed, broken,
ליט תביר ומשומת בר	and banned Bar Tit, Bar Tame in the name
טיט בר טמא בשם מרגיז	of Margiz Murifat and Istatmatey.[31]
מוריפת ואיסטטמתיה[31]	

In his commentary on the passage, Rashi infers from the context that *Bar Tit* is the name of the demon and that the spell calls for the demon to be "cursed, broken, and banned—ליט תביר ומשומת." The historical accuracy of Rashi's interpretation was recently corroborated by Christa

---

[30] The meaning of the repeated word דפקוק is uncertain. The strange sounding words of unknown origins which are repeated in magical spells are referred to by scholars as *voces magicae*.

[31] The citation is from the Oxford manuscript. The Vilna printed edition is replete with scribal errors.

Muller-Kessler, who discovered a similar formula on an incantation bowl from the Talmudic period:[32]

..לא תיתחזון ל[הלין] בר	You (the demons) shall not show your-
שרקוי ולנונדוך בת כפנאי	selves to Halyn son of Sharkoy and
{כפנאי} ולזדוי ברה לא	Nunduch daughter of Kafnay and
חברא ביממא ולא צותא	Zadoy their son, not a companion by
בליליה ליט ומשמת בר	night nor a companion by day, cursed
טיט ובר טמא אמן אמן	and banned is Bar Tit Bar Tame amen
סלה הללויה שריר	amen selah halleluyah sharir.)

The bowl uses precisely the same Aramaic phrasing ליט ומשמת to curse and ban the same demon, בר טיט ובר טמא for the clients listed on the bowl.

The Talmudic incantation concludes with the phrase בשם מרגיז מוריפת ואיסטתמתיה. The word בשם "in the name" followed by a list of various names, most often gods or angels, is found in almost every amulet and incantation bowl of the period. The amulet or spell derives its efficacy from the power of the god or angel invoked at its end. One of the names mentioned in the Talmudic passage is "Margiz" which, while not found on any incantation bowl, could mean lord of decrees, as it consists of the words מרי and גז—מרי for lord, and גז an abbreviation of גזר, decree.[33]

The Need for Precision

The next example highlights the connection between rabbinic law and magical formulae. This inscription, published and translated by Dan

---

[32] C. Muller-Kessler, *Die Zauberschalentexte in der Hilprecht-Sammlung, Jena, und weitere Nippur-Texte anderer Sammlungen* (Wiesbaden: Harrassowitz, 2005), 45.

[33] This abbreviation of the word גזר is found on another bowl. See Shaul Shaked, James Nathan Ford & Siam Bhayro, *Aramaic Bowl Spells: Jewish Babylonian Aramaic Bowls* (Leiden: Brill, 2013), 153.

Levene, was found on a bowl adorned with the image of a shackled demoness.[34] The bowl was created to offer protection for a specific family and its formula is modeled on a Jewish bill of divorce:

כתבית (7) גיטא דיכרי	I wrote a get (to) the male and female
וניקבתא משמתא מלויתא	ones, the accompanying demon who
דלויא ושריא ודירא בביתיה	accompanies and dwells and lives in the
דארדוי בר (8) כירכשידוך	house of Ardoi son of Khwarkhshidukh;
וכל שום דאית לה דמית	**and whatever name that it has** that
(חזיא) להון בחילמא	appears to them in a dream of the
דליליה ובשינתא דיממא	night and in the sleep of the day. And
ואנה כתיבנא עליכון גיטא	I have written you a divorce writ, a
(9) גיט פיטורין ושבוקין.	get of releasing and sending away.

Strikingly, the exorcising amulet is called a *get* and its language is patterned after the Jewish divorce document. Moreover, the particular phrase "and whatever name that it has"—וכל שום דאית ליה, is derived from Mishnah Gittin 4:2:

> In the beginning the husband would change his name, or his wife's name, or the name of his town or of his wife's town. Rabban Gamliel the Elder established that he should write [in the *get*] "The man so-and-so and whatever name that he has"; "the woman so-and-so and ever name that she has" because of *tikkun olam*.

Rabban Gamliel's enactment has generally been understood as a means to prevent any challenge to the validity of a *get* due to a name change. The author of the amulet, living in Babylonia hundreds of years after Rabban Gamliel's enactment in the Land of Israel, uses the same phrase to remove any doubt as to the identity of the demon from

---

[34] Dan Levene, *A Corpus of Magic Bowls: Incantation Texts in Jewish Aramaic from Late Antiquity* (London: Kegan Paul, 2003), 32–37.

which the client seeks protection. In so doing, the amulet's author implies that just as a *get* for the wrong woman will not achieve its desired aim, an imprecise incantation bowl has no more effectiveness than a blank shard of clay. The invocation of the Mishnah's halakhic language may indicate the diffusion of Rabban Gamliel's halakhic ruling into broader society.

The necessity for precision in magical formulae is also attested to in rabbinic literature. The following brief story appears as part of a lengthy discussion regarding demons and defenses against them (Bavli Pesahim 109b–112b). The passage opens with the Bavli's concern about drinking four cups of wine on Pesah, which seems to violate a Babylonian belief that it is dangerous to engage in activities involving even numbers (זוגות). As the Talmud explains, Ashmedai the king of demons is responsible for all even-numbered things (Pesahim 109b).[35] In this context, the following story appears:

בבלי פסחים קיא ע"ב	Bavli Pesahim 111b
(1) ההוא בר קשא דמתא דאזיל וקאי גבי זרדתא דהוה סמיך למתא.	(1) A certain town official went to relieve himself among the reeds that were near the town.
(2) עלו ביה שיתין שידי ואיסתכן.	(2) Sixty demons entered [him] and he was endangered.
(3) אתא לההוא מרבנן דלא ידע דזרדתא דשיתין שידי היא. כתב לה קמיע לחדא שידא.	(3) He went to a certain sage who did not know the reeds [held] sixty demons. He wrote an amulet for one demon.

---

[35] For more see Isaiah Gafni, "Babylonian Rabbinic Culture," *Culture of the Jews: A New History*, ed. D. Biale (New York: Schocken Books, 2002), 245–6.

(4) שמע דתלו חינגא	(4) He heard them rejoicing and singing
בגוויה וקא משרו הכי	as follows: Master's scarf is like that of the
סודריה דמר כי צורבא	scholars, but we have examined him and he
מרבנן בדיקנא ביה במר	does not know [how to] "bless."
דלא ידע ברוך.	

(5) אתא ההוא מרבנן	(5) A certain scholar came who knew that
דידע דזרדתא שיתין	the reeds [held] sixty demons and wrote an
שידי הוה כתב לה	amulet for sixty demons.
קמיעא דשיתין שידי.	

(6) שמע דקא אמרו פנו	(6) He heard them [the demons] say:
מנייכו מהכא.	Remove yourselves from here.

The story describes a town official who goes to relieve himself among the reeds where he is possessed by sixty demons.[36] The official turns to a sage for help but the sage is unaware that there were sixty demons in the reeds and writes an amulet for only one. The demons mock the sage for creating an ineffective amulet, singing: "Master's scarf is like that of the scholars, but we have examined him and he does not know how to 'bless.'" The demons deride the student because he dresses with the scarf of a rabbinic disciple but he does not know how to "bless," a euphemism for curse.[37] Subsequently another sage who is aware of all sixty demons writes an appropriate amulet, and the demons retreat in defeat.

This story offers two important lessons about magic and the rabbis. First, both the afflicted man and the demons assume that rabbis have experience and expertise in writing amulets to exorcise

---

[36] Manuscripts and genizah fragments include the verb איפני (to relieve oneself), clarifying what he was doing among the reeds.

[37] All traditional commentators understand "bless" as an actual blessing. However, in our opinion, the word "bless" is used here as a euphemism for curse. See for example Bavli Bava Metzia 59b and Kiddushin 30b.

demons. Second, we learn from the story that an amulet is effective only if it is directed at the specific demons causing the afflictions.[38] Here too, as with the incantation bowl, precision is essential in combating demons.

In this chapter we have considered just two examples of how the material remains of the incantation bowls can be used to deepen our understanding of the rabbis' involvement in the world of magic. Magic and rabbinic literature, as we have seen, were inextricably intertwined. A spell quoted in the Bavli references the name of the demon *Bar Tit Bar Tame*, and conversely, embedded in a text inscribed on an incantation bowl is a reference to the rabbinic laws of divorce. As artifacts, incantation bowls offer a powerful complement to rabbinic literature, for they are practically the only material remains left by the thousand-year Babylonian diaspora. The bowls afford a rare glimpse into the pervasive role that magic played in the actual lives of Babylonian Jews, both rabbis and non-rabbis.[39]

---

[38] See Bohak, *Ancient Jewish Magic*, 375–376.

[39] On the cultural exchange between Jews and non-Jews in the realm of magic see Shai Secunda, *The Iranian Talmud: Reading the Bavli in its Sasanian Context* (Philadelphia: University of Pennsylvania Press, 2014), 42–50.

AFTERWORD

In chapter 18 of Avot de-Rabbi Natan, R. Yehudah Hanasi contrasts the approaches of two great tannaitic sages, R. Tarfon and R. Akiva:

לרבי טרפון קרא לו גל
אבנים, ויש אומרים גל של
אגוזים—כיון שנוטל אדם
אחד מהן כלן מתקשקשין
ובאין זה על זה. כך היה רבי
טרפון דומה. בשעה שתלמיד
חכם נכנס אצלו ואמר לו:
שנה לי, מביא לו מקרא
ומשנה מדרש הלכות והגדות.
כיון שיצא שיצא מלפניו היה יוצא
מלא ברכה וטוב. לרבי עקיבא
קרא לו אוצר בלום. למה
רבי עקיבא דומה? לפועל
שנטל קופתו ויצא לחוץ:
מצא חטים, מניח בה; מצא
שעורים, מניח בה; כוסמין,
מניח בה; עדשים, מניח בה.
כיון שנכנס לביתו מברר
חטים בפני עצמן, שעורים
בפני עצמן, פולין בפני
עצמן, עדשים בפני עצמן.
כך עשה ר' עקיבא ועשה כל
התורה מטבעות מטבעות.

R. Tarfon he called, "A heap of stones. And some say, "A heap of nuts"—when a person removes one from the pile, they all go tumbling over each other. This is what R. Tarfon was like. When a scholar came to him and said: "Teach me," he would cite for him Scripture and mishnah, midrash, halakhah, and aggadah. When [the scholar] parted from him, he would leave filled with blessing and good. R. Akiva he called, "A well-stocked storehouse." To what might R. Akiva be likened? To a laborer who took his basket and went out. When he found wheat, he put it in [the basket]; when he found barley, he put it in; spelt, he put it in; lentils, he put them in. Upon returning home he sorted out the wheat by itself, the barley by itself, the beans by themselves, the lentils by themselves. This is how R. Akiva acted, and he arranged the whole Torah like coins.

345

R. Tarfon would overwhelm his students with an avalanche of sources without distinguishing between them. In contrast, R. Akiva would meticulously organize his learning, carefully separating between the sources in order to simplify the memorization process.

Like the paradigm of R. Tarfon, the Bavli is a massive repository of sources and teachings from different generations and of different genres, masterfully woven together into a single document. A student who approaches the text at face value will indeed leave "filled with blessing and good," thanks to the skillful redaction of the Talmudic editors. But our analysis of the sugyot in this book follows the approach of R. Akiva. We carefully isolate the different layers within each sugya, studying each in its own right, only then comparing them to each other. We uncover their literary development and halakhic evolution, identify the influence surrounding cultures had on the rabbis, and point to the profound impact that Talmudic redaction has had on Jewish thought, law and practice. In so doing, we seek to equip our readers with the skills to convert the massive corpus of the Talmud into "coins"—more manageable units that can become part of the common currency of educated Jewish scholars and thinkers. We hope that this book instills in our readers a deeper appreciation for the way in which modern critical techniques shed light on an ancient text, inspiring a new generation of students to turn and return to the Talmud's well-stocked storehouse.

ACKNOWLEDGEMENTS

The writing of this book has been a true labor of love, owing in large part to the participation of many individuals who have shared our enthusiasm for bringing academic study of rabbinic texts to a broader audience. We wish to thank them for all the assistance and encouragement they have offered us along the way. Various teachers, colleagues and students have expressed their support for the project and their eagerness to read the final product. We hope that they will be our readership, our marketers and our future collaborators. We would also like to single out a few individuals who have been particularly helpful:

First and foremost we want to thank our editor, Ilana Kurshan. Ilana edited both the content and the style of our work. We are deeply indebted to her for the quality and rapidity of her work. Additionally, Dyonna Ginsburg and Hanan Mazeh read drafts of various chapters and we would like to thank them for their comments and suggestions.

Dov Abramson and the Dov Abramson Studio designed the book, both its cover and the layout of its pages. We always wanted this book to be pleasing to the eye. If we have succeeded in this endeavor, all credit goes to Dov.

We would also like to thank Daniel Abrams for his help with all the technical aspects of bringing our work to publication.

We wish to thank our co-authors who contributed chapters or sections: Avigail Manekin-Bamberger, Alieza Salzberg, Shai Secunda, and Ethan Tucker. These scholars all enriched this book with their expertise and we were honored to collaborate with them.

From the moment we first discussed this book with Elie Kaunfer and Ethan Tucker, two of the Rashei Yeshiva at Mechon Hadar, they were immediately supportive of our efforts and enthusiastic about publishing the book. Mechon Hadar stands at the forefront of the rigorous and academic study of Judaism in a religiously meaningful setting. We are honored that such an institution shares our vision, and we look forward to continuing our work together in the future.

We would like to thank the Rogoff family, Lawrence and Patricia Schatt, and Sybil Shapiro for their generous support in publishing this volume.

This book has been a joint effort between the two authors. While each chapter began with one of us, continual discussion of the material and subsequent revisions largely obscure the original authorship. We have found that each of us has talents that the other lacks, and while it may be a cliché, working together has created a sum that is certainly greater than the parts.

Our cooperation in writing and producing the book has enriched both of our lives in multiple ways, and we have discovered that we have far more in common than love of Talmud. During this period, our families have gotten to know each other. Our five year old daughters have struck up an adorable friendship and so far we've attended a Kulp bat mitzvah and a Rogoff brit milah. We look forward to many years of study, work and friendship together.

Neither of us would be able to do what we love to do without the support and devotion of our spouses, Dara Rogoff and Julie Zuckerman. This book is dedicated to these two incredible women.

About the Authors

Joshua Kulp is one of the co-founders of the Conservative Yeshiva, where he has been teaching rabbinic literature for nearly twenty years. He is the co-author of *The Schechter Haggadah: Art, Literature and History* (2009). He is also the author of the material used in the Mishnah Yomit (now completed) and Daf Shevui projects. He earned his PhD in Talmud from Bar Ilan University.

Jason Rogoff is a faculty member at the Jewish Theological Seminary, the Rothberg International School of the Hebrew University and the Schechter Institute of Jewish Studies. He is also one of the co-founders of Yeshivat Talpiot. He earned his PhD in Talmud and Rabbinics from the Jewish Theological Seminary.

About the Contributors

Avigail Manekin-Bamberger is currently pursuing a PhD in Talmud at Tel Aviv University on the subject of magic and rabbinic literature. She completed her BA in Jewish studies and Talmud, and her MA in Talmud at the Hebrew University. She is a graduate of the Advanced Talmud Institute at Matan and teaches Talmud at Pelech High School in Jerusalem.

Alieza Salzberg is a faculty member at the Rothberg International School of the Hebrew University. She completed her MA in Literature and Creative Writing at City College and is a graduate of the Advanced Talmud Institute at Matan. She was also a founding member of Yeshivat Talpiot in Jerusalem. Her current academic work, in the department of Midrash and Aggadah at Hebrew University, analyzes legal narratives about virginity, found in the Bavli, from a gender studies perspective.

Shai Secunda is a Martin Buber Society Fellow at the Hebrew University of Jerusalem and earned his PhD in Talmud from Yeshiva University. He researches rabbinic and Zoroastrian literature, and is the author, most recently, of *The Iranian Talmud: Reading the Bavli in its Sasanian Context* (2014).

Ethan Tucker is President and Rosh Yeshiva of Mechon Hadar. He was ordained by the Chief Rabbinate of Israel and earned a PhD in Talmud and Rabbinics from the Jewish Theological Seminary and a B.A. from Harvard College. A Wexner Graduate Fellow, he was a co-founder of Kehilat Hadar and a winner of the first Grinspoon Foundation Social Entrepreneur Fellowship. He is the author, together with Micha'el Rosenberg, of the forthcoming book *Gender Equality and Prayer in Jewish Law.*

Made in the USA
Middletown, DE
26 September 2021